REFRACTIONS: *Essays in Comparative Literature*

BY THE SAME AUTHOR

THE GATES OF HORN:
A Study of Five French Realists

THE POWER OF BLACKNESS:
Hawthorne, Poe, Melville

JAMES JOYCE:
A Critical Introduction

THE OVERREACHER:
A Study of Christopher Marlowe

THE QUESTION OF HAMLET

CONTEXTS OF CRITICISM

REFRACTIONS

Essays in Comparative Literature

HARRY LEVIN

NEW YORK

OXFORD UNIVERSITY PRESS

1966

Copyright © 1966 by Harry Levin

Library of Congress Catalogue Card Number: 66-14477

PRINTED IN THE UNITED STATES OF AMERICA

For HENRY A. MURRAY

Preface

This volume brings together eighteen essays, all of them printed somewhere or other before, all but two or three of them written within the last five or six years. More often than not, they were framed to meet a particular invitation. Many of them were presented orally, as lectures or papers, before they were written down; several were contributed to symposia or commemorative discussions; two were prompted by recent publications which seemed to call for more than mere review. Consequently, such pertinence as they may hold is largely due to those colleagues and editors who provided the testing occasions, not to mention those audiences whose reactions offered the most helpful kind of feedback. I have tried to specify my thanks and acknowledgments in the headnotes prefixed to the articles as they follow, along with the appropriate indications as to the time and place of their first appearance. Republication would hardly be warranted if it took no advantage of its opportunities for self-correction and clarification. On the other hand, since the original dates are a part of the record, I have tried to restrain a succession of afterthoughts which —if allowed to prevail—would eventuate in a wholly different book or else no book at all. In some cases, where revision has entailed the elimination of footnotes, the major references are made clear in the text or the introductory note, while the minor ones may still be found in the earlier version of that essay.

Detached from the conditions that evoked them, these essays must now make a context for one another. In this, I trust, they will be assisted by the headnotes, by the sequence that the subject matter has more or less dictated, and by certain points of departure or return which are registered in the Index. Where diversity has been one of the animating concerns, it would be misleading to superimpose an *ex post facto* unity. I can regard the collection itself as a unifying strategy in relation to my other writing, since it fills in some of the many gaps with illustrative excursions and conceptual elucidations. But, though I should be gratified if the reader had one or two of those other books in mind, I could not and would not take it for granted. Insofar as they have been studies in depth, concentrated interpretations of writers and their works, perhaps they have earned me the privilege of ranging more broadly and generalizing more freely in this book. The single play discussed here in detail is probably Shakespeare's slightest; the only novel analyzed at length is Hawthorne's most discursive; the sole sketch of a literary career is devoted to my old teacher, Irving Babbitt. The discipline of comparative literature, which he did more than any other American to establish, has tended to focus its interest on interrelationships—traditions and movements, the intellectual forces that find their logical termination in *-ism*—rather than on the contemplation of individual masterpieces.

The special illumination of that perspective derives from its way of looking at all literature as one organic process, a continuous and cumulative whole. Yet, in shifting our attention from those objects which seem to have attracted it most concretely, we run the risk of obscuring them behind a set of abstract labels. There are also—I should like to show—grounds for hoping that the comparative method can throw light upon the esthetic and formal aspects, the styles and structures of literary craft. But criticism, particularly within the Anglo-American sphere, has suffered more from a lack of theoretical equipment than from its failures in appreciation. Here is where a broader outlook can help it to make its terminology more precise and its categories more meaningful. The re-examination of critical catchwords, with a view toward why they came into existence, what they have meant to those for whom their meanings have signified most, and how they have veered with the winds of semantic change, is a necessary basis for redefinition; and, unless we define our terms more rigorously, critics will go on playing games of their own with fuzzy concepts. Elsewhere I have attempted a definition of realism, based on detailed inquiries into both theory and practice, and summed up by the classical metaphor of a gate of horn. This has not left me less aware of that other area, prefigured by the contrasting metaphor of the ivory gate, which has connoted myth, dream, and the psychology of imagination.

Some of the pieces in the present volume, moving in a direction traced by studies of thematics, venture into that even more problematic area. Art, however, is created from the interplay of the realistic and the symbolic impetus; in any given artistic situation, there are components of each to be disentangled. No fiction is so utterly fantastic that it does not draw upon some background in experience, while no imitation is so literally exact in its reproduction of reality that it can afford to dispense altogether with fantasy. Sometimes, as in the instance of convention, an externally technical matter can become a mediating factor between literature and life. Seeking to formulate the connection between the two, I once had occasion to speak of literature as an institution in itself. This was no more than a means of reconciling the fact that it belongs and responds to society with the fact that it cannot express itself except through its unique and autonomous forms. Obviously, the formula applies to such social themes as I have been broaching: the role of women, the fate of expatriation, the consequences of noncensorship. Less directly, the application extends to the history of ideas and the evolution of genres. The traditional symbol for the relationship between society and literature has been the simplistic image of a mirror. But—to retain as much of the trope as we can, while making due allowance for intervening considerations—books are not reflections so much as refractions of life.

Refraction, according to the *Shorter Oxford English Dictionary,* is "the fact or phenomenon of a ray of light, heat, the sight (obsolete), etc., being diverted or deflected from its previous course in passing obliquely out of one medium into another of different density, or in traversing a medium not of uniform density." If we let that ray of light or heat stand for communication or expression, then we may assume that whatever turn it takes is determined by the nature of the medium. If we want to test the factual truth of what is communicated or expressed, we must gauge the angle by which it has been refracted; and then the correction of misunderstandings can teach us something about the respective languages, in the case of Shakespearean translation, or about the international climate, with American literature abroad. To put it more affirmatively: our world view is a response to an unremitting traffic in images, which are reshaped by the very circumstances of their transmission. From a more strictly critical standpoint, we are likely to be more concerned with the media that bring about the reshaping, and to accept their modifications of actuality as the metamorphoses of art. To refract an object, in the etymological sense, is to break it up, to break it down, to take it apart—in other words, to subject it to a thoroughgoing analysis. Hence it should not be too difficult or farfetched to transfer the term from physics to criticism. Nor should it be inappropriate if the critic's views seem, from a modish viewpoint, somewhat refractory.

In the long run, opinion seems to matter less than orientation, which is the common aim of these sundry sketches. One of my larger premises has been that culture itself is not exclusive nor twofold but inclusively manifold, that it is not the jealously flaunted perquisite of either the arts or the sciences, classics or moderns, East or West, but embraces them all in one varying continuity. To be educated is to be liberated, so far as one's personal limitations permit, from the provincialism of subcultures. We must start, of course, from our time and place; yet we scarcely know when or where they are located until we have taken soundings in the past and bearings from the horizon. Thus an American cannot understand himself until he begins to grasp the idea of Europe. Speaking and writing English with a difference, he approaches English literature from a distance, with elective sympathy rather than ancestral piety. He may indeed feel just as closely bound by cultural ties with the Continent. As a denizen of the twentieth century, he can no longer consider it a novel page of history; two of its three generations have been lived through already; and if he belongs—like myself—to the middle generation, he may well harbor doubts as to whether the very latest thing is the most modern. He should have no misgivings, nonetheless, about the present as a vantage point for taking stock of inherited treasure and accumulated research—a spectacle so absorbing and panoramic that conclusions from it are bound to be tentative and reports of it fragmentary.

H.L.

Cambridge, Massachusetts
September 15, 1965

Contents

REFRACTIONS: *Essays in Comparative Literature*

1   Semantics of Culture

A symposium on "Science and Culture" was held under the auspices of the American Academy of Arts and Sciences on May 10, 1963, with the participation of representatives from the sciences, the social studies, and the humanities. Their contributions were published under the editorship of Gerald Holton in the Academy's journal, Daedalus (XCIV, 1, Winter 1965), and subsequently as a separate volume by Houghton Mifflin Company. I was asked to introduce the discussion with the paper that follows, an attempt at historical definition of our central term.

"Every day, Sancho," said Don Quixote, "you are becoming less foolish and more sensible." "It must be that some of your worship's good sense is rubbing off on me," Sancho replied. "Lands which by themselves are dry and barren, if they are manured and cultivated, bring forth good fruit. I mean to say that your worship's conversation is the manure that has been spread upon the barren ground of my dry wit; the time that I have spent in your service and company has been the cultivation . . ."

And the harvest is, in short, a liberal education: the development of human personality through a systematic exposure to higher knowledge. Sancho Panza, as usual, sees farther ahead than his condescending master; his wit is truly as dry as the arid plain of La Mancha, and his earthy metaphor serves to place our problem in its elemental context. In the Spanish text of Cervantes the key-word is *cultivación*; its exact counterpart was not introduced into the English language until much later, because the word *culture* itself was still close enough to the soil so that it could designate a process rather than a product. *Culture*, imported from France as a synonym for tillage or husbandry, figures from the early fifteenth century — so unambiguously that the prefix in *agri-culture* did not need to be added for nearly two hundred years. Meanwhile English writers were not slow in extending a metaphorical application to the training of the intellect, which had been implicit from the original Latin in the Ciceronian "*cultura animi*." The *Oxford English Dictionary* cites a phrase employed by Sir Thomas More in 1510: "the culture and profit of their minds." Thomas Hobbes, who equated the education of children with "the culture of their minds" in his *Leviathan*, likewise referred to culture as training of the body under the Hellenizing influence of his translation from Thucydides. Subsequent meaning seems to have been broadened and sublimated to the point where the concept could be defined, by the Oxford editors, as nothing less than "the intellectual side of civilization."

French usage came to specify the object that was cultivated; thus the article in Diderot's *Encyclopédie* is limited to *"culture des terres"*; but the *Dictionnaire de l'Académie Française* of 1777 subjoins to its agricultural definition a figurative sense: ". . . se dit aussi au figuré, du soin qu'on prend des arts et de l'esprit." The word had already taken its artistic and intellectual turn when the Germans borrowed it from France; it is one of the ironies of linguistic history that *Kultur*, so heavily charged with the overtones of Teutonic nationalism, should have started out as a gallicism, and gradually changed its initial C to the more aggressive K. It preserved a uniquely patriotic aura for Thomas Mann, pamphleteering during the First World War, as opposed to the forces of *Zivilisation* on the other side: music and philosophy versus rhetoric and politics. Oswald Spengler shortly thereafter could take, as his touchstone for *Kulturgeschichte*, the difference between vitalistic cultures (Greece, Germany) and petrifying civilizations (Rome, America). In Russia it would seem that the term *kul'tura* has harbored certain western associations, sometimes merely denoting material amenities or — perhaps more characteristically — the absence of them: Gogol characterizes a slovenly inn as "uncultured because of the bedbugs." One of the sharpest issues between Stalin and Trotsky was whether Soviet culture should become proletarian and regional, or whether a Marxist culture should not be classless and international. The upshot was a victory for the social control of culture, rather than for the cultural regeneration of society.

Clearly, we are involved with one of those terms that have a way of touching off controversies. The *Kulturkampf* that reverberates at the moment is one which, over the past five years, has emerged from the common rooms of Cambridge University to enlist antipathies and sympathies throughout the educational institutions of the English-speaking world. It cannot really be said to have been started by Sir Charles Snow, whose Rede Lecture of 1959 on *The Two Cultures and the Scientific Revolution* was — in its good intentions — about as blandly unexceptionable as a commencement speech. Its earnest plea for intercommunication across the high table, as between exponents of the scientific and the humanistic disciplines, had frequently been voiced before and has been since, notably by J. Robert Oppenheimer. The fact that it slightly chided "the traditional intellectuals," while retaining full confidence in the scientists, explains some reactions to it *pro* and *contra* but docs not invalidate its attempt to strike a bicultural equipoise. Its incontrovertible argument came under the overlooked second half of its title, its recognition of the need to face the epochal changes wrought by science in our time. More problematic was its assumption of parity between a play by Shakespeare and the Second Law of Thermodynamics as twin tests of cultural literacy. Most educated laymen are vaguely aware of the general significance of the latter, even if they cannot recite Carnot's mathematical formula; whereas there are advanced physicists who, one gathers, have their doubts about it.

Energy was indeed transformed into heat three years afterward, when F.R. Leavis delivered his Parthian valedictory on the occasion of his retirement from a university lectureship in English at Cambridge, *Two Cultures? The Significance of C. P. Snow.* Granted that Sir Charles's views deserved to be more rigorously examined, it was not auspicious that the examiner began by pronouncing his subject "beneath contempt" on literary grounds, and proceeded to support his *ad hominem* arguments with the kind of intramural dogmatizing that has aroused the fervor of young disciples and the skepticism of professional scholars throughout the course of an embattled pedagogic career. But, when so equable and open-minded a critic as Lionel Trilling too joins issue with Sir Charles, we realize that *The Two Cultures* deserves at least one of the names that Dr. Leavis has called it: it is a portent. Beneath its well-meaning truisms there lurks one striking novelty, which has scarcely been tested by all the discussion: the implication that science can stand by itself as a culture. This assumes not only a total separation from the humanities but also an internal unity among the sciences. Anyone who has ever engaged in academic shop-talk will admit, with regret, that it all too soon reaches limits beyond which specialists in different fields — or even in differing branches of the same field, say mathematics or physics — find it difficult to communicate. And anyone who has tried to follow the public debate on the uses of nuclear energy will find it hard to believe that all scientists share the same premises.

However, there is nothing new in the basis of the controversy, and Mr. Trilling puts it into clarifying perspective when he reminds us that it was Matthew Arnold who gave the Rede Lecture in 1882. That became his well-known essay, "Literature and Science," much better known to most students of literature than the address to which it was intended as a rejoinder, "Science and Culture," by Thomas Henry Huxley. Huxley was arguing, six years after the founding of the Cavendish Laboratory, for the introduction of the sciences into higher education and against what he was not alone in regarding as a snobbish monopoly on the part of the classics. From a practical standpoint, and in the light of later developments, he does not sound unduly contentious when he maintains that "for the purposes of offering real culture, scientific education is at least as effective as an exclusively literary education." He does make certain naïvely positivistic assumptions, which scientific progression has since discarded, but which enabled Arnold to counterclaim that the layman needs to be acquainted only with the factual results of investigation and not with its experimental methods. Huxley stood closer to Arnold than to us in his Victorian belief that a secular revelation was near at hand. Insofar as he was proposing a more up-to-date version of revealed truth, he did not foresee how soon its momentary substance would be outdated by its inherent nature. The scientific revolution he heralded would make any given body of facts less significant than a continuing point of view.

Arnold was defending that position which he had made peculiarly his own in *Culture and Anarchy* (1869), where he saw culture both as a form of personal activity ("the study and pursuit of perfection") and as a collection of works to be studied ("the best which has been thought and said in the world"). He himself was committed to fighting a rear-guard action; his schoolmasterly voice got shriller as he felt himself constrained to repeat his old-fashioned lesson; and he must bear responsibility for making culture a curricular shibboleth, so that literary critics continue to bridle when they hear others using the word for purposes of their own. Hence they spurn the hand that Sir Charles has offered. They might do better by making common cause with our scientific colleagues, their fellow intellectuals after all, against the true Arnoldian enemy, the Philistines; for, if Arnold's prescription now looks as inapplicable as Huxley's overconfident materialism, his diagnosis of those anarchic influences which disorganize modern life seems clairvoyant, not to say understated. His pair of metaphors for the esthetic and cognitive objects of culture, Sweetness and Light, was derived from a hardboiled parable by Jonathan Swift, stating the case for the Ancients in opposition to the Moderns; but the connotation has softened appreciably, like Beauty and Truth themselves when jingled into a slogan. Similarly, the adjective *cultured* — or, for that matter, *refined*, which was once synonymous with *civilized* — has been relegated to the genteel vocabulary of the women's clubs. "The word of ambition at the present day," Emerson pontificated, "is Culture."

Mark Twain's chapter on gingerbread architecture, "Castles and Culture," in *Life on the Mississippi* expresses our native American suspicion of culture-faking, along with a grass-roots feeling that culture must be an importation to this country, more often than not from Great Britain. Consequently, such a culture-vulture as Ezra Pound can speak ambivalently of what he spells "kulchur," while a proponent of artistic modernism, Sir Herbert Read, can entitle a book *To Hell with Culture!* Yet self-improvement has always run the risks of falling into mere imitation or sheer affectation, and genuine culture has been kept alive by migrations as well as by traditions. Cultural deracination has taken various forms, many of them vain efforts to turn back the clock. The relative simplicity of the past, contrasted with the complexity of the present by Henry Adams and other Americans, instilled a mood of historical nostalgia. Still others, for whom the contrast was primarily geographical, artists and writers in search of picturesque backgrounds, expatriated themselves to the Old World like Henry James. T. S. Eliot seems to be both the exemplar and the preceptor of this retrospective movement in the twentieth century. His *Notes Towards a Definition of Culture* (1948) glance down at the problem from a hierarchical eminence, virtually identifying it with religion and ignoring science altogether. It is doubtless a consciously ironic anachronism that these notes should have been jotted down in the aftermath of the Second World War, when the next decade would be witnessing outbursts of angry young men, inroads of Americanization, and redefinitions of English culture by such levelers as Richard Hoggart and Raymond Williams.

Yet Mr. Eliot, unlike his Jamesian predecessors, has never romanticized his vista of latter-day England. His cultural orthodoxy does not necessarily fix its abode in cathedrals or castles, thatched cottages or ivy-covered ruins.

It includes all the characteristic activities and interests of a people: Derby Day, Henley Regatta, Cowes, the twelfth of August, a cup final, the dog races, the pin table, the dart board, Wensleydale cheese, boiled cabbage cut into sections, beetroot in vinegar, nineteenth-century Gothic churches and the music of Elgar. The reader can make his own list.

Mr. Eliot's personal list is a good index of the thorough degree to which he has been acculturated. For whom but a true-blue Englishman would the opening of the grouse-shooting season (the twelfth of August) be a meaningful and magic date? On the other hand, it may well take a foreign-born subject of the Queen to discern and savor the distinctively English quality in things that might seem merely undistinguished to those of us who are not connoisseurs. Of course, we could itemize their American counterparts: the World Series, the Rose Bowl, miniature golf, cheeseburgers, ice cream sodas, supermarkets, motels. Archaeologists of the future may speculate as to what sacrificial rites or orgiastic ceremonies might have been performed in our backyard barbecues and drive-in cinemas. Much that we might consider endemic, however, has become international. Pinball machines are a craze in Tokyo; a jukebox supplies the atmosphere for a novel by Jean-Paul Sartre; and our commercial hegemony is greeted abroad as "coca-colonization." The paradoxical notion of popular culture, standing somewhere between folklore and mass-communication, would seem to round out the etymology of the word by bringing it down to earth again — and to the lowbrow strata underlying the highbrow superstructures. The danger lies not in such stratification when it is clearly marked, but in the confounding of layers and the compounding of those tasteless amalgams which Virginia Woolf denounced as middlebrow.

The mutual incomprehension between scientists and scholars, so long as they more or less peacefully co-exist within the educational establishment, is by no means as unsettling as the gap between their aggregate minority of trained minds and the great majority of untrained minds. Here is a real disjunction between two cultures. It has been the focus of Dwight Macdonald's candid gaze for some two decades, during which he has diametrically shifted his critical viewpoint. In "A Theory of Popular Culture," which Mr. Eliot regarded as the best alternative to his own theory, Mr. Macdonald looked hopefully ahead toward some sort of integration between — to employ his categories — the masses and the classes. In his revised analysis, "Masscult and Midcult," he demonstrates and illustrates the extent to which popularization has become vulgarization. Drawing an analogy from the modern dairy, he tells us that our culture has been homogenized; the cream that should have found its place at the top has been diluted to a thin uniformity. It is reassuring to have so able a journalist as Mr. Macdonald on our side, but we professors cannot afford to be quite so intransigent. We are too painfully conscious that the study of perfection must work its way through a sequence of imperfect states. Since education proceeds from the lower to the upper levels of thought, teachers are never shocked by the large numbers who flounder complacently somewhere in the middle. Moreover, it seems rather sentimental to posit an uppermost level so aloof and inviolate from contact that we cannot imagine how anyone ever got there.

But, with all due reservation, the seriousness of the dilemma ought not to be minimized, and statisticians attest it more loudly than critics. It has not eluded Dr. Gallup's monitors, who polled the American public on cultural interests a year or two ago and produced the following paradigm:

	Men	Women
Went to theater	15%	20%
Went to concert	10	16
Visited art museum	17	17
Read a book all the way through	42	50
Paint in oils, watercolors	6	11
Play musical instrument	10	11
Went to football game	31	17
Went bowling	27	21
Watch TV westerns	74	61
Read comic strips	49	44

Not much Shakespeare here, and no Laws of Thermodynamics. The phraseology is revealing, inasmuch as it has to be specified in words of one syllable that half of the women, and somewhat less than half of the men, read at least one book "all the way through" during the year. We should not be surprised that the curve of taste ascends from the sporadic practice of painting and music, through the desuetude of the theatrical medium, to the popularity of the comic strip and the quasi-universal appeal of the televised western film. What is most significant, if not more surprising, is that the divergence of the sexes, within the broader pattern, corresponds to our cultural dichotomy. It would appear that our mores are still tribal; our squaws go in for the arts and our braves for athletics. (It would be enlightening to compare statistics from other countries, say Russia.) Additional figures show that the incidence of patronage for the theater and the concert-hall is considerably higher than average among our college graduates. The correlation should be encouraging for educators, so far as it goes; and the United States government promises further encouragement through a National Culture Foundation, which should raise the Gallup percentages — and possibly reduce the sexual imbalances — by officially sponsoring performances at Washington. Sponsorship of this kind has hitherto been something less than an instrument of national policy, especially when compared to France, whose *services culturels* have proved so strategic in upholding French prestige during periods of declining political impact.

Our field of observation is one which, operationally speaking, has no little effect in determining the vantage point of the observer. George Orwell's meat — comic postcards, advertising media — would have been Matthew Arnold's poison. High culture has traditionally been the proud possession of an elite, a mandarin class: the Arnoldian "remnant" suggests, as Oxford itself did to Arnold, defensive battles in losing causes. Its Oxonian canon has been a noble one, well worth fighting for: indubitable "Greats," *litterae humaniores*, the Greco-Roman heritage. It has been a mark of caste as well. It has constituted a good deal more than an ornamental framework of reference; for centuries it provided the West with its norms of behavior, prototypes of action, and criteria for evaluation; hence its reduction to simply another learned specialty has been a loss for culture in general. Through the greater part of European history, the collected ideas and surviving experiences of classical antiquity have functioned as the basic educational program, *paideia*, which comprised for Werner Jaeger the one, the only culture. Ethnologists were bound to regard that view as too ethnocentric. J. G. Frazer, who might be said to have annotated the classics by amassing barbarian lore, signalized a transition in this respect. If there was now a plurality of cultures, the next step was to recognize a relativism of standards. A culture-bound Euro-American might still risk the value judgment that Jaeger's Hellenes were more relevant and interesting to himself and his fellow citizens than Malinowski's Trobriand Islanders, or echo the nineteenth-century parochialism of Tennyson: "Better fifty years of Europe than a cycle of Cathay."

Nonetheless, it gives one pause to read a recent and fascinating book by Peter Matthiessen, *Under the Mountain Wall*, a firsthand account of a Stone Age people living today in valleys isolated by the New Guinea mountains, the Kurelu. Their tools, it seems, are utterly primitive; their clothes are all but nonexistent; but, like dueling students at German universities, they enjoy showing off their wounds. As for their weaponry, it is so ineffectual — bows and arrows and bamboo spears — that their wars are essentially sporting events; the fighters are greatly outnumbered by the spectators; and the game is called if anyone gets killed. Denizens of a nuclear-powered culture may be prompted to ask themselves Herman Melville's question, "Who is not a cannibal?" The relativistic approach of the anthropologists is well presented through a survey issued under the auspices of the Peabody Museum at Harvard and lately reissued in paperback, *Culture: A Critical Review of Concepts and Definitions*, by A. L. Kroeber and Clyde Kluckhohn, who between them very nearly succeeded in capturing our term for social science. Moving from cultures in the plural toward a broadly central conception, they unavoidably differ from their humanistic forerunners by stressing the collective at the expense of the individual. The older outlook stressed the dynamic aspect of self-cultivation rather than the static transmission of behavioral patterns. Culture was *Bildung*, a goal to be strenuously achieved rather than a *donnée* to be passively accepted. It was not simply a state or condition but, in the formulation of Dr. Johnson's dictionary, which quotes Richard Steele's periodical, the "Art of improvement or melioration."

Arnold and the Arnoldians, for all their ethical aims, had more and more tended to shift their emphasis from the individual's pursuit of perfection to the accumulated corpus of great books, from the act of cultivation to the cult of received opinion. Civilization, to paraphrase Montaigne, is something men carry within themselves. The human being remains the measure of the humanities; yet they are likewise subject to those pressures, technological, economic, and otherwise, which lead us to project an image of man being acted upon rather than of man acting for himself. Under the limiting circumstances, the anthropological attitude toward culture has a good deal to recommend it, particularly as it was spelled out by E. B. Tylor in *Primitive Culture* (1871): ". . . that complex whole which includes knowledge, belief, art, law, morals, custom, and any other capabilities and habits acquired by man as a member of society." The key-phrase repeated by several of Kroeber and Kluckhohn's other spokesmen is "complex whole." That science should play a role of ever-increasing importance within this aggregation of varied concerns, none of them wholly autonomous, ought almost to go without saying. But that it should be, or ever become, a culture by itself is even less tenable than the proposition — which only a Wildean paradox could defend — that art alone makes culture. Furthermore, it is dangerous and divisive to interject the number two, as Sir Charles Snow duly warned us when he did so. It would be better to acknowledge the coexistence of further subcultures, a multicultural pluralism — or better still, *e pluribus unum*, a unity out of variety, one large heterogeneous culture democratically split up into numerous professional lobbies.

This is a less discouraging and, I believe, a more realistic model than Sir Charles's tense polarity, and he himself is a lively illustration of the fact that the two worlds can converge. Much of that convergence, it should be noted, has taken place for him within the humane or humanistic or humanitarian sphere: in the recruitment and supervision of scientists and in fiction or drama about them. It seems to be an intrinsic feature of the situation that most of the dialogue between the sciences and the humanities must take place within the latter domain, not only because of our humanistic ignorance — which we trust such converse will modify — but because all scientists are human beings before they are anything else. We may rate the Laws of Thermodynamics with the plays of Shake-speare, if we are giving out posthumous Nobel Prizes for incommensurable achievements; but *King Lear* happens to be an accessible experience to everyone who knows the language, since it seems to address us so directly, while one must have learned a special language in order to appreciate Carnot. Obviously, one may experience the phenomena he has described without the benefit of his descriptions, which are laws because of their very detachment from the accidents of our existence. Art is such by virtue of that characteristic which the Scholastics called quiddity, that whatness which makes an object its unique self, and which is in itself of greater interest than anything that we could say about it. If applied science is what we like to call *know-how*, then theoretical science is *know-why* — another line of adverbial inquiry — and the arts and the humanities seek answers to the substantive questions, *what* (Montaigne's "What do I know?") and ultimately *who* (Who am I? Who are you?).

Such a polymath as Jacob Bronowski can minimize the difference between scientific and artistic truth, or between the experimentations of a Rutherford and a Rembrandt. In his last book, *Literature and Science*, the late Aldous Huxley reaffirmed the viability of certain middle roads. Under the conciliatory heading, "The Art of Science," in a special issue of the (London) *Times Literary Supplement*, Sir Charles Snow has amplified and modified his earlier case. He has withdrawn his thermodynamic test. His reconsidered criterion for scientific literacy would be taken from biology rather than from physics. This would bring it somewhat closer to the layman's orbit of curiosity, and the term *culture* already has its own currency in the biological sphere. He would also now admit the possibility of a third culture, to be hopefully drawn from the social sciences; and, if his allusion to that *tertium quid* is tactfully vague, this should help to obviate further reprisals from both the scientists and the humanists. One would not wish to see this gesture of conciliation incite another free-for-all. Yet there may be a mediating factor in the social scientists' acceptance of science as an ideal,

which is frankly approximated much more often than it is successfully attained. Physical scientists, one suspects, could make the
same admission without losing face. The actual attainment of such
an ideal is, in its searchingly analytic nature, beyond the apprehension of most other men. We must and do admire it; but Sir Charles
cannot have it both ways; by that very token, we cannot blame
ourselves and most other men for not apprehending it.

The structure of scientific knowledge is vertical, so that its investigators progress through research to discovery, building on the
work of their predecessors and guiding their students from one stage
to the next. To mark a rough geometrical distinction, it might be
counterstated that the structure of humanistic knowledge is hori-
zontal; it is so broadly based and so widely spread that everyone
must touch it at some point, however rudimentarily. To think of
the two modes of knowledge as existing on the same plane may, in
consequence, verge upon fallacy. Their relationship could be more
consistently outlined by a pyramidal diagram. At its base would be
programs in General Education, which colleges have developed to
counterbalance the mounting drives toward specialization. "Woe
to the specialist who is not a pretty fair generalist," Samuel Butler
admonished, "and to the generalist who is not also a bit of a specialist." Insofar as the scientists are the specialists, they need the
generality of the humanities; but there is another sense in which
the reverse may be true, and the specializing humanists need to
come to terms with the mechanisms of the universe. Such adjustments and corrections are mutually possible as long as the several
branches of learning are represented on the same faculty, or within
the alphabetical context of an encyclopedia. The very words we use
can either unite or divide, and their histories are records of unifica-
tion or subdivision. Thus the German rubric *Wissenschaft* subsumes all lines of scholarly inquiry and confers the nominal status
of a science on them.

Understandably, the Latin *scientia* did not differentiate between
book-learning and the other kinds: arts and sciences nestled together, and were interchangeably labeled, in the medieval Trivium

and Quadrivium. Nor did its English derivative until well into the eighteenth century, when *science* was more narrowly applied to what had previously figured as natural or experimental philosophy; and it was not until the mid-nineteenth century that its practitioners would be singled out as *scientists*. These semantic shifts run parallel to currents of ideas, which in turn reflect the changing enterprise of learning as a whole, and can be most aptly exemplified by a glance at that characteristic British institution, the Royal Society of London for Improving Natural Knowledge. Although the unabridged title invokes the traditional concept of culture as improvement, it is deflected toward a fresh range of subject matter. Accordingly, a charter member, John Evelyn, could write of "cultivating the sciences and advancing useful knowledge." Evelyn has survived as a man of letters; so has Samuel Pepys through his diary, though he belonged as a government official; and their fellow members, John Dryden and Abraham Cowley, were unabashedly poets. If we re-examine the Society's earliest rosters, we are likely to be struck by the large proportion of members who would not be retrospectively classified as scientists. Christopher Wren would not be, though he amply qualified as Astronomer Royal. Whereas Robert Boyle and Isaac Newton, who unquestionably would be, were theologians as well as experimentalists.

Bishop Sprat, in his contemporaneous *History of the Royal Society* (1667), testifies that its membership was to draw upon "all the professions" — plus, above all, nonprofessionals, "gentlemen free and unconfined." It would be their comprehensive purpose "to make faithful records of all the works of Nature or Art which can come within their reach." They were thereby expected to realize the well-rounded ideals of Renaissance humanism, and in particular the proposals of Francis Bacon, for organizing and centralizing all the provinces of knowledge. But the very success of their specialized investigations was destined to exert a decentralizing force. Their *Philosophical Transactions* grew less and less philosophic, until in 1887 they were subdivided into a physico-mathematical and a strictly biological series. In the meantime, two other cultural organizations have separately and belatedly appeared to fill in their respective gaps: the Royal Academy of the Arts in 1786, the British Academy for the scholarly disciplines in 1902. The American Academy of Arts and Sciences should be congratulated for continuing to foster a meeting of minds across the broadest area. The American Philosophical Society has also retained its wide interdisciplinary scope. Our government-sponsored institutions divide into the National Academy of Sciences, on one hand, and the Academy-Institute of Arts and Letters on the other. France's immortal Academy is mainly literary, though it includes a few scientists and generals, while its surrounding Institute embraces four lesser academies, preponderantly humanistic: Sciences, Sciences Morales et Politiques, Inscriptions et Belles-Lettres, and Beaux-Arts.

The Royal Society, founded a generation after the Académie Française, never attempted to exercise a surveillance over artistic tastes; but it did commence with a comparable interest in, and a decisive influence on, the state of the language. This — it needs no Lévi-Strauss to remind us—is a fundamental aspect of culture, though it resists legislation and in our country has been left to private entrepreneurs. Their latest contribution, the third edition of the Merriam-Webster *New International Dictionary,* has provoked a war of words involving a conflict between scientific and humanistic principles. The editors have viewed themselves as linguistic scientists and construed their task as descriptive rather than prescriptive: a tabulation of living speech without regard for historical precedent or normative usage. In basing their canvass so largely on commonplace examples, where diction tends to be imprecise and vocabulary limited, they may have diminished the expressive capacity of the American English they expound. Their definitions of culture, which are generous enough to include "beauty culture," are illuminated by a single quotation from a twentieth-century historian. However, no dictionary could transfix a word which casts so many-sided a penumbra of signification, or chart the vicissitudes of an idea which has stimulated such thoughtful and forceful reactions on the part of such diverse witnesses. To scan their testimony is to step back a pace or two from history and from society, to pass in review the determining conditions of man's relation to them and theirs to him.

To step back a few paces farther would be to contemplate the drastic changes that underlie those conditions, to speculate upon contingencies where the imagination is hard put to keep up with advancing technology. Naturally we think of books as the principal medium of culture, and our thinking is framed by the five-hundred-year span between ourselves and the invention of printing. The manuscript culture that preceded it necessarily differed in intellectual structure, and functioned on a much narrower social base. Today book culture, with all that it opened up for the literate individual, seems to have reached, if not passed, its apogee. For the moment, thanks to the paperback explosion, its instruments are more widely and cheaply available than ever; and yet this facile plenitude adds to the problems of housing and handing on knowledge. The libraries of the future will not be designed to foster erudite browsing; their stores of televised microfilm will perforce be controlled through self-limiting catalogues. Scholarship, as we know it, is already giving way to data processing and information retrieval. As for the introductory stages of learning, if their guide is to be the teaching machine, the consequences must be at once more uniform and more circumscribed. Culture is increasingly conceived as a hoard set aside by man, to be tapped at the dictates of occasion. Man himself becomes less and less a culture-bearer, more and more a codifier of programs and manipulator of electronics. Harbingers of audiovisual culture, such as Marshall McLuhan, promise us gains that will more than offset the incidental losses. Willingly we cede to them the mantle of prophecy.

Like the foregoing paper, this one also had its origin in a symposium at the American Academy of Arts and Sciences. The original conferences in May 1958 were organized and animated by Henry A. Murray, who edited the consequent issue of Daedalus (LXXXVIII, 2, Spring 1959) and the augmented volume, Myth and Mythmaking, published by George Braziller in 1960. Here, too, my assignment was to present a kind of semantic introduction. I am sorry that I was not aware until later of a paper by Herbert Weisinger bearing exactly the same title and published in the same year as mine, which he has republished in The Agony and the Triumph: Papers on the Use and Abuse of Myth (East Lansing: Michigan State University Press, 1964). That subtitle reflects a confessed ambivalence toward an approach which is treated with much acumen and learning. Professor Weisinger's attitude might be summed up in his truly Baconian apophthegm: "Pandora's box is myth; opening it is science." His essay, "Some Meanings of Myth," is a methodological critique of recent mythography as it has been applied to literary study. I should be happy to see my essay serve as an introduction to his.

A famous work of American mythology, which affords an object lesson to those rash enough to go fishing for mythical monsters, is introduced by a Sub-Sub-Librarian, who presents a sequence of more or less relevant extracts and cross-references. Such is the pedantic role allotted to me in the ensuing discussion: "a mere painstaking burrower and grubworm," in Melville's phrase. If my handful of citations suggests the range and richness of the field, or if it indicates some of the hazards that students might do well to avoid, it will have served its purpose. As a reminder of earlier speculations and a welcome to further contributions, much of what I have to say will be obvious and all of it will be provisory.

We could hardly begin without recognizing that we are beset on all sides by verbalism. We cannot even talk about our subject without indulging in "the myth of myths," as we have been admonished by Paul Valéry, for whom the very essence of myth was talk. "Myth," according to Valéry, "is the name for everything that exists, or subsists, only to the extent that speech is its cause." That is a fairly objective definition of the nonmythical as whatever exists independent of speech; it invites us to pursue the mythical into subjective realms, and to pin it down with a more detailed semantic inquiry.

The primordial meaning of our word was "word": *mythos*. Add *logos*, and you get "mythology." Thus, in a certain sense, the science of myth also means "the word of words," which should be a caveat against tautologies and other excesses of verbiage. An exploded example is the hypothesis of Max Müller that all myths were originally derived from words through a species of allegorical etymology. We may agree that language conditions thought; but may we agree that language antedates thought? Rather, we must assume that both language and thought are shaped by habits of prelogical or metaphorical thinking — primitive metaphysics as systematized by Ernst Cassirer in the second volume of his *Philosophy of Symbolic Forms*. It is an incidental irony that, although Max Müller did not succeed in accounting for myths by words, he circulated a word which went on to beget a myth, the dangerous word "Aryan."

Mythos is used for "word" or "speech" in Homer and the Greek poets, as differentiated from *logos*, "tale" or "story." As such, it became a technical term of literary criticism, signifying plot, which Aristotle held to be the most important feature of tragedy. The Latin equivalent, *fabula*, may signify the whole dramatic work, and has its own derivative in "fable," which comes down to us with moralistic overtones. Henry Murray's point is well taken, when he takes exception to the phrase "purely fictitious" in the primary definition of the *Oxford English Dictionary*. Here, I suspect, the lexicographers have superimposed a conception more germane to latter-day rationalism, a concept which J. G. Frazer was to hold. Vico was at pains to point out that *mythos* is often glossed by the ancients as *vera narratio*. Invention, exaggeration, and falsification were subsequent meanings.

Tragedy, which began in ritual, drew its fabulous plots from an inherited body of narrative lore, which was regarded as roughly true on the plane of universalized experience. The notion that

writers should create their own plots, *ad hoc* and *ex nihilo*, is relatively modern and possibly misguided. Shakespeare, although his
sources were more eclectic, would not have thought of inventing
the stories he dramatized any more than Sophocles had done. The
Hamlet of the one was no more original than the Orestes of the
other; and, unless the diffusionists can prove the descent of Hamlet from Orestes, we are confronted with a striking instance of
what Clyde Kluckhohn would term "cross-cultural universals."
The hazard of such universality is the reduction of all myths to the
same cast of characters, as attempted by Robert Graves and others
in the wake of the Cambridge school of anthropologizing classicists.

Whereas the derivatives from *logos* have attached themselves to
the sciences, or "-ologies," *mythos* and its verbal congeners have
been associated with religion. Retrospectively and scientifically, we
stress the etiological aspect of things and look upon myths as symbolic answers to questions raised by man's curiosity about causes:
e.g. the thunder must be the voice of Zeus. Theogony and cosmog-
ony, not to mention metaphysics, abound in discredited hypotheses
for explaining natural phenomena — which, of course, are supernatural until they have been satisfactorily explained. Even the
metamorphoses fabled by poets can be regarded as prescientific
gropings toward biological evolution. Perhaps we read back our
own concern with etiology, in asking ourselves the why, whence,
and how of myth.

The process is mysterious enough to deserve the designation of
mythopoesis, a technical term for imagination at work. Actually,
poesis is neither more nor less than making; a poet, etymologically,
is a maker; and poetry is, quite literally, make-believe. The term
"fabulation," which some of us have used to designate the storytelling faculty, should make clearer how the function of mythmaking relates to other forms of mental activity; for *la fonction
fabulatrice*, as Bergson locates it, stands midway between the
strictly cognitive and the obscurely intuitive; and it is out of that
limbo between rational intelligence and the unconscious that
fictions are generated.

Now there are two ways of looking at a fiction: we can consider it as a deviation from fact or as an approximation to fact. Fact must always be the criterion; and when the facts are under control, we emphasize the degree of deviation; but when we are out of touch with the facts, we utilize fiction to explain the unexplainable by some sort of approximation to it. "For as hieroglyphics came before letters," Bacon has said, "so parables came before arguments." We might well add that Plato's myths are notable examples of argument reverting to parable. Continually, in some such fashion, we must rely on imaginative constructs to fill in the gaps of our knowledge. "Fabulous thinking," as Santayana put it, "is a natural prologue to philosophy."

By and large, the writers of Greece and Rome were rather Pickwickian in their acceptance of mythology. So far as they could, they moralized or rationalized or allegorized the embarrassing misbehavior of their Olympians. Ovid's mythography — or, for that matter, the Norse pantheon of Snorri Sturlason — is highly sophisticated, if not downright skeptical. At its most serious, it asks for no more than that willing suspension of disbelief which Coleridge would call poetic faith. It was precsiely because the classics were based upon fictive themes that they survived the mythoclastic rigors of early Christianity. Myths were pagan and therefore false in the light of true belief — albeit that true belief might today be considered merely another variety of mythopoeic faith. Here is where the game of debunking starts, in the denunciation of myth as falsehood from the vantage point of a rival myth.

Classical myths could be rescued by allegory, prefiguration, or other devices of reinterpretation; but they could not be accepted literally. For Yeats, as for so many other poets, they would frankly be "embroideries." They had long been the *ornements reçus*, the conventional embellishments recommended by neoclassical critics. On the other hand, Boileau had declared that the Christian mysteries were improper subjects for works of fiction, which should properly deal with the fictitious, and not with the truths of revealed religion. Milton disregarded that injunction, at his peril, in *Paradise Lost*; yet, though he made a personal allusion to Galileo, he fell back upon the quasi-mythical system of Ptolemy when he came to describe the machinery of the cosmos.

This accords with the assumptions of many evolutionary theories of culture: that poetry is essentially a product of a primitive age, and that it will in due course be superseded by the application of reason to the different fields of human endeavor. Such theorists as Comte and Hegel come to mind in this connection, yet the attitude was already formulated during the Battle of the Ancients and Moderns in the latter years of the seventeenth century. The pioneering Modernist Fontenelle, in his essay *On the Origin of Fables*, suggested then that mythology was a kind of ignorant philosophy. He himself would become a kind of tribal hero to the anthropologists for having likewise suggested that classical myths and those of the American Indians be studied comparatively.

Fontenelle's rationalistic tendency had been anticipated by that ancient author whose name has been handed on as a virtual synonym for mythoclast, or dispeller of myths, Euhemerus. The lost work of Euhemerus seems to have been devoted to an exposure of the gods as no more than deified men: Zeus turns out to have been a king of Crete, long dead and buried and apotheosized. Curiously, this euhemeristic tract seems to have been cast in the form of a romance, some sort of imaginary journey. The attitude it expressed, euhemerism, reduces myth to legend; and legend, after all, can easily be reduced to exaggerated history.

The historical approach was set forth in 1725 by the monumental treatise of Giambattista Vico, *Principles of a New Science According to the Common Nature of Nations*. Vico proposed that mythology be read as protohistory. He discerned in myth not only the outlines of his spiral theory of progress, but a key to the so-called Homeric problem and a working model for the development of law. The personification of forces of nature through the Olympian deities represented a naïve stage of knowledge, which Vico called "poetic wisdom." Just as the early peoples had founded the arts during the childhood of the race, so late generations gave birth to philosophers who were maturely developing the sciences.

Vico's ardent disciple, Benedetto Croce, has claimed that his master resolved the age-old quarrel between poetry and philosophy. If he accomplished that object, he did so by apologizing for mythopoesis. He remained a man of the Enlightenment, and shared its interests in disentangling fact from fiction; yet he showed how mythoclasm could be employed, not simply as a means of exposing imposture, but as a technique for interpreting phantasmagoria. It would be wielded as a scholarly instrument for the examination of superstitious yet significant misconceptions, when Ottfried Müller brought out his *Prolegomena to a Scientific Mythology* in 1825.

Mankind, having outgrown its mythical adolescence, felt itself increasingly able to get along without myths. If the other religions were mythical, so was Christianity, David Strauss maintained in his far-reaching *Life of Jesus*. As for poetry, it was interesting enough, from an esthetic or archaeological standpoint, but it was technologically obsolescent. Poets lamented, with increasing pathos, that great Pan was dead, that the gods of Greece had gone into exile or underground, or that the woods and streams had lost their nymphs and naiads. Myth itself was defunct, a thing of the past; and the realization engendered another myth, the nostalgic myth of pastoralism.

Karl Marx, afterward to be denounced by his enemies as a mythologist, announced that any mythology was bound to be incompatible with the results of the Industrial Revolution. Indeed, the distance was vast between Mount Olympus and the city of Manchester. Yet when Ralph Waldo Emerson visited Manchester in 1848, he noted in his journal that modern mythology would have to be industrial, mechanical, parliamentary, commercial, and socialistic; moreover, that its "mythagogic names" would be Astor, Fulton, Arkwright, Peel, Russell, Rothschild, Stephenson, and Fourier. Emerson's generalization stands up better than most of his illustrations; for the men he names were primarily contrivers and not exemplars.

Emerson was really seeking tutelary spirits, lay saints for a secular epoch, in accordance with principles laid down by "Uses of Great Men," the introduction to his *Representative Men*. His friend Carlyle came closer to the mark — that is to say, the significance of public roles, the relationship between myth and cult — in his comparable set of case histories or hagiographies, *Heroes and Hero-Worship*. One of their common illustrations, common to all minds formed in the nineteenth century, was that of Napoleon, who was both contriver and exemplar, and who managed to become the mythographer of his own myth.

The Romantic Movement — to sum it up in our terms — may be conceived as a mythopoeic revival. Ideologues like Herder argued the need; critics like Friedrich Schlegel pointed the way; metaphysicians like Schelling reconstructed a transcendental world view; philologists like the brothers Grimm resurrected the old Nordic war-gods. It is no mere historic accident that this impetus originated in Germany, or that it found itself pitted against the more classicized culture of France. Nativism led to nationalism, as we can unhappily bear witness, with Wagner's tetralogy for its artistic climax and Hitler's Nazism for its political *Götterdämmerung*. "Poetic politics" was Vico's polite expression for what we have come to recognize as the Big Lie.

Georges Sorel was the theoretician of myth who placed it in its ideological context. To his *Reflections on Violence*, which expounded the syndicalist doctrine of the general strike, he appended a postscript which analyzed Lenin's myth of world revolution; and he lived to confer his benediction on Mussolini's melodramatic legend of Rome restored. Sorel perceived that social movements enlisted their adherents by envisioning themselves as struggles on behalf of an ultimately triumphant cause. This did not mean that the test would be the future; whether utopian or millennial, that would be pie in the sky. "Myths must be judged as means of acting upon the present," asserted Sorel — in other words, for their effectiveness as propaganda.

I leave it to our colleagues among the social scientists to face the problematic consequences of this view. I shall only venture to remark, in passing, that it is characteristically Gallic in the stress it puts upon the factors of contrivance and calculation. It is instrumental rather than apocalyptic, in treating the myth as a means rather than an end. With the Germans, the very opposite seems to be the case; and, consequently, they have tended to be a nation of mythopoets or — at least — mythophiles; whereas one has only to read the newspapers in order to realize that the French are a nation of mythoclasts. The current regime of General de Gaulle is a desperate effort to reverse their habitual direction, as is the anticlimactic career of André Malraux.

In the standard French dictionary of Littré, the third meaning given for *le mythe* is "that which has no real existence." Thereupon the lexicographer has expanded an afterthought: "It is said that, in politics, justice and good faith are myths." This edifying sentiment may help us to understand why French schoolboys are so customarily cynical. A recent critic, Roland Barthes, in a book entitled *Mythologies*, discusses sports, films, gadgets, elections, and the sensations of metropolitan journalism. "Mythology," M. Barthes theorizes, "is an accord with the world, not as it is, but as it wants to be."

It was the absence of the deflated myths of the Old World, and the comparative mythlessness of the New World, that inspired our American Dream; and it was a French immigrant to this hemisphere, Hector St. John Crèvecoeur, who voiced the most poignant hope for a new breed of men, *Homo americanus*. In the third of his *Letters from an American Farmer*, Crèvecoeur asked, "What is an American?," and answered by sketching out his ideal portrait, a cross between savagery and civilization which would have Cooper's Leatherstocking as its fictional protagonist, Walt Whitman as its messianic bard, and Frederick Jackson Turner as its historiographer.

The emergent figure has been much exploited, notoriously in the case of Davy Crockett, the politician presenting himself as folk-hero. Henry Nash Smith has chronicled numerous other heroes of the backwoods and the frontier in his comprehensive study of

the West as symbol, *Virgin Land*. A suggestive sequel is the monograph by R. W. B. Lewis on the concept of native innocence, *The
American Adam*. Both of those closely interrelated myths, it would
appear, have been extinct for some time. Even the Horatio Alger
myth, *The Dream of Success*, which Kenneth Lynn has retraced
through the writings of the muckraking naturalists, has been losing
conviction. We Americans have experienced the Fall, for better
or worse, and have lost our intellectual virginity. At the moment,
our favorite myth seems to be that of Original Sin.

Mr. Lewis' theme, the American Adam, converges with an energetic statement from Victor Hugo, who compares the formation
of types in art with the creation of Adam in life itself. Inevitably,
we shall be discussing Jung's archetypes and — it is intimated —
probing beyond them into the ultimate Ur of unconsciousness.
Hugo, the mythopoet of the Napoleonic myth who became its
mythoclast, offers this insight into Shakespeare: "A lesson which
is a man, a man with a human face so expressive that it looks at
you and its look is a mirror, a parable which nudges you, a symbol
which warns you, an idea which is nerve, muscle, and flesh, . . .
a psychic conception which has the concreteness of fact, . . .
that is a type."

That is how Shakespeare's exemplary figures — Romeo, Shylock,
Falstaff — have succeeded in embodying such diverse ways of life.
And that is why Russian writers of the nineteenth century, while
creating Adams of their own, recreated "A Lear of the Steppes,"
"A Hamlet of the Shchigri District," or "A Lady Macbeth from
Mtensk." Richard Chase, in his dissertation, *Quest for Myth*, has
given us a lively and informative survey of accumulated opinion;
but when Mr. Chase equates myth with literature, he has been
carried away by the zeal of the mythological critic for linking
everything with everything else. Myth may be unwritten literature,
if you like; and if that is a contradiction in terms, it has been
made meaningful by the researches of Milman Parry and Albert
Lord into the oral epic.

Myth, at all events, is raw material, which can be the stuff of literature. Insofar as this implies a collective fantasy, it must be shared. The ontogeny of dream recapitulates the phylogeny of myth — to restate a well-known Jungian axiom in the diction of biology — a possible explanation of why the individual psyche can be so deeply receptive to certain pre-existing trains of imagery. Yet if we have lived through all of the world's mythologies in embryo, then the synthetic and syncretic "monomyth" of *Finnegans Wake* proves — if it proves nothing else — how difficult it is to recapture our foetal memories. Conversely we may wonder whether any single person, even so intense a poet as William Blake, could fabricate and promulgate his own mythology. A private myth, for all the looseness of critical usage, cannot but be a contradiction in terms; and Blake's prophetic books and Yeats's *Vision* ought properly to be labeled pseudomyths.

We can test these paradoxes when we discuss mythical parallels in contemporary literature. Such parallels have been freely forthcoming whenever the moderns have conjured with the classics: the hybrid Euphorion, created by Goethe in the image of Byron, identifies himself with his classical prototype in his dying breath: "Icarus! Icarus!" Similarly, Joyce's artist-hero, Stephen Dedalus, sees his fate prefigured in his mythagogic name. Through these devices of identification, T. S. Eliot observed in his review of *Ulysses*, the modern world is made possible for art. But, when they have been so explicitly sustained by artists so consciously versed in psychology or anthropology, they impress us as commentaries rather than texts.

Thomas Mann's lecture "Freud and the Future," which deals more directly with Mann and the past, speaks for "the mythically oriented artist." The prelude to the first volume of his Joseph cycle, correctly titled *Tales of Jacob* in the British edition, is a remarkable excursion into the racial memory. Yet *Joseph and His Brothers*, as a whole, is a sophisticated version of Genesis, not a primitivistic reversion to it. It is not dissimilar, in that respect, to many other adaptations from the Bible, such as Racine's *Esther* and *Athalie*. Indeed it follows the curve that Flaubert projected for later novelists when, bored with the nondescript subject matter of his own day, he immersed himself in patristics and hagiography.

Conscious revivals may prove to be less revelatory than unconscious survivals. Literary achievements are never quite so personal or unique as they may seem, but generally more traditional or conventional. The most powerful writers gain much of their power by being mythmakers, gifted — although they sometimes do not know it — at catching and crystallizing popular fantasies. Thus Dickens' novels enthrall us again and again by taking us back, recurrently and obsessively, to the old folktale about the Babes in the Woods. Oliver Twist, Little Nell, David Copperfield, Esther Summerson, Pip, and his other waifs have to cope with the wicked witches of sullen bureaucracy and greedy industrialism. And *Hard Times* might almost be Dickens' response to Emerson's plea for a myth of Manchester.

In a stimulating footnote to his book of essays on magico-religious symbolism, *Images and Symbols*, Mircea Eliade exclaims: "What an inspiring study it would be, to bring to light the real spiritual function of the nineteenth-century novel which, despite all scientific, realistic, or social 'formulas,' remained the great repository of degraded myths!" Professor Eliade's idea is luridly illuminated by Mario Praz's *Romantic Agony* (more accurately described by its Italian title, *La Carne, la morte, e il diavolo nella letteratura romantica*), which shows the extent to which devils and vampires and other survivors from demonology still pervade the decadent fiction of the eighteen-nineties. We are still inclined to think of the novel as the most immediate, circumstantial, and individualized of artistic forms, the faithful mirror of actualities. We need to be reminded that it contains the elements, and continues the functions, of myth.

This may encourage us to believe that the underlying patterns are timeless, however their ephemeral contexts may change; or it may imply that modernity, which has become so much less modern than we used to believe, has not yet dispensed with the socio-cultural processes behind folklore. Such a motif as the Other-worldly Bride may be forgotten, except by professional folklorists or medieval antiquarians. Yet some antiquarians of the future, looking back at Emma Bovary, Anna Karenina, Hedda Gabler, and Carol Kennicott, may discover that all of those heroines exemplify one of the most persistent motifs of the past century: *la femme incomprise, die misverstandene Frau,* the Misunderstood Wife or — since English does not convey the ambiguous implication — the Unappreciated Woman, indeed a degraded myth.

Myth, insofar as it touches us, adapts itself to the permutations of history. The contrast between Homer's Odysseus and Tennyson's Ulysses is nearly as complete as if the two had no genetic affinity. Moreover, when the latter sums up his credo — "To strive, to seek, to find, and not to yield" — he seems to be affirming a temporal kinship with an altogether different protagonist, Goethe's Faust. *Faust* is probably the most elaborate literary crystallization of any myth we have had — or, more exactly, any legend, stemming as it does from a vaguely historic personage and surrounded as it is with numerous and revealing analogues. By comparing it with varying versions, we can distinguish the thematic structure of the mythic entity from traits acquired through the impact of successive reworkings.

All the accretions ultimately belong: the Protestant warning of the Lutheran *Faustbook,* the catalogue of Renaissance learning in Marlowe's *Dr. Faustus,* the self-fulfillment of the nineteenth-century individualist with Goethe, the relapse into guilty genius with Mann. Faust is throughout a *magus,* an intellectual and a heretic, who obtains through magic what is forbidden by Christianity; in breaking the taboo against such knowledge, he comes to resemble the primal Adam or the Titan Prometheus. Damnation, the predicated consequence for him as for Don Juan, withers away with the fading of orthodox eschatology. The eternally feminine component seems to enter the story at a later date. Much of this may seem accidental or idiosyncratic; yet the resulting complex of themes is so typical that Spengler employed the epithet "Faustian" to characterize the trend of Western civilization.

There is a contemporary movement which aims to "demytholo-gize" religion. More frequently, in other spheres of thought, the aim is now to remythologize. This may be attributable to the re-action against the harsh pressures of history in favor of that time-lessness whose rhythm is envisaged by Professor Eliade as "eternal repetition." Significantly in 1935, when I. A. Richards revised his manifesto of 1928 on *Science and Poetry,* he amplified his treatment of belief and footnoted his reference to myths: "Not necessarily a derogatory word." Through his intervening study of Coleridge in 1934, he had been moving from his empirical premises across "The Boundaries of the Mythical" to a position whence he could affirm: "Without his mythologies man is only a cruel ani-mal without a soul." All that remained was for Northrop Frye to propound a methodology for criticism grounded upon the cycle of season myths.

In this second half of the twentieth century, face to face with a decline in the literate arts and a rise in the extraliterary and audiovisual media, myth would seem more influential than ever, as experts on communication and public opinion will demonstrate. Meanwhile, one final quotation should subsume and underline the basic distinction that I have been trying to draw between mythoclasm and mythopoesis. "Science is the critique of myth," wrote William Butler Yeats in a letter to his fellow poet Sturge Moore. "There would be no Darwin, had there been no Book of Genesis." When a society comprising as many scientists as the American Academy of Arts and Sciences entertains such a topic sympathetically as well as critically, it is a perspicuous sign of the times. The pallid Sub-Sub-Librarian now concludes and withdraws, leaving his colleagues to embark on their oceanic adventure.

This essay was originally written for a collection by various hands which I edited as the twentieth volume of the Harvard Studies in Comparative Literature, Perspectives of Criticism (Cambridge: Harvard University Press, 1950). As another venture into critical lexicography — the method of defining key-terms by analyzing what they have signified to those who shaped their significance — it is closely related to my studies of "classical," "tradition," and "realism," which have been reprinted in Contexts of Criticism (Cambridge: Harvard University Press, 1957). It may serve as an excursus, amplifying and fortifying a point which I touched on too lightly in my "Literature as an Institution," subsequently incorporated into the first chapter of The Gates of Horn: A Study of Five French Realists (New York: Oxford University Press, 1963). But I hope it may have been serving a broader purpose of clarification, given both the unexamined diffusion of the present term and the diffuseness of some of its recent contexts; and I have been reassured by the published dissertation of Robert M. Browne, Theories of Convention in Contemporary American Criticism (Washington: The Catholic University of America, 1956), dealing chiefly with poetry and with the so-called New Critics. During the fifteen years since my notes were set down, the tendency toward conventionalization seems to have been playing a more and more explicit role in the arts: for example, the restaging of Wagnerian music-drama at Bayreuth. The following reprint omits my original footnotes, absorbing the principal references into the text. An Italian translation appeared in Inventario (Autumn 1960).

I

The history of criticism may seem at times to be something of a logomachy. This is perhaps because it faces the problem of dealing, in a fixed and limited set of terms, with a complicated and endlessly changing body of phenomena. Inevitably, when older schools are questioned and new movements arise, they engage in controversies over words; catchwords are attacked, slogans bandied, and neologisms deployed with the unflagging energy of language itself. Thus the same word means different things to differing critics. To cite the obvious instance, "romanticism," Irving Babbitt's poison, is Jacques Barzun's pap. It follows, not that the concept is meaningless, but that it is both broader and subtler than the endeavors of its interpreters to pin it down. To compile its multiple meanings and balance contradictory interpretations has therefore proved highly enlightening; but we need not stop, as Arthur Lovejoy would, with an irreducible plurality of definitions. No single formulation or simple pattern may cover, to anything but a rough approximation, a process so organic and continuous. But the common emphasis of the various romanticists on organism and continuity, as René Wellek reminds us, is in itself a clinching illustration of the attitudes they shared.

As for the classicists, it is mainly when viewed from a retrospective distance that they seem so consistent, so unanimous, indeed so urbane. We have only to glance at any of the commentaries on Aristotle's *Poetics* to realize how vast an area of verbal argument has been glossed over by their principles. Both adjectives, "classical" and "romantic," serving as a pair of labels, do little more than distinguish each from the other. Yet each is associated with a train of characteristic words, whose development may be historically traced and whose significance may be critically analyzed. Literary discourse acquires precision and perspective in the measure that it gains control over such words. It is charted by such landmarks as the sudden arrival of "originality," the gradual retirement of "imitation," the strategic vicissitudes of "imagination." Comparable changes have been taking place in our critical vocabulary during the century that separates the romantic period from our own day. Our failure to register them explicitly, to test them and prove them, to examine the circumstances that prompt them and the intentions they convey, may well be one of the sources of present confusion.

Contemporary criticism is nothing if not word-conscious. Yet we may observe, more regretfully than reproachfully, that our critics are not so semantically strict with themselves as they are with other writers. William Empson has taught them to perpetrate, as well as to discriminate, ambiguities. John Crowe Ransom has provided them with "texture" — a word which, though it sounds concrete and craftsmanlike, leaves a good many impressionistic loopholes. Kenneth Burke has concocted an eclectic diction, heavily fraught with italics and hedged with quotation-marks; by tinkering with terminologies, he has produced some very ingenious gadgets and some rather clumsy contraptions. I. A. Richards, having translated *katharsis* into the language of modern psychotherapy, has acknowledged the inadequacy of his translation. Repentance, it must be added, has carried him all the way back to Plato and the Bible. How far from them, for all our wishful talk about apparatus and method, can we be said to have come? Can we specify the impact of experience, on a reader or a writer, by opaquely referring to sensibility? Do we know more about what goes on, between one mind and the other, when we call it tension? Are opposites to be logically reconciled by the easy device of ambivalence? Though we shy away from value judgments like "great" and "good," we are always bestowing the accolade of "distinguished" — distinguished from what?

In default of immediate and positive answers to these questions, we need not conclude that criticism has been moving backwards or standing still. We need merely remember that, since its latest vantage point is for better or worse our own, we are in no position to draw conclusions. We can gauge directions, however, by projecting a curve which is based on a series of *loci critici* from the recent and remoter past. In pursuing one particular idea, together with the term that denotes it, we can hardly pretend to be definitive; for it has been the nature of that idea to evade definition, to take things for granted, to presuppose tacit acceptance. Nor can we be exhaustive in a matter which gathers importance with current esthetic discussion. We can take a few soundings and cut across categories, since the term "convention," which occurs in post-romantic contexts, has neoclassical associations. Since it not only facilitates the processes but establishes the motifs of art, it transcends the question-begging dichotomy of form and content. Since it depends upon the relationship between author and public, it opens up a viable channel to historians of style and taste. But, like all words that come to be widely used, it stands in increasing danger of obfuscation. The following examples and comments are set down in the hope of illustrating its utility and of possibly contributing toward its clarification.

II

Our starting point, then, is its currency today. This can be demonstrated *a fortiori* by reference to *Life*, a periodical more conscientiously devoted to photographic sensation than to verbal nicety. A recent editorial (August 15, 1948), campaigning for a more eupeptic brand of American fiction, attacks what it chooses to call "the slumming convention." It thereby echoes, as we shall see, the earlier counterattack against naturalism: the accusation that, in revolting against genteel conventions, the naturalists simply introduced hard-boiled ones. The significant, though questionable, implication is that *Life's* millions of readers — or rather, whatever proportion of its spectators can be counted upon to read its editorials — would appreciate the force of that paradox. Further examples could be multiplied by browsing at random through little magazines and scholarly journals. The most suggestive text that casually presents itself is a sentence from a review of a current novel in a popular weekly, by a critic whose usual writing is equally notable for common sense and responsible employment of the King's English. "Every novelist has his own conventions," writes George Orwell in *The New Yorker* (July 17, 1948), "and, just as in an E. M. Forster novel there is a strong tendency for the characters to die suddenly without sufficient cause, so in a Graham Greene novel there is a tendency for people to go to bed together almost at sight and with no apparent pleasure to either party."

Our first reaction is provoked by the final clause. Nothing could be farther from what convention implies, when we speak of it in ordinary conversation, than the twofold tendency that Mr. Orwell ascribes to Mr. Greene's characters. Clearly there are conventions and conventions, and the kinds invoked here conform more

closely to literary impulse than to social habit. It is precisely their
departure from what he regards as a social norm to which Mr.
Orwell takes exception, not so much on the grounds of propriety
as of probability. In the past it has more commonly been propriety,
the other kind of convention, which has rendered a novelist's treatment of sexual relationships improbable. In the one case personal
vagaries, in the other moral constraints, exaggerate or distort a
basic pattern of human behavior. But exaggeration or distortion
may inhere in the medium: it was thus conventional, in early romances, for heroes and heroines to die of love. This is not to say,
as Mr. Orwell says of Mr. Forster's characters, that those deaths
are inadequately motivated — nor that they are required by poetic
justice in expiation of a fate which was worse, nor that they are
gratuitous sacrifices on the altar of tragedy or desperate stratagems
for terminating a story. We must ask not what motivates the characters, but what the situations express; for when the means of
expression is inadequate or incomplete, the materials must be oversimplified, the effects externalized.

But when Messrs. Forster and Greene, with all their technical
adroitness and psychological sophistication, stray beyond the credulity of their readers, is it relevant to appeal to the license of convention? The novel began, with *Don Quixote*, by ridiculing the conventions of romance. We like to think that modern novelists are
unconstrainedly expressive, informal to the point of amorphousness,
"lawless" in André Gide's phrasing. To be reminded that they
observe laws of their own is therefore to admit that artistic media
are never quite free from some degree of formality. To add, with
Mr. Orwell, that certain conventions are peculiar to certain writers
is to give the term an unconventional twist. Few words have been
more loosely construed in latter-day criticism than "myth," as applied to the efforts of single individuals to promulgate their unique
imaginative constructions. A private convention, like a prefabri-
cated myth, is a contradiction in terms; neither, after all, can be
unilateral; just as genuine myths presuppose beliefs, so conventions
rely on prior awareness and widespread acceptance. The former

are warranted by a body of ideological assumptions, the latter shaped by a series of material conditions; and tradition is another name for the mechanism by which both are assimilated, organized, transmitted. The artist who lives in an untraditional epoch, like Blake at best, can only create pseudomyths. And the very refusal of critics like Mr. Orwell to accept a pattern of fictional behavior, the reader's disagreement with the writer's premise, relegates it to the category of pseudoconvention.

Now where the reader's sense of actuality corresponds with the writer's account of it, no special agreement between them is necessary. So sensitive a relationship, however, can all too easily be strained by either party. Originality, at the other extreme from conventionality, has very often manifested itself through unwillingness to abide by the preconditions and presuppositions to which the public clings. Critics, more often than not, have approached that conflict from the traditional side. They are therefore being somewhat inconsistent when they use the term "convention" pejoratively. The point at which they ordinarily apply it is wherever literature would seem to diverge from life. Such a divergence, when exemplified by the pastoral, was professedly unrealistic. But when writing that professes to be realistic is termed conventional, the problem of defining convention is augmented by the problem of agreeing on a definition of reality. This is not to be discovered, according to the editors of Life, in disillusioned novels of slums or wars. Yet what attests, more spectacularly than the Luce publications, that journalism and photography can be conventionalized? Alerted against the pseudoconventions of our contemporaries, we hesitate to identify works of the past with the realities of their respective periods. It may be that the Greeks had as brusque a notion of courtship as Graham Greene. On the hypothesis that they did, John Dennis tried to prove that love was conventionally slighted because it could not be realistically represented in classical tragedy.

If mere technique were directly correlated with real experience, the concept of convention would never have been called into being.

It traces its origin to imperfection — not to the fault of the craftsmen, but to the limitation of the craft. Since art never imitates
nature quite perfectly, in a one-to-one correspondence, there must
be a margin of error: an allowance for unnaturalness, a residue
of artificiality. Though this may result from numerous causes and
appear in innumerable guises, it has two related and recognizable
phases: it stereotypes life and it humanizes technique. The first
phase includes stock characters, standardized scenes, recurrent
themes — an example which subsumes them all is the *commedia
dell'arte*; another, closer at hand, the detective story. The second
phase is harder to discuss, and in greater need of discussion, because
it involves devices of presentation, modes of stylization, restrictions
of form. Formal terms have an ambiguous way of associating themselves with their incidental content. Thus "genre" begins by desig-
nating an artistic type, or perhaps a style, and ends by character-
izing a type of painting wherein the subject is more important than
the style. Yet the adaptation of any subject matter to the requirements of craftsmanship must, to some extent, enlist the aid of
convention. And every convention, however formalized, occupies
a plane where the discrepancies between matter and manner can
be circumvented; it upholds a covenant through which technical
factors and human variables, in the most literal meaning of the
two words, come together.

III

From the Latin roots for "coming together" to the modern instances just cited, the word "convention" has a long and varied
semantic history which can barely be outlined here. Though its
connection with literary criticism is of fairly recent date, it probably owes its wide European circulation to Roman law. Conventions as quasi-parliamentary bodies, empowered to call the king
himself to account, played a decisive part in seventeenth-century
England and eighteenth-century France. Conventions as nonpolitical treaties, deeply rooted in the theory and practice of international

relations, continue to operate in such matters as copyright. Over the centuries the area of connotation has broadened to cover a range of extralegal, socio-cultural applications: to extend the contractual principle, in short, into many different fields of human activity. This is the general significance that critics have been attempting to specialize for the purposes of esthetics. It is not accidental that convention was clearly discerned in the plastic arts before it began to figure in discussions of literature. And, like so many of our critical terms, it was well established in French before it appeared in English. *C'est convenu.* For those whose frame of reference is Anglo-American, however, the *Oxford English Dictionary* is the immediate authority to be consulted. The fact that, among the many meanings it records, the one we seek is only vaguely comprehended, does little to lessen the need for fuller discussion.

The first of two major categories, into which the definition breaks down, is devoted to "the action of convening" in its political and diplomatic aspects. The second, which more especially interests us, is concerned with "agreement, conventional usage." Ten subsidiary definitions are elaborated in roughly historical order, of which only the last two make any reference to the arts (an eleventh disposes of compounds). This is the ninth: "General agreement or consent, deliberate or implicit, as constituting the origin and foundation of any custom, institutions, opinion, etc., or as embodied in any accepted usage, standard of behavior, method of artistic treatment, or the like." The tenth follows: "In a bad sense: Accepted usage become artificial and formal, and felt to be repressive of the natural in conduct or art: conventionalism." This last variant, now obsolescent, is illustrated below with a quotation significantly chosen from Harriet Martineau's *Society in America* (1837). "The incubus of conventionalism" was apparently the English feminist's phrase for a state of mind which our native satirists would subsequently particularize. What is most significant is that no form of the word seems to have been employed in a nontechnical sense before the later years of the eighteenth century. It would then seem that the wave of individualism and the cult of nature associated with Rousseau, along with the concomitant distrust of etiquette and customary observance, helped to make men more explicitly conscious of social convention.

By failing to distinguish between social and artistic convention, the Oxford lexicographers have somewhat confused the chronology. Out of the Romantic protest against everything conventional, the critical usage emerged; hence its initial coloring was bound to be pejorative. The single literary citation that appears in the *OED* is late enough to observe historical neutrality. The year is 1879, the writer Matthew Arnold: "The Germans . . . were bent . . . on throwing off literary conventions, imitation of all sorts, and on being original." Here "imitation" and "original" are historically related to the issue he is describing; but presumably Arnold, a hundred years after the event, is pioneering in English when he links them with the continuance or rejection of convention. Not until we compare the cited fragment with the text of Arnold's essay, "A French Critic on Goethe," do we appreciate how directly the term has been imported from the Continent. The ellipsis conceals the pertinent fact that Arnold was virtually paraphrasing Edmond Scherer's account of the *Sturm und Drang:* "Il s'agissait de s'affranchir des conventions classiques, spécialement de l'imitation de la France," Scherer had written in *Etudes de littérature contemporaine* (1872), and had gone on — followed by Arnold — to discuss the substitution of romantic for classical models. Possibly Scherer's background gave him a cosmopolitan insight; very likely he was prompted on this occasion by his subject, Goethe. We shall find that, though the Germans implicitly grasped the idea of convention, they never quite assimilated the key-word.

The priority of the French can readily be documented, coinciding as it did with the adoption of the term into art criticism. Thus *convention* has no place in Lacombe's *Dictionnaire portatif des beaux-arts* (1759), but is fully discussed with respect to painting in Watelet and Levesque's *Dictionnaire des arts de peinture, sculpture, et gravure* (1792). This is at least fifty years in advance of

England, where it is ignored by Elmes's *Dictionary of the Fine Arts* (1826), and only the adjectival form is touched upon by Fairholt's *Dictionary of Terms in Art* (1854). By this time, its meaning had been more authoritatively stated in Ruskin's *Stones of Venice* (1851), as instanced by the *OED*: "Representation is said to be conventional either when a confessedly inadequate imitation is accepted in default of a better, or when imitation is not attempted at all, and it is agreed that other modes of representation, those by figures or by symbols, shall be its substitute and equivalent." These chary remarks are borne out by Ruskin's application of the term. Since nature was his esthetic ideal, under whose auspices he placed even Giotto, convention was destined to become his *bête noire*. He even lectured on "The Deteriorative Power of Conventional Art over Nature" (1859), and argued — from his own low estimate of Oriental art — that the Orient had produced no great civilization. He did not seem to be aware of how richly convention was typified in his venerated Gothic. It remained for another generation, schooled in the neater symmetries of Renaissance and Baroque, to give the term a sympathetic inflection through such spokesmen as Geoffrey Scott and T. E. Hulme.

In contrast to the English, who habitually take a vitalistic attitude toward artistic creation, the French have never hesitated to stress its mechanical details. Turning to them, we can also expect a sharper formulation of the problem at hand. In France, where the Convention made revolutionary history, the word itself seems peculiarly at home; and the special denotation that concerns us occupies an important place in the standard definition. "Accord tacite pour admettre certaines fictions ou certains procédés. La peinture, le théâtre offrent plusieurs conventions." This is Littré (1863), who amplifies — logically, if not chronologically — by indicating certain nuances: "Manière fausse de certains artistes. Dessin, couleur de convention." Now it happens that the official admission of words into the French language can be more or less accurately dated, because of the surveillance exercised by the Academy and the periodic revision and republication of its dictionaries. In the fifth edition of the *Dictionnaire de l'Académie* (1811), as in previous editions, *convention* is broadly defined without mention of its artistic or literary implications. In the sixth (1835), after reprinting the same generalities, some new illustrations are added: "Dans l'architecture il y a des ornements de convention. Dans beaucoup de pièces de théâtre, les paysans parlent un langage de convention. La comédie italienne a plusieurs personnages de convention."

Hence the date of acceptance coincides with the heyday of romanticism. On the other hand, the French Academy embodies the very spirit of convention — we cannot yet say the letter — so thoroughly that, even in this case, we must allow for a lag. We are justified in supposing that the new sense of the old word would never have received academic recognition had it not been introduced by more unconventional minds a generation or two before. We encounter it earliest in the criticism of that prescient thinker, versatile writer, and dramatic innovator, Diderot. In the second dialogue of his *Paradoxe sur le comédien*, expatiating on the differences between nature and art, the first speaker criticizes the monstrous unreality of theatrical characters.

LE SECOND.   Mais pourquoi ne révoltent-ils pas au théâtre?
LE PREMIER.   C'est qu'ils y sont de convention. C'est une formule donnée par le vieil Eschyle; c'est un protocole de trois mille ans.
LE SECOND.   Et ce protocole a-t-il encore longtemps à durer?
LE PREMIER.   Je l'ignore. Tout ce que je sais, c'est qu'on s'en écarte à mesure qu'on s'approche de son siècle et son pays.

But this passage is more prophetic than influential: written around 1770, it was not actually published until 1830. And though it anticipates nineteenth-century usage, it retains a tentative and metaphorical tone, as if Diderot were deliberately transferring the expression from law or diplomacy to the theater. The alternative, *protocole*, as his editor Ernest Dupuy points out, is elsewhere utilized in Diderot's writings on art. His attitude is intermediate, both recognizing and questioning the authority of convention, regarding it as one of those encrustations of the past which progressive enlightenment might confidently be expected to eliminate.

A work of much larger scope and influence, Madame de Staël's *De la littérature* (1800), was an agent of transition in this respect as in so many others. Contrasting the artificial grandeur of Racine's protagonists with the primordial simplicity of the Greek tragic heroes, the Swiss intermediary declared: "Tous les poètes ont peint ainsi les caractères, avant que de certaines habitudes monarchiques et chevaleresques nous eussent donné une nature de convention." The final turn of phrase — which was perforce omitted from the contemporary English translation (1803) — is almost a contradiction in terms. In a later chapter it attains the status of an axiom: "La nature de convention, au théâtre, est inséparable de l'aristocratie des rangs dans le gouvernement: vous ne pouvez soutenir l'une sans l'autre." Here it is worthy of note that the anonymous translator, seeking an English equivalent for *convention*, was obliged to render it by "conformity." Madame de Staël may be said to have carried the nonconformism of Rousseau from social institutions to literary genres. She believed that literature was perfectible; that works of the imagination, by repudiating all contrivance and acknowledging no limit, became the unimpeded vehicles of philosophy and sensibility. Convention, which for Diderot was a gentleman's agreement, had for her become a universal oppression; it was she who equated the *ancien régime* in politics with neoclassicism in the arts. It was Stendhal who turned her fundamental antithesis between Latin and Germanic writers into propaganda for the emergent romantic drama.

Not less ahead of its own time, not less paradoxical than Diderot's posthumous dialogue, Stendhal's *Racine et Shakespeare* was engendered in the controversy over the English Shakespeareans performing at Paris. It dismissed not only the classical unities and the rules of the French Academicians, but the "exigencies" and "necessities" of the stage itself, with a sweeping pun: "*habitude profondément enracinée.*" But, with the legal metaphor that Diderot had used to explain the excesses of theatricality, the same set phrase that Madame de Staël had attached to the tyranny of custom, Stendhal, in the classical mood that led him to recommend the style of the Civil Code, counseled respect for language — "*qui est une chose de convention,*" he added, in a footnote to the second of these two pamphlets (1825). In an unpublished essay, comparing the Italian language with French, he had already developed that penetrating insight: "Une langue est une convention; il faut que plusieurs millions d'hommes conviennent . . ." However arrant his individualism, he accepted the obligation to reach an understanding with his fellow men. He would be regarded, by the posterity he addressed, as more of a realist than a romanticist; in the long run *Racine et Shakespeare* foreshadows the Naturalists by conceiving the proscenium as an invisible fourth wall. Its naturalistic prediction that verse would yield to prose was soon to be parried by the arch-romantic Hugo; and Hugo's preface to *Cromwell*, without naming convention, would show an appreciation of its role. Though Stendhal realized that the stuff of the theater was illusory, he held that the greatest playwrights offered their audiences moments "d'illusion parfaite." In defining that illusion, ironically enough, he had recourse to Dr. Johnson's apology for Shakespeare. Still more ironically, he did not realize how he was thereby redefining convention: "l'imagination du spectateur se prête avec facilité aux suppositions du poète."

IV

Although the very name conveys a suggestion of the transient, the pretentious, and the superficial, convention has — as Stendhal glimpsed — an underlying purport which, instead of setting up barriers, draws men together. Since words are not the same as things, communication depends upon arbitrarily substituting the one for the other; each art, each genre exists by a prearrangement of available signs, a shared vocabulary of symbols; and what is true of verbal expression is even truer of the plastic arts, where the medium is more concrete, the representation more selective, the limitation — as Lessing demonstrated — narrower. When three dimensions are expressed by two, when the whole spectrum is reduced to black and white, when floral designs subserve architectural needs, when the human figure bends to the conformation of ivory or jade—when, in a word, the picture or sculpture challenges a visual comparison with its object, it soon exposes the process of conventionalization. Conventions are less evident in literature, as long as they are still working; they are seldom recognized until they have been nearly outgrown. Thus the invocation to the muse, which fulfilled a functional purpose as long as the epic was oral, survived as a conventional ornament of the literary epic. The recognition of convention, we have seen, historically coincided with its repudiation. Paradoxically, it was discovered by romanticists and realists who flouted it; while classicists and neoclassicists, who had embraced it, had done so unconsciously.

It was more or less assumed that conventions were survivals which, with the esthetic emancipation of mankind, would wither away. Some cultures were more conventional than others, to be sure, but they were commonly regarded as primitive or backward. The hypercivilized French were exceptional, for convention was the pivot around which their development revolved; they were at once its exemplars and its critics. Inevitably, when they rejected it, they turned for guidance to their nonconformist neighbors, the English, and to the notorious unconventionality of Shakespeare. Because the drama is plastic as well as literary, because it is both the most social and the most technical of forms, because it brings real and artificial components into such striking juxtaposition, it provided an arena in which the critical issue could be fought out. Pleading for the Shakespearean mode, in the preface to *Cromwell* (1827), Victor Hugo undertook to distinguish, "d'indiquer quelle est la limite infranchissable qui . . . sépare la réalité selon l'art de la réalité selon la nature." Stendhal's refusal to make this distinction had led him to attack dramatic verse: if and when the Cid speaks in prose, Hugo answered, why should not logic and realism equally compel him to speak in Spanish? Art cannot give us *la chose même* except by resorting to artifice; the theater has its trick mirrors, its optical illusions; the playwright, like the painter, manipulates techniques and calculates impressions. As for the unities: "L'unité d'ensemble est la loi de perspective du théâtre."

Convention thereby repeated the ancient principle of *ut pictura poesis*. The next step was for dramatic criticism to set forth its own version of the laws of perspective. This was very largely the contribution of Francisque Sarcey, the shrewd and popular critic of *Le Temps*, whom forty years of play-reviewing equipped with a technician's point of view and a highly professional concern for the "well-made play." During the summer of 1876, when the theatrical season had fallen off, Sarcey devoted his weekly column to sketching an "Essai d'une esthétique de théâtre," which later served as the introduction to his collected reviews, *Quarante ans du théâtre*. His point of departure was the basic condition the artist must face: in painting, the flatness of the canvas; in drama, the presence of the audience. Consideration for the latter explained those asides, soliloquies, and other conventions which differentiate what happens on the stage from the way it might happen in actual life.

Il ne faudrait pas donc simplement affirmer que le théâtre est la représentation de la vie humaine. Ce serait une définition plus exacte de dire: que l'art dramatique est l'ensemble des conventions universelles ou locales, éternelles ou temporaires, à l'aide desquelles, en représentant la vie humaine sur un théâtre, on donne à un public l'illusion de la vérité.

Frankly considering the dramatist an illusionist, Sarcey used *tricherie* synonymously with *convention*. Earlier and elsewhere he had pointed out that sentiments could be just as conventional as actions. Consistently, as an exponent of the single impression, he justified the classical separation of tragedy and comedy. Few unwritten books have as tantalizing a sound as his projected history of theatrical conventions.

In popularizing the term, Sarcey eliminated its disparaging overtones and increased its usefulness for matter-of-fact description. Hereafter the younger Dumas, even while attacking social conventions, could freely acknowledge his dependence on theatrical ones; and could defend himself, in the preface to *L'Etrangère* (1879), by describing all art as "une convention perpétuelle." Meanwhile the naturalistic school was assaulting tradition, and soon the Théâtre Libre would attempt to replace the *pièce bien faite* by the *tranche de vie*. Stanislavsky, reversing Diderot's paradox, would teach his actors to identify themselves emotionally with their roles, and would preach that convention (*uslovnost'*) was the very opposite of truth (*pravda*) and the very epitome of everything the Moscow Art Theater sought to avoid. The pros and contras were cogently stated by the literary historian, Charles-Marie Des Granges, in a pair of articles, for *Le Correspondant*, suggestively entitled "Les Conventions du théâtre naturaliste" (1904). He observed that the Naturalists were primarily novelists, impatient with the technicalities of a stricter medium. "Zola et ses collaborateurs, en prétendant chasser certaines conventions, en ont acclimaté d'autres." Whereas the old ones had been aristocratic and sentimental, the new ones were lurid and proletarian. Yet, "*convention pour convention*," Des Granges conceded that Naturalism had accomplished for its time the valued function of recalling the theater to the source of art, nature.

Tolstoy, whose career was an emphatic protest against the unnatural, was able to render grand opera ridiculous by merely taking its conventions literally. Wagner, one of the targets of *What Is Art?*, was being quite as literal when he installed the most realistic and up-to-date machinery at Bayreuth. Though Ibsen was praised and blamed for coming so dangerously close to reality, his meanings have been subsequently pursued to the plane of symbolism: Nora Helmer's tarantella has become a rite of liberation for her sex, and Eilert Lovborg, with vine leaves in his hair, is hailed as a reincarnation of Dionysus himself. Are the butlers and telephones and expository ruses of drawing-room comedy any less conventional than the choruses and messengers and *confidentes* of a statelier drama? If what the modern playgoer contemplates is a room with the fourth wall removed, why must its furniture always be facing that wall, and its occupants take such pains to balance one another? Does convention really tend, with the progress of art, to

undergo technological obsolescence? Or does each succeeding period re-enact its peculiar conventions? Clearly some compromise is
called for, such as Sarcey's distinction between the permanent and
the ephemeral. Differences of degree, as between France and England, and between the eighteenth and nineteenth centuries, were
noted by Henry James. Something could be said, he wrote of "The
London Theatres" in 1877, for that "conventional" quality which
they had been losing: "there was at least a certain method in its
madness; it had its own ideal, its own foolish logic and consistency."

The extent to which their respective traditions have lasted may
be reckoned by contrasting the grand manner of the Comédie
Française with the casual understatement of the British stage today.
Critics like Stendhal and historians like Taine, believing that this
contrast is inherent in the difference between blank verse and the
rhymed alexandrine, assume that it has always prevailed. Even
Bernard Shaw, that unconventional master of convention, accepts
it and plays upon it in his preface to *Overruled* (1912), where the
subsections deal with such topics as "The Convention of Jealousy,"
"The Limits of Stage Presentation," and "Our Illusive Scenery."
Under the rubric of "The Pseudo Sex Play," comparing Molière
unfavorably with himself, Shaw flings out and pulls in this twirling
sentence:

A play about the convention that a man should fight a duel or come to
fisticuffs with his wife's lover if she has one, or the convention that
he should strangle her like Othello, or turn her out of the house and
never see her or allow her to see her children again, or the convention
that she should never be spoken to again by any decent person and
should finally drown herself, or the convention that persons involved
in scenes of recrimination or confession by these conventions should
call each other certain abusive names and describe their conduct as
guilty and frail and so on: all these may provide material for very
effective plays; but such plays are not dramatic studies of sex; one might
as well say that Romeo and Juliet is a dramatic study of pharmacy because the catastrophe is brought about through an apothecary.

If a play is "about a convention," that must be a social convention;
a theatrical convention would be a part of the play. Yet the specific

instances that Shaw enumerates are clichés of behavior more likely to be observed on an old-fashioned stage than in everyday actuality. Shaw's deliberate method is to confound the two conventions so that their upholders, as he presents them in his plays, seem at once stuffy and stagey. Their antagonists, who are his protagonists, consequently seem to be all the more sensible and natural. But Shaw's common sense is at times so antiromantic that it becomes antitheatrical, and confuses the gesture with the emotion it symbolizes: "On a French stage a kiss is as obvious a convention as the thrust by which Macduff runs Macbeth through."

A self-conscious series of parodies (for example, *The Critic*) and burlesques (the Savoy operettas), conventionalizing the conventional as it were, characteristically reveals the English distaste for any kind of histrionic distortion. The fact that Shakespeare's audiences included the middle class, while Racine addressed himself to courtly circles, may help to account for the comparative realism of the Elizabethans. Again, Restoration drama was aristocratic, and took place — according to Lamb's well-known essay, "On the Artificial Comedy of the Last Century" (1822) — in an artificial world of make-believe. Lamb had a keen perception of stage illusion, of the "tacit understanding" between actor and audience, of "the barrenness of the imaginative faculty in the productions of modern art." But the gap between reality as he knew it and imagination as embodied in Shakespeare evoked an especially British paradox — that the greatest dramas ought not to be performed. Lamb therefore transposed them to narrative and anthologized their purple passages. His dramatic essays, as collected by Percy Fitzgerald, frequently hint at convention: "that symbol of the emotion which passes current in the theatre for it." In his own person Fitzgerald, a play-reviewer rather than an armchair critic, contributed a practical volume called *Shakespearean Representation: Its Laws and Limits* (1908). In *The World Behind the Scenes* (1881), he pioneered by laying bare the conditions, the tricks, and the "conventionalities" of the English stage.

Taine's *Histoire de la littérature anglaise* (1863–7) was a naturalistic sequel to the romantic manifestoes of Hugo and Stendhal; the subject attracted him because it seemed free from the neoclassicism that shackled French literature; like all too many commentators — and unlike his *Normalien* classmate, Sarcey — he equated Shakespearean drama with life itself; and because he was looking for documents rather than models, he confounded theatrical tradition with historical truth. Thus, forgetting that feminine roles were played by boys, Taine naïvely inferred that Elizabethan women had had a certain masculinity. Actually, it could be maintained that Shakespeare's plays are more conventional than Racine's, since they take so much more for granted and incarnate so many traditions. At all events, their twentieth-century interpreters have tried to reconstruct the vast and complicated framework of convention within which Shakespeare operated. Though he ignored the *liaison des scènes*, he observed what has been called "the law of re-entry": he carefully synchronized exits and entrances with changes of scene. Since neither he nor his fellow playwrights bothered to formulate the rules they worked by, it has been the helpful task of such scholars as W. J. Lawrence to sift the antiquarian and textual evidence. More recently these findings have been utilized for critical purposes in such books as Miss M. C. Bradbrook's *Themes and Conventions of Elizabethan Tragedy*. E. E. Stoll, in analyzing Shakespearean characterization, has followed the lines laid down by Sarcey's analysis of Molière; and although Shakespeare's characters transcend the conventions in which they were cast, Professor Stoll's method has proved an effective counterweight to the tenuous psychologizing of the romanticists.

French criticism made convention a weapon for offensive and defensive use in contemporary polemics. Anglo-American scholarship made it an instrument for the reinterpretation of great works composed in obsolete forms. It was made the basis of an invidious and iconoclastic comparison by William Archer in *The Old Drama and the New* (1923). Translator of Ibsen, colleague of Shaw, spokesman for a modernism which has since become somewhat dated, Archer endeavored on behalf of these allegiances to debunk the Elizabethan and Restoration dramatists. Drama comprised two elements, he declared: "faithful imitation" and "wilful exaggeration." Its evolution, from Webster to Galsworthy, was a gradual "purification"; extraneous matter, lyrical and operatic, had been — in Archer's slippery phrase — "sloughed off"; and the theater had progressed from a maximum to an "irreducible minimum" of conventions. To this T. S. Eliot, in "Four Elizabethan Dramatists: A Preface to an Unwritten Book" (1924), retorted: "Mr. Archer confuses faults with conventions." Eliot found it easy to reconcile Archer's attitude with Lamb's, since both consented to a divorce between drama and poetry. But where the Elizabethans were too conventional for Archer, they were too realistic for Eliot: only one English play, *Everyman,* escaped the disintegrating force of "unlimited realism" and came "within the limitations of art." That exception may throw some light on the limitations of *Murder in the Cathedral* and *The Family Reunion.* In his subsequent "Dialogue on Dramatic Poetry," Eliot relates this doctrine to his other orthodoxies by deploring our modern lack of social and moral, as well as artistic, conventions.

V

Thus far we have been concerned with explicit enunciations and clear adumbrations of our term. To look beyond the term is to pursue an idea so comprehensive and ubiquitous that, in full justice to it, the history of criticism ought some day to be rewritten. All that these sketchy paragraphs can do is to indicate certain points which are connected by the word, and certain gaps which are filled in by the concept, once it has been enunciated. Probably that connection was first established by Sarcey's more erudite and imaginative fellow critic, Jules Lemaître, when, in *Corneille et la Poétique d'Aristote* (1888), he pointed out that what Corneille called *"fictions du théâtre"* were known to latter-day writers as *conventions.* Conventions, of course, are implicit in any critical system; but not until the Romantic Movement, which honored

them more in the breach than in the observance, was it necessary
to name them; classical critics merely referred to "the rules." The
change in terminology is significant because it emphasizes the difference between compulsory enforcement and voluntary acceptance. It parallels the transition in political thought from natural
law to the Rousseauistic doctrine of social contract. Classicism
itself, with its codes and academies, its judgments and legislations,
is — as Irving Babbitt put it in *Rousseau and Romanticism* — "a
great convention." What need was there to designate the basis on
which so widely accepted a body of principles rested? Adherence
to custom or violation of propriety could, in the specific instance,
be dealt with under the heading of *decorum*. Yet literature is increasingly conscious of its own exigencies and, long before it recognized convention, it made use of a cognate expression: *les conven-
ances*.

We may say without drastically simplifying the classicists that,
in balancing the rival claims of talent and technique, of subject
and medium, of the living and the literary elements in a work,
they exhibit either a Longinian or a Horatian emphasis. Clearly
convention is on the side of the latter, with its norm of *usus*, its
catalogue of *colores*. Aristotle, who was broad enough to comprehend both positions, attributed esthetic experience to the interplay
of two fundamental instincts: *mímesis* and *harmonía* (1448b). As
a philosopher, he was primarily interested in the problem of imitation — that is, in the external relationship of art to nature — and
this preoccupation is reflected at length in the thinking of other
critics. Nonetheless the *Poetics*, in some detail, goes into the internal relations of artistic form, describes the physical conditions
under which genres developed, and even prescribes appropriate
meters, stylistic techniques, scenic practices, and so forth. With
practical injunctions, rather than theoretical formulations, ancient
rhetoric and medieval *dictamen* paid their respects to convention.
But convention excludes invention, which sooner or later reasserts
the claims of the other side: the real thing, the "nameless grace,"
the *je ne sais quoi* that is never quite conveyed by the descriptive

and prescriptive tradition of the *Ars Poetica*. Hence the neoclassical rediscovery of the "sublime," which in its turn was tamed by the romanticists. Sublimity was brought down to the conventional plane that beauty occupied in Burke's antithesis, *The Sublime and the Beautiful*, while the "grotesque" supplied that inventive element which Hugo found characteristic of modern realism.

The classical ideal, as formulated by Longinus and others (193r), was posited on the perfect correspondence of nature and art. To the extent that this ideal had been realized, conventions had been allowed to pass unnoticed. As long as the artist had treated probable subjects and overcome the inherent difficulties of his medium, there could have been no question of artificiality: *artificiale*, for the critics of the Italian Renaissance, meant simply artistic. Rhyme ideally corresponded with reason, according to Boileau, and Pope made little distinction between copying models and imitating nature. But neoclassicism, by over-insisting upon the rules, went from "nature methodized" to denatured method; and thereupon romanticism drew its heavy line between the artificial and the natural. When Thomas Campion attacked the irrationality of rhyme, when Dryden condemned a dramatic personage for stepping out of his role, their term of reproach had been "inartificial." Naturalistic critics, pledged to eliminate artifice from the arts, would have left off the privative prefix. In the actual instances the criticized fault was more cogently defended, on the grounds of convention, than it could later have been; for meanwhile the body of opinion on which judgment hinged, no longer coming together, was falling apart; and the old consensus, its basis in common sense, was breaking down into disputed tastes and subjective impressions. It grew accordingly harder to evaluate, by any objective canons of correctness or probability, how closely a given representation approximated the object represented. The distance that now revealed itself between them was the province of convention.

If art and nature were anywhere united, Friedrich Schlegel declared in "Über die Grenzen des Schönen," it was in the theater. Yet the drama of Elizabethan England and of Spain's Golden

Age, which proved so convincing to romantic generations, had been severely censured by contemporaries for its lack of verisimilitude. To the Platonic charge that poets were liars, much echoed in the Renaissance, apologists like Sidney had replied by differentiating poetic from literal truth, and by according the poet "liberty . . . to frame the history to the most tragical conveniency." Toward the plays of his age, however, Sidney took as censorious a view as Cervantes took of Lope de Vega, or as the French Academy would take of the *Cid*. Corneille, like Ben Jonson, was caught in a midway position between a heritage of indigenous conventions and the superimposition of classical rules. He regarded the dogma of the three unities as an effort to repudiate the persisting convention (or fiction) of the simultaneous scene. The Italian promulgator of that dogma, Lodovico Castelvetro, bore witness to the development of the proscenium, the adaptation of perspective to the stage, and the use of scenery to create a pictorial illusion. Castelvetro really took nothing for granted; if he sanctioned verse, his reasons were strictly functional: because he believed it carried better than prose. He believed that spectators, having literally accepted the setting as one particular place, should never be asked to consider it another; and, above all, that the time they spent in the theater should actually coincide with the timing of the dramatic action. Seldom can such positive recommendations as the unities of time and place have been founded on such negative considerations as an unwillingness to try the faith of the audience.

Classical precept, with Horace, had warned against straining credulity by melodramatic improbabilities: "quod ostendis mihi hic, incredulus odi" (188). The neoclassical unities articulated a rational and realistic program for avoiding possible confusions and arbitrary discontinuities. But, while predicating a mentally immobile spectator, they demanded from him an incredible agility in following the crowded events of an "artificial day." The multiple scene that Sidney ridiculed, where Europe confronted Asia across the same stage, was scarcely any more conventional than the situation Dryden looked askance at, where a farfetched suc-

cession of public events had to take place in the king's bedchamber. Dryden's *Essay of Dramatic Poesy* is an equable study
in opposing conventions: ancients against moderns, French against
English, Elizabethan against Restoration, rhyme against blank
verse. In his *Defence of the Essay* Dryden pushed his arguments
much further. "Bare imitation" should be heightened by artifice;
playwrights, like painters, should avoid "too near a resemblance";
insofar as drama was fiction rather than truth, it should be judged
by imagination rather than reason. In appealing "to every man's
imagination," Dryden paved the way for Dr. Johnson's preface to
Shakespeare, with its decisive appeal "from criticism to nature."
If nothing more immutable than "the laws which custom had prescribed" kept tragedy and comedy apart, Johnson saw no objection
to their intermingling. And, if the spectator could once imagine
himself in another time and place — "Delusion, if delusion be admitted, has no certain limitation." Unity was just as conventional
as multiplicity. When Johnson spoke of delusion rather than illusion, he kicked the stone; he reminded audiences that, under any
circumstances, the stage was a stage and the players were merely
players. To transcend the unrealities of art required that deliberate
effort which Coleridge would call for: "that willing suspension of
disbelief . . . which constitutes poetic faith." More specifically,
Coleridge would define "stage-illusion" in his Shakespearean
lecture-notes as

a sort of temporary half-faith, which the spectator encourages in himself and supports by a voluntary contribution on his own part, because
he knows that it is at all times in his power to see the thing as it really
is.

None but the most naïve, like Partridge at Garrick's play, could
mistake the reproduction for the reality. Connoisseurs could feel,
with the Abbé Du Bos, that their awareness of form brought higher
satisfactions: "que l'art de l'imitation intéresse plus que le sujet
même de l'imitation . . . Que le plaisir que nous avons au théâtre
n'est point produit par l'illusion." Artists, encouraged by Sir Joshua
Reynolds, could make "professed" or "allowed deviations from

nature," and thereby perfect "the natural imperfection of things."
Art could be nature's master instead of its slave; and convention
could be the hallmark of artistry, instead of the sign of imperfect
mastery. These were the changing conceptions that came to a head
when Schiller, uniting Greek with Shakespearean tragedy, revived
the chorus in *Die Braut von Messina* (1803), and justified his experiment with a prefatory note which — in essence — was a plea
for convention. Schiller reconciled this with the quest for freedom
by envisaging reality as a constraining force and imagination as
liberation, "eine gewisse Befreiung von den Schranken des Wirklichen." Since art realized its ideal by idealizing the real, he maintained, the artist should scorn illusion and oppose naturalism.

Der bildenden Kunst gibt man zwar notdürftig, doch mehr aus kon-
ventionellen als aus inneren Gründen, eine gewisse Idealität zu; aber
von der Poesie und von der dramatischen ins besondere verlangt man
I l l u s i o n, die, wen sie auch wirklich zu leisten wäre, immer nur
ein armseliger Gauklerbetrug sein würde. Alles Aussere bei einer dramatischen Vorstellung steht diesem Begriff entgegen — alles ist nur
ein Symbol des Wirklichen.

This passage links our original semantic inquiry with the broader
questions we have since encountered. The word *konventionell* is
here employed, in the more traditional and superficial sense, on
the very occasion when a more dynamic and profound idea of
convention is being put forward. The French derivation of the
word is underlined by its context; the German equivalent, *Über-
einkunft* or *Vertrag*, seems to have been a neglected possibility;
in recent Shakespearean scholarship *Konvention* is virtually inter-
changeable with *Stilform*. It is perhaps worth noting that, where
the American translation of *The Birth of Tragedy* speaks of "conventions," Nietzsche has used the more general term, *Wesen*.
Nietzsche, however, echoing Schiller and heralding Wagner, lifted
the whole subject to a high plane of generality when he asserted
in *Die Geburt der Tragödie*: ". . . es sei nicht genug, dass man das
nur als eine poetische Freiheit dulde, was doch das Wesen aller
Poesie sei."

VI

The foregoing definitions could be supplemented, and the aplications could be multiplied indefinitely, but already they range from one extreme to the other: from limit to license. At one extreme, we make allowance for technical faults, crude materials, restrictive conditions. At the other, we become aware of willful irregularities, self-conscious liberties, specialized virtuosities. Between these poles of under- and over-development comes a central phase where the disparity between art and nature seems to disappear, where difficulty has been overcome and mannerism has not yet set in. Such, in rough outline, is the history of most artistic genres — for example, of Western painting from the Italian Primitives to the School of Paris. Frequently, too, the career of a great artist falls into such a pattern. Goethe described the part that convention plays in the apprenticeship of genius when he wrote: "In der Beschränkung zeigt sich erst der Meister." If genius is distinguished by originality, convention is what originality is distinguished from. "Invention" — the old rhetorical term for "imagination" — may be the most exact antonym for our term; and we may well agree that convention without invention would be undesirable; but we seldom realize that the converse is quite unthinkable. We are still the heirs of the Romanticists, and our basic unit of esthetic discussion is still personality. Our literary history is largely collective biography; and though stylistic criticism has taken some promising steps, it still conceives its subject too exclusively in terms of personal expression. Convention, more broadly conceived, is collective style. Whereas new movements are propelled by individual talents, the vehicle of convention is tradition.

We live, however, in what Thomas Mann's *Doktor Faustus* has called "a time of broken-down conventions" (*zerstörten Konventionen*). This is at least as true of society at large as it is of literature; our critics, social as well as literary, register a growing fear of disintegration on every plane. Some of them look upon civilization itself, in Irving Babbitt's phrase, as "a great convention," whose survival depends upon the revival of old-fashioned doctrines and outmoded institutions. Their critique of naturalism, in philosophy, scientific experiment, and the arts, has retroactively extended through the Enlightenment to the Renaissance. Over that period they rightly discern a consistent and accelerating tendency to cast off conventions in every genre and approach the goal of literal reproduction. The accumulation of technique, and indeed of technology, made it possible to reproduce directly things which heretofore had been conventionally rendered. Perspective and the unities, as we have seen, converted the spectator of a dramatic performance into the witness of an actual event. But each medium, though it be more fluid than the last, has its limitations. If not with the discovery of the silent film, then surely with the introduction of sound, art might be said to have completed its illusion of reality. And if our films are unimaginative in their use of music, perhaps it is because they are afraid of spoiling the illusion. Hence any burst of song must be realistically motivated; there can be no hint of the operatic, unless perchance the scenario includes a visit to the opera. Such thoroughgoing literalness, which finds its usual theme in the life-story of a composer or singer, is destined to be defeated by convention; for the truth turns out to be rather uneventful and must therefore be twisted into conformity with the conventional standards of Hollywood entertainment.

The film is more successful in its mechanical aspects which, like all smoothly operating conventions, are seldom discussed; audiences more or less consciously understand that lapses of time and changes of place are betokened by certain tricks of cutting; and the association we make between moving lips on the screen and words which emerge from the public address system is convention at its purest. When Daguerre developed photography, it discouraged painters from competing with reality and encouraged a keener sense of the peculiarities and potentialities of canvas and pigment. Similarly, the cinema released the drama from its subservience to the claims of realism. The dramaturgy of Bertolt Brecht — which

cultivates esthetic distance by rebuffing emotional identification
— is a striking, but by no means unique, return to the formalities
of an earlier or more exotic stage. In 1916 William Butler Yeats
announced that he was going to Asia for a more distant, a more
aristocratic, a more symbolic form. In admiration for the Japanese
Noh plays, Ezra Pound went so paradoxically far as to repudiate
"Western convention of plot." Granted that every culture has its
own conventions, it was precisely the strictness of Japan's that
attracted such bohemian westerners as Lafcadio Hearn; but though
a writer can reject his native convention, he cannot arbitrarily and
eclectically choose another with complete success, as Pound's later
Cantos demonstrate.

On the way conventions are formed and break down, an authoritative light has been thrown by John Livingston Lowes's *Convention and Revolt in Poetry* (1919), which may in turn have drawn
some inspiration from an article, "Originality and Convention in
Literature" (*Quarterly Review*, January 1906), by the exponent of
folklore and balladry, Francis B. Gummere. Professor Lowes, the
accomplished interpreter of both Chaucer and Coleridge, was
equally sympathetic to the manifestoes of Imagism then resound-
ing. Knowing that "revolt is perennial," he welcomed "the new
poetry" as the sort of reaction that had occurred before and would
occur again — for he also knew that conventions, though differing
in detail, were similar in behavior. His cyclical interpretation of
poetic trends seems to have been richly corroborated a generation
afterward. Today, when Amy Lowell is no longer "the most modern of the moderns" and *vers libre* is more quaint than revolutionary, her cousin writes in metaphysical strophes and other young
poets outvie one another in sestinas and pantoums. While the
avant-garde fights a rear guard action, the experiments of the 1920's
are assimilated by slick middlebrow periodicals; and while documentary journalism proves to be stranger than fiction, serious novelists once again feel free to abandon the realistic for the historical
and legendary, the mythical and fantastic. Walt Whitman, for
whom convention was incompatible with democracy, inevitably

failed in his program to "express the inexpressible," since expressibility presupposes the replacement of a vague emotion by a concrete image — a symbolic process which is also conventional, if and when the symbolism is accepted.

Convention, as Paul Valéry redefined it in *Variété*, is a mysterious difference between impression and expression. When Thomas Campion proposed — on behalf of a stricter convention — to liberate English poetry from the shackles of rhyme, Samuel Daniel opposed him on the basis of tradition, custom, and example. When Valéry defended those voluntary chains, "les exigences d'une stricte prosodie," he did not assume that reason accorded with rhyme. He argued in 1920 that language naturally offered too little resistance; that it must be artificially framed by rules; that art, after all, is a game in which man seeks to satisfy "un instinct de l'artificiel." The Aristotelian instinct of "harmony," so long subordinated to "imitation," has thus been reasserting itself. By turning Aristotle upside down, and maintaining that nature imitated art, Oscar Wilde had overstated the case for convention; but he had re-emphasized its primary importance and its subsequent neglect. With the decline of the nineteenth-century view that the secrets of nature had all but yielded themselves to the human mind, it appeared that all knowledge — even science — reposed on no greater certainty than convention. The truth, it now appeared, was less likely to be biological than mathematical. The eminent mathematician, Henri Poincaré, who considered Euclidean geometry "une sorte de convention de langage," adapted this concept to scientific method in *La Science et l'hypothèse*. The result was a positivistic distinction between the framework of man's assumptions and the structure of the universe: the so-called laws of nature, if not arbitrary, were conventional.

Meanwhile, at the opposite pole, Benedetto Croce has polemicized against convention from his well-known anti-empirical point of view. Hesitating over the term in his *Estetica*, Croce writes: "However if there are to be conventions, something is necessary which is not conventional, but is itself the agent of convention...

This is the spiritual activity of man." And this is the kind of thinking that leads to idealism in philosophy and intuitionism in esthetics; that begs the questions Poincaré's empiricism has faced, and sets critics off on a futile quest for the inexpressible. To merge the arts with all the intangibles that enter into the spiritual activity of man, to overlook the work in favor of the author, is to forego our best opportunity for understanding what expression is and how it functions. Technicalities, however limited, help us more than generalities — particularly when they concern the relations of technique with history and society. The socio-historical approach needs to be balanced — not canceled out — by methods of formal analysis. We could do much worse than borrow a leaf from the books of the Russian formalist school — let us say from Victor Shklovsky, whose critical point of departure is "the knight's move" (*khod konya*), "the convention of art." Without questioning the ultimate importance of whatever lies beyond, we may humbly remember that there are no short cuts to it, and that conventions are avenues which lead from us to it, if not from it to us. Our position is brought home to us by the plea of Shakespeare's Chorus in *Henry V*: "Piece out our imperfections with your thoughts."

Writers in exile have been among the most impressive witnesses to human experience. Though the testimony of their writings or their biographies is uniquely individual in each case, history has lately been accumulating so much of it that it speaks with the voice of our time. Yet there has been little attempt to grasp its collective significance, as I pointed out in a bibliographical note too skimpy to be worth reprinting here. That exceptional critic, Georg Brandes, began his Main Currents in Nineteenth Century Literature with a volume wholly devoted to the émigrés of the late eighteenth century and the role they played in instigating the Romantic Movement. It will take many such volumes, probably written by many collaborators, to chronicle the literary migrations of the twentieth century on a scale commensurate with their importance in our lives. The paper that follows, though it does no more than sketch a background, was prompted by the timeliness of this theme. Delivered at Washington University, Saint Louis, under the auspices of the Oreon E. Scott Foundation, it was published in a volume of the Washington University Studies entitled Essays in Comparative Literature (1961). An abbreviated version, given as a talk for the Third Programme of the British Broadcasting Corporation, was printed in The Listener (October 15, 1959).

Books are said to have their fates; but seldom can these have been signalized by so immediate and so intense a discussion as that which surrounded the publication of Doctor Zhivago and the subsequent award of the Nobel Prize to Boris Pasternak. This double event has had a different reception from readers in the West than what it has had from nonreaders in the East. The novel illustrates its theme, which — I take it — is the survival of individuality against crushing odds, by demonstrating that artistic values and critical standards have actually survived in the Soviet Union. That idea, as it turns out, is unthinkable to the majority of Russian writers today; hence they met together and loudly clamored for the deportation of Pasternak. He in turn, after having accepted and then rejected the accolade of the Swedish Academy, addressed an appeal to Premier Khrushchev — a letter touchingly reminiscent of those poetic epistles which Ovid addressed to the Emperor Augustus. Having been deported to the shores of the Black Sea, where he would end his days among the Goths, Ovid had vainly pleaded for the privilege of returning to Rome. His case was cited by Russia's greatest poet, Pushkin, when he too was rusticated at the behest of the Tsar; but Pushkin, unlike Pasternak, had been forbidden to travel abroad. And even Ovid, though in exile, could console himself with the thought that his poems were read at Rome; whereas, though Pasternak was allowed to continue precariously in his homeland, his book cannot be read by his compatriots. The exile is *Doctor Zhivago*.

In his letter to that party official who seems to decide such matters personally, Pasternak went so far as to say: "A departure beyond the borders of my country is for me equivalent to death. . . ." The shock of this statement is somewhat alleviated if we remember that, during the years when he could not appear as a poet in his own right, Pasternak employed his skills in translating Shakespeare. The little we know about Shakespeare does not suggest that he, too, was ever threatened with exile; yet there are few significant human problems which, in his sympathetic way, he has not envisaged. Consequently a literary exile, James Joyce, could view his own situation as reflected in the Shakespearean mirror, and could observe: "The note of banishment, banishment from the heart, banishment from home, sounds uninterruptedly from *The Two Gentlemen of Verona* onward till Prospero breaks his staff, buries it certain fathoms in the earth, and drowns his book." Banishment from the heart sounds most poignantly when Romeo is parted from Juliet. Banishment from home sounds most powerfully when, as the gates of Rome are closing behind him, Coriolanus shakes his fist at his fellow citizens and shouts: "I banish you!" But Pasternak, in equating death with expulsion, seems to have had in mind that lyrico-dramatic scene in which Richard II pronounces against Thomas Mowbray, Duke of Norfolk, "the hopeless word of 'never to return.'" Whereupon Mowbray's protest against his doom becomes a poet's tribute to his medium:

The language I have learnt these forty years,
My native English, now I must forgo;
And now my tongue's use is to me no more
Than an unstrung viol or a harp,
Or like a cunning instrument cas'd up
Or, being open, put into his hands
That knows no touch to tune the harmony . . .
What is thy sentence then but speechless death,
Which robs my tongue from breathing native breath?

There is, of course, an alternative possibility. Like Mowbray,
Pasternak considered himself too old to live out his life in a foreign tongue; at an earlier stage of his career he had considered the
question of emigration and, like Dr. Zhivago, decided against it.
Had he chosen that course, it would have led to a further alternative: whether to go on writing in Russian for the dwindling en-
claves of refugees, with small hope of reaching an audience within
one's relinquished country, or to take up an untuned verbal instrument, to write as well as one could for the audience of one's
adopted country. That choice is strikingly personified by another
writer whose recent novel has brought him into the public eye;
who, while living in Berlin and Paris during the twenties and
thirties, published a series of Russian novels and tales under the
pseudonym of Sirin; and who, after coming to the United States,
has been writing in English under his own name, Vladimir Nabokov. It is not surprising that a feat of such virtuosity should be
characterized by a high degree of stylistic self-consciousness, that
it should sound the note of banishment and indeed run the gamut
of displacement, or that it should find its consummating theme
in an illicit union between a decadent European and an infantile
American. A less brilliant but equally striking example of the artist
as a displaced person, and of his art as a celebration of vaga-
bondage, is the case of the gallicized Irishman, Samuel Beckett,
and his breakdown of civilized discourse into an absurdly scurrilous
dialogue between two tramps awaiting an advent which never
arrives. Deracination has become so common that it has its professional spokesmen, such as the Anglo-Hungarian journalist,

Arthur Koestler. The Alsatian poet, Iwan Goll, has rechristened the modern author with the generic name of *Jean Sans Terre*, John Landless.

The situation, then, is not unexampled; and these are simply extreme expressions of the deracinated culture, the metic condition, the polyglot misunderstanding of our time. Joseph Conrad, whose centennial we celebrated not long ago, left a Poland dominated by Russia and emerged as a major English novelist. But Conrad was less interested in England than in the tropical outposts or fugitive ports of the British Empire, just as he was less interested in adventure than in the exploration of restless consciences seeking refuge there. And since Conrad had never been a Polish novelist, he was not faced with Nabokov's linguistic decision. "My private tragedy . . . ," the latter concludes in his postscript to *Lolita*, "is that I had to abandon my natural idiom, my untrammeled, rich, and infinitely docile Russian tongue for a second-rate brand of English, devoid of any of those apparatuses — the baffling mirror, the black velvet backdrop, the implied associations and traditions — which the native illusionist, frac-tails flying, can magically use to transcend the heritage in his own way." Obviously, Mr. Nabokov is much too modest; he has kept a trick or two up his sleeve; all too few of his contemporaries, born to English wordplay, can prestidigitate with it as he can. Yet even here, in this elegant and eloquent sentence, his flying "frac-tails" reveal a certain resistance to perfect assimilation. Whether by lapse or design, he has used the gallicism *frac* where Anglo-American usage would have said "coat-tails," if the old-fashioned magician chose to wear a frock-coat. ("Frocktails" turn up in *Ulysses* but not in the *Oxford English Dictionary*.)

Mr. Nabokov remains, for our surprise and delight, a Continental dandy. If, as he half admits, his book itself is a record of his love affair with the English language, he would also recognize that no latter-day romance can be quite so passionate as first love. Of this, too, he has spoken in a poem, a remarkable *tour de force* explaining to English readers—in the meters of Russian poets —

how inexplicable is the magic of their poetry. And here he speaks as a disinherited prince, a banished Duke of Norfolk as it were:

> Beyond the seas where I have lost a sceptre,
> I hear the neighing of my dappled nouns,
> soft participles coming down the steps,
> treading on leaves, trailing their rustling gowns.

Others, particularly among the Slavs, have taken a similar retrospect. An eminent Polish man of letters now settled in New York, Joseph Wittlin, has promised to give us an outline of what he calls the physiology of émigré literature. If we may judge from his introductory paper, "Sorrow and Grandeur of Exile," delivered at a meeting of the International P. E. N. Club, Center for Writers in Exile, American Branch, and published in the *Polish Review* (Spring-Summer 1957), it will be a searching analysis. Mr. Wittlin is profoundly aware of the dangers that waylay the alien writer in ghetto-like colonies, and of the haze of sentimentality that is likely to blur his retrospective glance. But the sorrow is counterpoised by the grandeur in an impressive number of cases which Mr. Wittlin discusses with firsthand authority, where placelessness became a path to timelessness and isolation a pedestal for stature. One of the most interesting phenomena is what Mr. Wittlin describes as "the return of words," those echoes which haunt the exile's imagination long after the sounds have ceased, because they reverberate through the hollow corridors of memory.

Such a phenomenon is jauntily acted out when Mr. Nabokov conjures up glimpses of his lost estate, where parts of speech champ in the ghostly stables or stroll along the terraces dressed in outmoded finery. One or two other illustrations of what he elsewhere calls "the science of exile," broadening the scope of our inquiry, may help to convince us that the return of words is a timeless experience for any displaced poet, and that his cultural problem naturally tends to assume a linguistic form. A pertinent one is that of Heinrich Heine, dying by inches in Paris, *in der Fremde,* and dreaming about the oaks and violets of his fatherland. "Ich hatte einst ein schönes Vaterland." His dream was vocal as well as visual;

it caressed him with words of love in lyrical German; but alas, they sounded too good to be credible; it was only a dream. "Es war ein Traum." Another is that of García Lorca, the Spanish poet in New York, writing his poems of solitude during his days as a graduate student in the gregarious purlieus of Columbia University. His observation, while contemplating the sleepless city at night from Brooklyn Bridge, was precisely the corollary of Heine's: that this life was not a dream. "No es sueño la vida." Both poets bear witness to the wide span that separates the brusque reality of here and now from the treasured remembrance of elsewhere and otherwhile.

However, our most illustrious exemplar must be Dante, whose imaginary pilgrimage through hell and purgatory and heaven was paralleled by his actual wanderings from city to city after having been expelled from his beloved Florence. In his great dream-vision and in his other writings, he cannot refrain from lamenting his earthly predicament. In the *Paradiso* he is greeted by the spirit of his great-great-grandfather, who prophesies that Dante will taste the bread and climb the stairway of strangers. Still more moving, because it occurs at an unexpected moment, is Dante's allusion in *De Vulgari Eloquentia*. There, within the dryly technical context of his Latin argument for composing in the vernacular, he quotes several specimens of word order, including this one: "I sympathize with all who are loyal, but especially with those who, languishing in exile, only revisit their native land in their dreams." Whereupon, suddenly, a syntactic relationship is charged with a deeply personal emotion. It was remarked of Ugo Foscolo, who was driven from Venice and died at London, that — in repeating a pattern set by Dante — he had turned exile into a characteristic institution of Italian literature. But though the city-states bred and drove away more than their share of poet-patriots, the institution was no more Italian than it was confined to literature. The history of civilization itself could be reckoned by an endless sequence of migrations, from those which have strewn their relics throughout the Homeric epos to those which account for our presence on this continent.

Somewhere in the dark backward behind them all looms the

archetype of a Paradise Lost, a glimpse of a primeval garden or
ideal realm from which mankind has been exiled for its sins. The
Judeo-Christian tradition has constantly looked back toward that
original idyll and ahead toward a Paradise Regained. A patriarchal
leader, guiding the children of Israel out of the wilderness, brings
the law down to them from Mount Sinai, beholds their promised
land from the top of Mount Pisgah, but is fated to die in exile.
An apostolic scribe, himself an exile from Rome to the island of
Patmos, thereon is vouchsafed a divine revelation which will terrify
and illumine half the world. A psalmist tunes his harp to the plain-
tive harmonies of tribal captivity:

> By the waters of Babylon,
> There sat we down, yea, we wept,
> When we remembered Zion ...

Thence again we witness a dispersion; the promised land fades
into time remembered; and again the words return from their
place of origin, from Zion to Babylon:

> How shall we sing the Lord's song
> In a strange land?

Exile has been regarded as an occupational hazard for poets in
particular ever since Plato denied them rights of citizenship in
his republic. His attitude, prompted by the belief that they could
exercise a demoralizing influence over other citizens, might have
been invoked by Augustus in banishing Ovid. Ovid mentions two
charges against himself: "*carmen et error,*" a poem and a mistake. What the mistake was we cannot be sure, though it might
have been a scandal involving the Emperor's daughter and her
circle. We know that the poem was Ovid's *Ars Amatoria*, a work
which is not without beguiling qualities, but which cannot readily
be defended on moral grounds.

Later exiles of literary men have usually been incurred through
their errors in public rather than private behavior, or through
works which were politically rather than morally subversive. Ovid
apart, to banish a writer because of his writing seems essentially a

modern procedure, attesting as it does the spread of literacy and the impact of the printing press. Dante was connected with a losing political faction; Cervantes was captured at sea and imprisoned at Algiers; both of them suffered for their actions rather than their words. Heine, on the other hand, would be speaking metaphorically when he asked to be inscribed as a soldier in the war of liberation. It may well have been Voltaire who made that metaphor possible, who acted directly by writing, and who thus transformed the pen into a dangerous weapon by making his readers realize the effects of propaganda. Exile had been, for the young Voltaire, a liberal education. His sojourn in England, after his arbitrary imprisonment in the Bastille, had taught him the power of free speech and other benefits which he conveyed to France through his *Lettres philosophiques*. Afterward, as a sage of the Enlightenment, he established its haven at Ferney, a retreat for himself and a sanctuary for the persecuted, whence he sallied forth to be their champion. It was conveniently located near the Swiss border, across which he could escape to his neighboring estate whenever his quarrels with the monarchic regime made French soil too hot for him.

Voltaire was able to rise above nationality, and to administer rebuffs on occasion to kings, because at heart he remained a citizen of the international Republic of Letters. That conception went back to the epoch when all of Europe had been unified by a single language and a transcendent culture, Latinity. The wandering clerks of the Middle Ages, the peripatetic humanists of the Renaissance, Petrarch journeying between Rome and Avignon, Erasmus lucubrating at Basel or Cambridge, all belonged to the same community of minds and all felt at home wherever they encountered their fellow intellectuals, regardless of regional origins. Their principle, as enunciated by Cicero, was *"ubi bene, ibi patria."* For the truly wise man, there could be no such thing as exile. Educated men from different countries could not regard one another as foreigners, so long as they all possessed the passport of Latin. Exile could never have attained its full meaning until the rise of nationalism, with its ensuing confusion of tongues. Nor, until then, could the feeling of homesickness have been fully appreciated. Men have always been moved by local pieties or collective ideals, to be sure. But it was not until 1688, in a medical dissertation presented at Basel, that Johannes Hofer diagnosed the symptoms of the malady henceforth known as nostalgia or *Heimweh.*

Especially susceptible to this disease, which seemed to result from sudden changes of climate, were the Swiss when traveling abroad. It could likewise be brought on — or so we gather — by the national cow-call, the *ranz des vaches*, in a syndrome that Rousseau has conscientiously detailed in his dictionary of music. More broadly defined, it was recognized as *la maladie du pays*, the geographical counterpart of a historical complaint which was later to be distinguished as *le mal du siècle*, a sense of having been born at the wrong time. *Dépaysement*, a sense of having gone to the wrong place, or — more positively — the yearning for one's homeland, was closely associated with the general growth of interest in the landscape and with the special cult of mountains in Switzerland. Cosmopolitanism, ignoring the countryside, glorifying the metropolis, and urbanizing the arts, had been a force for centralization in matters of taste. Exoticism, branching out in centrifugal directions, shifted the artistic emphasis from an escape to a search and turned the exiled into explorers. The historic turning point was the French Revolution, along with its psychological reaction, the Romantic Movement. In its wake, aristocratic émigrés from the capital of classicism discovered the primitive luxuriance of America with Chateaubriand or the metaphysical profundity of Germany with Madame de Staël, and they brought their discoveries back with them upon their remigration.

The revolutions of the nineteenth century were thoroughly enmeshed with its innovations in the sphere of esthetics. In nations still conspiring to attain full identity, to overthrow autocratic governments and embrace democratic principles, artists were prominent among the conspirators; and having once accepted revolutionary views, they soon became revolutionists in their own media.

Wagner was exiled along with Marx from Germany; Mickiewicz voiced the hopes of Poland to western sympathizers, as Kossuth represented those of Hungary or Mazzini those of Italy. The interplay of personality among such stateless persons, with their uprooted families and hospitable friends, is richly exemplified in the career of Alexander Herzen and his *ménage*. It is hard to draw the line between such exiles who wrote in the interest of politics, who were incidentally men of letters but mainly ideologues, and others who were primarily authors exiled because of some political activity. But we can distinguish their enforced fate, proscription, on the one hand, from expatriation or voluntary exile on the other. England, with its spacious traditions of toleration, played the logical host to Huguenot scholars and other victims of religious persecution. Under British rule, the French-speaking islands of Jersey and Guernsey could become virtual sounding boards for Victor Hugo's opposition to Louis Napoléon.

> Bannis! bannis! bannis! c'est là la destinée,

Hugo chanted in *Les Châtiments*, his poetic castigation of his despotic enemy,

> Ce qu'apporte le flux sera dans la journée
> Repris par le reflux.

He had the unique satisfaction of seeing the tide of despotism ebb, the flux yield to the reflux, and consequently of completing the heroic cycle of exile and return, returning to the democracy that his efforts had done so much to confirm.

Hugo's destiny had a much happier ending than that of Ovid or Dante, Heine or Mickiewicz, or the many other poets to die far from home. Still others died abroad as expatriates, but not as proscripts. Keats, that passionate pilgrim to Italy for reasons of health, would only be living there a few months; in his last letter he asserted that his real life had passed, and that he was already leading a posthumous existence. To see his burial place among the ruins in the beautiful Protestant Cemetery at Rome "might make one in love with death," wrote Shelley, echoing a line from Keats's "Ode to a Nightingale" ("I have been half in love with easeful Death"). Shelley himself, within the following year, was buried near that spot. Having left a domestic scandal behind him in England, Shelley had taken up his abode in "The Paradise of Exiles" — for so he saluted Italy in a poem based upon his conversations with Byron, who had done the same thing for the same reason shortly before. Byron's faculty for self-dramatization made him Shelley's "Pilgrim of Eternity," the very prototype of the expatriate, whether posing in the foreground of famous monuments as "self-exiled Harold" or straying eastward from Eden across the face of the earth with Cain or ending a hero of the war for Greek independence — where, it would now seem from his most comprehensive biography, Leslie Marchand's, he was a British observer rather than a military leader and was killed by doctors rather than Turks.

"England," he might have confessed as the home-loving Cowper did, "with all thy faults I love thee still." The worst of those faults, the one that expatriated Byron, was what he satirizes under the heading of "cant." But the more he renounces England, the more English he seems, in spite of his frequent temptations to belong to other nations. The Englishman seems to carry his Englishness with him wherever he goes, as if it were the patent portable bed that Byron took along with him to Greece. Robert Browning, who transported Elizabeth Barrett to a new life in Pisa and Florence and Rome, there created his own genre of verse, a cross between Shakespeare's soliloquies and Baedeker's travelogues. Yet when he expressed his "Home-Thoughts, from Abroad," it was in a simple lyric: "O to be in England / Now that April's there!" One is bound to admit that another month, possibly even March, might not have evoked so spontaneous an outburst of nostalgia. A young man, in that mood of inverted provinciality which is fostered by the pathos of distance and the drabness of one's own surroundings, dared to tell Browning: "There is no romance except in Italy." Browning is reported to have replied: "Well, I should make an exception of Camberwell." And if an exception is to be made of

Camberwell, Browning's prosaic suburban London birthplace, anyone else might well make an exception in favor of wherever else he happened to be born.

Modern writers have quickened our awareness that there are no memories so vivid, no impressions so indelible, as our recollections from early childhood; and these are most perfectly preserved when we are far away from the localities we associate with them, where our home-thoughts can be touched off from abroad by a season of the year or some fragment of mental association. The irony of the expatriate's lot is that he dearly pays for his *Wanderlust* with his *Heimweh*. His psalm of Babylon is dedicated to his remembrance of Zion — or, for that matter, Camberwell. But the long view need not be the nostalgic one; it can provide a vantage point for perspective. Ibsen wrote *A Doll's House* at Amalfi, of all places; from a terrace overlooking the Mediterranean, he could envision the Helmers' stuffy apartment in Christiania; no wonder his Nora dances the tarantella. Peer Gynt claims that he is Norwegian by birth but cosmopolitan in spirit; yet it has been remarked, and I believe it, that one must be a Norwegian in order to understand *Peer Gynt*. Stendhal, who introduced the word *touriste* to his countrymen, shuttled back and forth between France and Italy, writing *La Chartreuse de Parme* in Paris and *Lucien Leuwen* — his unfinished novel of French provincial life — while he was consul at Civita Vecchia. By his testamentary instructions, his epitaph describes him in Italian as a citizen of Milan; but his grave lies under the slopes of Montmartre.

Stendhal's Italy was an operatic principality, a great good place which never existed before or afterward on land or sea. More to the point, it was his critique of France. But the Germans too, more intensely than the French, felt this impulsion of *Sehnsucht nach Italien*. The opinion of Browning's young Englishman, that romance was impossible anywhere else, was the premise upon which Hawthorne grounded his last completed work of fiction, *The Marble Faun*. Yet Hawthorne had devoted nearly all of his previous stories to showing that romance was possible in New Eng-

land. If Italy was the paradise of exiles, it was because that land of
citrons and myrtles embodied *The Dream of Arcadia* — to cite the
title of Van Wyck Brooks's current study of those American artists
and men of letters who made it their studio and their inspiration.
Meanwhile, while foreigners were settling in the Italian art-cities,
the real Italy — the nation soon to be united by the Risorgimento
— was sending its writers into exile. The cycle of expatriation revolved to turn two young American poets into French symbolists,
Stuart Merrill and Francis Viélé–Griffin; it came full circle when
the most remarkable of the Symbolistes, Rimbaud, migrated to
Abyssinia where he gave up poetry for business. Here we begin
to encounter a hidden aspect of our subject, which may be defined
as spiritual exile. It was not for nothing that Pasternak was accused, by his Soviet comrades, of belonging to an internal emigration.

Alienation from the heart, from home, can occur without benefit of travel. Flaubert, in his monastic retreat from the bourgeoisie,
affirmed that the artist ought to be a man without a country.
Melville, after sailing the seas, immured himself, feeling more
and more like an outcast and telling his diminishing readers to
call him Ishmael. Poe — by Baudelaire's interpretation — was a
foreigner in his own country, wholly alienated from a culture which
was rapidly becoming one vast counting-house. Baudelaire professed similar attitudes toward himself and toward France. He
longed not so much for a definite destination as for "anywhere out
of the world," for a love which resembled a land:

> Là, tout n'est qu'ordre et beauté,
> Luxe, calme et volupté.

His invitation points toward an escapism which would take more
active voyagers to South Sea islands and other exotic places, continuing the quest of Western man for that pastoral state which
his own development has outdated. The problem for the American author in relation to his environment has been studied, again
by Van Wyck Brooks, in a pair of companion biographies, *The*

Pilgrimage of Henry James and *The Ordeal of Mark Twain*. To stay at home was by implication an ordeal, a trial by unequal combat against the massed forces of philistinism, commercialism, and *embourgeoisement*. As for pilgrimage, it was merely the other horn of the writer's inevitable dilemma.

"Your letter made me homesick," wrote Henry James from Berne to William Dean Howells in Cambridge, Massachusetts, "and when you told of the orchards by Fresh Pond I hung my head for melancholy. What is the meaning of this destiny of desolate exile — this dreary necessity of having month after month to do without our friends for the sake of this arrogant old Europe which so little befriends us?" James admired and envied his friend Howells, who had given up his consulate in Venice to immerse himself in the American scene. However, he showed greater admiration for his fellow expatriate, Turgenev — an admiration not shared by Russian nationalists. One of the latter, Dostoevsky, calling upon Turgenev during a trip to Baden, advised him to procure a telescope and train it on Russia in order to familiarize himself with his material. James never needed such ironic advice, since he was not a local colorist.

We're the disinherited of Art! We're condemned to be superficial! We're excluded from the magic circle! The soil of American perception is a poor little barren artificial deposit! Yes, we're wedded to imperfection! An American, to excel, has just ten times as much to learn as a European! We lack the deeper sense! We have neither taste nor tact nor force! How *should* we have them? Our crude and garish climate, our silent past, our deafening present, the constant pressure about us of unlovely conditions, are as void of all that nourishes and prompts and inspires the artist as my sad heart is void of bitterness in saying so! We poor aspirants must live in perpetual exile.

Such is the exclamatory plaint of the ineffectual artist in "The Madonna of the Future." But the narrator's retort completes the Jamesian dialectic:

You seem fairly at home in exile . . . and Florence seems to me a very easy Siberia. But do you know my own thought? Nothing is so idle as to talk about our want of a nursing air, of a kindly soil, of opportunity, of inspiration, of the things that help. The only thing that helps is to do something fine. There's no law in our glorious Constitution against that. Invent, create, achieve. No matter if you've to study fifty times as much as these. What else are you an artist for? Be you our Moses . . . and lead us out of the house of bondage!

Making a virtue of his dreary necessity, James took as his primary theme the consequences of expatriation for manners and morals. To hover between two worlds was, paradoxically, somewhat confining; yet it is hard to imagine his delicate characters subsisting in any less rarefied atmosphere. There were times, he admitted to his brother William, when he grew "deadly weary of the whole 'international' state of mind." But he goes on to state that if outsiders wondered whether he was an American writing about England or an Englishman writing about America, "far from being ashamed of such an ambiguity I should be exceedingly proud of it, for it would be highly civilized."

James could conceive of his Anglo-American world as a single totality because he had the advantage of crossing and recrossing a frontier where no language barriers existed. This alien American, by becoming a British subject, was belatedly following the footsteps of those colonials or provincials who traditionally have sought and gained their literary fortunes at London. So, to a considerable degree, was T. S. Eliot after him. It was a significant reversal of direction for the leading English poet of the next generation, W. H. Auden, to be naturalized as an American citizen. Since the last war, indeed, the respective role of the province and the mother country have been all but reversed. Yet Mr. Auden retains his British accent, even while he is rendering the rhythms of jive and jukebox; whereas Mr. Eliot, even when he is revisiting Anglican shrines, can recall the flow of the Mississippi past his nursery windows in Saint Louis. A change of nationalities has its problems, even if a change of languages is not one of them. James found it difficult at times to be certain whether he was observing national traits or the universals of human nature. André Gide has helped to resolve that difficulty by suggesting that the most national writer may also be the most universal. He cannot altogether uproot himself nor completely eradicate his background; but he can come to understand it more clearly by working at some distance from it, yet looking homeward, bearing it continually in mind, as did James Joyce.

Silence, exile, and cunning were Joyce's stratagems for flying by those nets of language, nationality, and religion which he felt were ensnaring his compatriots and bogging down their hopes for an Irish Renaissance. As a boy in Ireland he would look up at the clouds journeying westward from the Continent, and would hear noises sounding like strange words, and would long to live in foreign capitals. After his first pilgrimage abroad, he thought of facing the ordeal at home: of being what Swift had been, a spiritual exile, an emissary to provincial Dublin from the Republic of Letters. Instead, he took the opposite course; and, quartered successively in Trieste, Zurich, and Paris, he achieved for Dublin the most minute and massive evocation that any city has ever had in literature. Through the return of words, the recapture of memories, he liked to think that he was forging an esthetic conscience for his race. He was likewise striving to re-create, out of the particulars of his time, a timeless myth, a universal mythology. Joyce's career was beset with misunderstandings on all sides and at every level. Yet through his books it culminated in a vicarious homecoming, a monumental act of understanding. He was more fortunate, in this respect, than many of his contemporaries, for whom alienation was not a voluntary artistic gesture but a compulsory political sacrifice. For them there could be no deliberate choice between being nonpolitical and becoming *engagé*.

Once again in our century as of old, Thomas Mann has aptly reminded us, the storyteller has had to pick up his tent and pursue a nomadic star. Mann's own evolution has been exemplary: from the nationalism of his North German roots by way of his American citizenship to the internationalism of his last years in Switzerland, the locale of his cosmopolitan novel, *Der Zauberberg*. His youthful hero, Tonio Kröger, living at Rome and yearning for the North, between two worlds and at home in neither, exemplifies the artist as expatriate. His Biblical protagonist, Joseph, gifted and accursed, at odds with his treacherous brethren and only reconciled to them after his recognition by strangers in strange lands, prefigures the artist as proscript. Proscription from totalitarian regimes and occupied territories has had the effect of scattering literary exiles across the world. In general, this exodus has been westerly, often reaching its terminus in our hemisphere. Along the way there have been numerous casualties, and the terminus has not always been a readjustment; sometimes the adaptation has been worse than the failure to adjust. To cite a few instances from the large German contingent in the United States: the suicide of Ernst Toller, the long silence of Bertolt Brecht, and — on the other hand — the popular success of cruder writers like Franz Werfel or Erich Maria Remarque.

Some of those reverses may have been our fault, our own failure to adjust, to appreciate unfamiliar merit. Our treatment of intellectual refugees has not been that of the Goths with Ovid; rather, we have been compared by Mann to the Egyptians, treating Joseph with suspicion and reverence. We should be grateful for all the cross-fertilization that has been brought about by this new Diaspora: the dispersion of talents, the dissemination of ideas in the arts and sciences, and the notable enrichment of our universities. Nor should we forget that, psychologically speaking, every abandoned homeland is a Zion and every place of exile a Babylon. And we should sympathize with that poem of Berthold Viertel in which he regrets that, while the ice covers Europe, he cannot sing of sunny California. In the meantime, from the other side, temporary expatriation has played a major part in the experience and training of American writers and artists. Though the international theme has strategically shifted since the death of James, its permutations have gathered reflections in fiction from Thomas Wolfe, F. Scott Fitzgerald, Sinclair Lewis, Ernest Hemingway, and Katherine Anne Porter — to mention only the most established names.

Members of the so-called "lost generation," who strove and stayed
on the left banks between the wars, they found themselves; and
most of them found their way home.

The great exception is a painful one to discuss, because it involves the vagaries of a mind to which we are much indebted for
poetic invention and critical discernment. With Ezra Pound, the
writer's alienation from society has been pushed to a stage which
has been designated by legal indictment as treason and by medical
diagnosis as insanity. Its special irony is that it started from art-
for-art's-sake and culminated in the very grossest of propaganda.
"I have beaten out my exile," he announced to the "remnant en-
slaved" at a premature juncture of his career. "Born," as another
of Pound's autobiographical poems declares,

> In a half savage country, out of date;
> Bent resolutely on wringing lilies from the acorn,

he gravitated via Bloomsbury and Montparnasse to Italy, where a
sense of social commitment, perversely twisted, somehow caught
up with him; and he exchanged the lilies of Browning for the up-
to-date acorns of Mussolini. But in his collected letters, *Patria Mia*
— as he used to call his half-savage country — has its revenge; for
the farther his viewpoint ranges afield, the more his style falls into
the phony dialect and the analphabetic spelling of the Yankee
cracker-barrel philosopher. His *Cantos* are centos, *disjecti membra
poetae*, a babel of archaisms, genealogies, misquotations, mistranslations, smutty jokes, and purely decorative ideograms, eked
out with powerful and poignant lyrical fragments which graduate
students will be piecing together for years to come, in compensation for that brief academic career which he interrupted but never
quite lived down. Released from durance in an asylum at Washington, he has returned to Italy and to definitive exile, a more
tragic figure than any of the precedents we have been considering
because he uprooted himself and so irretrievably banished all hope
of homecoming. In his heyday, the twenties, one of the little magazines he edited was appropriately named *The Exile*. He has won

that epithet with a vengeance. Yet when he now speaks, he speaks only for himself and his idiosyncrasies — as in his farewell declaration that 160,000,000 citizens of the United States should be in madhouses.

The voice that sounds the note of banishment most eloquently and most authoritatively today belongs to a poet whose life has been a far-flung peregrination and whose work is a pure distillation of rootlessness, its disembodied traditions and shifting perspectives. The poetry signed with the *nom de plume* of St.-John Perse is written by Alexis Léger, a retired French diplomat, born on a coral isle near Guadeloupe, who came to reside in Washington during the war. His path has crossed Pound's with a curious symmetry; and some of his later poems are dated from islands off the coast of New Jersey and Maine. Perse's best-known poem, *Anabase*, might be read as a timeless and placeless epic of nomad races and anonymous hordes, overrunning the roads of the world and storming the fabled ruins of civilization on a voyage of conquest — or is it discovery? The gates of exile open wide, the ultimate headlands of exile loom behind every page of his writing. In *Poème à l'étrangère*, which registers his response to the Alien Registration Act, the exiled poet listens to church bells overseas and the returning words speak to him in his own language, naming a street in Paris: Rue Gît-le-coeur, the street where the heart lies. In *Exil*, his most explicit apostrophe to the numberless others who share his plight, he inquires: "*Qui sait la place de sa naissance?*" Which of us nowadays really knows the place of his birth?

Though this apocalyptic vision is too intensive to be contemplated for long by home-keeping souls, it enlarges our limited awareness by admonishing us — just as Coriolanus admonished the Romans — that there is a world elsewhere. The most creative minds are those capable of keeping that other world in sight; and it is by no means easy, given the more or less comfortable provincialism of our usual worlds. Marcel Proust, in a sort of Platonic parable, offered the explanation that artists and saints, discoverers and prophets, seem like foreigners when they appear in our midst because they observe the higher laws of *une patrie perdue*. To some extent, the old Republic of Letters may still survive in this concept of a lost fatherland. "The Republic of Letters," noted Alfred de Vigny, "is the only one which can be composed of truly free citizens, for it is formed of isolated thinkers." Such isolation need not mean sheer withdrawal, but that detachment of the one from the many which is the necessary precondition of all original thought. The relation between the poet and the multitude, according to Vigny, is a perpetual ostracism. That is a hard lot, and this has been a sad chronicle; yet it is not a disheartening one, I believe, since exile has often proved to be a vocation, reinforcing other gifts with courage and looking forward to a final triumph of independence over conformity.

The centennial of Jakob Burckhardt's Cultur der Renaissance in
Italien *(1860) — known in English as* The Civilization of the Renaissance in Italy *— was the occasion of a conference held at the University of Wisconsin–Milwaukee. Some of the approaches to the subject
made in more recent years were reviewed by six participants from the
respective standpoints of history, philosophy, science, fine arts, Romance languages, and English literature. This concluding paper is
reprinted, with grateful acknowledgment, from the published record
and bibliography of the conference edited by Tinsley Helton,* The
Renaissance: A Reconsideration of the Theories and Interpretations
of the Age *(Madison: University of Wisconsin Press, 1961).*

"The ages of the past for us, my friend, constitute a book with
seven seals." So Goethe's Faust, the tired scholar, warns his eager
disciple, Wagner. "What you call the spirit of the ages is really
our colleagues' spirit reflecting the ages." This perception explains
why the concept of the Renaissance, as it was formulated a hundred years ago, should inevitably have reflected the *Zeitgeist* of
Jakob Burckhardt, with all its libertarian ideals and its naturalistic
values. Similarly and even more obviously, in the Comte de Gobi-
neau's imaginary dialogues, Julius II, Raphael, and their contemporaries became mouthpieces for the esthetic hedonism of the late
nineteenth century; while Frederic Seebohm's *Oxford Reformers*
came somewhat closer to the latter-day Oxford Movement than to
the age of Colet, More, and Erasmus. The Renaissance was bound
to shine back brightly through the mirror of the Risorgimento,
which could reckon its final triumph from 1859. Italy — for such
English sympathizers as Byron and Shelley, the Brownings and
the Rossettis, Walter Pater and J. A. Symonds — had become the
fountainhead of culture in the West, the traveler's endless museum, the expatriate's second homeland. For the England of the
Cinquecento, it had been a source of horrifying and fascinating
corruption, the breeding place of Machiavellian intrigues and
Popish impostures, of poison and pox. Italianate Englishmen,

though we may retrospectively view them as farsighted and public-spirited intermediaries, were regarded in their day as proverbial devils incarnate. Whereas the modern British or American impression of the Italian Renaissance might be succinctly conveyed in this stage direction from a neglected closet drama by Max Beerbohm's friend, "Savonarola" Brown:

Re-enter Guelfs and Ghibellines fighting. SAV. [Savonarola] and LUC. [Lucretia Borgia] are arrested by Papal officers. Enter MICHAEL ANGELO. ANDREA DEL SARTO appears for a moment at a window. PIPPA passes. Brothers of the Misericordia go by, singing a Requiem for Francesca da Rimini. Enter BOCCACCIO, BENVENUTO CELLINI, and many others, making remarks highly characteristic of themselves but scarcely audible through the terrific thunderstorm which now bursts over Florence and is at its loudest and darkest crisis as the Curtain falls.

At this stage, we need scarcely labor the point that the historiography of the Renaissance has mirrored the preconceptions of its historians: their belief in progress, their trust in science, and their concern with genius. Indeed the point has been so heavily labored, the last generation of scholars has reacted so austerely against its predecessors, that we may well ask what are the commitments that have determined their own reinterpretations. Is not this revisionism a part of a broader reaction against that liberal and positivistic outlook which, on the whole, has prevailed since the Renaissance? Failure of nerve, denigration of intellect, loss of confidence in the democratic process and in the material world, reversions to dogma, both political and theological — are these the criteria by which the Renaissance is now to be reassessed and evaluated? Clearly, the Organization Man can have little in common with *l'uomo singolare*. On the other hand, the very glass through which today we may see the Renaissance darkly has brightened our picture of the so-called Dark Ages. Scholarship invariably has a vested interest in continuity, if not an entrenched suspicion of novelty. Justifiably assuming that nature makes no sudden jumps, it has filled in missing links and recovered significant layers of thought through

its habit of discerning earlier Renaissances. Assimilating these re-
discoveries, Ernst Robert Curtius, in his *European Literature and
the Latin Middle Ages*, has demonstrated the persistence and amplitude of classical tradition during that period. Yet the demonstration, depending as it does on the recurrence of standard topics or
rhetorical commonplaces, ends by attesting the lack of originality
and the static uniformity that had long been ascribed to the Middle Ages by far less sympathetic or erudite critics.

There may be further significance in the fact that the late Professor Curtius, whose previous studies were notable for their sympathy with the living cultures of Europe, should have devoted his
culminating work to the reconstruction of "a medievalistic humanism." Under the pressure of National Socialism, he was able to
maintain his integrity as a scholar by retreating to the more remote past. Under other pressures of our time, less intense but
rather more widely diffused, it may be that our surviving humanists
are becoming engaged in a general retreat from modernity. Arnold
Toynbee, for whom the long view is so often a dim one, refers
to the present as "the Post-Modern Period." Mr. Toynbee's interpretation of the Renaissance has not been so much discussed as
some of his other views, possibly because it is not encountered
until the ninth volume of his massive *Study of History*. By then
he seems to have completely relinquished the broad-minded empiricism of his opening volumes in favor of a mystagogic tone and
a highly apocalyptic message. The Renaissance — here undergoing
its severest devaluation — is merely another example, and for him
a flatly unsuccessful one, of "Contacts Between Civilizations in
Time." This aprioristic judgment seems to be a reflection of
Toynbee's ardent philhellenism, his Oxonian ideal of ancient
Greece. Considering the claims of Renaissance humanism to have
revived that spirit, he naturally finds that they cannot quite abide
a literal comparison. It is surprising that a polymath versed in so
many cultures should be such a purist, so little concerned with the
creative aspects of cultural synthesis or with the unforeseen consequences of what he calls "a transfusion of psychic energy." What

Toynbee seems unwilling to grant is that an imperfect restoration may bring about an important innovation.

Second temples are seldom like the first; but some are more commodious or elaborate, and a few may even be more beautiful. Our subject, however, tends to characterize itself in terms of one persistent organic metaphor. The idea of a rebirth of civilization after a barbarian interval was self-consciously voiced from the very outset. It was applied particularly to the revival of learning, as in the most famous letter from Erasmus to Leo X. Thence Vasari extended it to art, while adapting it to the vernacular, and drawing an explicit analogy between artistic development and the biological cycle. Now the natural sequence of birth, growth, and death is easily transferred from organisms to human institutions; but the conception of something like bodily resurrection requires an additional measure of faith. Refusing to accept it, Mr. Toynbee substitutes *revenant* for *renaissance*, thereby emphasizing his opinion that the ghost of a dead civilization had not returned to life. But, in ringing the metaphorical changes on necromancy, he approximates the characteristic legend created by the Northern Renaissance out of its aspirations toward the classics: Faustus evoking the shade of Helen of Troy. Goethe, reverting to this theme, which he conceived as the archetype of modern man, presented a Faust who boldly disregarded his own warning; who, upon rejuvenation, opened the seven-sealed book of the past; and whose child by Helen of Troy, Euphorion, was the apt embodiment of both classical and medieval traditions. It is well to keep that symbolic figure in mind, if we retain any hope of reconciling the arguments for a pagan and a Christian renaissance, or if we remember that any given interpretation of this protean phenomenon can call forth its Counter-Renaissance.

When we turn specifically to England, we need not be put off by such a yoking of opposites; for English culture is traditionally capable of muddling through by modifying extremes, and of adjusting theoretical problems to pragmatic solutions. What Paul Elmer More once described as "The Paradox of Oxford," that

profound interaction between the classics and Christianity, shaped
the enduring pattern of education. Its dynamic tension is to be
felt in the great conflicts that Milton dramatizes; and yet the
components have been so fully digested that he can allude, in the
last line of the *Epitaphium Damonis*, to "the thyrsus of Zion."
Matthew Arnold charted this oscillation by generalizing about
Hellenism and Hebraism. Less uncompromisingly than Toynbee,
he envisaged the Renaissance as a Hellenistic resurgence, unhappily subordinated in England to the Hebraistic influence of the
Reformation. It was Arnold, too, who proposed — in a footnote
to *Culture and Anarchy* — that our term be anglicized into *Renascence*. His proposal has never gained widespread acceptance; we
still seem to prefer the French original; and our usage suggests that
the basic conception has remained slightly foreign and somewhat
exotic to Anglo-American sensibilities. Granted that Italy provided
the impetus, and that France was the most complete and immediate conquest, we trace the countermovement from the Germanic
countries. Where, then, should we place England? At the periphery,
with Spain? If we do so, we should not forget that those two
peripheral nations were engaged in deciding between them the
shape of our own world, or that Britain's most conspicuous achievement during this era was to attain the imperial hegemony for
which the fanfares resound through Hakluyt and Purchas.

J. M. Keynes, in his *Treatise on Money*, ventured upon a curious
aside, while discussing the influx of gold from the Americas during
the sixteenth century: "We were just in a financial position to
afford Shakespeare at the moment when he presented himself."
This is as crass an application of economic determinism as any
Marxist has ever perpetrated, and it does not add very richly to our
store of Shakespearean commentary; but it offers a useful reminder
that commercial prosperity was as much a precondition of the
English Renaissance as were its responses to intellectual currents
from the Continent. Understandably, the transmission of the new
learning had been retarded by the cultural lag. R. R. Bolgar, in his
recent survey, *The Classical Heritage and Its Beneficiaries*, assigns

an amateurish and marginal role to the English humanists. Their transitional endeavors, as studied by Walter Schirmer, Roberto Weiss, and others, form a chronicle of patronage and collecting, and find their memorial in Duke Humphrey's Library at the Bodleian. Poggio, the first of the visiting scholars, was disappointed by his visit to Cardinal Beaufort. Erasmus, two generations afterward, was enthusiastic about his sojourn; but his correspondence overflows with scholarly compliments, especially when addressing his good English friends. When the study of Greek was finally introduced into the university curriculum, it was vociferously opposed by a party of academic diehards known as Trojans. The basis of their objections, if we may believe John Skelton, was utilitarian, not to say philistine:

> But our Grekis theyr Greke so well haue applyed,
> That they cannot say in Greke, rydynge by the way,
> How, hosteler, fetche my hors a botell of hay!

But Skelton, the Trojan laureate, making a parrot his spokesman for the old Latin scholasticism, grudgingly bore witness to the rise of the Hellenists and the decline of the Schoolmen:

> *In Academia* Parot dare no probleme kepe;
> For *Graece fari* so occupyeth the chayre,
> That *Latinum fari* may fall to rest and slepe,
> And *syllogisari* was drowned at Sturbydge fayre;
> Tryuyals and quatryuyals so sore now they appayre,
> That Parrot the popagay hath pyte to beholde
> How the rest of good lernyng is roufled up and trold.

Today we meet humane proponents of neoscholasticism who seek to identify the scholastic with the humanistic. Various other philosophies have attempted similar identifications; but humanism, Professor Kristeller reminds us, was actually a program, not a system. If there was any single position shared by the many divergent minds that we group together, it was their critique of the scholastics. It was not for nothing — though grossly unfair to the subtle doctor, Duns Scotus — that they passed the word *dunce* on to us as an epithet for a stupid pupil. Their revulsion from their pious forerunners was not irreligious or necessarily secular; it was animated by the zeal of reformers, whether Protestant or Catholic. Although paganism held attractions which the poets dulcetly expressed, there were no practising pagans in Tudor England. Everyone was, at least nominally, a Christian, though the question of which denomination all too frequently could become a matter of life or death. Catholics and Protestants both had their martyrs; most of the conflicting doctrines of the Continental Reformation were preached; yet the central issues between church and state were blunted by a political settlement that hinged upon the contingencies of a royal scandal. By another ironic twist of circumstance, the leading opponent of that settlement happened to be the pre-eminent English humanist: a lawyer who hated legalism, a parliamentarian who propounded theology, a wit who wore a hair shirt, a convicted and executed traitor who has latterly been canonized as a saint. The many-sidedness of Sir Thomas More has endowed him with different meanings from differing viewpoints. It was unified by the historic insight that made him at once a traditionalist and a utopian.

The most distinctive aspect of English humanism was its pedagogical emphasis, its earnest and energetic didacticism, its resolve to bring up the sons of the gentry on *litterae humaniores,* its enterprise in founding schools as well as colleges. By and large, as compared with their professional colleagues across the Channel, the English humanists tended to be clerics rather than laymen, schoolmasters rather than scholars. John Colet might lecture on the exegesis of the New Testament; William Grocyn might question the authenticity of the Pseudo-Areopagite; yet, contrasted with the ranging erudition of Guillaume Budé or the incisive method of Lorenzo Valla, their activities look relatively parochial. Their scholarship seems to have been rather biblical or patristic than strictly classical; and later, when English presses started to print, they turned out translations rather than editions of texts. There is an overwhelming contrast between Caxton's list of vernacular romances or books of devotion and the series of *editiones principes* issued contemporaneously by the Aldine Press in Venice. But these disparities are accounted for by the gap between island and mainland. Never more than an outpost in the days of the Roman Empire, far away from the sources of Greek manuscripts, England had to go through a long discipleship before it attained — in the seventeenth century — its full sense of mastery over the classics. Meanwhile, while it was importing much of its scholarly apparatus, native printers were freer to publish popular material. Here a glance at the *Short-Title Catalogue* of Pollard and Redgrave should be supplemented by a browse through Louis B. Wright's *Middle-Class Culture in Elizabethan England*, with its dense accretion of testimony as to the assiduous — if undiscriminating — reading habits of the average citizen.

It is well to be aware of the average, although *Geistesgeschichte* is more keenly interested in the exceptional — and ought to be, in dealing with a time when, as Donne would put it, "every man alone thinks he hath got / To be a Phoenix." Mr Wright's epitome of epitomes — his rereading of almanacs, handbooks, jestbooks, pamphlets, broadsides, and other modes of subliterature — shows that the sparrows greatly outnumbered the phoenixes. Furthermore, it implies that the division between highbrow and lowbrow readers goes much farther back than our experts on mass communication may realize. Think of the Cambridge don, Gabriel Harvey, learnedly annotating his polyglot collection of folios. Then think of Captain Cox, the stonemason of Coventry, who took such pride in his well-worn assortment of chapbooks. The difference is that his reading was essentially medieval, for the most part watered-down romance and printed balladry; whereas Harvey, when he was not being a classicist, prided himself on his up-to-date conversance with the Continental Renaissance. Our tendency to medievalize the Renaissance leads to giving the Coxes more weight than the Harveys; and, since there must have been a good many more of the former than of the latter, it can be justified on sociological grounds. Here the literary historian must face the choice between illustrating the everyday walks of society or analyzing its landmarks of art and thought. He is greatly helped by the valuable Tudor and Stuart collections gathered by research libraries in this country; but he is also swayed by their presence toward an antiquarian approach and uncritical tastes; and he is tempted to concentrate more and more on writers of lesser magnitude, who underline for him the most derivative and pedestrian features of their age.

Some years ago, in 1943, *Studies in Philology* published "A Critical Survey of Scholarship in the Field of English Literature of the Renaissance" by Rosemond Tuve. During the half-generation since, there has been much more research in this area, and most of it has followed directions pointed in Miss Tuve's suggestive *état-présent*. Her starting point was the realization that descriptive bibliography has virtually become an exact science, and has accordingly systematized the techniques of editing. Given these substantial contributions, she continued, "It may be, indeed, that the field of English studies now needs students who will use the bibliographies fruitfully and read the editions perceptively more than it needs students who will add to their number." Miss Tuve went on to indicate other desiderata and possibilities, notably in the history of ideas; above all, she affirmed a need for reconsidering and redefining, within the perspective of English studies, the idea of the Renaissance itself. Stimulated by such encouragement, students of English have been moving toward the history of ideas, and tracing the literary reverberations of philosophical concepts. But this means that the philosophy involved is secondhand, while the literature is liable to be of the second rank; what remains primary, in such monographs, is their bibliographical documentation, grounded on firsthand access to rare items in the Folger, Huntington, Newberry, or Houghton libraries. As for a redefinition of what the Renaissance meant to England, Miss Tuve's challenge has not been taken up. This reluctance seems to be connected with the feeling that, whatever it may or may not have been, the Renaissance originated abroad; and that our duty to it does not extend beyond noting the indigenous responses to its specific importations.

We have noted the somewhat insular, albeit high-minded, character of English humanism. We could go on to record the flowering of letters in the vernacular — the sonnet, and other verse forms or prose experiments — as if it were a series of transactions in comparative literature. But that story has been repeated often enough; and foreign debt, in the more considered accounts, has been redressed by native affluence. Such is not the case if we shift our ground to the plastic arts. Painting and sculpture seem to have been mainly reserved for imported talents: Holbein, Torrigiano. Music, on the contrary, was enjoying its brief and brilliant heyday; its affinities were never closer with the sister art of poetry; and William Byrd could vie with the best of European composers. Yet English architecture, proving its rule by the Palladian exception of Inigo Jones, seems to have proceeded directly from the flamboyant Gothic to the Baroque with little intervention on the part of the Renaissance. In lieu of a more relevant set of esthetic principles, pains have been taken "to apply chiefly to English poets and dramatists the definitions of style lately formulated for interpreting the fine arts of the Italian Renaissance." This is the stratagem of Wylie Sypher, in an attractively illustrated paperback volume entitled *Four Stages of Renaissance Style*. It would be pleasant if Heinrich Wölfflin's *Kunstforschung* could furnish us with a ready-made and all-embracing formula; but even within its own field, the verbal abstractions do not always seem precisely adequate for the concrete artifacts they undertake to describe; and when they are arbitrarily invoked to label works of unique complexity and variety, without the slightest regard for distinctions in medium or provenience, the result is no more than impressionistic small talk.

Indeed, it seems peculiarly farfetched when we recall that English writers had their own canons of style, which they acquired from thorough training in the art of rhetoric, and which are being effectively reapplied to their work by such scholars as Miss Tuve. Moreover, we should do better — *mutatis mutandis* — to emulate the analyses, rather than to echo the categories, of the art historians. One of the ablest among them, E. H. Gombrich, in an inaugural lecture "Art and Scholarship," has put forward a methodological caveat against "the physiognomic fallacy," which he defines as our "tendency to see the past in terms of its typical style." No physiognomy has ever stamped its image more indelibly upon an era than the face of Elizabeth I. Perhaps this is why the catchword *Elizabethan,* which sometimes tacitly usurps the reign of her successor, fits much better into many contexts than *Renascence* or *Renaissance.* After the baronial wars of Lancaster and York and the religious struggles under the earlier Tudors, English morale was centralized not only by the length and stability of her regime but by her charismatic personality: Bessy, Astraea, Gloriana, England's Eliza, the Virgin Queen. The most impressive of her personal qualities was, of course, her sex; it lent a special effulgence to the atmosphere of courtly compliment surrounding the monarch, and evolved a *Lebenstil* which affected the styles of all who practised the arts, from portrait painters to choristers, from sonneteers to balladmongers. The proud consciousness of living in one of the world's great epochs was enunciated in their tributes, and acted out by the triumphal pageantry that has its annals in Nichols' *Progresses and Public Processions of Queen Elizabeth.* To be sure, we need not take the epoch at its face value; and we shall do well to avoid the kind of pseudo-gusto that sentimental professors are prone to indulge in whenever they talk about "the spacious times."

Though we cannot maintain that the state was a work of art in the hands of Burleigh or Walsingham, we can observe the statesmanship of such literary works as the *Mirror for Magistrates, The Faerie Queene,* and Shakespeare's chronicle plays. They may be regarded as physiognomic, insofar as they helped to establish an official tone. But the other side of court patronage is censorship, which enforced public conformity to the controlling image. Nevertheless we hear from nonconformists, some of them strategically vocal. Forthright heresies were illicitly printed under the pen name of Martin Marprelate. Sir Walter Ralegh and several fellow skeptics became the object of an investigation. Shakespeare's company got into trouble with the Star Chamber for the allegedly subversive implications of *Richard II*; like many among the intellectuals, he may have shifted his sympathies from Elizabeth to Essex during her declining years. Much of this unofficial testimony deserves consideration *a fortiori*, if we are looking for signs of historical change. The counterargument to it was phrased with shrewdness and eloquence when Douglas Bush inquired: "But is Marlowe's half-boyish revolt against traditional faith and morality more, or less, typical and important than Hooker's majestic exposition of the workings of divine reason in divine and human law?" Professor Bush's Alexander Lectures of 1939, *The Renaissance and English Humanism*, had a healthily sobering effect upon the temptation to paganize the Renaissance. His own high seriousness enabled him to isolate the peculiar combination of virtues that More and Milton share with Arnold. When he dwelt on Christian Humanism, he was propounding what was then a heuristic paradox. Pushed to the extreme by others, it has since become a neo-orthodoxy, an ecumenical fold into which, one by one, freethinkers as wayward as Marlowe himself have been driven back.

Faced with my eminent colleague's alternative, I would not presume to choose between two such incompatible witnesses. One would have to be in favor of sin to deny that Hooker was more typical. His *Ecclesiastical Polity*, majestic but fragmentary, is accepted as an authoritative exposition of Anglican doctrine, though it did not refute the Puritans very decisively or stave off dissent in England. History, in spite of the learned and judicious, does not always take the *via media*. Marlowe was an authorized spokesman for no one but himself — or rather, for nothing but his grandiloquent characters. Yet he could not so spectacularly have mastered the drama, most social of arts, if he had not caught and projected certain moods which some of his contemporaries were feeling and thinking. Whether these were more, or less, important than traditional adherences is a value-judgment which depends on whether the historian is looking forward or backward. That the iconoclastic playwright and the moderate theologian should have coexisted, drawing upon the resources of the same language and — to a con-

siderable extent — the same frame of reference, is in itself a joint
testimonial to the diversity and the richness of the period. Hardin
Craig's *Enchanted Glass* stands out, among handbooks to the intellectual background, because it is based on a seasoned appreciation
of these fruitful differences. Efforts to reconstruct "the Elizabethan world-picture" can mislead us by selecting one-sided evidence,
quoting passages out of dramatic context, schematizing particulars
which may be problematic or equivocal, and superimposing a
simplistic unity. Thus no attempt to discuss the climate of opinion would be complete if it did not cite Ulysses' speech on order
from *Troilus and Cressida*, or — to be more precise — the first
half of that speech, stressing "degree, priority, and place."

Now the speaker of the passage is not William Shakespeare himself nor his choric surrogate. Ulysses is the wily strategist of the
Greeks, who are less sympathetically treated than Shakespeare's
Trojans, and Ulysses' other long speech is dedicated to the theme
of opportunism. Here, after he has outlined the ideas of order that
frame the play, he treats them as a set of norms which are currently
violated. Far from reaffirming the *status quo*, he reveals the abyss
that so closely underlay the surfaces of Elizabethan awareness.
The hierarchies were threatened; the great chain of being was
questioned; chaos could all too readily come again.

> Take but degree away, untune that string
> And hark what discord follows! Each thing meets
> In mere oppugnancy. The bounded waters
> Should lift their bosom higher than the shores
> And make a sop of all this solid globe.

The nightmare must have come close to home for Shakespeare's
audience in the microcosmic theater known as the Globe. Thence
Ulysses continues, envisioning the cosmos as an unappeased struggle for power, such as would shake the Stuarts from their throne
before too long, and would conform to Hobbes's description of the
natural state. The divine right of kings is being undermined by
the naturalism of *homo homini lupus*.

> Strength should be lord of imbecility,
> And the rude son should strike his father dead;
> Force should be right; or rather, right and wrong
> (Between whose endless jar justice resides)
> Should lose their names, and so should justice too.
> Then everything includes itself in power,
> Power into will, will into appetite;
> And appetite, an universal wolf,
> So doubly seconded with will and power,
> Must make perforce an universal prey,
> And last eat up himself.

Tragedy and comedy both have their technical means for restoring harmony after discord; and Shakespeare's carefully ordered endings have led his Hegelian interpreter, A. C. Bradley, to read his tragedies as object lessons in cosmic optimism. But surely his climactic scenes are visions of disorder, where conflict in the soul and schism in the body politic are matched by the to-and-fro-conflicting elements. When Ulysses alludes to "commotion in the winds" and "raging of the sea," he sets the stage for *King Lear* and *The Tempest*. Menenius Agrippa, in *Coriolanus*, calms the Roman populace with his fable of the Belly and the Members; yet its hierarchical moral, so edifying to Tudor and Stuart authoritarians, is less vivid than its protest on behalf of the underdogs; while the ideology of the hero is so ambivalent that it has not only prompted critical debates but incited theatrical riots. Other Shakespearean heroes or villains — and the line between them is sometimes as imperceptible as it is in actual life — are individualists who defy the stars, denounce Fortune, and deify Nature. For Hamlet, the feudal scheme of things is disjoint and out of frame; his hesitation, in setting it right, is motivated by skepticism and civilized compunction; the doubts that surround him, as he writes to Ophelia, encompass the Ptolemaic universe: "Doubt that the sun doth move."

We are not likely, after reading Willard Farnham's substantial work, to ignore *The Mediaeval Heritage of Elizabethan Tragedy*. But Erich Auerbach, that percipient reader, stated the situation more cogently than most of Shakespeare's commentators: "There is no stable world as background, but a world which is perpetually reengendering itself out of the most varied forces." Though the static world view survives as an ideal, its presuppositions are continually modified by the dynamics of experience. Shakespeare's grasp of this process aligns him with Cervantes, and has encouraged critics like Theodore Spencer to approach him by way of the metaphysical dichotomy between appearance and reality. Realism, as abstracted by the Middle Ages into *universalia ante rem*, was an affirmation of otherworldliness; the nominalistic shift from abstraction to particularity, which is taken to signalize the Renaissance, is nowhere more obvious than in the drama. It is exemplified with striking concreteness in the allegorical person of the Vice, the conventional agent who tempts the protagonist and escorts the Seven Deadly Sins through the morality plays. In Shakespeare's hands he is transmogrified into the inimitable Falstaff, "gross as a mountain, open, palpable," whose excess flesh is the warrant of his humanity, and who personifies the forbidden pleasures so persuasively that he all but leads us too astray. Morality is foreordained to win out, true enough, and Falstaff will be supplanted by the Chief Justice in the Second Part of *Henry IV*. But he will have presented, in the First Part, his case for the life of the senses: "Banish plump Jack, and banish all the world!" The trilogy that centers on Henry V adheres to the medieval formula for the Education of a Prince, just as Shakespeare's tragedies are Falls of Princes in outline. But Prince Hal has been humanized by his fraternization with the colossal clown, and democratized by what he has learned at the tavern and on the highroad.

The function of the theater, so Shakespeare held, was to show "the age and body of the time" its "form and pressure." To the extent that he succeeded in doing so, we may take his success as our strongest proof that the Renaissance stimulated the expression of personality. Dramaturgy has never worked on a comparable scale to produce so varied a sequence of *dramatis personae* or to exhibit the varieties of emotion in such convincing detail. His faculties of characterization were sharpened by the very books he drew upon: by the psychologizing of Plutarch, the self-questioning of Montaigne, the rampant individualism depicted in Italian *novelle* or British chronicles. His principal instrument, the English language, ranged the gamut from forensic resonance to colloquial immediacy; and he mixed his styles as deliberately as he mingled verse with prose, clowns with kings, or the comic with the tragic. It is this intermixture to which we owe his most poignantly realized effects, and which — as Auerbach has remarked — is only paralleled by the emergent drama of Spain. It is likewise the reason why the neoclassicists criticized Shakespeare for outraging decorum, and why the romanticists in their turn would praise him for combining the grotesque with the sublime. Both schools made the mistake of considering him a natural genius, for better or for worse; whereas, the more we learn about the conventions that guide his medium, the more we come to respect his conscious artistry. The more we learn about his playhouse, the less it seems to resemble a half-timbered innyard and the more ornate it seems to have been, with its classic pilasters and parti-colored hangings. Stage-historians, like George Kernodle, have made us realize how complex a structure was the Globe. Contemporaneous travelers, like Thomas Coryat, testified that the theaters of Venice looked "very beggarly" when compared with London's "stately playhouses."

We now know that Shakespeare received many benefits from the type of education the humanists had been preparing. Any condescension toward his attainments comes with an ill grace from our unclassical age, and is thoroughly crushed by T. W. Baldwin's 1300-page monograph, *William Shakspere's Small Latine and Lesse Greeke*. These two volumes, along with related studies, set forth step by step the infiltration of classical precepts, examples, themes, and devices, tracing their assimilation into a popular form which was heterogeneous but by no means amorphous. That, from its five-act construction, should be self-evident. The playwright of *Coriolanus* did not parade his vernacular classicism as explicitly as the playwright of *Sejanus*; yet Ben Jonson was also a nonuniversity man, who had earned the satisfaction he took in his ample Greek and more Latin. Jonson's use of the classics telescoped those successive stages — translation, adaptation, imitation, emulation — which, more directly in France, would link humanism with neo-classicism. But to the contrary, in the opinion of C. S. Lewis, this progression was so direct in England that it did not affect the Elizabethans: ". . . the great literature of the fifteen-eighties and nineties was something which humanism, with its unities and *Gorboducs* and English hexameters, would have prevented if it could, but failed to prevent because the high tide of native talent was too strong for it." Professor Lewis' pronouncement, with its obscurantist attitude toward humanism and its vitalistic attitude toward talent, is fairly characteristic of his *English Literature in the Sixteenth Century Excluding Drama.* Its half-truth could be supported by citing humanistic pedantries; but it would be confounded by mentioning Roger Ascham, whose lifework was a bridge between the Erasmian Reformers and the University Wits.

Ascham, who was Elizabeth's own tutor in Greek and Latin, contributed both theoretically and practically to the formation of solid vernacular prose. The roaring intonations of Thomas Nashe are heard in the chorus of writers extolling the Cambridge discipline that Ascham had inherited from Sir John Cheke and handed on to them. The legitimate heir of Ascham's treatise, *The Scholemaster,* was Lyly's *Euphues,* half courtesy-book, half novel of manners. As for the primordial tragedy of *Gorboduc,* it was worthy of Sidney's approval; and — what is more pertinent — it was, quite specifically, a forerunner of *King Lear.* English hexameters may have been an unsuccessful experiment; but their by-product turned out to be the major vehicle for English poets, blank verse. And though the Scaligerian unities were more honored in the breach than in the observance, they are strictly upheld by such masterworks as *The Alchemist* and *The Tempest.* Mr. Lewis' commitment to Anglo-Catholicism and his zest for whimsical polemic are manifest from his introductory chapter under the tendentious rubric "New Learning and New Ignorance." He does not altogether abandon the shibboleth "Renaissance," as H. O. Taylor did with his *Thought and Expression in the Sixteenth Century;* but he does reduce its definitions to absurdity; it "can hardly be defined except as 'an imaginary entity responsible for everything the speaker likes in the fifteenth and sixteenth centuries.' " Thereupon he inverts the formulation by proceeding to make that entity responsible for many things he dislikes. The business of the literary historian, he tells us, "is with the past not as it 'really' was (whatever 'really' may mean in such a context) but with the past as it seemed to be to those who lived in it: for of course men felt and thought and wrote about what seemed to be happening to them."

This would appear to be a sound historiographic precaution; the parentheses and the inverted commas properly warn us against the dangers of subjectivity. Yet, in practice, Mr. Lewis himself comes nearer to that kind of synthesis against which Faust warned Wagner: the spirit of the interpreter rather than the interpreted. Thus the very notion of *renascentia* is discounted because it was "a Renaissance legend," in spite of the well attested fact that it seemed to be happening to the humanists. Machiavelli is similarly played down, both as a thinker and as a legend, and an effort is made to confound those two roles. But they were securely separated by Mario Praz and others, who have recorded the Machiavellian impact on the Elizabethan imagination; while G. N. G. Orsini has shown that Machiavelli's own writings were thoughtfully read by many Englishmen, above all by Bacon; and it has even been suggested that Machiavelli's methods were consciously put into action by Thomas Cromwell. For Mr. Lewis, "the repudiation of medieval principle goes farthest" in *The Prince.* "But for that very reason," he frankly adds, "Machiavelli is not very important." This is not the first time that the problem of the Renaissance has been met by begging the question of importance — important for what? to whom? and why? Mr. Lewis is less dogmatic, but equally subjective, in his critical and scholarly judgments; he queries the ascription of *Lucan's First Book* to Marlowe because "it is of very great merit." Marlowe's greatest poetic achievement is, "of course," his *Hero and Leander*. The *of course* is Mr. Lewis' *sic probo*. What qualified Marlowe so magnificently as a writer of erotic epyllion "incapacitated" him as a tragedian. Consequently, Neptune's amorous assault on Leander is preferable to the soaring periods of Tamburlaine or Faustus.

But such preferences are not promulgated *ex cathedra*; for the book's title expressly excludes the drama, which is to be covered by a companion volume where amends to Marlowe might appropriately be made. This distribution of labor among the authors of *The Oxford History of English Literature* accords with a wider trend among sixteenth-century specialists, who slice their century into vertical halves, and among colleges offering separate courses in dramatic and nondramatic literature. Nondramatic is, to say the least, a nondescript category, covering — as it must — everything from Latimer's sermons to Campion's airs, and including much that was fossilized or out of contact with the main stream. We need not call it *Hamlet* without the Prince, but we may notice how it favors reactionary depreciations of the Renaissance. Significantly, E. M. W. Tillyard ignores the stage in his rather unsympathetic brochure, *The English Renaissance: Fact or Fiction?* Conversely, the dramatic category presents a unified *évolution de genre* toward secularization, individuality, naturalistic portrayal, and formal invention, which makes it the most expressive art of the period. In excluding Shakespeare's plays, we are judging that period without listening to its finest voice — unless, of course, we happen to prefer Shakespeare's erotic epyllia. Mr. Lewis subdivides his vertical half-century in accordance with its three generations. The first, which he terms "Late Medieval," is a congenial one for him; and the designation is not unsuitable for More and his friends and enemies. It is the second that surprises and shocks us with its proclamation of anticlimax: "the Drab Age." Although the adjective may suit Tusser or Churchyard, it unfairly bedims the luster of Wyatt and Surrey. We have come down a long way from those hopeful chapters which used to herald the colorful freshness of the mid-century.

The drabness is comparative, since the third age is truly an

illustrious fruition, which Mr. Lewis designates as "Golden." By
this, I take it, he does not mean a *siglo de oro*, an age which basks
in its literary pre-eminence, though such aspiring critics as Francis
Meres were laboriously pointing out English counterparts of the
classical Greats. Mr. Lewis seems rather to have in mind a stylistic
touchstone, a quality of innocuousness, innocence, or naïveté, as
distinguished from the more sophisticated traits of Metaphysical,
Romantic, or modern poetry. The chief exemplar of that style is
Spenser, who can illustrate it even while he is conjuring with the
pastoral myth of the Golden Age:

> But antique age yet in the infancie
> Of time, did liue then like an innocent,
> In simple truth and blamelesse chastitie,
> Nc then of guile had made experiment,
> But voide of vile and treacherous intent,
> Held vertue for itselfe in soueraine awe:
> Then loyall loue had royall regiment,
> And each unto his lust did make a lawe,
> From all forbidden things his likeing to withdraw.

The stanza is not nearly as picturesque as Spenser can be, yet it
smoothly chimes as it formally manipulates the archaic diction of
mellow commonplace. It is typically ambiguous in its dalliance
with the forbidden things it is renouncing, and typically unam-
biguous in ending on the dominant note of lawfulness and withdrawal. Spenser was no innocent himself; his pamphlet on Irish
affairs is somewhat Machiavellian; his poetic fairyland is ambushed
not only with dark conceits but with pagan seductions and foreign conspiracies. Yet virtue triumphs; danger is always averted; allegorical evils are bested by more powerful magic; and beauty in
distress is rescued by knightly prowess, through the paternalistic
surveillance of Prince Arthur, and to the greater matriarchal glory
of the Faerie Queene. Despite the devious narration, its moral
schematism and its regimented symmetry make the poem a perfect
monument to the Elizabethan cult of order — and not less so
because it is only half finished, or because its ultimate fragments

are preoccupied with the theme of mutability. Spenser was as con-
versant with Ariosto and Du Bellay as with Chaucer and Malory,
but he is always more solemn than his models. Mr. Lewis is doubtless accurate in classifying his work as neo-medieval. The compound may or may not be a compliment; it makes him sound a
little like Horace Walpole or William Morris; and indeed his
antiquarianism did not endear him to contemporaries more immersed in the contemporary, like Ben Jonson. At all events, Mr.
Lewis left no doubt where he would stand when, in *The Allegory
of Love*, he summoned up Spenser as "the man who saved us from
the catastrophe of too thorough a renaissance."

Whether he accomplished this Arthurian mission by prolonging
the Middle Ages or by trying to revivify them is again an arguable
matter. Certainly his depiction of them was as mythical as the
most fervid hypotheses about the Renaissance. Insofar as it moved
toward avenues of escape, it was pursuing the course that Sir
Philip Sidney had counseled and taken. Sidney's *Apology for
Poetry* answered the attack of the Puritans by appealing to a neo-
Platonic argument: that poets' fantasies were improvements on
nature, turning her brazen world into one of gold. *The Countess
of Pembroke's Arcadia* is Sidney's re-creation of that golden world,
as *The Faerie Queene* is Spenser's, and as it is glimpsed in Euphuis-
tic fiction or in the court masque. Regret for the Golden Age was
a classical *topos*, which does not figure among the medieval *topoi*
surveyed by Curtius; unlike them, it was altered and developed,
once it had been reanimated by the sixteenth and seventeenth centuries. Perhaps its crucial restatement is the chorus from Tasso's
Aminta, where the rustic idyll of peace and plenty is intertwined
with a paean in praise of free love. In Montaigne's essay, "Of the
Cannibals," it sets off a train of primitivistic speculations, foreshadowing the ethics of Rousseau and the science of anthropology.
This is the version gently burlesqued by *The Tempest*, and counterbalanced there — in Shakespearean fashion — with Italianate
intrigue and cynical worldliness. The ripest context may well be
Don Quixote, where the foolish knight declares his motive in a
resplendent discourse; but, unlike Spenser's knights, he has no

chance of converting baser metal to gold. Through all these variations, there runs a strain which is primarily elegiac. But gradually this conventionalized nostalgia for the past is augmented by a detailed criticism of the present, and elegy is outweighed by an impulse to satire.

A facile jack-of-letters like Robert Greene could rush from one sphere to the other, interrupting an Arcadian romance to launch a journalistic exposure of the London underworld. But the official mode was aureate, long after the deaths of Sidney and Spenser or the old Queen herself; not inappropriately, the *Arcadia* may have been deathbed reading for Charles I. The satirical undercurrent came to the surface during the closing years of the sixteenth century, when other self-critical symptoms of a *fin du siècle* were being cultivated, such as melancholia, religious conversion, and New Philosophy. The satirists were silenced by episcopal decree, and their publications were burned. This did not allay the disquietude of which they were symptomatic, and which became increasingly articulate as English literature entered the seventeenth century. Between the golden idealization of things and a more realistic apprehension, there was bound to be a lively interplay. Among the sparks it struck are the paradoxes of the Metaphysical poets and the speculations of Stuart prose. Milton, with his power of harmonizing incongruities, placed the golden world, which was his Eden, at the center of a much vaster universe, which had witnessed the rule of dissidence. With Milton, we reach the verge of another historic divide. Crisis of conscience, dissociation of sensibility — we may not have found the right phrase for it, but it can be definitely recognized; and we can trust our medievalizers not to push the Middle Ages beyond the Glorious Revolution of 1688. Their claim on the Spenserian tradition seems to me valid enough, though it also seems to qualify Spenser's position as an innovator and a seminal influence. Possibly we may agree that the Renaissance was, for him and his anachronistic school, a recessive element, naïvely borrowed from Continental literature and eclectically blended with native precedent.

That it could generate fresh ideas and wholehearted innova-

tions was discernible here and there, but it cannot have been lumi-
nously apparent until the Jacobean period reaped what had been
sown by some Elizabethans. King James lacked the charisma of
Queen Elizabeth; but he was a more conscientious patron, whose
memory is most happily preserved by the Bible associated with his
name. He, and not his predecessor, was a sponsor of the Shakespearean troop; if we set *Hamlet* apart as a sort of prologue, Shakespeare's preponderating work should be correctly listed as Jacobean;
and so should that of most other writers who bestride the two
continuous reigns. James's death, plus the troubled accession of
Charles, halted a plan for founding an English Academy, along the
lines that would soon control the Académie Française. Fortunately
for English literature, it was not institutionalized in that manner;
and, from the advantage of becoming decentralized, it gained
depth as well as breadth. In the sense of being extremely reflective
and introspective, inclining to the systematic in thought and to the
highly wrought in art, the Jacobean span could be looked upon as
a Silver Age. That its best minds doubted themselves is more to
their credit than if they had been historically complacent. They
brooded heavily over one question which had perplexed the
thoughtful, ever since men had seriously begun to contemplate
the past: whether they were lesser men than their forebears,
whether nature had fallen into a state of decay. Within a few
years, that would be the subject of the Quarrel between the Ancients and the Moderns; and within another century, the outcome
would be historicism — the recognition that each individual culture is best understood in the light of the changing conditions that
have uniquely shaped it. Most of us are still attempting to work
in that light today.

   The idea of progress no longer commands our undivided confidence; but, by a leap of the historical imagination, we must
project ourselves back to the point of time when it began to prevail over its alternative, the idea of decadence. The opportunity
for men to set their sights by the future instead of the past, or to
outdistance the ancients through the very accumulation of modern

knowledge, had its acknowledged apostle in Francis Bacon. Bacon, partly for biographical reasons, partly because he used art to elevate science, has not fared well with other men of letters; yet, after the disparagement of Pope, Macaulay, and Lytton Strachey, he will survive the slurs of Mr. Lewis. Bacon's essays, the latter asserts, are "a book for adolescents"; their relation to Montaigne is "quite unimportant." The *Essays* are discussible, to be sure, but not with profit upon so toplofty a plane of maturity. What is worth observing, in Mr. Lewis' terms, is that it was Bacon who implemented that too thorough renaissance which Spenser had impeded. The great renovation, for the pragmatic English, was the program of discovery set forth in the *Magna Instauratio*. We know all too well where it led: to the Royal Society, the *Encyclopédie*, utilitarianism, positivism, and other products of scientific experimentation, good and bad. But we must imagine a moment at the beginning, when — as Bacon exhorted James I in *The Advancement of Learning* (1605) — the instruments were being tuned:

And surely, when I set before me the condition of these times, in which learning hath made her third visitation or circuit, in all qualities thereof; as the excellency and vivacity of the wits of this age; the noble helps and lights which we have by the travails of ancient writers; the art of printing, which communicateth books to men of all fortunes; the openness of the world by navigation, which hath disclosed multitudes of experiments, and a mass of natural history; the leisure wherewith these times abound, not employing men so generally in civil business, as the states of Graecia did in respect of their popularity; and the state of Rome in respect of the greatness of their monarchy; the present disposition of these times at this instant to peace; the consumption of all that can ever be said in controversies of religion, which have so much diverted men from other sciences; the perfection of your Majesty's learning, which as a phoenix may call volleys of wits to follow you; and the inseparable propriety of time, which is ever more and more to disclose truth; I cannot but be raised to this persuasion, that this third period of time will far surpass that of the Grecian and Roman learning: only if men will know their own strength and their own weakness both; and take one from the other light of invention, and not fire of contradiction; and esteem of the inquisition of truth as of an enterprise, and not as of a quality or ornament; and employ wit and magnificence to things of worth and excellency, and not to things vulgar and of popular estimation.

This many-faceted sentence comprehends the pitfalls as well as the possibilities, while its context modestly deprecates Bacon's own contribution to coming events. If he has been eclipsed by the philosophers for whom he cleared the way, that in itself is a justification of his progressive credo. He was not, nor could he have been, a scientist himself; rather, by systematically completing the humanistic critique of scholasticism, he gained for empiricism an unprecedented measure of intellectual respectability. His thinking and writing reveal the lawyer at every turn; the fact that both More and Bacon were trained for the law indicates how broadly the legal substratum underlies English culture. Bacon, too, sketched his ideal commonwealth, his *New Atlantis* which — for better and worse — has had more fellow travelers than Utopia. When he speaks of the traders from his happy island as "Merchants of Light," he leaves us with a symbol of the belated yet determining role that Englishmen played in the Renaissance, the mediating practicality that reshaped its ideas into those of the Enlightenment. The eye of his visionary kingdom, Salomon's House, is his model for all future laboratories, libraries, art museums, research institutes, educational foundations, and science fiction. "The End of our Foundation," announces the wise old director of Salomon's House, "is the knowledge of Causes, and secret motions of things; and the enlarging of the bounds of Human Empire, to the effecting of all things possible." Such an end fell somewhat short of attainment under the British Solomon, James I; and it still does, even in this land of ours which Bacon called "the great Atlantis." But incidental failures or subsequent divagations mean less, in the long run, than Bacon's — or Shakespeare's — continued allegiance to what D. G. James has described as their "dream of learning." It is a dream which we have the privilege of sharing.

Shakespeare in the Light
of Comparative Literature

The well-known theme to which, I hoped, this paper might add a few variations is further enriched for me by its personal association with two distinguished European scholars. Shakespeare à la lumière de littérature comparée was the title suggested by the late Jean-Marie Carré, when he kindly invited me to address the Institut de Littérature Comparée at the University of Paris in the spring of 1953. Lecturing in American universities several years afterward, I found myself brought back to the topic with an enhanced awareness of its prismatic qualities: not only do the adaptations serve to bring out intercultural refractions, but the translations offer an instrument for the study of poetic style. Hence when a Festschrift was planned for Mario Praz, who has edited an Italian Shakespeare among his other scholarly and literary accomplishments, I was happy to pay my respects through these observations.

Goethe had the grace to mark one of his returns to a favorite subject with the caption *Shakespeare und kein Ende.* For that forthright expression, with its Teutonic admixture of reverence and despair, J. E. Spingarn could propose no happier English translation than "Shakespeare Ad Infinitum." Evidently we are entering a domain where familiar shapes are subjected to sea-changes. Of the making of books or speeches or essays concerning Shakespeare, the end is nowhere in sight. As we move into the fifth century of the Shakespearean epoch, that dénouement seems farther away than it can ever have seemed before. Reckonings of performance and publication on a world-wide scale are taken yearly by the *Shakespeare Survey* in England, the *Shakespeare Jahrbuch* in Germany, and the *Shakespeare Quarterly* in the United States. There is even, along with newsletters devoted to breathless bulletins about Scott Fitzgerald and other near-contemporaries, a *Shakespeare Newsletter*. Clearly it is not Shakespeare whose existence needs to be justified at this point. Rather it is comparative literature which must abide our question, and perhaps my caption would make more sense if it were reversed to read: "Comparative Literature in the Shadow of Shakespeare."

Whether comparative literature remains a marginal discipline, as it has been until quite recently, or becomes — as some of us feel encouraged to hope — a central one, may conceivably hinge upon its capacity to deal with artists of larger stature than Madame de Staël. Not that I would presume to challenge the jurisdiction of the English department over its most highly valued treasure; but the very circumstances of language, culture, and history that made Shakespeare so English a phenomenon could not be fully appreciated without overstepping his native boundaries. There are times when we must relinquish the pedagogical microscope for the telescopic view — or, to put it more bluntly, ask ourselves Kipling's question:

> What shall they know of England
> That only England know?

Nor is the field of comparative literature as much of an innovation as its elliptical name and its current spread might seem to suggest. Its critical practice can be traced back as far as that famous Greek treatise *On the Sublime*, which not only compares Demosthenes with Cicero but cites a passage from the Pentateuch, thereby bringing the Old Testament within the range of Greco-Roman literary criticism. It is within this larger frame of reference, further enlarged by nearer and by more distant ranges of literature, that we must seek an ultimate place for the greatest masterpieces.

When Thomas Fuller looked back across a generation, from the mid-seventeenth century to Shakespeare's lifetime, he compared Shakespeare with three classical authors: Ovid in poetry, Plautus in drama, and Martial in the warlike sound of his surname. Fuller's quasi-military parallel is no more extravagant or extraliterary than some of the farfetched comparisons that now and then find their way into our scholarly journals. Some of these are worthy of Shakespeare's Welsh captain, Fluellen, when he eulogizes Henry V by comparing him with Alexander the Great:

There is a river in Macedon, and there is also moreover a river in

Monmouth. It is called Wye at Monmouth; but it is out of my prains what is the name of the other river. But 'tis all one; 'tis alike as my fingers is to my fingers, and there is salmons in both. . . . I speak but in the figures and comparisons of it.

Such reasoning compels us to agree with the lately installed Professor of Comparative Literature at the Sorbonne, M. Etiemble, who has so emphatically proclaimed in the title of his inaugural pamphlet: *Comparaison n'est pas raison*. No, comparison is not the same thing as reason; and if the fortuitous jingle in French has aroused false hopes, it has pointed the way to undeceptions; whereas in English we have known all along that, with humanistic subjects, the logic is not necessarily inherent; if there is to be methodological rigor, we ourselves must achieve it.

Shakespeare's master of malapropisms, Dogberry, warns us that comparisons are odorous, if not odious. And Falstaff denounces Prince Hal, after a bout of unsavory similes, for being "the most comparative, rascalliest, sweet young prince." Whether the "comparative" goes with the "sweet" or the "rascalliest" is impossible to determine with any certainty. The kindliest attitude toward our present concern that we could wrest from Shakespeare would probably be no more encouraging than an amused tolerance. Yet relevant comparison may be — must be — an instrument of analysis and a criterion of evaluation. Shakespeare had to undergo a certain amount of invidious comparison with Ben Jonson and others before he was found to be *primus inter pares*, and with leading writers of other countries before he was declared to be incomparable. Paragons would not attain their unique positions without benefit of the comparative process — a process exemplified by Samuel Johnson's announcement that the excellence of Shakespeare's works was "not absolute or definitive, but gradual and comparative." Since Shakespeare lived about two centuries before literary history had been systematized, and incidentally nationalized, the original effort to place his work was framed by a double perspective: on the one hand, his English contemporaries and predecessors, and, on the other, the ancient classics.

The compilation of Francis Meres, *Palladis Tamia, or Wit's*

Treasury, published in 1598, is often adduced as a terminal date for
the number of plays it lists. More ambitiously, it strove to be an
intellectual survey of its era, albeit somewhat Procrustean in its
approach, and proceeded to "a comparative discourse of our English poets with the Greek, Latin, and Italian poets." Its method
was to demonstrate, by all too specific analogy, item for item, that
the English moderns could match the achievements of the ancients.
Hence it could be retrospectively viewed as a preliminary skirmish
in what, a hundred years later, developed into the Battle of the
Books. Meres, like Fuller afterward and many of Shakespeare's
earlier admirers, set much store by his erotic poems: "The sweet,
witty soul of Ovid lives in mellifluous and honey-tongued Shakespeare." Among Meres's other analogues the most important, because they were jointly applied to Shakespeare alone, signalized two
different counterparts for his dramaturgy: "As Plautus and Seneca
are accounted the best in comedy and tragedy among the Latins, so
Shakespeare among the English is most excellent in both kinds
for the stage."

In an early display of versatility, he had ranged the spectrum
from *The Comedy of Errors* to *Titus Andronicus*. His repertory
would be described by Polonius: "Seneca cannot be too heavy, nor
Plautus too light." Elsewhere the Elizabethans paid lip-service to
the Greeks; but, as is evident here, their models were Roman. Ben
Jonson's condescending reservation, that Shakespeare had small
Latin and less Greek, has misled many readers less learned than
Jonson — or, for that matter, than Shakespeare. Scholars have employed much learning to take the measure of Shakespeare's relative
ignorance, and have more or less concluded that he knew no Greek
at all, but that — measured by our unhumanistic standards — he
had a fair background in Latinity. It is sometimes regretted that
he had no acquaintance with Aeschylus and Sophocles. Yet imitation of consummate masters tends to produce lesser works, while
writers of the second rank may serve as stimulating examples to be
transcended. Obviously, it is more rewarding to study the influence
of a minor on a major writer than to retrace a chain of causation

which begins with unmatched brilliance and trails off into epigone mediocrity. The emulation of Shakespeare has had a debilitating effect upon all later attempts at poetic drama in English.

How the silver decadence of Seneca contributed to the golden flowering of drama in the sixteenth and seventeenth centuries — the paradox of abundant vitalities springing belatedly out of constricted agonies — is the impressive topic of a recent symposium, *Les Tragédies de Sénèque et le théâtre de la Renaissance*, edited by Jean Jacquot. Rather verbosely combining metaphysics with melodrama, not unlike that popular pessimist of our own day, Jean-Paul Sartre, Seneca offered his readers and hearers a paradigm for a dramatic relationship between the individual and the universe. Shakespeare deepened this relationship by shifting his emphasis from the turbulence of the universe to the consciousness of the individual. The observance of Senecan conventions helped to shape his tragic form; but, since his five-act structure was superimposed, it led toward unclassical complications. The structural norm for modern plays would seem to be three acts rather than five; and it could be argued with support from such theatrical technicians as Freytag and Granville Barker — it has indeed been argued by W. J. Lawrence — that Shakespeare, left to his natural devices, might have evolved a three-act play along more straightforward lines.

To attain the canonical five acts, the main plot had to be eked out with subordinate plots. This brought in a good deal of indigenous matter, whose origins could be sought in folklore and ritual rather than in more literary sources, and consequently have been overlooked until not long ago. However, the tendency of comic interludes to parody the more serious episodes may be the most distinctive and deeply rooted characteristic of the English stage. The sudden transitions from tragic to comic and vice versa, which outraged classicists and emboldened romanticists, were deliberate effects, not random jumbles. They were based upon a new esthetic of contrasts, appropriate to a climate which favored hybrid growths, and not upon the old unities, which had never been so firmly fixed as their proponents contended. The resulting intermixture of styles, under Shakespeare's full control, carried poetry closer and closer to the immediacy of reality — as innovating poets have attested, from Victor Hugo to Boris Pasternak. But with such witnesses we anticipate Shakespeare's bequest, whereas our initial glance should be directed toward his heritage.

If he has come to belong — as Benedetto Croce affirmed — to the common patrimony of culture, it should likewise be acknowledged what a rich inheritance came his way. The negative fact of not having studied Greek or even attended a university matters much less, in the long run, than the positive fact of having lived in a period which attached its highest values to books, the arts, and the pursuit of knowledge. An occasional slip or anachronism dwindles into insignificance before Shakespeare's ready command of so many professional vocabularies. He conjured with the apposite Latin tags, more especially in the early plays. He understood French well enough to risk a bilingual scene or two, not to mention a risqué joke or two, in *Henry* V. Some of his characters smatter a *lingua franca* of Italian, Spanish, and strange locutions from outlandish dialects. We roughly understand what Pistol means when he rants, "*Si fortune me tormento, sperato me contento.*" And we are just as baffled as Parolles by the "terrible language" of his tormentors, sheer double-talk and yet a demonstration of Shakespeare's linguistic virtuosity: "*Oscorbidulchos volivorco.*" Above all, he could draw upon series of translations which relayed the belles-lettres of the Continent to him with all the creative impetus of their age.

In the large assortment of reading that scholars have pieced together through internal evidence, two major writers stand out as kindred minds: Plutarch, the Greek biographer of the Romans, translated by the Frenchman Amyot and retranslated by the Englishman North, and Montaigne, the French psychologist of the self, whether or not in Florio's translation. Shakespeare could hardly have chosen better guides to human relations and to introspection. No English writer, apparently, meant so much to him.

He had to be a wide reader in order to pick up his subjects in some of the far-flung places where he encountered them. The rule holds true that he seems less inspired when his source was another major writer: consider Chaucer, for instance, and *The Two Noble Kinsmen*. *Troilus and Cressida*, where Homer stands behind Chaucer with Chapman between, may constitute an exception. But it may be observed that Shakespeare's chief masterworks, except for *King Lear*, were not derived from English originals. (*King Lear* is primarily Celtic, of course, and *Macbeth* is on the border in more ways than one.) There may have been more artistic challenge for him in dramatizing a slight or obscure *novella*. In any case, genetics are always more interesting when they involve cross-breeding.

The game of source-hunting is still worth playing when we can learn something from it about Shakespeare's technique of adaptation, and particularly when it illuminates the means by which imagination renews itself, the permutation and transmutation of themes. Old-fashioned believers in original genius have been duly shocked by Shakespeare's habits of composition, forgetting that the Aristotelian word for plot was *mythos* or that Henry James himself scanned the *Times* and listened to gossip for his *données*. Nothing can be created by human beings *ex nihilo*: such is the lesson so harshly imparted by *King Lear*. When painters were cut off from mythology and forced to dream up their own subject matter, rather than simply to depict what patrons had commissioned, they turned to impressionism, expressionism, and abstraction. The pressure on playwrights to invent their own stories out of their heads has latterly been pushing them farther and farther toward the cultivation of novelty for its own sake, or else throwing them back upon the haphazard resources of their subjective selves. Conversely, more traditional writing rests on the shared experience of mankind, as digested into narrative and expressed through varying forms.

Count Gozzi, generalizing from his association with the *commedia dell' arte*, observed that there were no more than thirty-six dramatic situations. Schiller thought there ought to be more than that, according to Goethe; but, when Schiller tried to enumerate them, he could not account for so many. We need not conclude that Shakespeare's artistry was reducible to the thirty-six categories ticked off in Polti's easy handbook of playwriting. Folklorists refine the enumeration by recognizing as many as 10,000 motifs. The esthetician Etienne Souriau has devoted a mind-extending book to 200,000 dramatic situations. The point is that these are finite, however numerous; there are just so many combinations, though they may be recombined and modified to give the impression of infinite variety; and we may leave the tabulation to our colleagues' computers. The raw material, the basic fabric, which Shakespeare liked to call "stuff," has a life of its own which can be charted by what used to be called *Stoffgeschichte*. We may well prefer to regard his treatment of a given theme as definitive, yet we shall appreciate it better for an awareness of the variations that have been played upon it: the underplot of *The Merchant of Venice*, for example, and the story of the three caskets in ancient and modern, oriental and occidental lore.

The tale of Romeo and Juliet is traceable, through the poem of Arthur Brooke that Shakespeare used, to a collection of Italian tales by Matteo Bandello. Since it was independently used by Lope de Vega for his tragicomedy, *Los Castelvines y Monteses*, it affords us an unparalleled opportunity for the controlled observation of what differentiates Shakespearean tragedy from the Spanish drama of the Golden Age, where the focal interest dwelt upon the families, the formalities, and the happy ending. From a broader standpoint, the basic motif of the tryst in the tomb is a Renaissance incarnation of the classic myth about Pyramus and Thisbe, which Shakespeare had read in his Ovid and burlesqued in his *Midsummer Night's Dream*. Furthermore, on the very highest plane of generality, Romeo and Juliet have common features with, and striking divergences from, Tristan and Isolde and many another pair of star-crossed lovers whose love is consummated by death. The organic totality of literature itself, insofar as it can be comprehended through its dynamic processes and its related configurations, must — in the last analysis — prove greater than any single author, even one who is generally acknowledged to be the greatest.

Thematic studies have much light to throw on characterization, as well as plotting. Critics of the late eighteenth and nineteenth centuries — periods when prose fiction flourished more than stage drama — tended to read Shakespeare's plays as if they were novels, identifying closely with the characters, and looking for more intimate details and more elaborate continuities than the dramatist had needed to supply. Twentieth-century criticism has endeavored to restore the balance by methods that the trenchant American scholar-critic, E. E. Stoll, termed "historical and comparative." These entail some danger of reduction: to reduce a character to his prototype — Falstaff, say, to the *miles gloriosus* of comic tradition — is to undermine his individuality. But, perceptively handled, they foster discernment: to discern the archetype from which a character gains his strength, as Gilbert Murray did in his essay "Hamlet and Orestes," is to show how literature gains its subliminal effects. Hamlet, for descriptive purposes, invokes several figures of mythology: Hyperion, Pyrrhus, Vulcan, Hercules (it remained for the Freudians to bring in Oedipus). Hamlet has himself walked out of his part into the sphere of mythological personification, like Falstaff, Othello, or Shylock with their respective tutelary attributes.

Thus Turgenev could localize a self-conscious personage as "A Hamlet of the Shchigri District," and could set up his own antithesis between Hamlet and Don Quixote as the alternative confronting all Russian writers and their protagonists. Tolstoy's Prince Andrey is Hamlet-like, his Pierre is Quixotic; Turgenev himself is a Hamlet, Dostoevsky a Quixote. Tolstoy's stubborn resistance to Shakespeare was a poignant irony, since he is one of the few observers of his fellow men who has manifested a comparable breadth of sympathy. George Orwell has explained the *contretemps* by pointing to the tormented destiny that ended by casting Tolstoy in the role of Lear. The very need of the Russians to come to terms with Shakespeare, or else to fight him off, registers the extent of his diffusion and assimilation. Their Shakespearean scholar, Mikhail Morozov, informs us that *Othello* alone has been played in sixteen Soviet languages. Shakespeare was introduced into Russia under the imperial auspices of Catherine the Great, who — in adapting *The Merry Wives of Windsor* — adapted the staple of Falstaff's diet, sack, by substituting a homely local beverage, quass. That may be a trivial detail, yet it illustrates the crucial distinction between what is universal in Shakespeare's appeal and what is merely particular: the universality of thirst and the particularities of the endemic potables for quenching it.

Shakespeare's international ascendancy is not unrelated to the peculiar cultural and linguistic position of England, notably its interdependence and interplay with the Romanic and Germanic cultures and languages. Here two books, both written about two generations ago, both of them pioneering contributions to comparative literature, have served as guideposts and remain object-lessons: *Shakespeare en France sous l'ancien régime* by Jules Jusserand and *Shakespeare und der Deutsche Geist* by Friedrich Gundolf. The contrast between them aptly mirrors the divergent fortunes of Shakespeare in France and Germany. Jusserand, a scholar by avocation and an Academician by predilection, was a diplomat accredited to England and to the United States. Gundolf was a professor at Heidelberg, more concerned with letters than with philology, and in close touch with the poetic circle of Stefan George. His study is philosophic and lyrical; Jusserand's is urbane and anecdotal; taken together, they virtually personify the variance between *Geist* and *esprit*. If Jusserand's is a fairly shallow book, it is because the contacts between Shakespeare and France were comparatively superficial during the two centuries to which his investigation is limited.

These are filled in with social documentation and rounded out with national generalizations, which are both shrewd and amusing; but the confrontation was strongly antipathetic, from the earliest allusions to the revolutionary epoch. Such a mutual repulsion has its significance for the history of taste, to be sure; and there have been English neoclassicists, notoriously Thomas Rymer, who were much more pigheadedly anti-Shakespearean than Voltaire. Voltaire's case is a complex one, which has been thoroughly investigated by later students and which is amply articulated through his collected works, since he kept returning to Shakespeare obsessively. Starting from a youthful enthusiasm for all manifestations of English liberalism, it turned into a sense of rivalry after he had aided Shakespeare to win a hearing in France, and culminated in a jealously nationalistic antagonism when Shakespeare was being hailed as a god of the theater. If the admiration and the reservation were balanced in Voltaire's catchphrase, "a barbarian of genius," then he put his hand upon the scales when he added that Shakespeare had more barbarism than genius.

This was a triumph of culture over language, though it would be hard to say which culture over which language. With ironic symbolism, Voltaire's chair at the Académie Française was filled upon his death by Jean-François Ducis, who was best known for his adaptations of Shakespeare. These are all the more remarkable because Ducis was utterly unacquainted with English, though he claimed to derive inspiration from portraits of Shakespeare and David Garrick on his writing-desk. The version of Ducis most performed and admired was his highly classicized Hamlet. Therein the ghost is decorously mute; the prince swears revenge on an urn containing his father's ashes; and the play is dedicated, in a tearful epistle, to the ashes of the playwright's father. The old king, it transpires, has been killed in a crime of passion by none other than his queen, who finally kills herself. Her accomplice, Claudius, is the father of Ophelia — inasmuch as Polonius is no more than a Racinian confidant — so that this Hamlet, like the heroes of Corneille, is faced with a clear-cut choice between his love for the heroine and his own family's honor. It requires no further manipulation of the plot for him to survive the carnage and mount the throne.

Well, it should not surprise us that every nation beholds its

118 REFRACTIONS

visage in Shakespeare's mirror. On the other side of the Rhine, after Goethe had recreated a Hamlet in the neurasthenic image of Wilhelm Meister, the radical poet Freiligrath would declare: *"Deutschland ist Hamlet!"* It will be conceded that, though the role has been more happily acted and the identification is far from complete, certain affinities have been stronger in Germany. Hence Gundolf had a richer and more sympathetic body of testimony to cover than Jusserand. At the outset, the German critic felt compelled to redefine the concept of influence — which has functioned as so jejune an entry on the ledgers of comparative literature — in terms of its etymological derivation, *Ein-fluss*, the inflow of a vitalizing current which changes the whole nature of the mainstream. He went on to show how that fusion had enabled German literature to free itself from the long French dominance, and how characteristically its emerging spokesmen had reacted to the Shakespearean stimulus. The independent Lessing had made Shakespeare a rallying-cry for the critical campaign against neoclassicism, as well as an exemplar for practising playwrights to emulate.

Shakespeare could be looked upon as the calm at the center of the *Sturm und Drang* — that tempestuous movement which produced so many plays that sound like exaggerations of his. His most successful emulator was Schiller, whose rendering of *Macbeth* is properly *geistlich*, with the witches fulfilling his notion of a Greek chorus, and the Porter's drunken monologue deleted in favor of a solemn hymn to the sunrise. Yet Shakespeare's chronicle-plays were the inspirations for the grandiose pageantry of *Maria Stuart* and the *Wallenstein* trilogy. What was lacking may have been hinted by — of all people — Karl Marx, when he distinguished between Schillerizing and Shakespearizing: between mere ideological mouthpieces and completely dramatized personalities, in brief, between propaganda and purer art. Shakespeare's pre-eminence in the world's drama was securely established by the critic mainly responsible for the standard German translation, August Wilhelm Schlegel, in his Vienna lectures of 1808, *Vorlesungen über dramatische Kunst und Literatur*, which seem to have had

more impact on Coleridge than the latter was willing to acknowledge. The German and the English currents, in their reflux, con-
verged to shift the tide in France after the Revolution, and after
that retarded classicism which was temporarily upheld by Napoleon's authoritarian tastes.

Now the word *romantic* is an anglicism. Its adoption into Continental languages ran parallel to the spreading cult of Shakespeare,
which, as it moved across Europe, brought out the latent nationalistic self-realization of the literatures that responded to it.
Significantly, that word made its first French appearance in the
prefatory discourse to the first full-scale French translation of
Shakespeare by Pierre Letourneur in 1776. This was the occasion
for the rear-guard action expressing Voltaire's extreme protest, his
letter to the French Academy. In a footnote contrasting *romantique* with the usual adjective *romanesque*, and with its synonym
pittoresque, Shakespeare's exponent defended his neologism on the
grounds that it conveyed a more emotional response to nature.
Immediately afterward it was employed, still rather self-consciously,
in a volume on the appreciation of picturesque landscapes by the
Marquis de Girardin, a friend of Jean-Jacques Rousseau. Thence
the arch-romanticist seems to have picked up what was to become
his shibboleth; for *romantique* was naturalized into a context describing the Swiss landscape in the fifth of Rousseau's *Rêveries du
promeneur solitaire*, written in 1777 but published posthumously.

During that same year, at the height of the American Revolution, the English critic Maurice Morgann took up Voltaire's challenge, and predicted that Shakespeare would soon be enacted on
the other side of the Appalachian Mountains. His voice would ring
through riverboats and mining camps. But there is an inevitable
lag between the emergence and the acceptance of revolutions in
the arts. It was not until 1830, with the première of Hugo's *Her-
nani*, a drama which owed more to Shakespeare than to its French
forerunners, that Romanticism made its triumphant arrival in the
capital of its enemies. It took an English battering-ram to breach
the wall of French classicism, as Sainte-Beuve would phrase it,

before a native Romanticist could carry an audience. Hugo had tried and failed, with his pseudo-Shakespearean *Cromwell*; the preface was more telling than the play. That, in turn, had been preceded by Stendhal's manifesto, *Racine et Shakespeare*, which had borrowed some of its ammunition from Dr. Johnson's magistral defense. Stendhal, without paying much attention to either dramatist, had pitted them against each other as programmatic symbols of authority and autonomy, offering his compatriots the choice between obsolescence with Racine and modernity with Shakespeare.

The actual cross-fertilization occurred during the eighteen-twenties when a celebrated English troop of actors played Shakespeare at Paris, with after-effects that are memorialized in the painting of Delacroix and the music of Berlioz, as well as in literature. Berlioz' frenzied courtship of the fascinating Irish actress, Henrietta Smithson, reverberates through his sequence of Shakespearean compositions. His operatic version of *Much Ado About Nothing* was tactfully rechristened *Béatrice et Bénédict* because the French title of Shakespeare's play might have been construed as a reflection upon his musical style: *Beaucoup de bruit sur rien* could be too pointed a comment on the orchestration of the new school. Shakespeare, then, could awaken fresh talent in France as he had been doing in Germany. Yet, though he was now welcomed, he was never quite at home in the garb prescribed for diplomatic visits. Desdemona's controversial handkerchief, scorned as a vulgarity by the purists, was replaced in Vigny's *More de Venise* with an innocuous scarf and an impeccable bracelet. Meanwhile the Germans, at the opposite pole, had become so acculturated that they fell into their provocative habit of talking about *unser Shakespeare*.

That usage might be warranted as a claim of spiritual kinship, so long as it could be advanced for other languages with their own possessive pronouns, and while the English *our* retains its priority — in other words, so long as Shakespeare transcends any one nationality by appealing to all. The German claim could be substantiated by a vast corpus of commentary, yes, but more appropriately by a living record of presentation in the theater. This could not have been accomplished without a translation which, while remarkably faithful to the original, has come to occupy an honored niche in German literature. The circumstance of using a text which dates back no more than one hundred and fifty years means, of course, that their Shakespeare is closer to them by some two hundred years than our Shakespeare is to us. Moreover, it is not for nothing that the two languages are structurally interrelated. When Juliet invokes Apollo's chariot, for instance, she speaks of "fiery-footed steeds," which does not sound quite the same as *"flammenhufiger Gespann"* or even "flame-hoofed team." Yet it comes close because Schlegel has managed to capture the compound epithet, where Salvatore Quasimodo is forced to string the words out in Italian: *"cavalli dai piedi di fuoco."*

As a little exercise in comparative stylistics, let us concentrate on a well-known and problematic line which distressed Pope and other English rigorists because it perpetrated a mixed metaphor: "Or to take arms against a sea of troubles." The German flows just as naturally, and somewhat more regularly: *"Sich waffnen gegen eine See von Plagen."* Here too the Russian of Pasternak's translation seems no less accurate, though perhaps more compressed. But the image could never accommodate itself to the rules of French logic and clarity. If Pope balked, you can imagine Voltaire's objections. He undertook to rethink the entire soliloquy, while conferring the dignity of alexandrines upon it:

> Demeure, il faut choisir et passer à l'instant
> De la vie à la mort et de l'être au néant.

Thus Hamlet's existential dichotomy is rounded out with a flourish more characteristic of Sartre; and, since an anticlerical is speaking, it will not surprise you that — among the other ills that flesh is heir to — Voltaire goes out of his way to drag in lying priests (*"nos prêtres menteurs"*). The impulse of French translators is to qualify Shakespeare's trope by neutralizing one component or the other, modifying "take arms" to *"lutter"* or *"s'insurger"* and "a sea

of troubles" to *"un monde de douleurs"* or *"la mer orageuse"* — or
else abstracting both, as in Letourneur's rendering: *"se révoltant
contre une multitude de maux."*

Yet a more concretely literal rendering, in the most widely circulated French Shakespeare, that of the poet's son, François-Victor
Hugo, sounds at once odd and prosaic: *"s'armer contre une mer de
douleurs."* (Here we must blandly ignore the collocation of syllables, *mer de*, which Voltaire played upon for a scatological snicker.)
As Hamlet goes on to remark, "There's the rub" — and the figure
from bowling, for an unfavorable inclination of ground, slows
down, if it does not stop, the translators. Again they try to generalize the dilemma: "the rub" becomes *"l'obstacle"* or *"l'embarras."*
Others introduce metaphors of their own: a reef (Guizot), a gulf
(Ménard), a question-mark (Montégut). Dumas is unwontedly
laconic and colorless: *"Ah! tout est là!"* In the second volume of
the Pléiade Shakespeare the editor, André Gide, prints eleven versions of the *être ou ne pas être* passage, but not his own, which
takes the unexpected step of transporting the catachresis from
warfare to horsemanship: *"mettre frein à une marée de douleurs."*
In his previous translation of *Antony and Cleopatra*, Gide has been
more resistant to the Shakespearean afflatus. There the succinct
tribute of Enobarbus,

> Age cannot wither her nor custom stale
> Her infinite variety,

is decompressed and divided into two heavy commonplaces: *"Les
années passeront sans la flétrir. Son extrême diversité met au défi
la lassitude."* One is reminded of those Academicians who criticized
an exuberant line from *Le Cid*, *"Ses rides sur son front ont gravé
ses exploits,"* by patiently instructing Corneille that, though
wrinkles denote the passing of years, they cannot strictly be said to
engrave exploits.

"There's the rub" — reverting with Gide to *Hamlet* — becomes
"C'est là le hic." That is to say, a metaphor from sport is transposed to a bit of scholastic jargon. Since the *hic* is an abbreviation

of the Latin "*Hic est quaestio,*" it is basically a repetition of Hamlet's "That is the question." But the transposition from an athletic to a bookish expression is revealing, as we shift from England to France. Every barrier of untranslatability in language is a genuine index of disparity in culture. Shakespeare seems to provoke a certain stylistic intransigence, even on the part of the flexible Gide, who does not brand Shakespeare a drunken savage as Voltaire did, but tells us that the reader undergoes "*une sorte d'enivrement verbale.*" Though such poetic intoxication can be exhilarating, it deviates at its peril from sober prose. The contribution of *Hamlet's* latest French translator, the gifted poet Yves Bonnefoy, has been to round out the cycle by utilizing in earnest what Voltaire had conceived as a reduction to absurdity, and literally rendering our troublesome line: "*ou de prendre les armes contre une mer de troubles.*" This willingness to adapt the French to Shakespeare, rather than to adapt Shakespeare to the French, sets the tone for the *Hamlet* of Yves Bonnefoy.

This would not be a viable strategy if the French convention were not changing at the hands of such poets as M. Bonnefoy. English poetry has an open diction, an *ouverture* which — in his critical comments — he opposes to the *fermeture*, the closed diction of conventional French poetry. What has happened during the past half-century, as we might learn from comparing translations, has brought French literature closer to a Shakespearean openness of form. As it were, some spirit has been breathed into the letter. At all events, whatever we lose through these international transactions can be regained with interest whenever we return to the reading of Shakespeare at first hand. Yet that reading, even for natives of English, is not just an unimpeded projection from the page to the mind; it is rather a gradual unfolding, which varies from person to person and stage to stage in the amount of meaning it reveals. Since all comprehension is at best an approximation, we must pursue our object from our varying distances. And, since even Shakespeare's puns are "a lively feature of his work," they need not be written off when the translator is as

resourceful as Mario Praz in his command of both languages involved (*"Shakespeare, Il Castiglione et le facezie"*).

To pinpoint the areas of probable misunderstanding is a valuable aid to potential understanding. Those refracted images disclose much about the cultures between which they mediate. The
intervention of Shakespeare has acted as a touchstone for bringing
out positive aspects of German romanticism and negative aspects
of French classicism, although the Germans did not understand
him as well as they thought and the French are coming to understand him better. The quality — or should it be the quiddity? —
whatever confers on poetry its uniqueness is, by definition, untranslatable. The poem addressed by Hamlet to Ophelia pivots upon
an ambiguity which is peculiar to English, the use of the verb *to
doubt*. Two accomplished and indefatigable linguists, Erika and
Alexander Gerschenkron, have studied one hundred translations
of this quatrain into sixteen languages. Their forthcoming article,
"The Illogical Hamlet: A Note on Untranslatability," is a devastating chronicle of evasions, circumlocutions, misconstructions,
and downright mistranslations, which leaves us wondering what
can come out of a process wherein so much is lost, beyond the
self-congratulation of those who may happen to have been born
into Shakespeare's language — or, at least, our demotic dialect of it.

The answer, I would suppose, is that every reincarnation must
assume its own autonomous form, though it has been brought to
life by Shakespeare's inimitable touch. "Every historical period
finds in him what it is looking for and what it wants to see." Such
is the warrant, at any rate, for a widely heralded, currently published, and already influential book, *Shakespeare Our Contemporary* by Jan Kott. As a Pole, Professor Kott has honorably suffered
under both the Nazi and Soviet regimes. That may explain why he
does not want to see any meaning at all in history. Instead he looks
for, and naturally finds, an anachronistic panorama of meaningless-
ness in Shakespeare's histories. He finds no humor in the comedies
or anywhere else, while tragedy is displaced by grim grotesquerie,
since moral choices must confront alternatives which are equally

absurd in the world Professor Kott envisions. Accordingly, the book that Hamlet reads is not by Montaigne, as some scholars like to believe, but by Sartre, Camus, or Kafka; while *King Lear* is subtitled *Endgame* and updated for Samuel Beckett's Theater of the Absurd, where dialogue subsides into endless monologue, will power is smothered in inertia, and the stormy heath shrinks to the asphyxiating proportions of a pair of garbage cans.

Shakespeare, thus roughly handled and forcibly subpoenaed, bears witness to the anger, the cruelty, and the violence of our own times. Nevertheless, there are other contemporary interpreters to whom his lessons seem more optimistic. Writing to commemorate his quadricentennial in the Soviet literary journal, *Novy Mir*, the orientalist Nikolay Konrad accepts the tragic sense of history as a bond between Shakespeare and the Russian soul, with the implication that Stalin was cast as Macbeth or Richard III. But Professor Konrad sees the blood and terror as an expiation which clears the air for more humanistic perspectives. Meanwhile, the West German periodical *Akzente* has marked the jubilee with a curious article by that brilliant novelist Günter Grass, compendiously entitled "Pre- and Post-History of the Tragedy of Coriolanus from Livy and Plutarch through Shakespeare to Brecht and Me." What Herr Grass gets out of Shakespeare or reads into him — "*herausgelesen und hineingelesen*," in his own phrase — is something more than a parody of the pedantic *Quellenforschung* conducted by German professors; it is an attack against Bertolt Brecht on charges of political opportunism, using techniques of burlesque which Brecht applied to other writers, and taking its departure from his last production, a Marxist revision of Shakespeare's play.

Coriolanus, somehow one of the few plays by Shakespeare that never seem to get produced in Soviet Russia, is wryly characterized by Herr Grass as an ever green, and therefore sour, apple ("*dies immergrüne, aber sauer Apfel*"). Truly it seems to affect its audiences with the kind of social tension, the conflict of ideologies, the very class struggle it dramatizes. Riots broke out when Max Reinhardt produced it during the nineteen-twenties in Berlin, and a

French cabinet fell when it was presented in the mid-thirties at the Comédie-Française. *Julius Caesar,* another one of Shakespeare's public inquiries into the hazards of Roman citizenship, has elicited similar repercussions from time to time, most pointedly when Orson Welles costumed it in Fascist uniforms. It was first translated into Japanese for liberal and patriotic reasons in 1884, the year of Japan's new constitution; but it was not acted until 1901, when a performance — Kabuki-style in Tokyo — seems to have been generally regarded as alluding to an explosive train of events touched off by the assassination of a reactionary politician. When a Swahili version of the same play was recently published by Julius K. Nyerere, the Premier of Tanzania, it was reported to have stressed the understandable moral that conspirators come to bad ends. The echoes must intensify to a crescendo, when a Tanzanian or a Japanese Cassius exclaims:

> How many ages hence
> Shall this our lofty scene be acted over
> In states unborn and accents yet unknown!

Carrying prophecy to the point of fulfillment, in purporting to look ahead, those lines hark back to Shakespeare himself, even while they look beyond him — and with him — to ancient Rome. Through them he takes his stand in our cultural firmament, encompassing so much of what has gone before, enkindling so much of what comes after, that we are bound to take our bearings from him. The dependence of latter-day writers upon his igniting spark was indicated and exemplified by Vladimir Nabokov, when he named his last English novel with an oblique allusion to *Timon of Athens:*

> The moon's an arrant thief,
> And her pale fire she snatches from the sun.

Most of us, as students, feel more at ease with the microcosm of Shakespeare's text than in the bedazzlement of such cosmic vistas. Yet comparative literature can help us to realize how much of our light is reflected from his radiance, how many of our luminaries can be viewed as his satellites. In short, it can teach us to reckon the larger magnitudes, to recognize the stars by discerning the constellations. As distinguished from the specific study of individual authors, it must place its stress on interrelationships rather than on objects in themselves. But a literary object owes its existence to a network of such relationships, not least to those that link it with ourselves.

7   Two Comedies of Errors

This is a small illustration in some detail of what has been broadly adumbrated in the foregoing sketch, circumstances having provided an unforced comparison where the telescope could be replaced by the microscope. The comedy of Plautus is interesting in itself, though chiefly for its conventions and stylizations. Shakespeare's early comedy, compared with his later plays, seems slight indeed; but when we compare it with its Plautine source, we are struck by the extent to which he has elaborated and enriched it. The confrontation throws into bold relief both the comic universals and the uniquely Shakespearean touches. My remarks were presented as the opening lecture of the Shakespeare Seminar at Stratford, Ontario, in 1963, and were published in the Stratford Papers on Shakespeare edited by B. W. Jackson (Toronto: W. J. Gage Limited, 1964). An abridged and modified version forms the introduction to my edition of The Comedy of Errors in the Signet Classic Shakespeare (New York: New American Library, 1965). For the present republication I should like to express my thanks to Professor Jackson, Director of the Stratford Seminars, and to Professor Sylvan Barnet, general editor of the Signet Shakespeare.

To err is human; and if to forgive be divine, then at least it can be the temporary prerogative of the gallery gods; for it has also been repeatedly said that to understand everything is to forgive everything, and comedy may be described as an exercise in understanding. To put the matter more precisely, it is a planned confusion, created in order to be clarified: a series of misunderstandings brought about, under the guise of chance or contrivance, by the playwright himself — who is usually at pains to keep the audience alerted at every step, so that it will end by congratulating itself on having foreseen the hazards, seen through the wiles and ruses, shared in the solution of the dilemmas, and taken a thoroughly enlightened view of the whole benighted proceeding. Comedy was defined for Shakespeare's age by Sir Philip Sidney as "an imitation of the common errors of our life, which [the poet] representeth in the most ridiculous and scornful sort that may be, so as it is impossible that any beholder can be content to be such a one."

Sidney was propounding — and possibly straining — a moral argument, since he was engaged in the defense of poetry. Yet his definition suggests the relation between the spectators and the comic actor: there, but for the grace of God, go we!

We are invited to look down upon the buffoonery, to survey the scene from the sidelines in intellectual detachment, whereas we look up in an emotional identification with the tragic protagonist, tending as we do to identify ourselves with those whose qualities we most admire. Morally speaking, they are object-lessons, where the comic figures are awful examples. Not that our heroes cannot fall into error: as man strives, he strays, like Goethe's Faust. The ebullient Mayor of New York, Fiorello La Guardia, used to say, "I don't often make a mistake, but when I do, it's a beaut." This reservation could serve as a dividing line between comedy, with its many trivial mistakes, and tragedy, with its monstrously grand one. Think of *Macbeth*, of *Othello*, of *King Lear*; and if *Hamlet* seems to stand apart in this respect as in so many others, it is because the Prince tried so hard — albeit so ineffectually — to avoid making a big mistake. Your hero, for all his virtues, has his tragic flaw; and a single misstep, for him, has fatal consequences. Your buffoon is constantly waylaid by pitfalls, familiar and not terribly consequential, or else upset by pratfalls, from which he scrambles to his feet not very badly harmed, so that he may come closer to us — to the stuff of our experience — after all.

> For never was a story of more woe
> Than this of Juliet and her Romeo,

tragedy thus properly concludes, while Titus Andronicus is regarded as nothing less than "The woefull'st man that ever liv'd in Rome." Tragedy is by nature extraordinary; it envisages men and women as singular and superlative, as the most perfect paragons of woe. Comedy, having to deal with the ordinary and the realistic, is given to generalization. All this has happened before, and may happen again; take the long view; statistics never lie; and patterns of behavior are predictable. Orlando believes that he is in a most woeful plight; but Rosalind coolly surveys the lovers of classical myth — Troilus, Leander, and so on — and generalizes, "Men have died from time to time, and worms have eaten them, but not for love." Here we are dealing not with extremes but with norms, not with unique individuals but with typical cases. When a young lover says farewell to his lady because he must go off to the wars, the crisis may well enlist our sympathetic concern. But if, while that poignant scene is taking place, an identically similar scene is taking place on the other side of the stage, and both pairs of lovers are going through the same motions at the same time, and all four are singing a quartet to music by Mozart — why, then we cannot but shrug our shoulders and comment, "*Così fan tutte*, thus all women do, it's the way of the world."

Hence it is comedy which typifies, where it is tragedy which individualizes; where tragedy observes the nice distinctions between man and man, comedy stresses those broad resemblances which make it so difficult to tell people apart. The closer the similarity between them, the easier it becomes for us to confuse them. Blunders are most easily committed when two differing alternatives closely resemble one another, though the resemblance be no more than skin-deep. "Two faces that are alike," Pascal observed, "though neither of them excites laughter in itself, make me laugh when together on account of the likeness." It was this sentence of Pascal's that Bergson amplified into his cogent theory of laughter, which found its formula in the repetition, the duplication, and the mechanization of the humane and the natural: in fine, a vindication of reality as against artificiality. Now there is an inherent lack of dignity — I am almost tempted to call it a loss of face — in being indistinguishable from, in always being mistaken for, someone else. If that were your problem, you might well prefer to go on living in Ephesus or Epidamnum rather than to return to Syracuse, where you could scarcely hope not to be confounded with your twin; and the moral of the two comedies before us might simply be to let well enough alone.

Those two plays, spanning a distance of some 1800 years, belong to what is perhaps the oldest continuous tradition in drama or literature, and is therefore somewhat ironically known as New Comedy. It was already established when Menander crystallized its usages; by way of the *commedia dell'arte* it furnished prototypes for both Molière and Marivaux; and it is not yet dead so long as Zero Mostel finds his way down Broadway to the Forum.

> Whilst slaves be false, fathers hard, and bawds be whorish,
> Whilst harlots flatter, shall Menander flourish.

Such was Ovid's testimonial, as translated by Ben Jonson, another robust upholder of the tradition. This does not betoken the most elevated pinnacle of fame or the most elevating conception of human nature. Yet it does convey some notion of the stock types that keep reappearing in varied combinations throughout the repertory, motivated by a hard-boiled ethic — or, if you prefer, a single-minded psychology: "a niggardly Demea, . . . a crafty Davus, . . . a flattering Gnatho, . . . a vainglorious Thraso," each summed up by Sidney in a single trait. For, in that constricting geometrical world, motivation is mechanized, and human beings react like automata. The young are animated mainly by sexual appetites, as the old are by monetary considerations; while the perennial conflict between them is abetted by parasites, whose only object is feasting, and by slaves — so much cleverer than their masters — who expend the utmost resources of their cleverness to wriggle out of another beating.

Because of political pressures, New Comedy did not address itself to public issues as Aristophanes had done with his Old Comedy. Dramatists had turned from matters of state to private affairs, to the middle-class sphere of business. If the family was now the dramatic center, it was being decentralized and disrupted; and the dramatic action, so packed with previous events and offstage adventures, so limited in what actually happened on the stage, moved toward domestic reunion and enlargement. The surviving Roman comedies seem to have been adapted from Greek originals, subsequently lost. Their *dramatis personae* still have Greek names;

they wear the pallium and not the toga. The background of their escapades is not Rome; and if it is not Athens, still it Hellenizes — or, as the prologue to our play from Plautus announces, it Sicilianizes (*"non atticissat, verum sicilicissitat"*). In any case, the locale was some Hellenistic city — some Mediterranean seaport where fortune veered with the winds of trade, and where piracy, shipwreck, and naval warfare were items of daily report. Though the town changes from play to play, New Comedy is invariably an urban phenomenon. The architectural proscenium of the Roman theater, with its practical doors and upper windows and niches and statues, was a stylization of a street or a square, leading to a harbor on one side (the Piraeus) and to a marketplace on the other (the Agora).

Though that mode of presentation had been drastically transformed during the Renaissance, the Italian designers preserved these associations in the perspective vistas they devised. Pastoral called for woodland scenery, tragedy for temples and palaces, and comedy for shops and domiciles. Something of the tradition has persisted on the stages for vaudeville and burlesque, where a drop-curtain close to the footlights surrounds the fast-talking comedians with an atmosphere of downtown. It was theater in the flat, not in the round, accommodating a drama which was linear rather than plastic. The result may seem too thin for performance without music, as if Hart's libretto for *The Boys from Syracuse* were performed without Rodgers' score. Roman comedy, true to its emphasis on externals and appearances, seldom permitted more than the merest glimpse of what went on behind those inviting façades. The distinctive feature of its setting were the doorways, which represented conveniently neighboring houses. Between them flowed the continual traffic of characters, and most of their interchanges took place at the thresholds — whence other characters would emerge periodically, slapping their thighs and holding their sides, to bring us up-to-date by divulging the goings-on within.

Such a theatrical genre, depending so much upon monologue and narration, must sound rather static to modern tastes; yet the

Romans looked on Plautus as the master not of the *modus statarius* but of what they termed the *modus motorius*, the method of movement. He was the most popular of their playwrights, partly because of his racy language and frisky verse, but chiefly because of his sustained animation, which offered their comedians opportunities for slapstick, pantomime, and gags *ad libitum*. In short, he seemed to have that comic energy, that proverbial *vis comica*, which was to be so regrettably deficient in the later and smoother Terence. Terence, never the audience's favorite, was to achieve his greatest success as a text for schools, providing many centuries with a model of elegant style and a mine of sententious quotations. Shakespeare, in his day, was compared to both Plautus and Terence by his earliest critic, Francis Meres. Shakespeare may have had small Latin, by Ben Jonson's standards of erudition; but we cannot afford to be so exacting with him; and the internal evidence from his plays argues a fair acquaintance with certain standard Latin authors. There is even an accredited rumor that, before entering the theater, he had taught in a country school, where the curriculum would have consisted of very little else.

It was not surprising then that Shakespeare, as a journeyman playwright hitherto occupied with a cycle of unclassical English histories, should want to test the range of his medium by experimenting with a Latinate comedy, along with his early experiment in pseudo-Roman tragedy. "Seneca cannot be too heavy," Polonius would boast when announcing the Players, "nor Plautus too light." If *Titus Andronicus* is indeed a heavy-handed attempt at Senecan melodrama, *The Comedy of Errors* is surely a light-fingered rehandling of a Plautine original. It is not appreciably an improvement, according to Hazlitt. Yet A. W. Schlegel declared that Shakespeare's play was "perhaps the best of all written or possible *Menaechmi*." (And there were countless others, such as Trissino's *Simillimi*.) Without begging the question, let us consider those conflicting possibilities. We know that *The Comedy of Errors* was accorded a gala production by the legal gentlemen of Gray's Inn during the Christmas season of 1594, probably two or three years after it was first publicly produced. A contemporary record, which dutifully notes Shakespeare's debt to Plautus, tells us that the festive occasion prompted such crowds and confusions that "it was ever afterwards called *The Night of Errors.*"

The generic title of Shakespeare's play sorts with any comedy or revel, and it has a lost precedent in a *History of Error*, recorded as played in 1577. Indeed the key-word would almost seem to have had the force of a technical term. As a schoolboy, if not as a schoolmaster, Shakespeare could have read Plautus in the edition of Lambinus; so T. W. Baldwin has shown in his massive studies of Shakespeare's modest Latinity. It is noteworthy that the commentary of Lambinus on the *Menaechmi* marks each successive twist and turn of the plot with the Latin verb *errare* or the noun *error*. Moreover, there is another term which ought to be considered in this connection, and which was introduced by the Elizabethan fugleman, George Gascoigne, as the title of his play, *The Supposes*. By a coincidence worthy of two such comedies, *The Supposes* had likewise been acted at Gray's Inn in 1566. This was a free translation of the prose version of Ariosto's comedy, *Gli Suppositi*, and it was to furnish Shakespeare — who takes cognizance of "counterfeit supposes" in *The Two Gentlemen of Verona* — with the underplot for his *Taming of the Shrew*. Ariosto's title literally means "the supposed" in the masculine plural or, more colloquially, "the substitutes."

In the Italian literary comedy, the *commedia erudita*, which is another branch of New Comedy, there is always someone who is deceived and someone else who does the deceiving. One of the most famous is entitled *Gl' Ingannati*, or "The Deceived," and its twin brother and sister were borrowed by Shakespeare for *Twelfth Night*. Still another, more objectively, is entitled *Gl' Inganni*, or "The Deceits," putting its stress upon the process and not the persons involved. Gascoigne's supposes are the substitutions or deceptions of Ariosto's deceivers. Though Gascoigne does not invoke Plautus or Terence in his prologue, as Ariosto did, he formulates the device. These are not to be the suppositions, the premises or hypotheses, of scholastic disputation:

But, understand, this our Suppose is nothing else but a mistaking or imagination of one thing for another. For you shall see the master supposed for the servant, the servant for the master; the freeman for a slave, and the bondslave for a freeman; the stranger for a well-known friend, and the familiar for a stranger. But, what? [the explanation concludes, not very flatteringly,] I suppose that even already you suppose me very fond that have so simply disclosed unto you the subtleties of these our Supposes, where otherwise, indeed, I suppose you should have heard almost the last of our Supposes before you could have supposed any of them aright.

A prologue is hardly needed to start the game or give away the show. The respective poses of the supposed master and the supposed servant, et cetera, are spelled out by the exposition. If that is not explicit enough for the reader, the printed text (the quarto collection known as *The Posies of George Gascoigne*, with further wordplay on the metaphorical flowers of poesy) has twenty-five marginalia pointing out each suppose as it occurs in the play.

Thus, when the heroine confides to her nurse that her father's putative servant is the hero in disguise, the speech is overtly tagged "The first suppose, and ground of all the supposes." As they proceed, and the changes are rung upon the situations, the marginal epithets are varied. "A crafty suppose," "A knavish suppose," "A shameless suppose" — the adjectives serve more or less synonymously for the disguises, the intrigues, and the lies. When somebody is duly befuddled by them, it is "A doltish suppose." And it is paradoxically marked as "A right suppose" or "A true suppose" when anyone speaks more truly than he realizes, with the ensuing effect of dramatic irony. Among the many Italianate supposes, there is only one which can be classified as an error in the Shakespearean sense: a misconception brought about by accident rather than by deliberate manipulation. This is the circumstance whereby the servant pretending to be the master really turns out to be the long-lost son of the rival suitor; and it is highly significant that the quondam master, who is the *ci-devant* servant, curses the cruel and capricious goddess Fortuna for having revealed what he calls in his naïve pride "our subtle supposes."

In this regard, the comedy of *The Supposes* does not quite live up to the observation of Francesco De Sanctis on Machiavelli's *Mandragola* (or *Mandrake*): that chance plays no part there, that all the mischief is attributable to the malign contrivance of human will. "In the reproof of chance," Nestor will observe in *Troilus and Cressida*, "Lies the true proof of men." *La Mandragola* may well be one of the toughest plays ever written, just as Machiavelli's *Prince* may well be one of the toughest guides to politics; but, as such, it is no more than an extreme application of the tough-minded code that prevails throughout New Comedy. This, in turn, helps to explain why, when a certain W. W. (probably the minor Elizabethan poet William Warner) published a slightly abridged translation of the *Menaechmi* in 1595, it was characterized on the title page as "A pleasant and fine conceited comedy taken out of the most excellent witty poet *Plautus: chosen purposely from out the rest, as least harmful and yet most delightful.*" W. W.'s choice may throw some light on why Shakespeare chose the *Menaechmi* as the one object of his direct imitation within the sphere of Roman comedy; for it is altogether untypical in its all but complete reliance on chance and not on contrivance, not mischief but sheer luck. As the translator promises, it contains "much pleasant error."

True, it has its professional embodiments of greed and lust in the parasite and the prostitute; but even they intend no harm until their respective claims have been balked; and then the harmful truths, the tales they tell out of school, make clear that they too are victims of the general imbroglio. We are at the roulette table, not the chessboard, here. There is no plotting or counterplotting in a Machiavellian sense. The sole plotter is the playwright, and whatever that ingenious trickster hatches is fobbed off on us as a trick of fate, a practical joke on the part of providence. For here, with these *gemini*, the mistaken identity is not deliberately culti-vated through impersonation or disguise; it is not a pose, a suppose, or an imposture; it is a freak of nature, *lusus naturae*, which Cole-ridge advises us to accept as a postulate. And Coleridge philoso-phizes — as is his wont — about farce, distinguishing between it and proper comedy as the basis for a distinction between the possible and the probable. A set of identical twins, leading different lives, constitutes an improbable possibility. The distinction is sometimes drawn in terms of character and plot: farce tends to subordinate the former to the latter. Two characters sufficiently alike, so that each may fit interchangeably into the other's situation, cannot afford to possess distinguishing characteristics.

The *donnée* of Plautus, the initial improbability, was complicated to the very limits of the possible when Shakespeare dared to redouble his twins by providing his pair of protagonists with a brace of retainers and thereby to quadruple his *duplex* plot. If that was a reduction to absurdity, absurdity is man's lot as the Existentialists have redefined it, and what should a farce be if not wholly absurd? Shakespeare again used Plautus to outdo Plautus, drawing upon a play so frequently readapted that Jean Giraudoux could call his version of it *Amphitryon 38* — and that must have been a conservative reckoning. There, however, the double identities are not natural but supernatural. Jupiter, whose powers of metamorphosis endowed him with so many advantages in his amorous exploits, deliberately assumes the person of Amphitryon, in order to lie with Alcmena, the absent general's wife. Jupiter's equerry Mercury makes his appearance in the person of Sosia, Amphitryon's slave; and the opening scene, with those two opposite numbers confronting each other, heralds the scene of the homecoming general, where the false Sosia manages to keep the true Amphitryon out of his own house. These are among the most effective doorway scenes in Roman comedy.

But the play is not a comedy, strictly speaking; it is — and Mercury's prologue coins the term for criticism — a tragicomedy, because it commingles human beings and gods. Nothing short of a *deus ex machina* can resolve the husband's jealousy. The *tragicomoedia* is rounded out with the miraculous announcement that Alcmena has been delivered of two sons at once, Iphicles and Hercules, respectively the scions of Amphitryon and Jupiter, siblings who are far from identical. Unlike the anxious and suspicious

Amphitryon, who has the best grounds for his anxieties and suspicions, the two Menaechmuses are bland and blithe. In fact, the
first, a local citizen, begins by telling off his wife, in what appears to
be a Punch-and-Judy relationship. He is a solid man of affairs,
who later favors us with a monologue about his many clients; but
for the nonce he is resolved to put aside business for pleasure, the
working-day world for a holiday, a day off, a night out. The
hanger-on, Peniculus, smells it in the air: *"Furtum, scortum, pran-
dium"* ("Pinching, wenching, lunching"). Whether we name it a
lark or a bird of another feather — a bat, in Johann Strauss's slang,
Die Fledermaus — it presupposes a release from the rules, a dispen-
sation from the routine duties of existence: in short, that carnival
spirit which is the first condition of comedy.

By way of contrast, the other Menaechmus — Sosicles, the stay-
at-home from Syracuse, who has turned traveler in search of his
twin — makes a serious entrance, bent on his objective. With his
presence, the errors begin to operate, through the congenial modes
of feasting and love-making; and, since he is their beneficiary, he
gaily falls in with them. All work and no play would make Jack a
dull boy. Consequently the responsible John Worthing, J.P., in-
vents a younger brother, as a playboy role in which to indulge his
irresponsible whims, and christens him — with one of Wilde's
verbal paradoxes — Ernest. He is soon rivaled in this masquerade
by his frivolous friend, Algernon Moncrieff. So might every man
wish to have a surrogate self, whose actions would be freed from
inhibitions. Now Jack and Algy, in their act of the pseudo-Ernest,
are conspirators. There is no conspiracy whatsoever in Epidamnum,
despite the punning warnings of the visitor's slave Messenio that
no one ever escapes *"sine damno,"* without damage. The visiting
Menaechmus Sosicles, like Gogol's government clerk mistaken for
an inspector general, is wined and dined and bribed and courted by
the corrupt villagers. The larks drop, already roasted, into his
mouth.

Like the Russian Hlestakov, the Syracusan Sosicles accepts his
windfalls with insouciance; and, as he catches on a bit, he plays

up to his benefactors with more and more impudence. When he leaves the prostitute's house, and her maid runs after him with a chain to be left at the goldsmith's shop for repair, he quickly recovers from his surprise and inquires if there be not some bracelets to go along with it. The Epidamnian Menaechmus, who is like his brother psychologically as well as physically (environment seeming to count for less than heredity in their temperaments), has an analogous reaction when he is offered an unsolicited purse. When the stranger is taken for a madman through what he takes to be madness on the part of the wife and her father, he joins in the fun and feigns a mad scene to fend them off. All the knots are bound to be disentangled as soon as both of the Menaechmi encounter; but that fraternal reunion is suspensefully delayed; and when the brothers finally meet, the built-up impact produces on both sides — so to speak — a double take. It is Messenio who puts one and one together, explaining to his Menaechmus that the other Menaechmus is his mirror: *"speculum tuum."*

And it is Messenio who, on gaining his freedom, pronounces the last words: since his master's brother will be returning to their native Syracuse, there will be an auction of his goods and chattels — including, if there are any bidders, his wife. The *Menaechmi*, for all its climactic pacing, shows its age with Messenio's farewell speech, not so much in his conventional bid for the plaudits of the spectators as in its incidental revelations of ancient mores, the manumission of the slave and the callous treatment of the wife. *The Comedy of Errors*, omitting the Roman feature of the parasite, doubles Messenio into the two Dromios, who are presumably bondservants. It does not alleviate the number of beatings they receive; but these are matters of farcical convention rather than social custom; and besides, like the marginal glosses in Gascoigne's *Supposes*, they register the cross-purposes of the play. (Even Ariel, in *The Tempest*, observes the conventions of Plautine slavery.) As for the Roman matron, Plautus wastes no sympathy on her; her own father judges her from a one-sidedly masculine point of view; and she should be easily forgotten, since she is namelessly designated as *Uxor* or *matrona*, whereas even the *meretrix* has a trade-name, Erotium.

Shakespeare, in amplifying the wife's role, reduced the Courtesan's. The pivotal banquet is served not at her hang-out, the Porpentine, but at the home of Antipholus, the Phoenix; while he, a normally faithful husband, seeks out her company only after he has reason to suspect his wife. The latter, Adriana, inherits the Uxor's misunderstanding with her husband; but Shakespeare sublimates it to a plane of genuine, if too possessive, conjugal love. Moreover, he endows her with a sister, to be courted by the bachelor Antipholus; and Luciana proves to be a *raisonneuse*, a mouthpiece of moderation, so that the twins take their place in the great Shakespearean debate on marriage, along with Kate and Petruchio or Rosaline and Beroune or Beatrice and Benedick. Shakespeare's characters move, as usual, in a Christian ethos. The perplexed traveler swears, "as I am a Christian," and — approached by the Courtesan — echoes Christ bidding Satan avaunt. The change in the ethical climate may be noted by the shift from Epidamnum, which is nonetheless mentioned along the way, to Ephesus. Plautus' Syracusans fear Epidamnum because it is an emporium of sharp practice, peopled by rogues and harlots and standard comic types. Shakespeare's Syracusans are cautious too. "They say this town is full of cozenage," the traveling Antipholus warns himself.

Notwithstanding, the Ephesians he meets are not "disguised cheaters." They are, as the traveling Dromio puts it, "a gentle nation," who "speak us fair, give us gold." Shakespeare is more in his milieu where the setting is a room in the palace — or, better still, another part of the forest — than in the mercantile zones of New Comedy. It is not coney-catching but witchcraft and sorcery that envelop Ephesus in its mysterious aura. This is a place of strangers and sojourners, to echo the patron saint of travelers *in partibus infidelium*, the Apostle Paul. Not without pertinence, it has been suggested that Paul's Epistle to the Ephesians, with its injunctions for husbands and wives, and for servants and masters, may have been in the background of Shakespeare's mind. His far-flung romance of *Pericles* reaches its resolution in the famous Temple of Diana at Ephesus. Some of the elements of the late play are present in the early one, notably the vicissitudes of a family progressing through misadventure to recognition. Shakespeare as yet had no need of Gower's folktale; the story was latent nearer at hand in the *Captivi* of Plautus, where the old father, Hegio, seeks and recovers two sons captured and brought up elsewhere under the circumstances of two cities at war.

The framing figure of Egeon contributes an emotional tension, at the very outset, to what would otherwise have remained a two-dimensional drama. His protracted expository narrative — a specimen of the rhetoricians' *narratio* — is enlivened by the awareness that it is a plea, and probably a vain one, for his life. Rightly he blames his misfortunes on hap; for nowhere else in Shakespeare can a whole pattern of incidents be so directly traceable to sheer unmitigated contingency. Egeon is hopeless and helpless because he is hapless. But this is not to be a novel by Thomas Hardy; it is a knockabout farce, where bad fortune will change soon enough into good. The next scene not only offers a hint that the new arrival is one of Egeon's sons — through the mix-up of the Dromios — and that the other son is just around the corner, but virtually guarantees the ransom, since the sum mentioned in both scenes is exactly a thousand marks. Coincidence has already done its best, as well as its worst, and a happy ending was implicit from the beginning. Meanwhile, the sequence of farcical episodes has been framed by the tragicomic overplot; and Shakespeare, by enlisting our sympathies for the fate of Egeon, has charged the air with a suspense which cannot be resolved until the appointed hour of execution, five o'clock in the afternoon.

Both of the Antipholuses have appointments at that hour, one with the Merchant and the other with the Goldsmith; and since it is noon when the Syracusan arrives, and since the Ephesian Dromio gets into his troubles over the question of dinner-time, the time-scheme is firmly fixed within the course of the afternoon. There are frequent reminders of its passing, to reinforce the structure of occurrences. Adhering to the classical unities, as he does just once again in *The Tempest,* Shakespeare takes the traditional city street as his horizon, moving his characters back and forth from port to mart and in and out of the various doorways between. The play would seem to lend itself very conveniently to the simultaneous stage of a great hall, such as that of Gray's Inn, where three or four free-standing houses or so-called mansions would have corresponded to the labeled locations of the play: the Phoenix, the Porpentine, the other inn, the Centaur, and the ultimate abbey near the place of execution. On the other hand, the production at Stratford, Ontario, demonstrated how well the play could adapt to the multi-level mobility of an Elizabethan playhouse.

The problem of staging ought not to be unduly strained by the presupposition of identical twins. To be sure, the difficulty raised by the twins of two sexes in *Twelfth Night,* which would have been solved when both parts were acted by young men, is virtually insoluble in the modern theater. But, granted an approximate equivalence of stature, plus the same costuming and make-up, the Antipholuses and the Dromios ought to look enough alike to confuse the other characters without confusing the audience. After all, it is our premise that we are brighter than the people on the stage. In the Roman theater, where the employment of masks eliminated the facial disparities, Plautus had to give a tassel to Mercury and a feather to Jupiter so that they would not be confused with Sosia and Amphitryon. The festival at Stratford, Connecticut, I am told, has been casting the same actor as both twins, thereby combining histrionic virtuosity with artistic economy. This directorial tactic must create a bigger dilemma than the one it endeavors to solve, since the audience can never know the moment of catharsis, the visual illumination of seeing the two confusing elements discriminated from one another and exhibited side by side.

That way schizophrenia lies — which does not mean that it would be unproduceable in the Theater of the Absurd. It might turn out to be something in the vein of Pirandello, if not a drama-

tization of *Dr. Jekyll and Mr. Hyde*. But the actual predicament
is that of two personalities forced into the same role, rather than
that of one personality playing two roles, since the resident twin
has the contacts and continuities, and the roving twin intercepts
them, as it were. Their twinship is a sort of human pun. Tweedle-
dum has got to match Tweedledee, more or less, in order to be
taken for him; and yet, the less he feels like him, the more the
dramatic irony. Plautus did not discriminate between his two very
sharply; the discrepancies that emerged largely took the concrete
form of objects which fell into the wrong hands; otherwise the
interconnecting characters did not seem to notice much difference.
The married Menaechmus was angry from the first, so that each
new chagrin could be rationalized to his mood. The interloping
Menaechmus, though considerably bewildered, had no cause for
being dissatisfied with his reception. Neither of them was above
the temptation to profit from the *contretemps*; and the interloper
finally engaged in a stratagem of his own, when he pretended to
be a lunatic.

That sort of conduct is what we have agreed to label a suppose,
a deception which is cultivated rather than casual. The most
notable fact about Shakespeare's comedy is that it has no supposes,
only errors: only mischances, no contrivances by anybody except
Shakespeare himself. There is no parallel scene of pretended madness; Shakespeare must have been saving the theme for *Hamlet*.
Here the suspected madman, like Malvolio, protests his sanity. He
does not act; he is acted upon; and Shakespeare, ever the psychologist, makes a good deal more out of the attempted diagnosis of
demonic possession. He makes the exorcism so very painful, and
goes so far out of his way to substitute the grim-visaged schoolmaster, Dr. Pinch, for the Plautine Medicus that we sense a virtual
obsession possibly connected with Holofernes, the pedant of *Love's
Labour's Lost*, or with some other reminiscence from Shakespeare's
own teaching days. It is as if the nightmare came so close that the
misunderstood hero dare not pretend to be hallucinated. The customary rhetorical questions of comedy, in these mouths, become

questions of existential bewilderment or expressions of cosmic ver-
tigo: Do I dream or wake? Do we see double? Is he drunk or sober?
Is she a liar or a fool? Who is crazy? Who is sane?

Contrasted with this constant inner questioning, the caricature
of Dr. Pinch seems externalized. He is the sole humorous personage of the play, in the Jonsonian usage, a man of obvious quirks
and eccentric appearance; if the others are funny, it is because of
the plights they find themselves in. No, there is one other exception, though she is peripheral and appears but once on the stage.
Nevertheless New Comedy was capable of casting offstage characters in title roles, as with the *Casina* of Plautus. This heroine,
invoked indifferently as Luce or Nell, is generically a Dowsabell or,
for that matter, a Dulcinea — a kitchenmaid whose formidable
proportions are vividly verbalized by the wrong Dromio, her
brother-in-law, who is still quaking from the shock of having been
claimed by her as a husband. This is the vulgar parallel to Adriana's
claim upon her brother-in-law. Dromio's description of his brother's Nell, elicited by his master's queries as straight man, is a
set-piece in the manner of Launce or Lancelot Gobbo, and may
well have been assigned to the same comedian. With its geographical conceits, comparing the parts of her person to foreign countries,
it might almost be a ribald reversal of Othello's traveler's tales
when wooing Desdemona.

But it is by no means a farfetched gag, since it embodies — on
a more than miniature scale — the principal contrast of the play:
on the one hand, extensive voyaging; on the other, intensive do-
mesticity. In using an underplot which burlesques the main plot,
Shakespeare employs a device as old as Medwall's interlude of
Fulgens and Lucres, where the rival suitors have servants who court
the mistress's maid under the diagrammatic designations of A and
B. With Nell, as with the demanding Adriana, the normal approaches of courtship are reversed. The closest we come to romantic love is the sketchy relationship between her brother-in-law and
her husband's sister-in-law. Yet that is a good deal closer than
Plautus brings us; and though both masters are suitably mated in

the end, the concluding dialogue of the servants emphasizes the pairing of twins, not spouses. Parents and children are reunited, family ties are reasserted; but Dromio of Syracuse remains a free agent. His greatest moment has been the midpoint of the play, when he acted as doorkeeper and kept out his fellow Dromio, as well as that Dromio's master, the master of the house. This is the one point before the dénouement where Shakespeare permits his twins to meet and talk, and the door between them seems to keep the mutual visibility fairly obscure.

It is interesting that their brief colloquy reverts to the doggerel style of *Ralph Roister Doister*, the oldest English imitation of Plautus, in its stichomythic interchanges of rhyming fourteeners. This is the main scene (the first of Act III) that Shakespeare borrowed from the *Amphitryon* (the first of Act I), eking out the comedy of the *Menaechmi* with the underplot of the two Sosias to complete — with a vengeance — the Elizabethan requirements for a double plot. He develops it to the very pitch of the dramatic subversion that he has been exploiting, with the outsider inside and the insider excluded, the stranger in possession of the house and the householder cast into outer darkness. Both parties are translated, as Quince will affirm of Bottom, and they could not have been so completely translated, had they not been facsimiles to begin with. The most fundamental alteration that Shakespeare made in his Plautine material was to shift the focus from the homekeeping twin to his errant brother, whose sobriquet, Antipholus Erotes, may be a garbling of Erratus or Errans. The *Menaechmi* starts out with the other twin, and with the reassurance of familiar surroundings, into which the disturbing factor will be injected. *The Comedy of Errors* starts with the newcomer, and his impressions of strangeness: the witchery of Ephesus, not the bustle of Epidamnum.

Having a head start, and having to alternate scenes with Antipholus of Ephesus who does not appear until the third act, Antipholus of Syracuse has a much larger part: roughly 272 lines to the other's 207. The disproportion is even clearer between the parts of

the two Dromios: there the score is Syracuse 233, Ephesus 162.
The *Menaechmi*, though it is the shorter play, has fewer characters
and longer speeches; accordingly, its Syracusan twin has 251 lines,
whereas the Epidamnian twin has 300. We therefore tend to visu-
alize what goes on in the Latin play from the denizen's standpoint,
and what goes on in the English play from the alien's. Epidamnum
could be any old town, where everything should be in its place,
in situ; where everyone expects his fellow citizen, Menaechmus, to
go through the round of his habitual day. No one could suspect
that there was another Menaechmus, whose chance encounters
would lead to incongruities and discontinuities, except for his one
follower, who shares and compounds his perplexities. Ephesus is
another story, however. We are put off at once by the hostile reception of Egeon; and when the two other foreigners enter, Antipholus and Dromio, they are the first of those names whom we
have met.

We share their misgivings all the more readily because they too
have been risking their lives, and because the object of their travels
has so far eluded them. When this Antipholus gets caught up in
his brother's existence, it is as new to us as it is to him. We participate in an adventure; what might be matter-of-fact to an Epe-
sian is, for him and ourselves, a fantasy out of the *Arabian Nights*.
"What error drives our eyes and ears amiss?" he wonders, after
Adriana accosts him, reprimands him, and invites him to dinner.
And tentatively he resolves,

> Until I know this sure uncertainty,
> I'll entertain the offer'd fallacy.

Then, after dinner, smitten with Luciana, he asks her to unfold
the mystery:

> Teach me, dear creature, how to think and speak.
>   Lay open to my earthy gross conceit,
> Smother'd in errors, feeble, shallow, weak,
>   The folded meaning of your words' deceit.

But the undeception does not come about until all the participants in this "sympathized one day's error" — for so the Abbess sums it up — have sought the illumination of sanctuary within her Priory. In that cloistered serenity, far from urban corruption, the deferred recognition scenes can coincide at long last. The confessions and counteraccusations piece together a step-by-step recapitulation of how "these errors are arose." The maternal figure of the Abbess is something of a surprise, as Bertrand Evans points out in his recent study, *Shakespeare's Comedies*. Running through all of them, Mr. Evans finds their common structural principle in what he calls a "discrepant awareness." Characteristically, the humor springs from "the exploitable gulf spread between the participants' understanding and ours."

In Shakespeare's development of this resource, *The Comedy of Errors* is primordial, since it is his single comedy where the audience knows all, and all the characters are in the dark. Mr. Evans' suggestive analysis can be perfectly fitted to the *Menaechmi*. Plautus is always saying, "I told you so." But Shakespeare is always asking, "Can such things be?" The exceptional position of the Abbess not only rounds out the recognitions; it lays the spell of wonderment again upon the concluding scene; and it reminds us, as other touches do, of Shakespeare's romances. Even within the venal and angular precincts of New Comedy, he can make us aware of unpathed waters, undreamed shores, and things in heaven and earth that philosophy has not fathomed. Yet philosophers can tell us much, particularly about the processes of learning; and Bergson tells us much about *The Comedy of Errors* when, in his essay on laughter, he borrows a concept from optics and writes of "the reciprocal interference of series." At length we can put our supposes or errors down in scientific terminology. "A situation is invariably comic," Bergson explains, "when it belongs simultaneously to two independent series of events, and is capable of being interpreted in two entirely different meanings at the same time." It would be hard to conceive of a better illustration than the two

different series of events in the respective days of the two Antipholuses, and the ways in which they are imperceptibly crisscrossed.
Antipholus of Syracuse has no particular expectations or plans. He
derives a gratuitous enjoyment from the inexplicable services rendered and favors due his brother. This interference or substitution
induces a certain amnesia on the brother's part, when the bills
come in and the witnesses testify; naturally, he cannot remember
the items attested. As one error engenders another, suspicion is
bound to mount and disgruntlement spread, rising to their climax
in hot pursuit toward the madhouse or the jail, and ending at the
Priory. Now the brunt of these displacements is borne by Antipholus of Ephesus. Of all those discomfited, he comes nearest to being
a victim of the situation, since it is his situation, in the last analysis.
It is his routine which is broken up, his standing in the community
undermined, his normal expectations interfered with; and — to add
insult to injury — he is expected to pay for what he has been de-
prived of. In short, the rug has been pulled out from under the
very preconditions of his existence.

Other people's bafflement can be fun, and Plautus makes the
most of it. From our spectatorial overview, we need not worry too
much about what befalls whom. We are not playing blind man's
buff, we are watching the game. But Shakespeare, himself the
father of twins, makes us feel what it is like to be this or that
Antipholus — all the difference in the world, if we started by being
the other one — and the interplay of more or less exact counterparts ends by demonstrating *a fortiori* the uniqueness of the individual. When Adriana and her husband appeal to the Duke, the
stories they tell of their day's experience are mutually contradictory;
but the discrepancies would disappear if the shadow of the inter-
fering Antipholus were retraced through their reciprocal patterns.
(Latter-day readers or viewers may be reminded of the Japanese
story or film, *Rashomon.*) It has been a lesson for Adriana, brought
home by the gentle rebuke of the Abbess. For Antipholus of
Ephesus, it has been an eye-opening misadventure. Apparently, he
has never felt the impetus that has incited his brother and his

father to sally forth in search of him. Unconcerned with his found-ling origin, he rejoices in the good graces of the Duke and takes for granted the solid comforts of his Ephesian citizenship.

What greater shock for him, then, than to bring a party of fellow citizens home to his well-established household for lunch and to discover that household pre-empted by roistering strangers, to be shut out in the street, to have one's own door slammed in one's own face? Or is it one's own? The sense of alienation, that *Verfremdungseffekt* so characteristic of Brecht and of the twentieth-century theater, is all the greater when our image of ourselves depends for its corroboration upon a settled context, and when we come to realize — what tragedy teaches us — that it is our destiny to be displaced. When Messenio saw the two Menaechmuses together, he declared that water was not more like water. After Shakespeare has adapted the metaphor, it stands not for an easy correspondence but for an unending quest.

> I to the world am like a drop of water
> That in the ocean seeks another drop,

Antipholus of Syracuse confesses sadly, realizing that he is less likely to find a mother and a brother than to be irretrievably lost himself. Later Adriana, addressing him as if he were Antipholus of Ephesus, likens their imperiled love to a drop of water falling into the sea; and he has a similar exchange with Luciana. The Syracusan twin is conscious that he must lose his identity in order to find it; the Ephesian twin is not; but he must, and he does. And Dromio too — both Dromios, whichever is which — must undergo their crises of identity: "Am I Dromio? Am I your man? Am I myself?"

The essence of the predicament is embodied in a comic turn which must be as old as Plautus, which I once saw enacted at the Cirque Médrano, and which has been immortalized by the Marx Brothers in one of their films. It involves both an error and a suppose, a mistaken identification and a willful imposture. Two comedians happen somehow to be dressed alike; one of them, seeking concealment and meeting the other, takes refuge in pretending to be a mirror image; whereupon the other proceeds to test his authenticity by going through a series of gestures and grimaces which he is pretty clever at matching and mimicking; but sooner or later he betrays his autonomy by making the wrong response; and the jig is up; again the chase is on. Under the circumstances, it would be a relief to be quite sure that there were two men, not one — or, for that matter, that there was one man, not two, if we could only be sure. But, given the subjective mirrors of our introspection, can we ever be absolutely certain who we are? And, given the reduplicating devices that multiply the sameness of our lives, where, if anywhere, is there any room left for the otherness of unquestionable individuality?

Modern psychological fiction is haunted by doubles, sometimes as overtly as in the tales of Hoffmann, Poe, and Dostoevsky, or in "The Jolly Corner" of Henry James, where the Black Stranger turns out to be the self that might have been. The other self — best friend, worst enemy — stares back at the poets from Heine's pallid ghost (*"Du! Doppelgänger, du bleicher Geselle!"*) or Baudelaire's hypocritical reader (*"mon semblable! mon frère!"*). That *alter ego* may be daemon or devil, good angel or evil genius. It may be the retribution of conscience: Philip Drunk reprehended by Philip Sober — or, at the other extreme, the vicarious pleasure the artist enjoys in the playboy, the envy of Shem for Shaun. All this may well be a far cry from Plautine or even Shakespearean farce, to which we should be glad that we can escape. There all aberrations come home to roost and are sorted out by the happy ending; we acknowledge the error of our ways, and false suppositions are replaced by truths. No one really gets damaged in Epidamnum, and everyone enjoys a new lease of life when Egeon is ransomed and reprieved. Yet, as the philosopher Etienne Souriau concludes in his book, *Les 200,000 Situations Dramatiques:* "A comedy of errors — or of ignorances — is inherent in the condition of men, who are perpetually groping through moral shadows and playing a game of blind man's buff with their souls."

8   Reflections on the Final Volume of
The Oxford History of English Literature

This review-article was written for the first issue of a new periodical, Forum for the Modern Language Studies, published at St. Andrews University in January 1965. The death of T. S. Eliot, which occurred between the proofreading and the publication of the article, gave — I fear — a morbid edge to the question it raises about the limits of contemporaneity. It was not my intention to polemicize against the author or the book at hand, least of all against a multiform institution to which all students of English culture owe some degree of allegiance, as I have attested elsewhere. But Eight Modern Writers by J. I. M. Stewart (Oxford: Clarendon Press, 1963) does bring to a head certain problems: the academic study of recent literature, the arguable methods of literary historiography, and the differing scholarship of the different schools. It is reassuring to learn that Professor Alfred Harbage has now undertaken the Oxford volume on Renaissance drama.

Yeats, no doubt, had other notions of felicity when he looked forward to dining at journey's end (Volume XII) with Landor (Volume X) and with Donne (Volume V). Yet here they stand, all three among the rest, in serried uniformity if not in total completeness, aligned together behind the handsome blue and gold aegis of the Clarendon Press. Literary history may perhaps be conceived in epic terms as a journey to the underworld, where the illustrious shades are to be encountered and engaged in a continuing dialogue. Since the most difficult and demanding encounters are with those immortals who have died most recently, visitors who make the descent should be — like the author of this final volume, J. I. M. Stewart — at once intrepid and tactful. But, whereas there may be a sort of resurrection in establishing contact with writers who lived before our time, it would seem more like an inhumation to review the recorded achievements of men whom we might have known as living presences. Instead of watching the past being brought back to life, which is the principal outlook of scholarship after all, we sometimes feel as if the present were being embalmed and entombed.

That feeling may be a symptom of superannuation on our part, a grudging hesitation to admit that the quondam present has become the current past, or to acknowledge that somehow we have already rounded out two-thirds of the twentieth century. It may be that the brilliance of the first third, as we look back upon it through the unsettled middle years, has arrested the sensibilities of those of us who can draw upon our memories. Those who were born too late for that are in a better position to take upon themselves the duties and the prerogatives of posterity. For a number of years now twentieth-century literature has held an enlarging place in American universities, not only as a popular feature of the curriculum but as a special field for advanced research. It might well be hoped that anyone devoting himself to literary studies in any period, either as a student or as a teacher, would take a collateral interest in the literature of his own day. Conversely, he could not be expected to show much understanding of recent work without being fully grounded in what had preceded it. There the outlines have been traced and the labels applied, the categories laid down and the hierarchies set up.

Here, where the welter confronts us directly, quantities are as undetermined as qualities. That, of course, can be a stimulus, if not a discipline: to chart the confusion and gain a perspective untrammeled by clichés. But the problematic question remains whether or not the study of contemporary literature should be taught as a university subject, or whether it is a contradiction in terms like artists in residence or courses in "creative writing." T. S. Eliot, in spite of all that he himself has contributed to the subject in the way of text and commentary, issued a caveat against it a while ago. What we define as contemporary, needless to say, can be more broadly defined as temporary; it becomes historic soon enough; and the determination is effected by the sharpest of dividing lines, the one that separates the quick and the dead. It is the tendency to hold that line which makes academies so academic. This seems perfectly appropriate, given the pre-existing distinction between the academy and the forum, where the live issues are still being settled. For instance, although the Sorbonne will not accept a thesis on an author while he is alive, he is deemed worthy of scholarly treatment upon his demise. Candidates, waiting to post with dexterity to the doctorate, circled like vultures over the latter days of André Gide.

There is something to be said for the decent interval that, in modern painting, used to be symbolized by the Luxembourg as an antechamber to the Louvre — or, for that matter, by the Salons as antechambers to the Luxembourg. Our high-pressured era, however, has speeded up the transition between an age and all time. More and more we tend to reckon generations by decades, to regard our yesterdays as pages of history, to turn our journalists into historians and *vice versa*. We expect our critics to be tipsters, more concerned with pace than with duration; the measure of their wisdom is the quickness of their response to the perennial query, "Who's in? who's out?" It used to be assumed that an author's career terminated in a critical limbo whence, after due probation and gradual judgment, he would be assigned to the proper niche of fame or obscurity. We seem to have eliminated this lag. The case of James Joyce is particularly striking because it moved so quickly between the extremes of rejection and acceptance. It was as if, having been tried so severely throughout his lifetime, he ended by being accorded the classic status he always claimed. From the censor's ban to the scholar's preserve the distance was short for him, and it has been even shorter for his admirers from the little magazine to the learned monograph.

The repute of Henry James conforms to a more traditional pattern: a mixture of admiration and misunderstanding from his contemporaries, an interim of probationary uncertainty after his death, and then a posthumous triumph which has been all but complete, at least for the moment. Thomas Hardy and Bernard Shaw lived through their own eclipses by surviving their own best efforts, so that niches in the pantheon had long been prepared for them when they died. William Butler Yeats soared from strength to strength in a widening gyre which is still ascendant. Joseph Conrad, who enjoyed wide popularity as a kind of Slavic Stevenson, has taken longer to register in depth. D. H. Lawrence seems, in retrospect, the most prophetic of the figures before us; his sexual candor, his class-consciousness, and his other quarrels with his time and place seem to make him the very progenitor of today's angry young men. Among Mr. Stewart's *Eight Modern Writers* it is the choice of Rudyard Kipling, supported though it be by the contemporaneous record of impact and acclaim, which would seem to command less critical agreement than the others; but even here the images persist, the echoes reverberate, and the critics come around.

Mr. Stewart's inclusions and exclusions, he tells us at the outset, are "best not defended." His taste has been guided solely by "literary enjoyment" — a question-begging phrase which is best not pursued. The sheer bulk of the selective bibliography, largely compiled by another hand, does not merely justify his inclusions; it attests the close interplay between criticism and creation in our Alexandrian century, when poets supply their own footnotes and manifestoes are pondered in seminars. A further principle of selection may be implied in the varying length of the eight chapters, which range from 39 pages for Conrad to 128 for Yeats. Mr. Stewart, himself a Scotsman, is ironically aware of the ethnic disparities among his chosen eight. Three of these English writers were Irish-born; one was Polish, and another American. Of the remaining three, one is inseparably associated with India; another resided on three continents, and is buried in France; and only the oldest, Hardy, can be viewed as a deeply rooted Englishman. Now, if these are truly the most important English writers of their epoch, they might open the way for topical innuendoes about the suicide of a nation or the disintegration of an empire. But I would rather view the situation as a crowning example of cultural diffusion, a fulfillment of Samuel Daniel's vision:

> And who, in time, knows whither we may vent
> The treasure of our tongue, to what strange shores . . .?

In some ways it all seems a fitting resolution to that great synthesis of languages and cultures which originally went to make up

English, and which — we trust — will be duly chronicled when the first volume of *The Oxford History of English Literature* is finally published. At all events, the historian of Spanish, German, or Russian literature could hardly treat its twentieth-century phase without transcending the issue of nationalities. The international aspect of Mr. Stewart's octet is probably the most significant generalization that one could reach about them. But there are others: it is interesting, as well as chastening, to note that on the whole they are not university men. Joyce is the type of exception that proves the rule, Lawrence is not less so in his own way, and Harvard's claim to James — I am sorry to say — is quite nugatory. It is surprising and rather disappointing, in view of the freedom attained by women and their unprecedented professional accomplishment over the past three generations, that no woman writer has been admitted into Mr. Stewart's temple of fame. The safest generality is that each of his authors was an extreme individualist. If one thinks of any two of them together, the relationship seems antipathetic, like that of Yeats and Shaw.

The fact that their objectives, their methods, and their backgrounds have so very little in common may have encouraged Mr. Stewart to present his material in a sequence of eight almost airtight compartments, with a sketchy introduction of eighteen pages and no conclusion whatsoever. The problem of periodization, in the history of English literature, has been frequently met by naming each age for a highly characteristic writer. There exists a once-useful series of manuals comprising *The Age of Alfred*, *The Age of Chaucer*, *The Age of Shakespeare*, and so on through the successive ages of Milton, Dryden, Pope, Wordsworth, and Tennyson. We should be hard put to rechristen Mr. Stewart's period after one of his eight names. *The Age of Kipling?* No. *The Age of James?* Hardly. *The Age of Lawrence?* Well, who shall say? It is worth noting that the revised edition of the concise one-volume *Cambridge History of English Literature* has a supplementary chapter entitled "The Age of T. S. Eliot." Mr. Stewart recognizes *The Waste Land* as an epoch-making publication; yet Mr. Eliot plays no part in his book, except as an occasional off-stage voice, not because of his American birth but because he is not yet immured in Westminster Abbey or anywhere else.

Nevertheless, the happy accident of longevity, which has thus far spared him to us, could not have retroactively neutralized Mr. Eliot's importance for the literary history of the nineteen-twenties; and it seems even more farfetched to pretend that E. M. Forster, who is eighty-five years old and whose last novel was published forty years ago, is not ready to face the historian's reckoning. To depend so heavily on mere contingency is to run the risk of soon becoming outdated — if indeed it can be maintained that a literary history of England, published in 1963 and spanning the official dates from 1880 to 1941, which excludes Eliot and Forster and Aldous Huxley and Sean O'Casey and W. H. Auden and the Sitwells, could ever have been up-to-date. The lack of direction — or, what is worse, the resultant air of planlessness — is much more disconcerting than the handful of small inaccuracies that any sharp-eyed reader can pick up along the way. There is no need to defend Mr. Stewart's inclusions; some of his exclusions are best not defended because they seem indefensible. In his introductory remarks he explains the elimination of Arnold Bennett, H. G. Wells, John Galsworthy, and other Edwardians against whom the Georgians were reacting; and he, in his turn, has been influenced by the subsequent reaction against the ascendancy of the Bloomsbury Circle.

But *ubi sunt?* Oscar Wilde, George Moore, George Gissing, Ford Madox Ford — where are they now? What ever happened to Virginia Woolf and Katherine Mansfield? Surely their lifework ought to be more lasting than the snows of yesteryear. In what darkling morass of the Elysian Fields wander the wraiths of J. M. Synge, A. E. Housman, Wilfred Owen, Dylan Thomas, and Walter de la Mare? Who has decreed that they are no longer to be conjured with? Was not T. E. Lawrence a man of letters? Where will the student of the future find an apt page or two on the role of Wyndham Lewis or George Orwell or Joyce Cary? Certainly not in *The Oxford History of English Literature.* For all the recognition it affords, all but eight modern writers are no better off than Enoch Soames — that imaginary esthete of the nineties who, with the complicity of the Devil and Max Beerbohm, looked himself up in the British Museum catalogue of 1997, where he found that he had left no mark; he had written in vain. (The ghost of Max will have a slightly happier fate, since Mr. Stewart is fond of quoting him.) Some of my examples may belong to the second order of magnitude or even the third, as compared with Mr. Stewart's. Yet such comparisons call for thoughtful reconsideration; they cannot be settled by blackball.

Moreover, it has been the premise of his predecessors that there is a valid place in English literary history for a substantial aggregation of lesser lights, the Gowers and Dekkers and Fullers and Priors and Landors. Since Mr. Stewart's segment may exceed the previous periods in its scope, its variety, and possibly its excitement, he might have paid some attention to those originals and eccentrics who add their personal ingredients to its unique savor: oblique commentators such as G. K. Chesterton, T. E. Hulme, and Lytton Strachey or semi-successful experimentalists such as Dorothy Richardson, Ronald Firbank, or David Jones. "Mainly a history of literature," the jacket still proclaims, "*The Oxford History of English Literature* does not neglect the other arts, and it is also a history of ideas, political, philosophical, scientific, and social, in so far as these are expressed in the literature or assist the understanding of it." This twelfth volume figured in the announcements, like most of the preceding eleven titles, as a straightforward chronological rubric. It was a strategic retreat, and virtually an abandonment of the historical function, when the general editors permitted the title to be changed from the scheduled *Modern Literature* to the modest *Eight Modern Writers*.

Granted the integer, give or take one or two choices, readers could not seriously quarrel with the canon that Mr. Stewart has brought into existence. Any two critics would agree on six, if not all eight of them. When we reconsider the complexity of the milieu, the changing society, the intellectual developments, the conver-

gence of movements and personalities, we may well admire him for
his shrewdness in sidestepping so monumental a task. "On the
'threshold of a drama of ideas,'" he quotes Bernard Shaw, "an
accurate sense of period is essential." It is conspicuously absent
here. Landmarks and causes are mentioned now and then, but
never are they expounded or criticized. Only in the appended
chronology are we accorded a glimpse of the interrelationship
among lives and works and events. What is lacking is that ferment of -isms which makes Shaw's ideas dramatic, and which should
be the animating spirit of literary history. The sixty-year span between Gladstone's second ministry and the Second World War
saw revolutions in taste and ideology, art and psychology, science
and technology, public welfare and private conduct. Those were
the preconditions for putting the element of modernity into modern writing.

Individualistic and idiosyncratic as our *dramatis personae* undoubtedly were, it is possible to discern a common denominator in
their diverse responses to certain underlying challenges: problems
of testing tradition and reformulating belief, from Shaw's utopian
schemes to Hardy's encrusted archetypes, from Yeats's *Vision* to
Lawrence's gospel, from Kipling's imperialism to Joyce's esthetics.
But here the warp of continuity simply does not mesh with the
woof of cross-reference. Joyce is cited as a witness in favor of
Yeats's tale "The Adoration of the Magi." That tale was a source
of inspiration for Joyce's vital conception of the "epiphany." Yet
no mention is made of it when we come to the chapter on Joyce;
in fact, there is no discussion of that conception at all; and, though
the posthumously published *Epiphanies* are listed in the bibliography, they are not discussed in the text. Mr. Stewart jeopardizes
our confidence in his documentation when he quotes the last page
of the catechism in *Ulysses* and informs us that the final question,
"Where?," goes unanswered. Actually, Joyce took pains to supply
an answer in the form of a typographical device: a large black dot
which symbolizes the world itself, diminishing as it recedes into
space. Mr. Stewart seems to have used one of the unreliable texts

that omit this portentous detail, and the omission makes nonsense out of his explication.

Failing to unify its subject matter, his book might just as well — and less expensively — be eight of those pamphlets on modern writers put out under the auspices of the British Council and sold at one and sixpence apiece; like them, it could be most fairly judged by the light it sheds upon its respective subjects. We may leave the particulars to the reviewers; my present concern is with the presuppositions and implications. When a multiplicity of talents has been scaled down to a magic number, the assumption is that our canonical authors should be the touchstones of literary quality. When their dialectical relations with one another, with their environment, and with the cross-currents of thought are allowed to pass unemphasized, it is fair to assume that the emphasis should fall upon their artistry. Yet Mr. Stewart, if not scornful of art, is distrustful of the attempt to analyze it. The prefaces of Henry James are deprecated for "the obtrusiveness of their concern with technique." Conrad's increasing concentration on "treatment," which is blamed on James, is held to be "a debilitating factor in his art." Joyce's experimentation with form and style is greeted by a similar skepticism, and in the case of *Finnegans Wake* by a candid boredom.

Bored with technical analysis, Mr. Stewart enlivens his recital with metaphors drawn from the world of sport. He remarks in passing, not very felicitously, that Virginia Woolf "rode so gallantly at the stiffest fences." Those who prefer to look on life as a boxing match, rather than as a fox hunt, may be pleased and edified to learn that the Victorians "did well . . . not too quickly to throw up the sponge, but to remain fighting in the ring until the bell went." If such comments do not inspire a reinterpretation of Tennyson's "Ring Out, Wild Bells," they illustrate the extent to which Arnold's successors are willing to compromise with the Philistines. As a novelist himself, under the pseudonym of Michael Innes, Mr. Stewart is well known for many a mystery story; as a literary historian, dealing principally with works of prose fiction, his method is less an examination of craftsmanship than it is a renarration of narrative. A paragraph on a novel by James which is no more than an outline of its plot has — to say the least — a somewhat reductive effect, and the attrition is not much less when its victim is a novel by Conrad. To reduce plays to such literal-minded synopses altogether dulls the cutting edge of Shavian satire.

Poetry, to be sure, does not lend itself so readily to this anecdotal approach. Mr. Stewart, who discerns a Miltonic strain in Kipling's "Recessional," romanticizes his account of Yeats by seasoning it with allusions to Maud Gonne. There are twenty-three of these — to estimate from the index — as contrasted with five to Blake and two allusions to Shelley; proportionately, it could be deduced, there is more preoccupation with extraneous romance than with actual poetry. Not that biographical fact, or indeed the modicum of psychological speculation that is thrown out here and there, need be irrelevant to the practice of letters. The irreducible factor in literary history would seem to be the developing talent of the in-dividual author, which operates as a middle term between his cre-ations and the circumstances that usher them into being. The exfoliation of styles at a given time presupposes a flowering of personalities, so that the ensuing formal richness cannot wholly be accounted for on the grounds of a purely formalistic criticism. Thus history, with its component biographies, holds a key to the evolution of forms. History is thus a story in both a broader and a deeper sense than the twice-told narrations of Mr. Stewart.

*   *   *

How, then, do his anticlimactic efforts fit in with *The Oxford History of English Literature* as a whole? Chronologically speak-ing, they constitute the final volume; but, as circumstances will have it, this is not the last in order of publication; for the com-pleted project will comprise twelve volumes, two of which will be subdivided into two further tomes, adding up to fourteen in all. As of Mr. Stewart's publication date, a quarter of a century since the inception of the scheme, six volumes remain to be published. Meanwhile, *The Earlier Seventeenth Century, 1600–1660* by Douglas Bush, which first appeared in 1945 and reappeared in an amplified edition after seventeen years of valued service in 1962, has consolidated its place as the standard handbook for its central area. Unhappily, it will not soon be joined by a volume on *The English Drama, c. 1485–1642*, owing to the recent death of the scheduled author and co-editor of the series, F. P. Wilson. Another close companion, *English Literature in the Sixteenth Century, Excluding Drama*, does indeed exist; but, as I have ventured to argue elsewhere, it is a capricious piece of work which does justice neither to the Renaissance nor to its author, the late C. S. Lewis.

From the division of labor it is not clear to what degree the arrangement is by periods and to what degree by genres. An unpublished half-volume, *Middle English Literature*, is slated to precede two complementary tomes, *Chaucer and the Fifteenth Century* by H. S. Bennett and *The Close of the Middle Ages* by the late Sir Edmund Chambers. Mr. Bennett's half-volume is admirable as far as it goes; but it is both depleted and overlapped by the curious bifurcation that assigns the drama of the period, plus the anonymous poetry and the prose of Malory alone, to the slender and disjointed half-volume of Chambers. Two of the latest installments are sequels which fit together awkwardly, *English Literature, 1789–1815* by W. L. Renwick and *English Literature, 1815–1832* by Ian Jack. Professor Renwick justifiably voices a prefatory complaint on the "difficulty in keeping proportion." He deals austerely with twenty-seven years in 293 pages, while Professor Jack deals much more expansively with eighteen years in 643 pages. The difference of proportions, which is not warranted by qualitative or quantitative distinctions in the materials, allows about eleven pages per year for the first Romantic generation and thirty-six for the second. One reviewer has pointed out that Thomas De Quincey receives as much space as Jane Austen and George Crabbe together.

"Each volume or half-volume will be an independent book," the

prospectus announces, and that has turned out to be true for better and worse. But it goes on to announce that "the whole series
will form a continuous history from the earliest time to the present
day," and that must now be regretfully pronounced an exploded
hope. The volumes now available may be rated according to their
unevenly distributed merits; and we may continue to look forward
to such forthcoming volumes as that of Geoffrey Tillotson on the
Victorian age; yet as a collective enterprise, a coherent retracing
of a majestic train of traditions, a reinterpretation carried through
with consistent standards of criticism and scholarship, a monument
commensurate with its theme, it is not too early to admit that *The
Oxford History of English Literature* has been a failure. Should
we be surprised? Could we not have expected — along with the
excellences guaranteed by some of the collaborators, few of them
associated very closely with Oxford — such a dénouement? Oxford
may well be the navel of British culture. Assuredly, it practises
self-regard with an intensity which outdoes the Buddhists. But it
has never been very much of a center for studies in English literary
history.

Lectures and examinations in the subject seem to have been
introduced there belatedly, as were women students. The two
innovations, which struggled against the same entrenched opposition, may be said to have gone hand in hand. The honors school
was not introduced until 1894, and the professorship not until
ten years later (though the other Merton chair in English philology
was established in 1885, and the chair of poetry goes back to the
eighteenth century). This neglect was a direct consequence of Oxford's whole-hearted commitment to the noble and declining cause
of the Greek and Latin classics. Absorbed by *litterae humaniores*
so delimited, the dons left it to the German scholars — and to their
American pupils shortly afterward — to develop the academic field
of *Anglistik*. One cannot point to an English counterpart for such
pioneering investigators and founding fathers as Bernhard Ten
Brink or Francis James Child. The closest would be Frederick
James Furnivall, who was not attached to a university; rather, he

was involved in a Working Men's College at London, and in many other reforming institutions including the Early English Text Society and the New Shakespeare Society. Up to the last hundred years, the curatorship of English letters has been in the hands of amateurs and freelances, hobbyists and collectors, antiquarians and librarians.

Rhetoric and belles-lettres had been officially sponsored much earlier as a part of the philosophic tradition at Edinburgh, and not long afterward in the United States. In the latter half of the nineteenth century, chairs of English were set up at London and the provincial universities before they were instituted at Cambridge and ultimately at Oxford. As for the study of the language, the great dictionary that bears Oxford's name was inaugurated by the Philological Society — another of Furnivall's undertakings — and subsequently taken over by the Oxford University Press. The dictionary itself, the splendidly printed and carefully edited texts, the many reference works and secondary studies bearing that imprint have made that press a semi official custodian to which we owe esteem and gratitude. We pay it a tribute when we are shocked to see it revealing symptoms of human fallibility. Yet it may be symptomatic that the New Oxford Shakespeare did not survive its editor, R. B. McKerrow (a King's College, London, and Cambridge man), or progress beyond his excellent prolegomena of twenty-five years ago. Furthermore, with the newer editorial and bibliographical techniques and with transatlantic co-operation, authoritative critical editions tend to be printed increasingly by American presses — Chaucer, Spenser, Milton, Dryden, Johnson, Coleridge, Arnold.

Nor are we likely, when Oxford is our point of departure, to forget her sister university, whose scientific luster has not obscured her traditional ties with the major poets. The systematic presentation of history has been something of a Cambridge specialty. The dilemma of the modern historian, striving to interpret for himself, and for the general reader, the vast accumulations and the knotty technicalities of knowledge, has been poignantly dramatized by the career of Lord Acton, who never finished his own historical projects but projected the *Cambridge Modern History* and therewith marshalled those forces which came to be known as "syndicated scholarship." Such was the case with *The Cambridge History of English Literature*, which was organized by A. W. Ward and A. R. Waller along the same lines, with each chapter assigned to one of the leading authorities in its special field: W. P. Ker on the medieval romances, Charles Whibley on the Tudor translators, H. J. C. Grierson on Donne, Wilhelm Creizenach on the moralities, Emile Legouis on Wordsworth, J. E. Spingarn on literary criticism. Trends of research and opinion have shifted considerably over the past half-century, yet such articles can still be profitably read and respectfully cited.

The policy of letting the expert hold forth on his expertise is not without its pitfalls: J. M. Manly exploited the opportunity to propound his controversial views on the authorship of *Piers Plowman*, which were not to be substantiated as promised. On the other hand, this reliance on specialists broke down with the crucial chapters on Chaucer, Shakespeare, and Milton, all of which were allotted to that master generalist, George Saintsbury. Saintsbury (an Oxford man, who was professor at Edinburgh), with his Tory gusto and his all-embracing parentheses, was possibly the last man to take all literature for his province. The upshot of that catholicity was an impressionism which savored books at the same level of discrimination as the bottles in his famous wine-cellar. The intention of the Cambridge editors, as summarized in the reprint of 1932, was "to give a connected account of the successive movements of English literature, to describe the work of writers both of primary and of secondary importance, and to discuss the interaction between English and foreign literatures." They also intended to treat such allied subjects as journalism and oratory and to expand their orbit toward the dominions and America, which was soon to be covered by a satellite, *The Cambridge History of American Literature*.

They succeeded in providing encyclopedic coverage, subject to the ups and downs of so far-flung a venture. It might be thought that *The Oxford History of English Literature*, by allowing its fourteen contributors a volume apiece, would go farther toward supplying a connected account. But the actual jumps are shorter, and hence the disconnections seem less sharp, in *The Cambridge History of English Literature*, because the editors made their presence constantly felt by laying out and filling in the numerous contributions. The indispensible Cambridge bibliography has been brought up to date from time to time with supplements (and its Oxford editor has just brought out, for American consumption, a slapdash *Guide to English Literature*). The fifteen-volume Cambridge history, which terminates with the nineteenth century, and which was published between 1907 and 1916, continues to stand in need of an adequate replacement. In a peculiar sense, its momentary counterweight could be poised by the twenty-volume set of *Scrutiny*, which originally ran from 1932 to 1953 and has lately been reissued by the Cambridge University Press. This emergence is a form of canonization for an erstwhile little magazine, and its "editorial protagonist" — as F. R. Leavis describes himself in a "Retrospect" — is not backward in underscoring the irony.

Scrutiny has its share of the local and the ephemeral, and a compact selection from its best essays — such as the volume brought out by Eric Bentley in the United States, *The Importance of Scrutiny* — would be more impressive for purposes of rereading than the extended file. But it would not serve the ultimate purpose of catching the overtones of a movement in all their youthful zeal and pedagogical dogmatism. Between the veneration of his disciples and the deprecation of his colleagues, it is not easy for outsiders to understand what Dr. Leavis represents. Not that his ideas seem particularly novel, once we have accepted the coalition between Matthew Arnold and D. H. Lawrence. His "New Bearings" do not entail new departures, and firsthand evaluations are less in evidence than donnish revaluations in his quarterly. Many of the judgments it promulgates were already passed by T. S. Eliot, such as the attempted dislodgment of Milton along with the reinstatement of the Metaphysical poets, while in his emphasis on close

reading — the very process of scrutinizing — Dr. Leavis' forerunner was I. A. Richards, before he left the English for the American
Cambridge. But the program of reappraisal is all the sounder for
having such godparents; and the year-to-year endeavor to work it
into the Tripos, to transpose the critic's perception into the student's comprehension, can have been no dilettante's pastime.

The uphill character of the work may explain the tone of personal rancor or nagging provincialism, not infrequent in *Scrutiny*.
Its moral earnestness, even to the point of humorlessness, may be
preferable in the long run to Mr. Stewart's Oxonian prattle. The
extramural conflict is made polemically explicit by Mrs. Q. D.
Leavis in her review-article "The Discipline of Letters," on the
professional dilettantism of Oxford's Professor of English, G. S.
Gordon, and his predecessor, Sir Walter Raleigh. "*Scrutiny* was
essentially Cambridge's achievement," Dr. Leavis affirms, but with
the qualification, "in spite of Cambridge." Speaking of it as "our
outlaw's enterprise," he shows some propensity for eating his cake
while complaining that no one has ever offered him any. The Establishment has a way of absorbing its outlaws — especially in
England, it would seem to an admiring American — or possibly we
should say that the outlaws have a way of infiltrating the Establishment. Dr. Leavis' followers, under the editorship of Boris Ford,
have been rewriting the history of English literature — or should
we say recasting *Scrutiny?* — in the form of a *Pelican Guide*. Those
five paperbacks trace a critical line which seems likely to exert a
wider influence than anything in hard covers heretofore. Without
pretending to scholarly authority, the various contributory hands
display a common concern for the social implications of literature.

Insofar as these Cantabrigian shifts embody a revolution in taste,
the paradox is that the old regime was liberal, possibly too liberal
for its own good after the positivistic fashion of laissez-faire, while
many of the challengers are reactionaries who would impose a neo-
orthodoxy. Their vaunted "training in sensibility," as contrasted
with the old-fashioned philology that they scorn, cannot take other
than a subjective approach. This too will therefore pass in its turn,

by reason of its own rigidities and self-imposed limitations. At such an impasse it is comforting to remember that we always have the right to appeal, as Dr. Johnson did, from criticism to nature. It is the nature of revaluation not only to displace the *status quo* but to be replaced as criteria change and the wheel of fortune rounds its cycle. The unending flow of historical data is never arrested by the immediate standstill of critical dogma, and consequently the inconclusiveness of *The Oxford History of English Literature* may present a paradigm of its open-ended subject. Yet Johnson, writing as a critic rather than as a naturalist, had little use for Donne; and Pope played a thankless part in Arnold's sessions of the poets.

Historicism has made it possible for us to appreciate both Donne and Milton, as well as Pope and Wordsworth: to comprehend all writers of any significance within a conspectus extending broadly from their times into our own. The overview of literature *sub specie historiae* is a late and hard-won attainment of civilization, as can be inferred from a well-informed article by Robert Escarpit, "L'Histoire de l'histoire de la littérature." This article completes the three volumes devoted to the history of all literatures in the *Encyclopédie de la Pléiade* under the supervision of Raymond Queneau: Volume I, ancient, oriental, and oral literature; Volume II, occidental literature other than French; and Volume III, French literature and its dependencies. The scale of treatment suggests that even the French have not yet acquired complete objectivity; it demonstrates not so much the hegemony of their literature over all others as their predominance in the sphere of literary historiography. English literature is beholden to their endeavors — to the examples of Taine and Jusserand, Legouis and Cazamian — for a realization of its independence, a perspective on its waywardness from the models set by more classicistic literatures.

On its own ground, France has given the world a manual of manuals in Gustave Lanson's *Histoire de la littérature française* (1894), and an amplified and illustrated epitome a generation later in the collaborative history edited by Bédier and Hazard (1923).

Such collaboration lacks the discernment and consistency of one man's view, when that one man happens to be Albert Thibaudet; but Thibaudet concentrated his focus on the period between the Revolution and his date of composition, 1936. Literary history has its classics in other countries as well, though they are not plentiful anywhere. The finest of these may well be the *Storia della letteratura italiana* of Francesco De Sanctis, which is a work of art in its own right, but likewise a critique of Italian culture and society — an examination of the national conscience, in Croce's phrase. Though Wilhelm Scherer's *Geschichte der Deutschen Litteratur* is a more laborious effort, its varied strains are harmonized by the unifying figure of Goethe. Though V. L. Parrington's *Main Currents in American Thought* now seems incomplete and out of date, it is animated by a dialectic which has not ceased to be relevant.

By contrast the *Literary History of the United States*, which consolidates the advancing professionalism of the subject twenty years after Parrington, is much more comprehensive yet somewhat colorless. The proliferation of many literatures out of a single one under divergent conditions has its fascinating chronicle in Anderson Imbert's *Historia de la literatura hispanoamericana*. One of the most remarkable achievements in this line is the two-volume history of Russian literature by the exiled Prince Mirsky, written in English with a freedom and a subtlety which the unhappy author had to renounce after he was converted to Communism and returned to his native land. English literature is by no means deficient in ideological drama or cultural syntheses or integrating conceptions of other kinds; yet its sheer amplitude offers resistance to the generalizing processes of the historians; and its heterogeneity has discouraged those neat formulations which adapt themselves so easily to French literature. Significantly, the history of English poetry has been a fertile theme by itself, from the earliest precedent of Thomas Warton to the substantial interpretation of W. J. Courthope. Working in fifty-year units, Oliver Elton gradually extended his judicious *Survey of English Literature* from 1730 to 1880.

But even the ubiquitous Saintsbury, though he fathered a single-volume short history, worked at five-volume length with three collaborators, supplying volumes on the Elizabethan period and the nineteenth century, and leaving the others to Stopford Brooke, W. H. Schofield, and Edmund Gosse. We are probably long past the day when any one author could encompass the totality of the field with genuine authority, and David Daiches' recent *Critical History of English Literature* reads like a set of examination papers by a bright undergraduate. The compendious volume of Albert C. Baugh and four colleagues, *A Literary History of England*, like the similarly proportioned work by Hardin Craig and others, possesses the strengths and limitations of period specialization as practised by the last generation of American professors of English. At its best, it mirrors the special dedication and professional mastery of the collaborator, as in the separately issued sections on the Restoration and eighteenth century by the late George Sherburn; but the net effect is hardly less uneven or unintegrated than the papers at a meeting of the Modern Language Association of America. At the moment — and that may mean for the future — there are many valuable surveys of schools and problems; but there is simply no integral history to which serious students of English literature may be confidently referred.

In this there may be an implicit critique of literary history itself as a mode of expression or a tool of knowledge. To find a plane of discourse where artistic monuments and historic documents can meaningfully coexist, to render what respectively pertains to esthetics and to society, to schematize and categorize in setting forth the effects of originality and individuality, may prove to be a self-defeating task. When George Saintsbury published his *History of Criticism*, Irving Babbitt reviewed it under the heading, "Are the English Critical?" The question is far too sweeping to be affirmed or denied with any cogency; it is better left in the realm of rhetoric; yet it probes toward certain tendencies which are the chronic defects of great qualities. Empiricism, their grasp of the concrete object for its own sake, can lead to a distrust of all theorizing: "We murder to dissect." Vitalism, their respect for the immediacy and wholeness of experience, which has repeatedly made a virtue of defying analysis, thereby helps to explain why the English have never taken full measure of their incomparable literary heritage. They are entitled to reply, of course, that the rich subject resists definitive treatment; that the last chapter gets, at the very latest, a penultimate word; and that the lively autobiographer has no chance to write *finis*.

The American Voice in English Poetry

This address was delivered at a plenary session of the eighth congress of the Fédération Internationale des Langues et Littératures Modernes at Liège on August 30, 1960. With bibliographical footnotes and a summary of the discussion led by Professor F. E. L. Priestley, it was published under the auspices of the University of Liège in a volume entitled Langue et littérature (1961). During the five years since it was set down, we have lost our two most eminent poets, Robert Frost and T. S. Eliot; and there has been further change, but not — I think — any major reversal of trends. I may have underestimated the San Francisco school, in the light of its current impact abroad; but this would seem to be a socio-cultural, rather than an artistic, manifestation; and, in becoming internationalized, it would seem to have given up its nativistic impulsion. The comparative problem of diction in English and American poetry still needs to be critically recognized and examined at length. Sir Herbert Read, with his characteristic gift for sensing relationships while blurring distinctions, has touched upon it in an address to the National Poetry Festival at Washington in 1962, "American Bards and British Reviewers." Conrad Aiken, in "Poetry and the Mind of Modern Man" (Atlantic Monthly, January 1965), has given a valuable firsthand account of the search for a new stylistic medium. The most interesting recent contribution to American poetry, in its handling of voices from the subliterate to the hyperliterary, has been John Berryman's 77 Dream Songs.

My topic presupposes both the unity and the diversity of English as a literary medium. To refer to "the American language" would be to run the risk of taking H. L. Mencken's humorous exaggeration too seriously. American as such is really not even a dialect, in the sense that lowland Scottish has been for poets from Blind Harry through Robert Burns to Hugh Macdiarmid. The increment of local idioms and residue of archaic usages, the shifts of meaning and variations of spelling, fall well within the relation defined in principle when Noah Webster brought out *An American Dictionary of the English Language* in 1828. (It was possible for the most influential of English grammars to be brought out in 1795 by Lindley Murray, who had been born in colonial Pennsylvania and had migrated to England about a decade before his emergence as its grammatical arbiter.) In current practice, the main sources of divergence seem to be largely vocal. Poetry, if not spoken aloud, should be overheard in the mind's ear. Whether the presumptive speaker is English or American makes an enormous difference in the pattern of sounds, as a pair of phonograph records could easily demonstrate, and as the articulation of phonemes ought to make clear. It is not simply a matter of differing pronunciations, but of pitch and pace, which can vary so much more with the English than they usually do with us. American English is literally monotonous by comparison: that is to say, it comes closer to a monotone, and its rhythms are slower and more regular. Hence the British actor has more of an instrument for musical performance than the American.

Our Sidney Lanier, in *The Science of English Verse*, emphasized its underlying "speech tunes," but did not differentiate between those of the parent culture and those of its offshoot. Yet these ought not to have escaped the notice of a poet-prosodist; and W. H. Auden, who is also both a witness and a practitioner, has latterly remarked: "From Bryant on there is scarcely one American poet whose work, if unsigned, would be taken for that of any Englishman." I quote Mr. Auden's remark from his introduction to *The Faber Book of Modern American Verse*, which he compiled for British readers a few years ago. A few years before that, by collaborating with Norman Holmes Pearson upon a five-volume collection, *Poets of the English Language* (New York, 1950), he acknowledged the interrelationship of the two poetic traditions. Inclusion of the one within the other has become an editorial policy in an increasing number of current anthologies, and has more than once been facilitated through collaboration between editors of both nationalities. The recent volume edited by Lord David Cecil and Allen Tate, *Modern Verse in English* (New York, 1958), though it intermixes its selections chronologically, sums them up in separate introductions, with Mr. Tate asserting in his that contemporary "Anglo-American poetry . . . only by convention can be separated." Yet poetry exists by means of convention, and criticism must exercise a continual discrimination. When the great-

est of modern poets in English, the Irishman William Butler
Yeats, made his compilation twenty-five years ago, he limited *The
Oxford Book of Modern Verse* to British contributors on the
advice of an unnamed American poet, who warned him: "If your
selection looks representative you will commit acts of injustice."

That warning would seem to apply, with equal force, to any
anthologist who was unsure of his ground. There is a fair amount
of American poetry in *The Oxford Book of English Verse*, published thirty years before by Sir Arthur Quiller-Couch. There was
none in the canonical nineteenth-century compilations of F. T.
Palgrave and T. H. Ward. American poets could then be well
represented only by making their own collections, as did Bryant,
Emerson, and Whittier. There have, of course, been many professionally American anthologists, some of whom — like R. W. Gris-
wold and Louis Untermeyer — have also published separate
collections of British poetry for consumption in the United States.
Only two American poets — along with half a dozen French ones
— were represented in *Edith Sitwell's Anthology*, published in 1940.
In 1951, having meanwhile discovered the United States for herself,
Dame Edith made gracious amends with a *florilège* entitled *The
American Genius*. And in 1958, at the instigation of an American
publisher, she reunited the two strains in a single compendious
anthology, *The Atlantic Book of British and American Poetry*
(Boston, 1958). I should also mention the two-volume *Viking Book
of Poetry of the English Speaking World* (New York, 1941; revised edition, 1958), edited by the late Richard Aldington. It is
not to be inferred, however, that English editors recognize American poetry only when their selections are sponsored by American
publishers: for example, it is given considerable space by Herbert
Read and Bonamy Dobrée in *The London Book of Modern Verse*
(London, 1949).

It would be agreed, at all events, that American poets now possess
a mansion of their own in the vast and variegated house of English poetry. A comparable degree of autonomy is today being sought
by Anglo-Canadian poets, whose double problem is to keep independent of their neighbor as well as their mother country: wil-

ness *The Oxford Book of Canadian Verse* edited by A. J. M. Smith, a leading poet of Canada who has been teaching for many years at Michigan State University. Similar problems confront the Franco-Canadian poets, whose endeavors to keep in touch with tradition at a far remove are bound to seem less exciting than the French Negro poetry of Haiti or Senegal. The parallels with Spanish and Portuguese poetry overseas are even richer, given the circumstances under which the languages were multiplied and the cultures adapted in the Americas. But the novelty of newly developed countries, broadly speaking, seldom presents itself first in their literatures. It could be argued — indeed it is my argument in outline — that the Anglo-American cycle has moved from virtual homogeneity to self-conscious differentiation and back again toward a dialectical synthesis. More explicitly, this evolution begins in colonial dependence, with the colony weakly parroting the imperial tone; then it branches out into a search for identity, widely ranging and freely questioning; and finally it emerges in cosmopolitan rapport, into which the two cultures blend with still others. It is my congenial task to exemplify this progression.

The beginnings, of course, are wholly derivative. America's first poet, Anne Bradstreet, the English-born wife of a royal governor, would have written the same way — as she put it — "in either hemisphere." The Reverend Edward Taylor, the New England member of the Metaphysical school, followed such masters as George Herbert from a distance. Yet it may have been Taylor's provincial situation which fostered a manner unique in its homely and practical familiarity. He is fond of comparing infusions of grace to draughts of beer; his metaphor for an agitated heart is Satan's bowling alley; and his conception of Christ addressing the soul is rather more domestic than spiritual:

> Peace, Peace, my Hony, do not Cry,
> My Little Darling, wipe thine eye,
> O Cheer, Cheer up, come see.

The surge of revolutionary patriotism, retarded by the critical lag, expressed itself in highly conservative terms. Witness the Hudibrastics or the Pope-like couplets of the half-forgotten Connecticut Wits. Nevertheless, when Joel Barlow's epical *Columbiad* appeared in 1809, *The Edinburgh Review* was irritated not only by its egalitarian sentiments but also by its Latinate neologisms. The reviewer was as adept at transatlantic generalization as his successors are in *The New Statesman* or *The Times Literary Supplement:* "These republican literati seem to make it a point of conscience to have no aristocratical distinction — even in their vocabulary. They think one word just as good as another. . ." This testimony should modify the view that Barlow made no "attempt to create a new style," as stated by George Philip Krapp in his *English Language in America.* On the whole, it is surprising that so little attention has been paid to stylistics by scholars concerned with Anglo-American linguistics. The periodical *American Speech* seems to concentrate on the curiosities of syntax and dialect.

While *The Edinburgh Review* was putting *The Columbiad* in its place, William Cullen Bryant was starting to write the first poem that Mr. Auden and others would regard as unmistakably American. Ironically enough, when "Thanatopsis" was submitted anonymously to *The North American Review*, the editor, Richard Henry Dana, Sr., assumed that it must have been composed by an Englishman. "No one on this side of the Atlantic," he humbly reasoned, "is capable of writing such verses!" Bryant himself, in a lecture at the New York Athenaeum, spoke of the common language as "a transplanted dialect," imagined an English poet emigrating to America, and posed the rhetorical question: "Can anybody suppose that his poetry would be the worse for it?" On the contrary, the traditional styles would merely be extended to novel subjects; the new republic abounded in villages and graveyards sedulously invoked by indigenous Goldsmiths and parochial Grays; and the young Bryant, meditating over its natural wonders, presented himself in the guise of a minor Wordsworth. Yet, in turning away from "that proud old world beyond the deep," he faced a horizon more challenging than the Lake District:

> The unshorn fields, boundless and beautiful,
> For which the speech of England has no name . . .

No — we are reminded, as the succeeding lines describe their subject, "The Prairies" — that name was borrowed from the speech of France, by way of those *voyageurs* who charted our western terrain. Since the landscape is a major theme, place names are particularly significant. And although we have none with the special magic of Rue des Martyrs or Bleeding-Heart-Yard, as Stephen Vincent Benét pointed out in "American Names," European towns have nothing to match the hyphenated associations of Harrisburg and Spartanburg or the tribal memories of Painted Post and Wounded Knee. Yet Europeans could be just as sentimental about Indians as Philip Freneau or Henry Wadsworth Longfellow; and topographic allusion can become a superficial coloring, applied to gratify exotic tastes rather than communicate regional feelings, when the point of observation is far away. It was easier for Thomas Campbell to romanticize an American setting than it had been for native versifiers; never having visited the locality, he could embellish *Gertrude of Wyoming* by interpolating aloes and flamingoes. But the actual continent had its authentic flora and fauna; it had scenes for which its inherited language lacked phrases, and images which could not be placed within a frame of foreign reference. In his "Invocation to the American Muse," Benét protested:

> They tried to fit you with an English song
> And clip your speech into the English tale.
> But, even from the first, the words went wrong,
> The catbird pecked away the nightingale.

The protestation sounded here belatedly is the loudest note that runs through American poetry. It was singled out for counterattack by Edgar Allan Poe, whenever he criticized his nationalistic contemporaries. Appropriately, Poe's impact as a practitioner has been mainly felt in the international sphere. One of the questions not considered in his "Philosophy of Composition" is whether he himself would have read his most famous poem with a Southern accent, in which case the familiar refrain would have had two eroded consonants and an extra syllable: "Quoth the Raven,

'Nevahmoah.'" Although Poe's flights into outer space did not ultimately prove him to be un-American, he reduced the cult of place to absurdity by inventing his own topography — as Edward Lear would do in his *Nonsense Songs*. For in metrics they were fellow travelers: Poe might well have sailed away with the Jumblies to the hills of the Chankly Bore or dwelt upon the coast of Coromandel with the Yonghy Bonghy Bo. The only concrete fact about such landmarks as Mount Yaanek or the ghoul-haunted woodland of Weir is that they fill his inordinate need for rhymes — and they do not even do that in Mallarmé's prose translation. Mallarmé could scarcely have been judging the verbal effect of Poe's nervous syncopations and album-leaf clichés, when he characterized the poet's mission· "*Donner un sens plus pur aux mots de la tribu,*" or, in T. S. Eliot's paraphrase, "To purify the dialect of the tribe." Actually, Poe did more to adulterate than to purify the language. Mallarmé's pronouncement was a Symbolistic reversal of the Romantic thesis, as stated by Wordsworth, that poetry renews itself by adapting "the very language of common men." The late Wallace Stevens resolved this conflict of emphasis in one of his jaunty paradoxes:

> The poem goes from the poet's gibberish to
> The gibberish of the vulgate and back again.

The poet's gibberish, when he talks to himself, tends toward the more jejune artificialities of poetic diction; hence he regains his hold on reality by periodic immersions in the vulgate; and thus he re-enacts the classic myth of the giant touching the earth to increase his strength. The most decisive of these renewals came when Dante and the poet-critics of the Renaissance shifted from Latin to their respective vernaculars. English poetry, in particular, has maintained its vitality through a sequence of such stylistic renovations, accomplished by Chaucer and Donne in their varying times, by Dryden and Yeats as well as Wordsworth and Coleridge. The American poets carried through, on a larger scale and with

newer apparatus, the revolution stirred up by the English Romanticists.

Poetry would soon bog down into tameness, if it were not constantly striking out for what Robert Frost likes to call "wildness."
When the nightingale becomes a standard item of poetical decoration, then it is time to listen for the catbird — or, better, for the
hermit thrush whose song accentuates both *The Waste Land* and
"When Lilacs Last in the Dooryard Bloom'd." Insofar as Romanticism voiced forces of liberation, impulses toward expansion, and
a passion for nature, its program could be most fully worked out
— as exemplified by Walt Whitman — in "the States." Whitman's critical manifestoes, plus the organic accumulations of
Leaves of Grass, constitute its defense and illustration, and consummate a long series of literary declarations of independence. His
premise — that America itself is potentially a great poem — seems
to have been acquired from Ralph Waldo Emerson; but his nationalism is broad enough to allow for the realization that Goethe
had learned a similar lesson from Herder. The "great psalm of the
republic," keeping pace with its hopes, should be "transcendent
and new"; yet the migratory Muses should enrich it with fabulous
contributions from the Old World. As for the English language,
so full of imported treasures from the outset, so grandly lawless,
it "befriends the grand American expression." What is more: "It is
the medium that shall well nigh express the inexpressible." This
will presumably be an American feat; for in an anonymous review
of his own work, invidiously comparing its ruggedness with the
ennui of the gentlemanly Tennyson and "his British and American
eleves" (the unaccented gallicism hinting at their effeteness), Whitman adds insult to injury by dismissing them as "jinglers" and
"danglers."

The nation had all too many poetasters, imitating the genteel
graces of the cisatlantic Muse; and Whitman expressly provided
the shock of a counterexample by "leaving out the stock 'poetical'
touches" and sounding his "barbaric yawp over the roofs of the
world." His *Leaves*, as he confessed to a disciple, may have been

"only a language experiment." He could hardly have poured a more numerous or heterogeneous set of ingredients into his linguistic melting-pot. Words, "book-words," jostle against "words of earth," and the latter include *amelioration* along with *soil* and *air*. Names, Indian names, lend their primitive undertones: "Wabash, Miami, Saginaw, Chippewa, Oshkosh, Walla-Walla." But these are counterpoised by the foreign capitals — London, Paris, Brussels, Vienna, Constantinople, Saint Petersburg — of which the bard proclaims himself a *habitan* (his word is not quite French-Canadian). His smatterings of French and other languages are not more consciously flaunted than his Americanisms, his coinages, nicknames, and slang. But, in his subsequent and frequent revisions, neologism gives way to archaism; as the experiment succeeds, the vocabulary becomes more conventional; and it ends by proving, among other things, the undemocratic hypothesis that some words may be better than others for the poet's purposes. Perhaps Whitman's clearest success was in the range of his prosody. What Emerson took to be its "formlessness" proved to be, on closer scrutiny, its mode of expressive form. English poets had often balked at the constrictions of rhyme; free verse was the logical measure for a free country. One of those "Poets to Come" for whom Whitman set the example, Edgar Lee Masters, would underline the contrast in his epitaph for a poetaster surnamed Pettit by virtue of his littleness:

> Tick, tick, tick, what little iambics,
> While Homer and Whitman roared in the pines!

But iambic pentameter was hard to avoid, so firmly were Shakespeare's and Milton's rhythms imprinted upon the national consciousness. Emerson could jot down a page in his journal which, with a few slight adjustments, becomes a blank-verse effusion upon the seashore. Similarly, Melville has many passages which can be scanned by the rules of Shakespearean versification. Whitman finds his more flexible norms in the cadences of prose, and especially in public speech, not seldom in the eagle-screaming elocution of Fourth-of-July oratory. By preference he plays the orator; but by profession, like most of the ablest American writers, he has worked as a journalist. Journalistic coverage is combined with forensic declamation to give a broad documentary scope to his rhapsodies. Emerson categorized their style as a compound of the *New York Herald* and the *Bhagavad Gita*. He might have pointed to a sacred book much closer to home: it was the Bible first and last, for Whitman as for Blake, which inspired prophetic insights and supplied rhetorical patterns. Moreover, it was as true of America as it was of England that the parlance of everyday life had been permeated with, and dignified by, Biblical influence. The eloquence of Wordsworth's countrymen, according to Coleridge, was attributable to "the Bible and the liturgy or hymn-book." The hymn-book, as it unexpectedly happened, turned out to be a primary model for the most subtle and personal kind of lyricism. Most of Emily Dickinson's lyrics conform to the meters laid down in Isaac Watts's *Christian Psalmody*. The commonest is a four-line alternation of eight and six syllables — more precisely, of four and three iambs, like a slow ballad-meter. For instance:

> Indebtedness to Oxygen
> The happy may repay,
> But not the obligation
> To Electricity.

This is a far cry from the parish church, or from the pedagogical naïveté of "How doth the little busy bee . . . ?" The off-rhyme is Emily Dickinson's own, as is the poetic use of prosaic words. The use of polysyllables to accelerate and clinch the stanza is a device she may have picked up from the Metaphysicals: "Deserts of vast eternity." She has appropriated the terminology of science in order to comment upon a tragic experience which she has previously compared to a bolt of lightning. Elsewhere, her epithet for spring is "Experiment of Green." When she alludes to greenery as "Duds of Emerald," she invites comparison with Whitman, since "duds" — for shabby clothes — was one of his favorite vulgarisms. Her lapidary selection and careful juxtaposition stand out sharply against his easy profusion. If she coins a word, and she rarely does, it is a key-word which brings out a crucial significance. Thus it conveys a sense of arrested movement, when she considers

> The overtakelessness of those
> Who have accomplished Death.

Here the hopelessness of her single long-drawn-out coinage is balanced against her sense of death as an accomplishment. The inexpressible, by definition, may not be expressed; but it seems to be mystically contemplated from her interior world, or through her familiar ambience of household and garden, with all the microscopic intensity of the habitual recluse:

> Maybe — "Eden" an't so lonesome
> As New England used to be!

Here, as the trochees drop from speculations on paradise down to earth, the Yankee contraction "an't" (correct enough for *am not* but incorrect for *isn't*, and rather countrified in any case) twists a heartcry into a wry smile. Be that as it may, it is not the reaction of a regionalist. Emily Dickinson's isolation from her own day has enabled her work to survive with an air of modernity. As a woman, writing without view to publication, she did not need to be a spokesman for anybody except herself. While the expansive Whitman strove to be typical, she could attain uniqueness within the most exacting self-limitation.

It was for Whitman to strike an attitude. Most democratic spokesmen have shown an awareness of the roles they were playing — individualized embodiments of the common man — plus a tendency to simplify them, to talk down to their audience. Nathaniel Ward took part in Puritan controversy as the Simple Cobbler of Aggawam. Benjamin Franklin won his fame at home and abroad as Poor Richard. Politicians as notable as Lincoln had been concerned with projecting a popular image. Whitman was well aware that, before there could be a truly American body of poetry, there had to be a distinctively American role for the poet, and this would

not be an easy thing to improvise. Hence he programmatically re-
modeled his eccentric personality. He grew a beard, he affected
workingman's garb, and he had his portrait printed as the frontis-
piece to *Leaves of Grass*. It was a pose, if you will; but it was also,
like Baudelaire's dandyism, a way of life. The only way to cut
through the affectations of the "literats," for Whitman, was to be
"one of the roughs." His gesture accorded with romantic assumptions about untutored genius and folk inspiration. Incidentally, he
received some of his earliest and most generous appreciation from
England, which was proving particularly hospitable to picturesque
writers from the American West. Cincinnatus Miller, the so-called
Byron of Oregon, borrowing another Christian name from one of
his heroes, Joaquín, and wearing the costume of a mining prospec-
tor, was lionized in the drawing rooms of London. So was Bret
Harte, the Dickens of California. American critics saw through this
nativism fabricated for the export trade; it was their own polite
Anglophilia in reverse. "Sham slang and sham barbarism," commented Bayard Taylor, "are worse than sham refinement and
luxury."

In contrast to those émigré local colorists, Whitman created a
bardic figure, composite and archetypal, who is both the singer and
the song. The self in "Song of Myself" is not the author's ego but
rather his persona — that is to say, etymologically, his mouthpiece.
Its utterance is the voice of American singing in chorus, not solo:

> A call in the midst of the crowd,
> My own voice, orotund sweeping and final.

In spite of the sustained first person singular, we hear a multiplicity
of voices, the call of the crowd. The poet himself becomes, like
Shelley's forest, an Aeolian lyre which reverberates to the plucking
of diverse and random winds. "Lands of ensemble, bards of ensemble!" was Whitman's maxim in a letter to Emerson. Whitman,
by striving for a universal dialect, contrived an idiolect. Though he
paid lip-service to simplicity, his *patois* is extraordinarily complex.
It was for simpler poets to effect an adaptation to the vernacular.

In that connection, a strategic line could be traced through the writings of James Russell Lowell, since he kept his *Biglow Papers* apart from his more serious and less original verse. Lowell exploited the Yankee dialect with comic intent and satiric effectiveness. In the introduction to his *Second Series*, he analyzed and defended it at length, drawing upon his scholarship to emphasize how much of old England had survived in rural New England speech. He feared that the "mother tongue," as taught in American schools, stood in danger of becoming "a dead language." He chose to sharpen his political criticism by placing it in the mouth of one Hosea Biglow, "an upcountry man . . . capable of district school English but always instinctively falling back into the natural stronghold of his homely dialect." Between this "assumed character" and the polished man of letters who had conceived him, the gap was obviously wide. Lowell bridged it by introducing a personage closer to himself, Parson Homer Wilbur, who edits the satires with mock-pedantic commentary.

This had heretofore been the usual arrangement for regionalists and humorists writing in prose. Though they focused on the quoted speeches of some colorful and semi-literate type such as Sut Lovingood, as transcribed through clumsy phonetic spellings in the dialect of his region, he was presented and commented upon by an urbane and condescending narrator. Later, when writers took to the lecture platform, the two figures merged; the author himself impersonated his humoristic creation; Charles Farrar Browne was popularly identified with Artemus Ward, and Samuel Langhorne Clemens with Mark Twain. The final step — as predicted by the pioneering novelist, John Neal — was "learning *to talk on paper.*" It was decisively taken with *The Adventures of Huckleberry Finn,* when Mark Twain abandoned third-person narrative and plunged directly into the monologue of his youthful protagonist, thereby initiating a process which Ernest Hemingway would complete, and transforming the colloquial language into the literary norm. Poetry had to go through the same sort of development; and Whitman's part seems clearer if we align him with the humorous lecturers; but colloquialism was no more than a seasoning in his rhapsodic *pot-pourri*. John Greenleaf Whittier conscientiously celebrated the interests of his natal New England, but his style was ineptly literary rather than effectively colloquial. The austere framework of "Snow-Bound" is heavily decorated with European allusions in the manner of Longfellow. When Whittier sighed,

> Blessings on thee, little man,
> Barefoot boy with cheek of tan,

he was taking a Wordsworthian position and patting the child on the head. True, he went on to link himself with his object-lesson through a sentimentalized reminiscence: "I was once a barefoot boy." But mere nostalgia for childhood was not enough; there had to be a more whole-hearted identification with it; the onlooker had to become the participant. The American point of view in fiction has been characteristically connected with adolescence — or, at any rate, with related qualities of innocence, eagerness, and athleticism. There is usually something boyish in the aspect of America's heroes. E. E. Cummings closes his elegy on Buffalo Bill with the poignant query:

> how do you like your blueeyed boy
> Mister Death

Significantly, the title of Robert Frost's first book, A *Boy's Will*, is an echo from the refrain of Henry Wadsworth Longfellow's poem "My Lost Youth" — a refrain which is not less characteristic of Longfellow because, in his eclectic and academic fashion, he had translated it from "a Lapland Song." Mr. Frost, long established as the grand old man of American poetry, can readily play the role of the reminiscent interlocutor: "So was I once myself a swinger of birches." The barefoot boy has grown up and put on shoes; but he has remained on, or else returned to, the farm; and it is his voice that we hear. When Mr. Frost tells us, "I choose to be a plain New Hampshire farmer," he tells us how deliberate this choice has been — no less deliberate than Calvin Coolidge not choosing to run for President in 1928. For a native of San Francisco, who had gained his first recognition in England, spent many years on college campuses, and was actually living in Vermont when he penned that line, it could hardly have been an inevitable decision. Here was no Ettrick Shepherd, fresh from the tending of flocks, but a thoroughly "Literate Farmer," as keen as Hosea Biglow on politics and considerably keener on philosophy, whose plainness was the vehicle of his shrewdness. It was about as naïve as Vergil's eclogues, and almost as much of an impersonation as Browning's soliloquies, though with the years Frost's public figure has become inseparable from his poetic characterization. His liking for "the one state of ours that is a shire" implies a continuing bond with the English countryside. Indeed there are similarities between his poems and those of his friend and sometime Gloucestershire neighbor, Edward Thomas. The New England background is less a source of local color than it is a natural prospect for autodidactic lore and gnomic wisdom, and for such timeless dramas as happen alike to Hardy's or Edwin Arlington Robinson's villagers.

Mr. Frost is sparing in his descriptions; his adjectives are meager and ordinary; he addresses himself to the ear rather than the eye. He flavors his poems by making them conversations, which catch — as Ezra Pound was quick to discern — "the natural spoken speech." Mr. Frost himself has called them "talk-songs." Consequently, the reader becomes a hearer, a second person closely linked with the first. In the prologue to Frost's collected verse, "The Pasture," his farmer-spokesman invites us to accompany him on his daily round of farmyard tasks: "I shan't be gone long. — You come too." Yet he is a listener as well as a talker; his monologues *in propria persona* are interspersed with the gossipy dialogues of his rural neighbors. The talk digresses now and then into unpoetic garrulity: "What was I going to say?" Its Yankee inflection comes out in such rhymes as "sticks" and "creeks," or in the intransitive usage of the verb "to signify." But it likewise helps to revitalize such outmoded contractions as " 'tis" and " 'twas," and even certain inversions: "Something there is that does not love a wall."

The principal meter is a five-foot iambic line, either blank or rhymed, slowed down by the prevalence of spondees, monosyllables, or occasionally hypermetrical syllables. Observe how the following couplet hinges upon the contracted enjambment, and is speeded up by the repetition of a polysyllable:

> What if it wasn't all it should be? I'd
> Be satisfied if he'd be satisfied.

The following quatrain, which typifies the ironic detachment of Mr. Frost as a commentator, is cryptically titled "U.S. 1946 King's X." The date refers to the first American proposal for outlawing the atomic bomb. "King's cross" is a call for truce in a children's game, an adopted Briticism which the poet couples with an American child's cry of injustice, "no fairs." The epigram builds up to the anticlimax of another reduction to childishness:

> Having invented a new Holocaust,
> And been the first with it to win a war,
> How they make haste to cry with fingers crossed,
> King's X—no fairs to use it any more!

To a world of such complexities, the childish approach is manifestly inadequate. On the other hand, while industry has been superseding agriculture in New Hampshire and elsewhere, the homespun rustic has obsolesced into a figment of pastoral convention. Meanwhile most of the Southern poets, who once constituted the *Fugitive* group at Nashville, have taken flight northward. Nonetheless, it would be hard to imagine a Northerner writing the poems of, let us say, John Crowe Ransom. Other poets had spoken for various hinterlands, as James Whitcomb Riley did for the Hoosiers of Indiana, and even for another race, as Paul Laurence Dunbar and a good many since have done for the Negroes. The *vers de société* of urban wits, from Oliver Wendell Holmes to Dorothy Parker, cultivated a facile strain of informal urbanity. But the central problem was to capture the genuine voice of the city — "the blab of the pave," in Whitman's truncated phrase. Solutions ranged from the sprawling apostrophes of Carl Sandburg's

Chicago Poems to the kinetic particularities of William Carlos Williams' *Paterson*. As music quickened its beat from hymnology to ragtime, one could note the very transition in the revivalistic chants of Vachel Lindsay. Under the rubric of *In American*, John V. A. Weaver printed verses in metropolitan slang. One almost had to be a New Yorker to understand some of E. E. Cummings' phonetics: e.g. the nasalized blur of "yunnuhstan." However, with a few exceptions, notably Conrad Aiken's "Blind Date," such efforts were narrowly limited by their implicit class-consciousness. The use of dialects has almost always involved a certain condescension toward the subject matter, from the Greek pastorals of Theocritus to the Cockney ballads of Rudyard Kipling. Even a John Clare or a William Barnes, by occasionally writing in literate English, put imaginary quotation marks around his peasant lucubrations.

A farther-reaching social consideration was the increasing number of articulate Americans who were not of English-speaking ancestry, and who brought in lilts and accents from continental Europe. Others, like Longfellow with Dante and Bayard Taylor with Goethe, not to mention Bryant with Homer, reaped the fruit of their travels in translations. A Philadelphian who had studied in Germany, Charles Godfrey Leland, gave the migrations of 1848 their rowdy Minnesinger in Hans Breitmann, who could romp through a macaronic ballad where broken English was eked out with German words and French names:

> Dere woned once a studente
> All in der Stadt Paris,
> Whom jeder der ihn kennte
> Der rowdy Breitmann hiess.
> He roosted in de rue La Harpe,
> Im Luxembourg Hotel,
> 'Twas shoost in anno '48
> Dat all dese dings pefel.

Happily, there have since been more sophisticated exemplars of this multilingual trend. The English critic, Michael Roberts, in

The Faber Book of Modern Verse, suggested that, whereas his compatriots "take the language as they find it," American poets inherit a "European sensibility" in which there is "something of the dandy and the dilettante." Another English critic has recently given an invidious edge to that valid distinction by describing Wallace Stevens as "a cultural show-off" — a rather testy refusal to be amused by the playful bravura of the Pennsylvania Dutchman who toyed with "Le Monocle de Mon Oncle." Insofar as Whitman and the nationalists had founded a school of official rhetoric, their twentieth-century successors were bound to react by showing what cosmopolites they could be. Along with advertising slogans and other verbalistic excesses, E. E. Cummings repudiated ideological catchwords, infixing one of his parenthetic disclaimers into a sacred word: "democ/ra(caveat emptor)cy." His revolt against capitals, his calligramatic typography, and his syntactic transferences were all in the libertarian tradition, as were the more labored efforts of Hart Crane to aggrandize his lines with spellbinding verbiage and sesquipedalian malapropisms. But the Whitmanesque belief that a democratic art ought to express itself in open forms, which led to the cultivation of *vers libre,* was yielding to a revived concern for the stricter techniques. The dandies were gradually replacing the rhapsodes; and Whitmanism, for so long the mainstream, now pulsates chiefly through such undercurrents as the San Francisco school, where its once-confident yawps subside into howls and whimpers. In general, there has been a withdrawal to more detached vantage-points, academic more often than not, where the perspectives of internationalism prevail over nationalism and regionalism.

The movement that determined this direction was launched in London shortly before the First World War. Its exponents, who prominently included several Americans, designated themselves collectively as *Des Imagistes.* They were thereby proclaiming an affinity with *Les Symbolistes,* and with Gallic ideals of alembicated refinement as opposed to Anglo-Saxon notions of earthy reinvigoration. Ezra Pound, their polyglot fugleman, was a self-avowed anti-

Whitman, whose fastidious stylizations ended in an unpatriotic confusion of tongues and loyalties. While in England, he wrote more or less like an Englishman; but subsequently, during sojourns in France and Italy, his English seemed to get more and more American, parodying itself with nasal twangs and orthographic jokes. The reconquest of Britain that he heralded, "the American colonization," was accomplished by his fellow expatriate, T. S. Eliot. It could have been foreseen that, in that process, Mr. Eliot would himself be conquered, becoming more British than the British. His innovations might be said to have begun with his signature. To sign himself T. S. like a businessman, instead of Thomas Stearns, was to deviate from the triple-barreled stance of William Cullen, Edgar Allan, Ralph Waldo, Henry Wadsworth, Oliver Wendell, and John Greenleaf. Mr. Eliot's American boyhood had sensitized him to the sound of jazz and the noise of the machine; but when he came to orchestrate the metropolis, his scene was London. *The Waste Land* echoes an English "gramophone," not an American "phonograph"; but its climactic episode takes place behind an American "gashouse," not an English "gasworks"; while its rooster crows in Continental fashion, "co co rico," rather than with the Anglo-American "cock-a-doodle-doo." Such exclamations as "How his hair is growing thin!" seem unidiomatic to the point of sounding foreign. The *agon* of "Sweeney Agonistes" seems in part to be a conflict between Americanisms and Cockneyisms.

Mr. Eliot's later *Quartets* hymn American vistas as well as Anglican shrines, while his earlier poems recollect the United States with such idiomatic phrases as "dooryards," "vacant lots," or "city blocks." And yet it surprises us to be reminded, with "Sweeney Among the Nightingales," that Agamemnon's "stiff dishonoured shroud" re-echoes from Daniel Webster's "dim/Dishonored brow" in "Ichabod," and that therefore Whittier should be numbered — along with Donne and the Elizabethans, or Dante and the Symbolists — among Eliot's literary ancestors. Whenever Mr. Eliot is asked whether he is an English or an American poet, he replies with his usual astuteness: "Whichever Wystan Auden is, I am the

other." Yet Mr. Auden has not been Americanized to the extent
that the elder poet, moving from the periphery to the center, has
been Anglicized: Mr. Auden's course had to be more centrifugal.
Stylistically, he remains an Englishman, all the more fundamentally so in his casualness and his resourcefulness, albeit a much
traveled Englishman who fluently speaks many languages — including Americanese — with a British accent. He has parodied his
dilemma in "Refugee Blues." In his dialogue, *The Age of Anxiety*,
the scene is New York City; the verse form is Old English; and
the principal speaker is a wandering Jewess from England, whose
mental horizons are "dales" and "wolds," and whose Briticisms
("sentry-go," "gym-mistress") terminate in an echo from the He-
brew liturgy. At this point, younger poets may already look back,
with Donald Davie, upon "Audenesque" as "an idiom too dated,"
a synthetic diction. Yet Mr. Auden has been the consolidator of
fifty years' experimentation on both sides of the Atlantic, and has
set the conversational tone and the technical standard for emergent
generations in both countries.

To leaf through an anthology of English and American poets
under forty, edited by Donald Hall, Robert Pack, and Louis Simp-
son, is to get the impression that they all talk — very expertly and
almost interchangeably — the same *lingua franca*. Indeed, it is
hard to tell their provenience from the place-names they use; so
many Americans have been Rhodes Scholars, and so many Britons
Commonwealth Fellows. That Charles Causeley (English) should
compose a "Cowboy Song" today, albeit the cowboy is expected
"home by tea," seems no stranger than that Adrienne Rich (American) should indite an "Epilogue for a Masque of Purcell." Both
the Englishman Thom Gunn, who teaches in California, and the
American W. S. Merwin, who has lived much abroad, are classified
in a current number of the *Times Literary Supplement* as "transatlantic commuters." This convergence should prove most welcome, since it enables talent to gain a hearing in two worlds, and
most opportune, since it reinforces understanding between the
hemispheres. It brings to a full circle that mutual discernment

which Marianne Moore has so graciously bespoken. In her apt and comprehensive poem "England," the title does not denote the subject; rather, it is the first word of a sentence which rambles through stanzas, pausing briefly to mention Italy, Greece, France, the East, and — in each case — some appealing national attribute. America is the real theme, which is amplified by dwelling upon its evident lack of such distinctive attributes:

> the wild men's land; grass-less, link-less, language-less
>   country in which letters are written
> not in Spanish, not in Greek, not in Latin, not in shorthand,
> but in plain American which cats and dogs can read!

The flat pronunciation of the letter "a" alone — and Miss Moore might have instanced Emily Dickinson, rhyming "alms" with "New England Farms" — has produced "continents of misapprehension." But may it not be, she wonders, that those who misapprehend have not scrutinized the object closely enough? Excellence has been widely scattered throughout history and geography; and, after specifying a few unsuspected examples, the poet concludes:

> . . . should one not have stumbled upon it in America, must one imagine
> that it is not there? It has never been confined to one locality.

10   Statues from Italy: *The Marble Faun*

This was offered in tribute to the centennial of Hawthorne's death in 1964. It was read at his alma mater, Bowdoin College, on April 7, 1964, and published in the volume edited by Roy Harvey Pearce, Hawthorne Centenary Essays (Columbus: Ohio State University Press, 1964). I was glad to have the opportunity for attempting a more rounded appraisal of this exceptional novel than was possible in my thematic study of Hawthorne, Melville, and Poe, The Power of Blackness (New York: Alfred A. Knopf, 1958).

It is a salient fact of American fiction that much of it has been set in foreign parts: most of Melville, James, and Hemingway. Among the rest, nearly every important novelist has managed to write at least one expatriate novel. Since Nathaniel Hawthorne was so congenitally house-bound, so thoroughly identified with his region in almost everything else he wrote, he seems to provide the *a fortiori* case. Certainly *The Marble Faun* stands at some remove from his three other major novels, which came so close together some years before and constitute a kind of New England trilogy. Hawthorne's last completed work is by far his longest one, and he seems to have exercised an author's privilege in considering it his best. Henry James called that judgment into question, in his life of Hawthorne, while conceding that *The Marble Faun* was then probably the most popular of the four novels — the one that was widely sold in Tauchnitz and gift editions. James's revaluation may have had some effect on its declining status in the canon, as well as on the gradual heightening of critical interest in *The Scarlet Letter* and *The House of the Seven Gables*, if not in *The Blithedale Romance*. But *The Marble Faun* was destined from the first to date more than the others, because it was more dependent on changing tastes and literary conventions. Always a self-conscious writer, Hawthorne was never more so than here; yet the result is uncharacteristic because, so far from home and unsure of his ground, he had to reinforce the delicate outlines of an ambitious plan by drawing heavily on bookish precedent and unassimilated tradition.

In the typical odyssey of the man of letters, Italy is cast in the role of siren, whose dalliances have been celebrated by Goethe's elegies, Byron's declamations, Hans Christian Andersen's autobiographical fantasies, and countless other poetic tributes. The special attractions that beckoned American writers and artists seeking to fulfill their "dream of Arcadia" — especially that form of nostalgia which could be diagnosed as "Rome-sickness" — have been chronicled by Van Wyck Brooks. Historic and esthetic factors combined to make "the Pictorial Land" a brilliantly ominous backdrop for the intrigues of Gothic romance, and Hawthorne had made an earlier entry into this storybook realm through the poisonous garden of "Rappaccini's Daughter." For a novel with a Roman setting, his most influential exemplar was Madame de Staël's *Corinne, ou l'Italie*, with its gifted and ill-fated heroine, its cosmopolitan passions, its philosophic discourses, rhapsodic improvisations, and educational tours of the principal monuments. Margaret Fuller, during the Roman phase of her career, came to be regarded as a New England Corinne; and Hawthorne himself explicitly imitates a gesture from Madame de Staël when his lovers look for reflections in the Fountain of Trevi. He justified his choice of terrain in a preface, which — like his other prefaces — is also a plea for imaginative license and, more specifically, an apologia for his chosen genre, the romance, as opposed to the usual novel of manners or social observation. The operative paragraph has been frequently quoted; but, since Hawthorne is never more elusive or ironic than when he claims to be stating his intentions, perhaps it may be quoted once again:

Italy, as the site of his Romance, was chiefly valuable to him as affording a sort of poetic or fairy precinct, where actualities would not be so terribly insisted upon as they are, and must needs be, in America. No author, without a trial, can conceive of the difficulty of writing a romance about a country where there is no shadow, no antiquity, no mystery, no picturesque and gloomy wrong, nor anything but a commonplace prosperity, in broad and simple daylight, as is happily the case with my dear native land. It will be very long, I trust, before romance-writers may find congenial and easily handled themes, either in the annals of our stalwart republic, or in any characteristic and probable events of our individual lives. Romance and poetry, ivy, lichens, and wall-flowers, need ruin to make them grow.

Our reading of this passage is retrospectively slanted by the underlined and amplified paraphrase in James's critical biography, the famous litany of cultural landmarks whose conspicuous absence made the American scene such unpromising territory for the artist: no castles, no cathedrals, et cetera. This may have been a justification for James's decision in favor of what the ivied ruins seemed to promise, the direction pointed by the later Hawthorne and pursued by the early James in "The Last of the Valerii" and *Roderick Hudson*. But if we reread Hawthorne's statement in his own context, the key-phrase seems to be "without a trial." He had prodigiously tried to overcome the difficulties of which he is complaining; and, though he was never the man to relinquish his qualms, surely it may be said — and James would agree — that Hawthorne succeeded. Elsewhere he would have been the first to admit that he had been preoccupied most of his life with the delineation of shadows. Was there "no picturesque and gloomy wrong" to be discerned in the United States on the very eve of the Civil War? Writing from England where he composed his romance during 1859, basing it upon impressions noted during his previous year in Italy, and caught in the ambiguous position of an American between two worlds, he could only view them both with irony. It was dubious homage to the Old World to repair there in search of the sinister. As for the prosperous actualities of the New World, he had come to terms with them in his Custom House sketch prefacing *The Scarlet Letter*, before turning back again into that twilight America whither his European admirers preferred to be led.

He had been at his best in casting a romantic light on the commonplace, or in investing familiar objects with symbolic meanings. Noting down his visit to Arezzo, and to a certain well described by

Boccaccio, he expressed the modest hope that he might be remembered for his description of the town pump at Salem. He had tried and would try again, without success, to work out one or another of the related ancestral themes that had been haunting him during his English sojourn. In America the limitations of his material had stimulated him to ply the techniques of enhancement; in England there was so much paraphernalia, already so enhanced and overfraught with the trappings of association, that he found little or nothing to add. The traditional richness of the symbols seemed to keep him from making effective use of them. He was not near enough to his subject matter, as he had been in America, or far enough from it, as he might be in Italy. There he was too far away, Henry James would feel, and that feeling was doubly significant: "Hawthorne forfeited a precious advantage in ceasing to tread his native soil." Many years afterward, generalizing on *William Wetmore Story and His Friends,* James faced the problem more squarely with a sort of retraction: "the 'picturesque' subject, for literary art, has by no means all its advantage in the picturesque country." Hawthorne really could not be expected to improve upon the coloring of his Italianate scenery. Rather, he exploited it as a richly contrasting background for those somber characterizations which he was better qualified to portray.

Mrs. Hawthorne, in editing *Passages from the French and Italian Note-Books,* parenthetically affirmed that her late husband's insight "was only equalled by his outsight." Such wifely praise is well merited by the *American Notebooks;* and the two capacities are still commensurate, if somewhat bedimmed, in the *English Notebooks.* As for the Continental notebooks, we must await Norman Pearson's complete edition in order to judge them fairly. Yet it might be observed that the *Passages* highlight the hard-headed Yankee facets of Hawthorne's character, whereas his native journal disclosed more of the dreamy transcendentalist. Travel abroad brings out common traits in dissimilar compatriots, and Hawthorne as a tourist stood closer to Mark Twain than to a cultivated European who might have crossed the Alps for his *Italien-*

ische Reise. Though Hawthorne was more the shy puritan than the bumptious philistine, he remained painfully conscious of his provinciality. He did not guy the guides with Mark Twain's stock question, "Is he dead?" But Rome, as a city of tombs and vaults, the graveyard of past cultures, ministered congenially to his lifelong preoccupation with death. *The Innocents Abroad* could even find laughing matter in the grisly cemetery of the Capuchin Convent, elaborately decorated with human bones. Touring the adjacent church a decade before, Hawthorne had happened on one of those physical details which he cherished for their emblematic potentialities: a monk, laid out for burial, suddenly bleeding. Hawthorne had been in Rome less than a month, and here was a whole chapter for his new book: "The Dead Capuchin." Here was the body, then, but where was the mystery?

It seems to have been one of Sophia Hawthorne's editorial principles to omit the main passages that had been worked into *The Marble Faun,* so that her published text does not allow us much opportunity to watch Hawthorne at work. However, we can see him noting down such locations as the Virgin's Shrine, storing up such encounters as the buffalo calf on the Appian Way, and entertaining such conceits as the possibility of lodging in one of the papal tombs at Saint Peter's. We can even learn that his hero's tower room, presided over by the skull in the adjoining oratory, was actually the bedchamber of his fragile daughter, Una. The place that lends its landscape to the subtitle of *The Marble Faun, or The Romance of Monte Beni* is closely modeled on the antique Villa Montauto rented by the Hawthornes for two summer months at Bellosguardo, not far above Florence, where Fenimore Cooper had been — and Henry James was to be — among the various American sojourners. Now habitations are not merely backgrounds but often the very matrix of Hawthorne's fictions, which sustain a cloistered indoor atmosphere occasionally relieved by a breath of fresh air. *The Marble Faun,* though refreshed by a series of sylvan interludes in Tuscany and the Campagna, is set for the most part in the macabre and malarial capital. Hawthorne's strongly ambivalent attitude toward "the sad embrace" of Rome is tensely poised in the remarkable two-page sentence at the beginning of Chapter XXXVI. Spending two successive carnival seasons there, he reacted to the first with all his inherent austerity and participated rather more in the frolic spirit of the second one, as another strategic chapter attests.

Good American husband that he was, he had conscientiously accompanied his "artistic" wife around the monuments and through the galleries, and he had not neglected to do his sight-seeing homework in Murray's guidebooks. This was scarcely an adequate preparation, as he must in his modesty have realized, for acting as *cicerone* to a wide circle of Anglo-American readers eager to wander vicariously among the masterpieces. For all his antiquarian sympathies, he was very easily put off by the faded or encrusted state of so many primitive paintings — a response which, in his wife's estimation, simply asserted his own perfectionism. Actually, philistinism can seldom have ventured farther than the suggestion, in *The Marble Faun*, that it would be charitable to cover the frescoes of Giotto and Cimabue with whitewash. Yet fascination was not always overmastered by inhibition when Hawthorne confronted the female nude, in spite of Sophia's retroactive blue pencil. He lingered nervously over the sensual impenitence of Titian's Magdalen before he concluded, on a note of virtual self-reproof, "Titian must have been a very good-for-nothing old man." Most of the living artists he knew were Americans, and he knew them better as fellow New Englanders than as artists. Hiram Powers, the ingenious Vermonter in Florence, delighted him because he did not "put his life wholly into marble." William Story, the affable dean of the American colony in Rome, had originally turned from law to sculpture in order to execute a statue of his eminent father, Mr. Justice Story of Massachusetts. And when Hawthorne sat for his own bust, the sculptress was Miss Maria Louisa Lander of where else but Salem?

Under the circumstances, it was extremely bold of him to attempt anything in the nature of a *Künstlerroman*, and altogether unlikely that such an attempt would be highly seasoned by *Scènes da la vie de Bohême*. Though his artists have their studios which reflect their respective imaginations, their initial meeting place is a museum, the Campidoglio; and their further walks and talks together have somewhat the aspect of guided tours. Between the travelogue and the story, however, a neutral distance is kept; otherwise the characters would be dwarfed by the age and scope of their environment. The pathos of their individual strivings, as contrasted with the impersonal chill of the museum-world through which they stray, is emphasized in such chapters as "The Emptiness of Picture Galleries." Except for the beggars, the street urchins, and the omnipresent and invisible clergy, we meet few Roman citizens. Nothing beyond the occasional glimpse of a French uniform tells us — and Hawthorne himself seems totally unconcerned — that we are standing on the threshold of the Risorgimento. For nineteenth-century Americans, a trip to Europe was bound to become a return to the past — classical, medieval, or Renaissance in Rome, but never quite modern. The visual analogue for Hawthorne's art was that which Washington Irving had cultivated: the sketchbook of the traveling amateur draftsman, whose water-colors owe much of their gentle charm to the unfamiliar scenes they catch in so artlessly personal a fashion. Fortunately the vistas now opening up before Hawthorne had been familiarized through many a reproduction or set piece, so that he could more or less take their literal contours for granted and concentrate upon his psychological evocations.

In his preface he apologizes for having made fictional use of certain actual sculptures by his artist-friends. Such an acknowledgment failed to allay the wrath of Arnold Schönberg when Thomas Mann ascribed the twelve-tone system of musical composition to the demonic hero of *Doktor Faustus*. But Hawthorne's American sculptor, Kenyon, seems a mild and marginal figure by comparison, an observer-spokesman who is clearly related to the artist-inventors of Hawthorne's tales, endowed with similar powers of cold penetration, but not so obsessive and more urbane. His relation to the title character is that of counselor if not confidant, and there are moments between them that remind us of the all but psychoanalytic interchange between Chillingworth and Dimmesdale in *The Scarlet Letter*. In speaking of a title role, we are stretching a point, since the marble faun itself can be no other than that of Praxiteles, from which the narrative takes its Capitoline departure. The faunlike human being, Donatello, linked by the Florentine sculptor's name with his boyish David, is unquestionably a creature of flesh and blood. What comes into question — what gives the book its more didactic English title, *Transformation* — would seem to be his hard-won acquisition of a soul. The author of *A Wonder-Book* and *Tanglewood Tales* looked upon "this race of fauns" as "the most delightful of all that antiquity imagined." A story "with all sorts of fun and pathos in it" might be contrived about their intermingling with humanity. Hawthorne could be trusted to moderate the fun; and it remains a striking thought that he chose, in the very year of Darwin's *Origin of Species*, to celebrate "a natural . . . link betwixt human and brute life, with something of a divine character intermingled."

From the cerebral Hawthorne, attracted by the very paganism of the theme, Italy seems to have compelled a belated respect for the animal side of human nature — not in its uneasy coexistence with the spiritual side, but in a pristine purity of its own. Donatello, to the woman who loves him, seems "a creature in a state of development less than what mankind has attained, yet the more perfect within itself for that very deficiency." Strange, sweet, playful, friendly, rustic, wild, charming — Hawthorne's epithets make quite a pet of him. He may be a throwback to the childhood of the race, an atavism from the Golden Age, when all men were spontaneously happy because they lived in uncorrupted harmony with nature. Hence he has the gift, or has had it before his Roman exposure, of conversing with the animals. His lineage, both natural and supernatural, can be traced back to the Greek migrations, and also can be linked with a local Tuscan myth sadly involving a tutelary naiad. The ambiguity of his whole situation is invisibly symbolized by a train of speculation to which Hawthorne keeps coyly returning until the last sentence: whether or not Donatello's curly hair conceals the hirsute and pointed ears of a faun, not to mention whether he possesses "a certain caudal appendage." This tricksy sprite coalesces with the image of a contemporary who is hardly less vague, the Count of Monte Beni, a young Italian aristocrat who does not know his own age and has never read Dante. The romance about him was inspired, so the narrator informs us, not so much by the Marble Faun of Praxiteles as by Kenyon's unfinished clay model of Donatello's head, with its groping hints of his perplexity, struggle, and change.

For his pair of heroines, Hawthorne chose to reincarnate an old antithesis: blond for innocence and brunette for experience, as in The Blithedale Romance. Hilda, like the fair Priscilla, would have been called a White Lily by D. H. Lawrence; but where Priscilla's feelings were externalized, Hilda's are projected from within. "Her womanhood is of the ethereal type, and incompatible with any shadow of darkness or evil," says her fellow American admirer Kenyon, who has modeled a replica of her hand — even as Hiram Powers had of his little daughter's — and has put her into plaster as maidenhood gathering a snowdrop. Hilda is an orphan whose transparent virginity seems to have won her the unmolested freedom of the menacing city. She has not ceased to be, as Hawthorne does not tire of reminding us, a daughter of the Puritans. It is paradoxical and yet not inappropriate that she practices her own cult of the Virgin, tending the lamp at a shrine which adjoins her studio amid the doves on the roof top. Her pursuit of the arts, as Hawthorne intimates that a woman's should be, is sensitively appreciative rather than strikingly original; in short, her skill is that of a professional copyist. In vivid contradistinction to her, the other heroine, who comes as close as any character to being the real protagonist of the drama, is not only an ambitious painter but seems to specialize in forceful depictions of "the idea of woman, acting the part of a revengeful mischief towards man." Over and over again the subjects of her sketches compulsively re-enact the battle of the sexes, which invariably culminates in the grim triumph of aggressive feminism: Jael assassinating Sisera, Judith exulting over Holofernes, Salome with the head of John the Baptist.

Miriam Schaefer's family name accords her a doubtful advantage over the other characters, since it proves to be an assumed one. She proves to be indeed the darkest of Hawthorne's dark ladies. Though her fate is not so blankly tragic as Zenobia's at Blithedale, her origin is considerably more mysterious and her allure is appreciably more magnetic. Her appearance seems to have been suggested to Hawthorne by the sight of a raven-haired Jewess at a Lord Mayor's banquet in London some years before. Though the precise details of Miriam's identity continue to be shrouded in secrecy, she is evidently the hyphenated child of an Anglo-Jewish mother married into a decadent line of Italian nobility. Whenever the veil is lifted a little, the breath of a scandal is felt; but it is wafted to us so delicately that we can never be sure how far she has been compromised by it. She has experienced sorrow and suffering, obviously; but to what extent has she experienced sin? Can she be innocently involved and not be contaminated? Hawthorne exhibits his usual compunctions in equivocating between fatality and the responsible will. Artistic allusion conspires with historical innuendo to associate Miriam with the favorite Renaissance heroine of the Romantics, Beatrice Cenci, and with the dark doom of incest and parricide related by Stendhal and dramatized by Shelley. Historically speaking, it would now seem that the veritable Beatrice was less victimized by her father and more compliant in his murder than the notorious tale would have had it. Yet her tearful visage, as Henry Murray points out, "had been assimilated to the most moving theme of the current mythology of the heart, that of *abused female innocence.*"

Her portrait by Guido Reni in the Palazzo Barberini, which was rumored to have been painted shortly before her execution, was the most widely admired and the most commonly reproduced picture of the day. Pilgrims sought it out with a curiosity which could only be compared to the subsequent and slightly more sophisticated vogue of that *femme fatale*, the "Mona Lisa." "The History is written in the Painting," Charles Dickens had responded to it in his *Pictures from Italy*, "written, in the dying girl's face, by Nature's own hand." Miriam and Kenyon might well debate the merits of Guido's "Battle between Saint Michael and Satan," but his Beatrice seemed beyond the reach of mere art. She had dominated a recognition scene in Herman Melville's *Pierre* — "that sweetest, most touching, but most awful of all feminine heads," comparable in certain respects to the "maidens of tropical nations," Melville added, dreaming of the South Seas, and he eagerly procured a copy for himself at Rome in 1857. More significantly, he was to dramatize his relationship with Hawthorne through the reserved and enigmatic dialogue between Clarel, the hero of his long narrative poem, and Vine, the older man whose name embodies the metaphor that Melville later used in his monody on Hawthorne's death.

> 'Twas Vine, He wore that nameless look
> About the mouth — so hard to brook —
> Which in the Cenci portrait shows,
> Lost in each copy, oil or paint;
> Lost, or else slurred, as 'twere a hint
> Which if received few might sustain.

The Cenci portrait was a crucial link in the tenuous chain that bound Hawthorne and Melville together, an emblem of that sense of guilt for the world's corruption which they seem to have momentarily shared. Even Henry James, though cognizant of the disillusioning afterthoughts, could meditate on "our prolonged sentimental consumption of the tenderest morsel, as we have mostly felt it, in all pictorial portraiture." It is not surprising, then, that Reni's Beatrice became a talisman for Hawthorne, or that his recurrent adjective for her was "magical." Her influence was present already in the pathetic and poisoned decoy, Beatrice Rappaccini. In the notebooks, the expected tribute is duly paid: "It is the most profoundly wrought picture in the world." Yet Hawthorne, who repeatedly came back to see it, was shrewd enough to wonder whether the canvas itself would exert the same appeal if the beholder were unaware of the extraneous associations. Nevertheless, it is Hilda's supreme accomplishment, in *The Marble Faun*, to be able to copy the original and to capture all its nuances. More than artistry, her accomplishment presupposes affinity.

"She is a fallen angel," Hilda comments on Beatrice, " — fallen, and yet sinless." Miriam cannot let so naïve a contradiction pass by her unchallenged; and when she reminds Hilda of Beatrice's tragedy, Hilda becomes implacably severe in her condemnation: "Yes, yes; it was terrible guilt, an inexpiable crime, and she feels it to be so." Thus the conversation leads us back, as all occasions do, to Miriam's secret. This has its malign personification in her model, the villain of the piece, whose speeches are well-nigh inaudible and whose misdeeds are never quite pinned down. Visually, he is picturesqueness itself, "dark, bushy-bearded, wild of aspect and attire," ready to pose as saint or sinner without revealing his own personality. Hawthorne presents him enveloped in "Subterranean Reminiscences" and heralded by a legend of the catacombs not unlike the motif of the Wandering Jew: a man-demon restlessly seeking a companion in misery. Miriam is shadowed by her specter, is presumably blackmailed by his obscure claim upon her, and is threatened with an ostracism from which the ardent Donatello suddenly acts to deliver her. In the one decisive action of the plot, prompted by her glance of mute entreaty, Donatello seizes upon an opportune moment to plunge her evil genius down to his death — and afterward to his startling final emergence as the dead Capuchin, whose corpse turns out to be the accusing symbol of their crime. The height from which he has been thrown is the Tarpeian Rock above the Forum, whence the ancient criminals were dispatched. As for the timeless depth it overhangs, Miriam has just declared to Hilda: "The chasm was merely one of the orifices of that pit of blackness that lies beneath us, everywhere."

The deed, from which the doers recoil in spontaneous horror, has had an unseen and half-unseeing witness; and that is where Hawthorne, whose habitual stance is the aloofness of the detached onlooker, comes forward to score a Dostoevskian point. "While there is a single guilty person in the universe," so Hilda reproaches Miriam, "each innocent one must feel his innocence tortured by that guilt." Miriam, though she has not raised a hand, is implicated as Donatello's accomplice. Hilda, who unwittingly found herself looking on and registering the shock, feels caught up in a chain of complicity which runs around the world. Consequently it is her own self-portrait that she beholds in the pictured and copied lineaments of Beatrice Cenci, and the resemblance is generally remarked and variously interpreted when Signor Panini depicts her as "Innocence, dying of a blood-stain." In virginal discovery of evil, as a lone sufferer for the sin of another, she wanders through the labyrinth distraught until she finds herself at the utimate center, "The World's Cathedral," Saint Peter's, where she paradoxically endeavors to ease her Puritan conscience within the confessional. This episode would be even more extraordinary if it had not been anticipated by a novel which Hawthorne may well have read, Charlotte Brontë's *Villette*. There the issue is more centrally the romance between a Protestant heroine and a Catholic hero. Here it is more tangential, since Hilda cannot claim the Church's solace without embracing its doctrines, and her Kenyon will be shocked by the halfway lengths to which she seems willing to go. Yet it serves to discharge the mounting tensions between respect and suspicion which drew Hawthorne to, and repelled him from, the "Altars and Incense" of Roman Catholicism.

The two accomplices seem the less likely couple to have been drawn together. But Donatello has acted to share the burden of Miriam's moral estrangement, and Miriam is more than willing to share the moral responsibility for Donatello's act. Momentarily, during an interlude in the Borghese Gardens, he had shown her his bucolic world; he had set everyone dancing, whereupon her nemesis had interrupted the dance. What seemed to be Arcadia was Eden, after all, whose denizens were foreordained to fall and be expelled. Miriam and Donatello would seem to be bound forever by the serpentine coils of their guilty collusion, and we might expect them to take their further way like Adam and Eve — or like the young groom and bride at the end of "The May-Pole of Merry Mount." Yet Donatello's immediate reaction is to flinch from Miriam's tender advances; when she tests him by laying her hand next to his, he refrains from taking it; thereupon he must leave her and make a penitential retreat to his tower in the Appenines. There his sympathetic visitor and traveling companion is Kenyon, who in turn receives a clandestine visit from Miriam. His reserve has prevented her from confiding in him before, albeit she might have provided more inspiration than Hilda for the smoldering voluptuousness of that tigress-like Cleopatra which he has somehow been sculpting. Now, when Miriam pours out her heart to him, he is able to reassure her of Donatello's love. It is as if the crime had to take place and be fully assimilated before the passion could manifest itself and be consummated. The two experiences are so intertwined that Kenyon arrives at this severe, if tentative, verdict: "Worthy of Death, but not unworthy of Love."

Love, in a Hawthornesque efflorescence, blossoms among the ruins. The lovers are reunited under the blessing of the bronze pontiff who oversees the market place at Perugia; and though they subsequently disappear and reappear in altered guises, Hawthorne leaves their wanderings uncharted to give them privacy for sexual fulfillment. This, too, is marked by its symbolic statue — a fallen goddess, if not an angel, recovered from underground, pieced together, and hailed as the long lost and vastly more beautiful original of the Venus di Medici. Hawthorne's notebooks again contain an account of the excavations that gave him the notion, as well as an account of his prolonged flirtation with the Venus di Medici herself, standing "in chaste and naked grace" at the Uffizi in Florence: "I felt a kind of tenderness for her; an affection, not as if she were one woman, but all womanhood in one." So bemused was he by his morning communion with her that, after spending his evening with the Brownings, he could not help concluding his daily notation: "The Venus di Medici has a dimple on her chin." Melville, paying his respects in a lecture on "Statuary in Rome," had reminiscently likened her modest pose to that of the native maidens he had seen in the Typee Valley. In conferring an extra dimension upon his characters by associating them with counterparts in the sphere of art, Hawthorne resembles Proust. To be sure, his range is much more limited; his taste is insecure, to say the least. His preference for sculpture, rather than painting, lends his creations a tangible quality which they might otherwise lack. It also favors a marble whiteness over the colors on the painter's palette. He was emphatic in his objections to the flesh-tinted statues of the Anglo-Roman sculptor John Gibson.

Hawthorne may or may not have read Lessing's *Laokoon*, albeit the snake-entangled group at the Vatican could not but appeal to his allegorical instincts. Kenyon's esthetics are not unlike Lessing's, however, when he criticizes the "Dying Gladiator" and remarks that "in any sculptural subject, there should be a moral stand-still, since there must of necessity be a physical one." The approach of *The Marble Faun* is sculptural; the stasis of the ages is upon it; and its movement is reducible to a sequence of standstills or *tableaux vivants*. For a longish novel, it has a small cast: mainly the four characters introduced in the first chapter, plus the model whose protean disguises are not enough to enlarge the *dramatis personae*. Three of the four are artists in some degree and, therefore, primarily spectators: the sculptor, the painter, the copyist. The fourth, idly posing for them, would seem to be the most passive of all; yet his quick shove is the single burst of activity; and his psychic transformation could be rendered as a metamorphosis in stone. All of them strike attitudes and engage in colloquies: duets, trios, and quartets in varying combinations. The ambulatory pace and unwieldy pageantry put us in the mood for opera — let us say *La Vestale*. The construction of the book displays Hawthorne's neatly symmetrical workmanship. There are fifty chapters, each with its essayistic heading and its topographical shift. The fatal climax occurs betimes in Chapter XVIII, followed by a remorseful withdrawal extending through Chapter XXXV, and completed by an accelerating countermovement toward the center and toward an equilibrium. The total pattern may be roughly divided into three equal sections: the first is melodrama; the second, pastoral; and the third, carnival.

The style is more formal in conversation than in the author's narration, which does not differ much from the whimsical tone and speculative habit of the notebooks. In operatic or Shakespearean fashion, characters apostrophize situations or address themselves in streams of self-consciousness:

"Be quiet," said Miriam to her own heart, pressing her hand hard upon it. "Why shouldst thou throb now? Hast thou not endured more terrible things than this?"

The second person singular is warranted, here and elsewhere, by the assumption that some speeches have been translated from the Italian. Yet, though she professes to have thrown decorum to the winds, Miriam's heart-to-heart talk with Kenyon about Hilda — presumably in English — leaves something to be desired in the way of untrammeled expressiveness:

"Oh, you are right!" said Miriam; "I never questioned it; though, as I told you, when she cast me off, it severed some few remaining bonds between me and decorous womanhood. But were there anything to forgive, I do forgive her. May you win her virgin heart; for methinks there can be few men in this evil world who are not more unworthy of her than yourself."

It could not be argued that the spoken language sounds much more colloquial in Hawthorne's other writings, and it may be relevant to recall that he himself was noted for taciturnity. Yet, in his own person, he maintained an open and amiable relationship with his reader, whom he was fond of taking by the hand while discursively pointing out the sights, illustrating with anecdotes, and moralizing with symbols. Thus the first page of *The Marble Faun*, among better-known statuary, calls attention to a sculptured child between a dove and a snake — an allegory of "the Human Soul, with its choice of Innocence or Evil." A casual fig tree at the side of the road, twisted by the grasp of a clambering grapevine, becomes an object-lesson inviting a temperance lecture. Kenyon, who makes this observation on Hawthorne's behalf, is constantly being challenged by Donatello to supply a pat moral for each passing instance. Hence Kenyon plays the moralist at the conclusion: looking back at Donatello's involvement and retribution, he proposes a pair of alternative morals; but they are mutually incompatible, and Hilda is both too hopeful and too reverent to accept either of them.

The second, the theological alternative, has been more commonly accepted by critics. This invokes the Augustinian doctrine of *felix culpa*, the fault that bears a fortunate consequence. In the long run, it may be all for the best that the Faun blundered into his mortal trespass; it has taught him the ethical basis for distinguishing between good and evil; and, by struggling through that grim education, he has achieved a higher state. Such is the opinion that Miriam naturally holds. Accordingly the book becomes in essence a *psychomachia*, a conflict within the soul; there the Archangel and the Devil pursue their unending fight; and it is fitting that the bust of John Milton can be viewed in Kenyon's studio. "Did Adam fall, that we might ultimately rise to a far loftier paradise than his?" If we retain any doubt, if we follow Lawrence's advice for dealing with Hawthorne and "listen to the diabolic undertone," we should reconsider the prior alternative, which is based on naturalistic premises and opposes a pessimistic heresy to an optimistic orthodoxy, pagan degeneration to Christian regeneration. This entails belief in man as potentially a happy and healthy animal, whose "genial nature" could not but be warped by the serious pressures and complex demands of latter-day living. Such a conception looks forward to the hard primitivism of Nietzsche, rather than backward to the soft primitivism of Rousseau. Though Hawthorne's treatment of sex is ostensibly tepid — as we might expect from a son of the Puritans lately accredited to Queen Victoria — there are Lawrentian implications in the love story he does not tell but insinuates between chapters and behind scenes, which has its subterranean archetype in the buried and rediscovered fragments of Venus.

Conceivably those alternatives might be reconciled by being transposed into modes of twentieth-century thinking. That the Fall should give rise to self-improvement is a hypothesis which parallels Toynbee's theory of challenge and response in the growth of cultures. That civilization should be attained at the cost of a certain anguish fits in with the Freudian progression of consciousness from the id to the superego. Hawthorne's hero pays the price for evolving by literally undergoing imprisonment, while Miriam concludes by kneeling in prayer — meaningfully at the Pantheon, inasmuch as the frame of reference has broadened from the Catholic to the pantheistic. Her honeymoon with Donatello has ended, in the masquerade of a Contadina and Peasant, amid the "polluted flowers" and grotesque confusions of the carnival   a kalcidoscope which Hawthorne cleverly shakes, instead of carefully tracing his patterns to a detailed culmination. His ambiguous ending so mystified readers that he was forced to add an explanatory postscript to the second edition wherein he refrained again from explaining his ambiguous postulate. Understandably, he did not feel obliged to unravel everything like Mrs. Radcliffe, and he had gone further than ever before in moving "between the Real and the Fantastic." Yet it had been harder this time to stay on middle ground; he had oscillated between an archaeological reality and an allegorical fantasy; his vision of evil had become so generalized that even James would complain of vagueness. Hawthorne's defense would be Hilda's attack upon "this inclination, which most people have, to explain away the wonder and mystery of everything." And it is through Hilda's eyes, through her sense of wonder, that the final prospect is relayed to us.

Hilda is the precursor, not merely of James's international heroines, but of his private ambassador who discovers that Europe is more entangling than could be foreseen. She has not only shared the guilty knowledge of her two friends' transgression; she has been lured, through her duty of delivering Miriam's packet, into the Palazzo Cenci itself; for even Hilda must go underground, as it were; and during her incarceration, the Virgin's Lamp is extinguished. Hawthorne is loth to account for her temporary disappearance, except by opaque allusions to those clerical auspices which she had once besought and which seem to have the situation well in hand. Inevitably, she and Kenyon are brought together in their mutual loneliness. Homeward bound, she is still linked to the sphere they are leaving through Miriam's bridal gift, the Etruscan bracelet with its seven sepulchral gems. Hawthorne is never more himself than in the nostalgic paragraph where, mingling his sensibilities with hers, he contrasts the "crumbly magnificence" of Rome with the "native homeliness" of her New England village. Easing "the exile's pain," he loses no opportunity to bring the parable home by transatlantic cross-reference: the weather, the vegetation, the sanitation, the housing, the sociability, the wine versus the cider. It is an American who refuses to join in Donatello's improvised bacchanal; it is a less dignified member of our "Gothic race" whose confetti damages the dignity of a Roman Senator's coachman. And it is "An Aesthetic Company," a moonlight ramble of young American artists, which makes the Via Sacra reverberate to the choral strains of "Hail, Columbia!" When Kenyon goes back, the sculpturesque clouds will be his sole art gallery; yet he has seen no spectacle as gorgeous as a sunset in America.

Half a generation later, Roderick Hudson would opt for Europe, where his talent would fizzle out at Rome. His fellow sculptor, the Franco-Italo-American Gloriani, who is a cynic and seems at times a charlatan, would reappear at Paris in *The Ambassadors*, where he would personify the wise maturity of the artist who has intensely lived. If an innocent New World met a corrupting Old World to frame a beginner's formula for James, he could develop the corollaries and vary the complications: a refined example is the adjustment of the Italian prince in *The Golden Bowl*, who is so propitiously named Amerigo. From *Daisy Miller* (1878) to Tennessee Williams' novella *The Roman Spring of Mrs. Stone* (1950), we could trace the decline in American innocence. In William Styron's recent and powerful novel *Set This House on Fire*, the agent of corruption is an American; the Italian peasants are the true innocents; and a Hollywood company has appropriately been producing a film about Beatrice Cenci. Hawthorne, almost exactly a century before, intervened none too soon in repatriating his two expatriates; and his own return journey across the Atlantic took place not long after he had finished his romance. His four remaining years were not truly productive, doubtless for a complication of reasons. One of them may have been that what James suggestively calls the apple of Europe had turned—even more suggestively— into a "Borgia cup." At all events, though *The Marble Faun* may not be as compact or controlled as Hawthorne's former successes, there are moments when it reaches farther or plunges deeper. His horizons opened late in life; but it must have been a great satisfaction, for the contriver of "Drowne's Wooden Image" or "The Snow Image," to reshape his fancies in classic marble.

France-Amérique:
The Transatlantic Refraction

This short conspectus served to open a discussion of Franco-American literary relations at a meeting of the Modern Language Association in Chicago on December 29, 1963. It will be reprinted in a volume of essays on the subject edited by the chairman of that group, Professor Frederick J. Hoffman, having been printed meanwhile in Comparative Literature Studies, I, 2 (1964). I owe the quotation from Balzac's novel — transcribed from Melville's copy of the Katherine Wormeley translation — to my former student, Walker Cowen, whose Harvard dissertation on Melville's marginalia should be published before too long.

It is now thirty years since Bernard Faÿ inaugurated a chair in American civilization at the Collège de France. By assisting at his lectures, almost in the literal sense of the idiom, Gertrude Stein — with her assistant, Alice B. Toklas — was returning the extravagant compliments with which Faÿ had recently prefaced a translation of her turgid autobiographical novel, *The Making of Americans.* Younger Americans then at the Sorbonne found themselves occasionally crossing the Rue Saint-Jacques for that weekly reunion. Those were the opening months of the New Deal at home, and the sprightly lecturer succeeded in relaying its atmosphere of excitement. Yet, though he was nothing if not *au courant,* his course was geared to the clichés and cadres of a French academic syllabus. It never reached the regime of Franklin D. Roosevelt, at least not while I was attending; but I well recall that, in its vivid evocation of Theodore Roosevelt, a dynastic note was already sounded. T. R. was presented as a Grand Monarch, with a Spanish Question of his own, and Oyster Bay as his Petit Trianon. Just as Louis XIV patronized Molière, Racine, and Boileau, so our *roi soleil* had his court circle, whose common forename — conveniently for purposes of note-taking — alliterated with Harvard: Henry James, Henry Adams, and Henry Cabot Lodge. The rest was much in the same vein: familiar words to an unrecognizable tune. The stranger it sounded to us, and the farther it deviated from its sources in fact, the better it adapted to its new climate of preconception.

Bernard Faÿ has since disappeared into an oblivion which he sought and earned, after a desperate effort to exert his mediating talents during the German occupation. I mention him now, not merely because he exemplifies that distortion which distance lends to the view, but because his approach is happily uncharacteristic. A long and percipient line of French observers, stemming from Tocqueville, has viewed America not as a repetition of the feudal past but an adumbration of the democratic future. We might note that, as France itself has moved closer to those *Scènes de la vie future*, in the phrase of Georges Duhamel, the reports of its *voyageurs* have become increasingly severe. But, the more they have been put off by what they can only regard as the irrational elements in American life, the more they have been fascinated by the reflection of those elements in American literature. Far from minimizing the cultural differences, French critics have been notably receptive to the uniqueness of our major writers. Melville and Hawthorne, misunderstood in their homeland more often than not, met with contemporary appreciation from Philarète Chasles, Emile Montégut, and E. D. Forgues. Faulkner made a serious critical impact, before his compatriots had fully awakened to him, through the translations of Maurice Edgar Coindreau. Books by American authors have figured early and continuously in the English curricula of the French universities, where scholars have done more to interpret them than in any other country except our own, and not excluding Great Britain.

One country's image of another is likely to depend on its image of itself, particularly when its culture is as highly organized and systematically diffused as that of France. Our culture, from that vantage point, has seemed both antithetical and complementary. Thus our first ambassador, Benjamin Franklin, came to personify the *philosophes'* answer to the *ancien régime*. Conversely, it was the French emigrant, Crèvecoeur, who voiced Europe's hope for the United States as a place of asylum and a melting-pot of races. Chateaubriand dramatized the antithesis between the New World and the Old through the contrasting figures of the noble savage, Chactas, and his world-weary interlocutor, René. The significant contrast, in the American episodes of Chateaubriand's *Mémoires d'outre-tombe*, was between his social criticism and his romanticized landscapes. Perhaps because civilization could have but one center, for Frenchmen, they have been peculiarly susceptible to the attractions of the uncivilized. Their taste for the primitive and the exotic was aptly gratified by the Leatherstocking novels. Cooper himself preferred to treat more civilized material, but his reading public wanted more Indian-fighting, and consequently his treatment of *Bas-de-Cuir* became more and more idyllic. D. H. Lawrence draws an amusing picture of "*Monsieur Fenimore Cooper, le grand écrivain américain,*" dreaming about the pathless forest in a Parisian boudoir. The situation might serve as a paradigm for Franco-American literary relations: for Americans who go abroad only to rediscover themselves, and for cosmopolites who welcome them on condition that they remain outlanders.

The striking exception is Poe, who has indeed been taken to the bosom of French poetry, albeit on the problematic assumption that he was ostracized in his native land. His America was described by Baudelaire as "a vast cage, a big counting-house" — a large-scale application of those bourgeois influences which European artists were engaging themselves to flout. More than Poe's work, the legend of his life made him a generic literary hero, gallicized and virtually canonized by the diaeresis superimposed on his name: *Poë, poète, poésie*. The philistines were the *Eux* of Mallarmé's sonnet, while Poe remained the *Lui-même*, whose tomb would become a monument for all *poètes maudits*. Most of his own Gallic touches are superficial, such as the nonexistent Rue Morgue; but it seems pertinent that, when he chose to elucidate his mysteries, he chose Paris as their setting; and his paragon of ratiocination had to be a Frenchman, Monsieur C. Auguste Dupin. The cycle of the Symbolistes, which drew inspiration from Poe, counted among its adherents two Franco-Americans, Stuart Merrill and Francis Viélé-Griffin, and was rounded out by an Anglo-American epilogue in the person of T. S. Eliot. The light that it reflected back on its origin was not primitivism so much as decadence. A storm of black snow, reported from Michigan, seemed to the Goncourt brothers highly appropriate for "the land of Poe." Baudelaire had resolved the paradox by declaring that America was "young and old at once." Possibly, as Lawrence would speculate, it had rotted before it was ripe.

Southward, it could become a symbol of overripe tradition. Out of ancestral nostalgia Julien Green could raise a backdrop for *Sud,* where a psychological melodrama culminates in the outbreak of the Civil War. Yves Berger's recent novel, *Le Sud,* covers more ground, since it imposes a storybook Dixie upon an actual Provence, and — for geographical rather than sexual reasons — names its heroine Virginie. Yet the original idyll of youthful freshness, the recurrent sentimental dream of *la vie des fauves,* is not altogether lost today. It could be rediscovered in Chicago by Simone de Beauvoir, retreating from the café dialectic of *Les Mandarins,* which is dedicated to Nelson Algren. To Michel Butor, whose quest for novelty has driven him across most of the states in *Mobile,* the variety encountered is precisely as rich as the assortment of ice creams at Howard Johnson restaurants. However, the patterns of ordinary existence, with their neon lights and their jazz rhythms, no longer differ widely from one hemisphere to another. And the technological style of our epoch, whether or not we call it Americanization, has been reshaping artistic forms everywhere. Walt Whitman pioneered in liberating formal verse. Claude-Edmonde Magny's study of American novelists, which in turn has affected French fiction, *L'Age du roman américain,* might almost have been entitled *L'Age du roman cinématographique.* But Jean-Paul Sartre, hailing John Dos Passos as the inventor of this technique, simply reveals his own lack of conversance with Dos Passos' model, Joyce's *Ulysses.*

Shortly after the last war, on the occasion of his single visit to

the United States, M. Sartre argued very frankly: "There is one
American literature for Americans and another for the French."
Exercising their categorical flair, the French have established a
twentieth-century canon, *Les Cinq Grands*, comprising Faulkner,
Hemingway, Dos Passos, Steinbeck, and Caldwell. With due respect for all five, most American critics would look upon them with
varying degrees of admiration. Most of us were rather surprised
when John Steinbeck, following Faulkner and Hemingway, received the Nobel Prize in Literature. We should not have been;
we should have recalled that its first recipient was the banal Sully-
Prudhomme, and that the Swedish Academy is not more immune
to provinciality and propaganda than any other self-appointed literary authority. We could appreciate the sociological interest behind its first award to an American; for, though Sinclair Lewis
may seem homespun to us, he manifested a certain exoticism for
Europeans — as the Hungarian critic, Jean Hankiss, pointed out
in *La Littérature et la vie*. But the laureation of Pearl Buck —
which was more of a recognition for China — demonstrated that
well-meaning international sympathy, even at a second remove
and without artistic distinction, could be the sole criterion. In
Russia it is not surprising to see the party line determine the
vogue of foreign as well as Soviet books. Some writers, like Jack
London, gain more honor in other countries than their own: Mau-
passant, Anatole France, and Romain Rolland have exported better than they have endured in France.

The novels on Dr. Sartre's five-name shelf, he maintains, have
taught his compatriots — Camus, for example — the lesson of action. The French are by no means unaware that our literature
contains other works in a more analytic genre; but, having invented
that genre, they feel they have little to learn about it from us.
Hence the up-to-date *Histoire littéraire des Etats-unis* of Cyrille
Arnavon emphasizes the rougher and readier aspects at the expense
of Henry James's "Byzantinism." James, of course, had learned
many technical lessons from the French masters, and generously
acknowledged them in his criticism. Like Henry Adams, he as-

sumed the posture of a pilgrim genuflecting before the shrines of Gothic tradition. His vocation had been confirmed by a vision, his boyish dream-adventure of the Louvre, as interpreted by Leon Edel, wherein the Galerie d'Apollon became his "bridge over into Style." The esthetic spectacle of Paris, glittering before Lambert Strether like an iridescent jewel, held its ethical hazards, to be sure. James's American master, Hawthorne, on his brief and belated trip through France, had registered a comparable reaction to his initial *table d'hôte*. Hawthorne had decided that English cooking is "better for one's moral and spiritual nature," since it leaves you in no doubt that "you are gratifying your animal needs." Whereas, "in dealing with these French delicacies, you delude yourself into the idea that you are cultivating your taste while satisfying your appetite." Puritanism has seldom armed itself more sternly against less vicious temptations.

James, in a novel like *The American* or a tale like "Madame de Mauves," worked out classic parables of the encounter between American innocence and Continental sophistication, always conceived from the standpoint of a neophyte venturing beyond his depth. Guile at first hand, the accumulation of power, the mechanics of intrigue, the dynamics of enterprise, and the specific pitfalls of worldly experience may have seemed to subsist beneath his novelistic notice; all the more reason for admiring that writer whom he considered to have made the most of such themes, Balzac. Curiously enough, Balzac seems also to have been the novelist best represented among the books read by Melville during his silent years. One of the most emphatic of his frequent pencilings underscores a description of New York in *The Two Brothers*, an English translation of *La Rabouilleuse*: "a place where speculation and individualism are carried to the highest pitch, where the brutality of self-interest attains to cynicism, where man, essentially isolated, is compelled to push his way for himself and by himself, where politeness does not exist . . ." Melville had tackled the Balzacian problem of the young provincial struggling against the metropolis in *Pierre*, with equivocal results. The traditional vehicle of our nineteenth-century fiction, the romance, did not lend itself to the complex realities of modern circumstance. The process of adapting the form to the subject had to be helped by recourse to the French naturalists; Edward Eggleston was inspired by Taine, Frank Norris by Zola, and finally Theodore Dreiser by Balzac.

It was as the habitat of natural man that our continent had originally appealed to the French. Yet our men of letters, inhibited by nineteenth-century notions of gentility, sometimes envied the freedom of their Gallic *confrères* to explore all manner of subjects. James wrote a letter to Howells, after a heady evening in the circle of Flaubert, wistfully confiding that Edmond de Goncourt's latest yellowback would set out to investigate — if I may quote James verbatim — "a whorehouse *de province*." This would not do, as he hardly needed to comment, for the readers of *The Atlantic Monthly*. Half a century afterward, after the First World War, it would be the Americans who were breaking through the barriers of polite constraint and the French who were beginning to follow a transatlantic initiative. Doubtless those barriers had meanwhile been breaking down further. The point of intersection between the two literatures was Paris during its brilliant period of *l'Entre-deux-guerres*. Writers and artists of both nationalities, and of many others, fraternized there with consequences which have continued to fructify. Expatriation was an ideal apprenticeship for the lost-and-found generation of Hemingway. Henry Miller felt more at ease amid the seedy bohemianism of the Latin Quarter than in returning homeward to *The Air-Conditioned Nightmare*. Since the Second World War, *The Paris Review* has offered a showcase for promising newcomers, along with a forum for advice from their elders; but, contrasted with the footloose exploits of the twenties, it is bound to seem elegiac and secondhand.

Our problem has had no definitive resolution, nor is it reducible to an explicit formula. Howard Mumford Jones's study, *America and French Culture*, deals comprehensively with political, religious, and social backgrounds. It is not Professor Jones's fault that, in the thirty-six years since his volume appeared, there has been no second volume dealing with the American reception of French literature. There are a number of parallel studies from the other side, which would seem to show that intercultural exchange is contingent and episodic by nature. Meetings of first-rate minds are as rare as renderings by first-rate translators, and such shocks of recognition deserve to be studied for their own sake. The shift in atmospheric conditions, when moving between the hemispheres either way, produces a refraction which must be allowed for and reckoned with by comparative literature. A massive dissertation by Simon Jeune has just come out of the University of Paris, *De F. T. Graindorge à A. O. Barnabooth*, which surveys the roles played by American figures in the works of French writers between the Civil War and the First World War. The record is even more crowded than might be expected, and quite as entertaining up to a point. After that it can become depressing to watch the persistently rigid exaggerations reduced from types to stereotypes: the quaint *peau-rouge*, the happy *noir*, the bumbling *homme d'affaires*, the independent *jeune fille*. The two spokesmen mentioned in the title, as irony will have it, are typical of no one except their respective authors, Taine and Larbaud.

Yet we should have to be even more depressed if, turning around the telescope, we asked ourselves what conceptions of French character have penetrated to *outre-mer*. The spirit of finesse does not travel as well as the spirit of geometry. Taking the long view, we are apt to be struck by externals — and, in the case of France, by a conscious preoccupation with ceremony, form, and dandyism. Dr. Jeune's opposite number might have to call his thesis *From Monsieur Beaucaire to Monsieur Verdoux*, and to illustrate it from the old comic strip of Gaston and Alphonse. The theme of *An American in Paris* not only has been orchestrated by Gershwin, but is put through several maudlin variations each year by Hollywood. Our warmest friends in Dr. Jeune's *galère* have been such champions of material progress as Jules Verne, whereas such thoughtful pessimists as Renan are numbered among the foes of *l'américanisme*. Generalizing broadly about our literary interrelationship, we might say that the eastward trend across the Atlantic has been largely a traffic in images, whereas the ideas have tended to cross in the other direction. This means that our debt to France is primarily intellectual, a reckoning of methods borrowed by craftsmen or attitudes developed from ideologues. It is more than counterbalanced at the popular level by the credit — if not the discredit — that we have gained from France's interest in America as a perennial series of illustrations and impressions, an unending source of color and anguish, vigor and jargon, invention and syncopation.

The mirage of a Nouvelle France in this hemisphere, though it can still be momentarily conjured up by the nationalistic rhetoric of an André Malraux, began to fade away when Jefferson purchased the Louisiana Territory. Nor could there be any serious danger of an invasion which would leave the French culturally subservient, so long as their language is officially guarded by their Academy, and M. Etiemble wages his private war on Americanisms. The mutual attraction of the two cultures is that of opposites: ours has had a centrifugal movement, as well as an outward perspective, where theirs has had a centripetal tendency, along with an inside viewpoint. Consequently, others have always turned to them for precepts and examples of refinement, while their more robust spirits have frequently sought to escape from the effeteness of their own conformities. The avenues of escape have been pointing westward ever since Montaigne animadverted upon a South American cannibal. The American influence could be described, in the terminology of the Russian Formalists, as that process of deliberate estrangement which is characteristic of — and necessary to — all literatures when they have reached a stage of fixed conventions, facile elegance, and over-familiarity. Then they must renew their energies by being rebarbarized, and that is where America seems to come in. According to the aphorism of Mirabeau, an audience of foreigners constitutes a "living posterity." Should that make us skeptical in referring ourselves to the future, or should it give us pause when we next attempt to evaluate a book from abroad?

The title of this article is one which I also used for a brief section of The Gates of Horn; but, though the two discussions have the same starting point, they take off in different directions. My book was a study of realism, as manifested in the French novel during the nineteenth century and, more pervasively, as a main current of modern culture. According to the theory suggested and tested there, the realistic viewpoint is never as downright or total as it aspires to be. It is always preceded by an outlook which is at once more imaginative and less consonant with the empirical facts of a given situation. Insistence on the latter, in response to changing social and intellectual pressures, brought about the predominance of the realists and the use of fiction as a mode of knowledge. But the mode of imagination, which had certain prior claims on men's minds, is still a powerful recessive factor, and literature is compounded of both in varying degrees. Hence, when an issue of the Yale French Studies (XIII, Spring-Summer 1954) was devoted to French Romanticism, I was pleased to accept the invitation of Professor Henri Peyre to explore the other side of my binary metaphor. An Italian translation was printed in Inventario (May-December 1954). The article by Erwin Panofsky is cited from the Report of a Third Conference Held at the Graduate College of Princeton University on January 1–3, 1953. Robert Finch has since added some interesting details on the relations between Sainte-Beuve and Vigny in "Ivory Tower," University of Toronto Quarterly, XXV (October 1955).

Sunt geminae somni portae; quarum altera fertur
Cornea, qua veris facilis datur exitus umbris,
Altera candenti perfecta nitens elephanto,
Sed falsa ad caelum mittunt insomnia manes.

                                        Aeneid, vi, 893–6

I. THE GATE AND THE TOWER

Whenever the world is too much with us, as it so undoubtedly is today, the ivory tower has its advantages. These have been eloquently defended in a recent address to the Princeton Graduate Alumni by Erwin Panofsky. With his usual clairvoyance in calling attention to the idea that lurks behind the image, Professor Panofsky reminded his hearers that the original phrase, "tower of ivory," had been a rather hyperbolic metaphor for the neck of Shulamite in the *Song of Songs*; and that *tour d'ivoire* had been given its modern application by Sainte-Beuve, referring to the artistic isolation of Alfred de Vigny, in a verse epistle describing the state of French poetry in 1837. Professor Panofsky also suggested that the *turris eburnea* of the Vulgate might have been conflated in Sainte-Beuve's mind with Danaë's brazen tower as described by Horace, *turris aënea*. Perhaps, but it seems a little more relevant to detect a reverberation from Vigny's own *cor d'ivoire*, and to recall that infernal vision in Sainte-Beuve's *Volupté* where the philanderer is symbolically excluded from no less than three ivory towers. Even more to the point is that earlier article in which, saluting Alfred de Musset and the coming generation of Romantic poets, Sainte-Beuve characterized the work of Chénier and Lamartine as "two ivory gates to the new domain." Those gates were the traditional portals to the land of dreams, here by implication identified with Romanticism. By a further process of conflation, their insubstantial fabric, the ivory, was transferred to the tower, now the self-evident symbol of lofty solitude. It was as if Sainte-Beuve had said that the new domain, so full of potentialities just a few years before, was narrowing and shutting itself off again.

Now, traditionally speaking, there was only one ivory gate; the other was fashioned of horn; and this tradition has been traced back to prehistoric days when men worshipped in caves, the entrances to which were decorated with the tusks and horns of sacrificial animals. In the Stone Age, according to a British anthropologist, Miss G. R. Levy, the hornéd gate was seen as the dividing line between day and night, life and death, the human and the divine. In ancient but historic times, it was held to be the gateway to Hades or to the nether world of the Egyptian dead. Its diametrical opposite, facing eastward, was the chryselephantine portal associated with Mount Olympus or the rising sun. The classical lore and the archaeological data are gathered together and suggestively interpreted in E. L. Highbarger's monograph *The Gates of Dreams*. It would seem that the gate of horn was traversed by

the shades of the dead, when they returned to this world in order
to make revelations or prophecies; whereas the gate of ivory was
reserved for the gods who, more often than not, appeared to men
in delusive shapes and offered them ambiguous counsel. Hence
Homer can depict the twin gates, *passim* but notably in the
Odyssey (XIX, 562–7): the one of opaque ivory, through which
pass fictitious dreams, the other of transparent horn, which lets out
nothing but truth. This conception, which is reflected by many
other Greek and Latin writers, finds its definitive treatment in
Vergil's allegorical description of Aeneas returning from the underworld. The *locus classicus* in French literature is the chapter
on the divination of dreams from the Third Book of Rabelais,
where Pantagruel also cites medieval and humanistic authorities
on the subject, and Frère Jean makes an anticlimactic and inevitable pun upon the horns.

This skeptical view of the matter, it might be argued, is not
merely Rabelaisian; it is inherently French. When Molière's doctors ask Monsieur de Pourceaugnac what is the nature of his
dreams, his prosaic reply is: *"De la nature des songes."* Although
the *Roman de la rose* begins by distinguishing false from true
dreams, many French writers — basing their normative values on
reason, society, and material reality — tend to dismiss all dreams
as untrue or inconsequential. *Tous songes sont mensonges*, in the
words of the proverb. A semantic study of the word *songe* in colloquial or literary usage, or even a glance through the successive
dictionaries of the Academy, would show that its overtones were
largely pejorative. But it would be equally rewarding to trace the
word that has tended more and more to supplant it, *rêve*. Etymologically considered, this is the more specific and less honorific term;
significantly enough, it is a cognate of our English verb, "rave."
But it has improved its position since the arrival of the Romantics;
what was once the raving of a madman could become the *rêve
étoilé* of Hugo's Ruy Blas. Temperamental kinships, in some degree or other, have always been recognized between lunatics and
lovers, poets and dreamers, creative inspiration and varying frenzies.

of other kinds. Poetry, since Pindar, has been able to envisage life itself as the shadow of a dream. Spanish literature has been so mystically preoccupied with this theme that its constant burden is voiced in Calderón's proverbial title: *La vida es sueño*. Shakespeare, in his inimitable way, came to the same conclusion in *The Tempest*; but throughout his work he looked on death as a sleep, on life as a drama, and drama as a "dream of passion." The English language even retains a special verb for introducing poetic accounts of dream-visions, "methought," deriving from an obsolete root which is not that of "think." In characteristic contrast, the French verb *songer* has become a casual synonym for *penser*.

Classicism logically deprecated, yet it could not ignore, so universal a phase of human experience as dreaming. Montaigne's many-sided awareness had touched upon it in his essay *De l'expérience*; and Diderot's intention, in the perpetually surprising *Rêve de d'Alembert*, was "to give wisdom the air of folly." However, the prevailing skepticism, the fear of being duped, the hatred of the irrational, the cult of the matter-of-fact and the wide-awake, are typically summed up in Voltaire's dictionary under the heading *Somnambules et songes*. The mysterious aspects of life were mystifications, which the mind of the Enlightenment sought to expose. Due allowance must be made for another point of view, for the underground currents of Illuminism, and for such unclassical expressions of wonder and curiosity as C. G. T. Garnier published in his series, *Voyages imaginaires, . . . suivis des songes et visions, et des romans cabbalistiques*; but these were already manifestations of what — teleologically — we call pre-Romanticism. Although we may not agree with Irving Babbitt's interpretation of Jean-Jacques Rousseau, we can still take our bearings from his remark that "Rousseau's great discovery was revery." The all-important adjective *romantique*, making two of its first appearances in France, constitutes a highly significant link between his *Rêveries du promeneur solitaire* and the preface to Letourneur's translation of Shakespeare, which had appeared the year before. Shakespearean romanticism would not reach its apogee until Berlioz composed his Queen Mab rhapsody, which was appropriately suggested by a speech on the nature of dreams — Mercutio's rather Freudian explanation —from *Romeo and Juliet*. To understand the intervening trends, the new generation of self-professed somnambulists, we should have to look toward Germany, and to consider the illuminating examples that Albert Béguin has presented in *L'Ame romantique et le rêve*.

Taine, a later representative of the rationalistic and empirical attitudes, would deplore the French acceptance of German philosophy. "For the first time in history," he wrote in his *Philosophes français au dix-neuvième siécle*, "revery was metaphysical." For this uncharacteristic concern with the speculative and the transcendental, he offered a political explanation: under a series of repressive governments men were free to do little else except dream. Yet Taine, despite his keen interest in national psychology, neglected the psychology of the artist — that state of mind which, it could be maintained, owed its formation to German Romanticism. One concise example will serve our purposes: *Ritter Gluck*, a sketch written by E. T. A. Hoffmann at the crucial point of his career, when he turned from musical criticism to imaginative fiction. Much of it is a sequence of lively opinions and critical speculations; but the author's spokesman — whether he be the apparition of Gluck or, more probably, a lesser and later musician gone mad — remains a memorable figure; and thus the tale looks backward to *Le Neveu de Rameau* and forward to *Le Chef-d'oeuvre inconnu*. In order to become a great composer, the old man tells his interlocutor, one must turn aside from the broad highway. "One enters the realm of dreams through the ivory gate; very few get a single glimpse of that gate, even fewer get through it." And for them there are further pitfalls: "it is hard to get out of that realm." The effectual artist is he who crosses the interior and returns to the highway of life; but it is all too easy for the ineffectual dreamer to stay continually among the phantoms; and that way madness lies. No mention is made of the hornéd gate, for Hoffmann seems to believe that all dreams are potentially both true and false, and that the artist's task is to make them come true by recombining fantasies with actualities.

We are moving, then, away from Vergilian symmetry toward

something like Thomas Mann's one-sided conception of genius
as a deviation from the commonplace. Hoffmann's ideal seems
analogous to that of the youthful James Joyce: to mediate between
the world of reality and the world of dreams. Yet Hoffmann was
acutely aware, and the author of *Finnegans Wake* necessarily more
so, that mediation is increasingly difficult. In cultivating the dream
at the expense of reality, one ran the risk of upsetting the delicate
balance of the mind itself. Witness the striking instance of Hölderlin, one of those whose peculiar insight into the night-side of life
was ultimately bought at the price of his sanity. Witness, particularly, this comment of Théophile Gautier upon the chief visionary
among the French Romantics: "The progressive encroachment of
dream, little by little, made life impossible for Gérard de Nerval
in an environment where realities operated." This was alienation
with a venegeance. Gérard's literary testament, *Aurélia*, was published by Gautier and Arsène Houssaye in a posthumous volume
entitled *Le Rêve et la vie*. Its opening paragraph starts with an
almost classic invocation, and sweeps us directly into the depths
of unconsciousness:

Dream [*le rêve*] is a second life. I can never cross without a shudder
those gates of ivory or of horn which separate us from the invisible
world. Our first instants of sleep are the image of death; a shadowy
numbness grips our thought, and we are unable to notice the exact
instant when the *ego*, under another form, continues the work of existence. It is a dim vault which gradually lights up, and where pale
figures gravely motionless, who make their abode in limbo, emerge
from the shadow and the night. Then the picture takes shape, a new
brightness shines forth and animates these strange apparitions; the
world of Spirits opens up for us.

Thence the "*épanchement du songe dans la vie réelle*," the pursuit
of chimeras amid familiar scenes, proceeds on its zigzag course to
its destination, a madhouse. There the two doors to the cellar
resemble the subterranean entrance to the Pyramids — or again,
perhaps, the double gates of dream. The visions terminate in the
author's notion of writing them down, in "the idea of a descent

into Hell," in the fatal resolve: *"enfin forcer ces portes mystiques.
. . ."* He had wished, on the one hand, to "arrange [his] life deliberately like a novel." On the other hand, he had realized that
"the human imagination invented nothing which might not be
true in this world or another one." Realizing that the whole truth
consisted of more than facts, he had gone on to discover that fictions comprised a large part of it. He had corroborated Joubert's
maxim that illusion is an integral part of reality. Escape, for Gérard,
could only end in confinement.

II. THE TWO DREAMS

Dichotomies can be just as unproductive in esthetics as in metaphysics. *"L'imagination dispose de tout."* Yet long after Pascal
enunciated that principle, Coleridge — under the influence of Kant
— managed to effect his notorious subdivision between Fancy and
Imagination. Granted that the operations of the mind seem to take
place on different levels, the fundamental gap is that which divides
intelligence from existence. The latter comes first with modern
French philosophers, if not with Descartes; as Bergson pragmat-
ically remarked, *"avant de philosopher, il faut vivre."* Since even
intelligence cannot see far ahead, and cannot be trusted to guide
itself by social rather than egoistic motives, Bergson posited a sort
of instinct, which he called alternatively *fiction, fabulation,* or *la
fonction fabulatrice.* In his last book, *Les Deux Sources de la
morale et de la religion,* Bergson conceived this function as man's
continuous effort to fill in the gap, while incidentally creating
mythologies and institutions, ethics and arts. This accords well
with the psychoanalytic approach to dreams as a recapitulation of
myths. Ontogeny recapitulates phylogeny, as it were, in the domain
of fantasy. Whereas psychoanalysis studies dreamwork for what
it reveals of private motivation, Gaston Bachelard has been interested in its revelation of collective experience. In his five books
devoted to "the material imagination" — two to earth and one to
each of the other three elements — Professor Bachelard has traced
poetic imagery to some of its unconscious archetypes, and has

shown how the stuff of dreams can be no less tangible than matter itself. He has likewise shown how man bridges the gap between his mind and his environment, although his image-making faculties may take an active or a passive direction: toward either "reveries of will" or "reveries of repose."

Turning back toward Romanticism and Vigny, and to those *Réflexions sur la vérité dans l'art* that preface his *Cinq-Mars*, we find him developing a more or less Aristotelian doctrine to reconcile poetry with history. "In our troubled and contradictory hearts," writes Vigny, "we should find two needs which seem opposed to each other, but which — to my way of thinking — blend together in a common source: one is the love of the *true*, the other the love of the *fabulous*." If we identify the first need with the scientific intellect, the second is clearly the *fonction fabulatrice*, and Vigny's formulation comes close to Bergson's. Other poets would formulate this polarity in other terms: roughly it corresponds to the division of labor between Wordsworth and Coleridge in *Lyrical Ballads*. In his preface to *Les Rayons et les ombres*, Victor Hugo conceives the poet fixing one eye on humanity and the other on nature: "The first eye is called observation, the second imagination." This arrangement, which seems unduly schematic, is likely to result in a certain degree of strabismus. If Hugo attains an artistic wholeness, it is through the yoking of opposites: on the critical level through a synthesis of the grotesque and the sublime, in a famous chapter of *Les Misérables* through the formula of "mire but soul." Meanwhile the bestial actuality and the beautiful vision seem to be moving farther and farther apart, so that the younger Baudelaire can play upon their very incongruity, upon the running contrast between *Spleen et idéal*. Baudelaire escapes from the workaday world, not by madness, but by stimulants; he emulates both the alcoholic nightmare of Poe and the opium-eating revery of De Quincey. Sleep, which for Keats was the matrix of poetry, is "that adventurous voyage of every evening" in *Les Paradis artificiels*; and dreams are again of two kinds, which Baudelaire designates as the "natural" and the "hieroglyphic."

Baudelaire speaks as a proto-Symbolist; Professor Bachelard employs psychological language; yet neither takes us very far beyond Vergil's parable of a single and rather vague realm of phantasmagoria, communicating with outside spheres through a pair of adjoining entrances, one highly attractive, the other somewhat repellent in appearance. We may well take a monistic view of the source of dreams, the mental process of fabulation; but we are soon thrown back upon some sort of dualism when we seek to follow their effects. This is for the very simple reason that fiction, when confronted with fact, can do one of two things: accept or reject. It can either face the situation or seek to escape — "anywhere out of the world." Schiller based his strategic distinction between naïve and sentimental poetry on the assumption that the ancients were at home in their world; whereas the moderns, ill at ease, had the choice of reflecting the real in satire, like that of Voltaire, or else projecting the ideal in elegy, like that of Rousseau. More and more they expressed themselves in the idyll — which, as Schiller defines it, approximates to William Empson's definition of pastoral — and either harked back to a mythical golden age or else looked ahead to an ideological utopia. Nietzsche, as a student of the classics, knew that the Greeks themselves were subject to cleavages of this kind; and therefore he sought to distinguish the Apollonian dream from the Dionysiac intoxication. His disciple, Oswald Spengler, by changing the term "Dionysiac" to "Faustian," reverted to the problematic assumption that the ancients had been bland while the moderns were being peculiarly difficult. All of these antitheses seem to grope, with some consistency among themselves, toward a basic statement of the dialectical relationship between imagination and life, and to recognize that imagination is split within itself by a native tendency to withdraw and an enforced necessity to respond.

In this respect it may be compared with catharsis, the other side — the reader's or spectator's side — of the imaginative process, as it has been redefined by I. A. Richards: "Pity, the impulse to approach, and Terror, the impulse to retreat." Tragedy thus works through ambivalence, and it must keep a sensitive equilibrium between its conflicting emotions. It is Freud, however, who provides the widest extension and the deepest penetration for the concept symbolized by the twin gates. Out of man's hopes and fears are engendered his reveries and anxieties. Merely to indulge them may be productive of nothing but daydreams and nightmares. But here wish-fulfillment encounters the reality-principle, and the resulting compromise may turn out to be adaptation, invention, and sometimes creation. The writer is the man who, in consciously mastering his own fantasies, helps to shape the fantasies of others. It is this conscious mastery which marks the essential difference between great works of fiction and ordinary dreams.

> All' Dichtkunst und Poëterei
> ist nichts als Wahrtraum-Deuterei,

sings Hans Sachs in Wagner's *Meistersinger*, foreshadowing the possibilities of Freudian criticism even while evokng more primitive methods of divination. *Dichtung und Wahrheit* — it was the interpenetration of those two categories that led Goethe to unite them on the title-page of his autobiography. Innocence and experience, sense and sensibility — the alternative, in each case, implies development; but William Blake never lost his innocence, and Jane Austen was never lacking in sensibility. Those two gates, then, still seem as closely connected as the sense of wonder and the zeal for truth. One of them may be taken to represent the sentimental or the fabulous, the other to stand for the observant or the natural. But, however we phrase it, we end in the recognition that all great writers have passed through both of them.

For example, Balzac. He is usually listed with the Realists, and we naturally think of him as a man who traveled back and forth through the hornéd gate. Yet he was the contemporary and associate of the Romantics, and recent critics have taken increasing interest in the visionary aspect of his work. In 1830, which was a miraculous year for Balzac as well as for Romanticism, he brought out — among more important publications — a revealing story entitled *Les Deux Rêves*. It is simply the account of a social gathering in 1786, where the conversation happens to focus on dreams. One of the guests, an obscure lawyer, tells of a dream in which the ghost of Catherine de Medici has discoursed to him on matters of statecraft. Another, evidently a surgeon, has dreamt more prosaically about operating upon a patient with a gangrenescent thigh. When the time comes to leave, they are introduced to each other; their respective names it now appears, are Robespierre and Marat. With their portentous exit together, the tale breaks off. Both dreams are soon to converge in the sphere of action. Both — the romantic dream of the rhetorician, the naturalistic dream of the physician — are equally prophetic of revolution. Both are omnipresent in the *Comédie humaine*, metamorphosed, elaborated, and amplified, though seldom so carefully balanced or so explicitly set forth. A curiously similar episode is that central one in *Madame Bovary:* that scene in the alcove where the connubial reveries of the doctor and his wife are intimately pursued, where Emma dreams of lovers and Italian romance while Charles is dreaming of patients and domestic business. This twofold mode of perception, the consequence of Flaubert's habitual alternation between the vantage points of romanticism and realism, constitutes what Albert Thibaudet has aptly termed *la vision binoculaire*.

Early and repeatedly Flaubert declared, as he did in a letter to Louise Colet: " . . . one must live for one's vocation, climb into one's ivory tower, and there — like a dancing-girl amid her perfumes — remain alone with one's dreams." But he knew well that such a retreat was just as tenuously insecure as it sounded; and from time to time, for better or worse, he felt compelled to mingle with society, even as it was changing in his day. During his later years he confessed, in a letter to Turgenev: "J'ai toujours tâché de vivre dans une tour d'ivoire; mais une marée de merde en bat les murs à la faire crouler." The juxtaposition of contrasting views — not to mention contrasting odors — created a unique perspective, which was neither romantic nor realistic but a combination of both, which involved the techniques of self-delusion and undeception used simultaneously and intensively. But, in this sense, *le bovarysme* was not without precedent; indeed it was the response to a question involving *le donquichottisme littéraire*, raised by Jules Janin at the very outset of the Romantic Period, and pointing back to the primary example of Cervantes. The archetypal novel, *Don Quixote*, had been a critique of the fictitious; it had discredited the romances that preceded it by a technique of systematic disenchantment. This meant that Cervantes too had to practise the art of enchantment; for disillusionment presupposes illusion, and realism would scarcely have been conceivable without the preexistence of romanticism. The interplay of *engaño* and *desengaño*, so cherished by Spaniards, is not limited to any one country or to a single epoch; it is only another way of stating the endless dialectic of ivory and horn. Hamlet's problem looks modestly personal when he first answers his mother: "Seems, Madam? Nay, it is." But André Gide's translation, hypostatizing the simple English verbs, brings out the universal application: "*Apparence? Eh! non, Madame. Réalité.*"

III. THE WAKING DREAM

It has already been said that Taine neglected the special problem of the artist's psychology. Nonetheless, in *De l'intelligence*, the highly generalized outline of his psychological theories, he instanced the case of Flaubert, "the most exact and lucid of modern novelists." What interested Taine, in the composition of *Madame Bovary*, was the author's identification with his protagonist to the point of self-induced hallucination. Elsewhere Taine emphasized — perhaps over-emphasized — the objective forces that influence human behavior; here he dwells upon the subjective factors, and stresses the distinction between mental images and physical sensations. He goes so paradoxically far as to assert that "perception is a true hallucination, . . . an internal dream which happens to harmonize with external objects." Truth is not unattainable, but fable comes first; man dreams before he analyzes, and this priority seems valid historically as well as psychologically. "Two main processes are employed by nature to produce in us that operation we call cognition: one consists in creating illusions, the other in rectifying them." Hence the intellect has its revenge upon the *fonction fabulatrice*, and fiction becomes an analytic device for exposing fantasies, an *onirocritique* — to sum it all up in a succinct term borrowed from Guillaume Apollinaire. After all Flaubert, that penitent romantic, had finally succeeded in detaching himself from Emma Bovary. The mechanism of rectification, as Taine describes it, not only explains the effect of *Madame Bovary*; it also applies to *Don Quixote* and thence to many other realistic novels. It also helps to explain how realism manages to encompass within itself a large component of romanticism. Naturalism is less imaginative to the extent that it loses this component, which in turn — left to its own devices — tends to secrete itself within the more elusive domain of symbolism.

Again the two dreams are detached from each other. The oscillation of French literature, its ease in moving from one extreme to another, is strikingly illustrated when the final pages of Taine's *De l'intelligence* are cited in the opening pages of André Breton's *Premier manifeste du surréalisme*. There the intention is to exclude reality, to revel in hallucination, to cultivate the unrectified illusion. The romantic notion of the mad genius had included a hope for his eventual return from the land of dreams to the purlieus of humanity. Even the Symbolists envisaged a system of correspondences between their more mystical sphere and actuality. The Surrealists were the pure literary Don Quixotes, the *Pierrots lunaires* who refused to awaken from their dream. Gérard de Nerval's lucid intervals were his only weaknesses, when viewed from the oblique angle of the Comte de Lautréamont. It is more than historical coincidence that, while creative fantasy has been projecting itself farther and farther out of this world, this world has been becoming more drab and dull. "O poètes!" Hugo announced in *Les Voix intérieures*,

O poètes! le fer et la vapeur ardente
Effacent de la terre, à l'heure où vous rêvez,
L'antique pesanteur . .

But that announcement looks both ways; it suggests the possibility
that the awakening poet can be a Whitmanesque bard of the new
industrialism, as well as a dread lest poetry itself prove to be incompatible with the conditions of modern life. The latter view is taken
by Musset in a poem entitled *Les Voeux stériles*:

.. la fiction
Disparaît comme un songe au bruit de l'action.

This is the argument of poetic obsolescence against which Shelley
wrote his famous defense, an argument originally advanced by
Hegel and currently restated by Edmund Wilson. It followed that
beauty was a thing of the past, according to Flaubert; according to
his counterpart among poets, Baudelaire, beauty was always elsewhere. Rimbaud, who would ultimately be a voyager in exotic
countries, sought it first in dreams. He "dreamed up" — as we
might say today — "crusades, unreported voyages of discovery,
unchronicled republics, abortive wars of religion, displacements of
races and continents: I believed in all the enchantments." This
particular sequence from *Une Saison en enfer* almost reads like a
scenario for St.-John Perse's *Anabase*.

The true had been synonymous with the beautiful, for the classicists, for Boileau: "Rien n'est beau que le vrai. . . . " The binocular
vision of Flaubert and Baudelaire focused upon the contrast between truth and beauty. Truth seemed increasingly ugly to the
Symbolists, who tended to obscure it and concentrate on forms of
beauty which were frankly illusory. When Rimbaud hallucinated
himself, he saw "a mosque in place of a factory, a drum-corps of
angels, carriages on the highways of heaven, a drawing-room at the
bottom of a lake" — anything, the farther fetched the better, that
would displace the factory and discompose the obvious characteristics of daily existence. One of the heroes of *le bas romantisme*, the
murderer-poet Pierre-François Lacenaire, had also enjoyed his

escapist reveries — and for the most concrete of reasons, since he was confined to prison and sentenced to the guillotine. In his *Rêve d'un condamné à mort*, he sighed:

> Que l'on est heureux quand on rêve! . . .
> Sans dormir, rêver c'est charmant.
> En moins d'une heure, ainsi j'achève
> Le plus agréable roman.

And since his actual life had been as sensational as any *roman-feuilleton*, his daydream is one of simple domestic felicity. The usual romantic dreamer, conversely, escapes from the norms of comfortable routine through dreams of highly colored extravagance. But with the years, with the acceleration of events, with the successive encroachments of the irrational, common existence becomes extravagant. Heinrich Heine's irony depended upon the fact that his wish-dreams were all too obviously untrue: "Es war ein Traum." The ironies of Franz Kafka are grimmer because, to us in our century, no horror — not even the absurd situation of *The Metamorphosis* — can be dismissed as altogether fantastic: "Es war kein Traum." In one of his apocalyptic moods, Hugo foresaw how the sense of reality, under such pressures, might turn itself inside out: "Quel rêve horrible! c'est l'histoire!"

Therefore it seems not inappropriate for the twentieth-century artist-hero — as personified by James Joyce in *Ulysses*, the work of fiction that consummates the realistic trend — to make the declaration: "History is a nightmare from which I am trying to awake." It also seems understandable, from this point of view, why Joyce should have gone on to attempt a phantasmagoric chronicle of human subconsciousness in his gigantic dream-vision of *Finnegans Wake*. Even while *Ulysses* was being written, Henry James, who was then dying, described the onset of the First World War as "a nightmare from which there is no waking save by sleep." With the subtle deliberation that marked every choice he made, James chose an unabashedly romantic title for his last and unfinished novel: *The Ivory Tower*. "Doesn't living in an ivory tower just mean the most distinguished retirement?" is one of the questions it asks. But since this is Henry James, there are many others: the significance of the mysterious ivory cabinet, or of the crass financial documents it evidently conceals, or indeed of the scene being set in America after so many novels located abroad. James demonstrated, as Flaubert had done and Joyce would do, that retirement can be the most serious commitment. In the heyday of Romanticism a keen-eyed Frenchman, Alexis de Tocqueville, had noted that the American imagination devotes itself "either to conceiving the useful or representing the real." His comment throws light on James's esthetic expatriation. But Tocqueville is more broadly illuminating when he observes two opposing tendencies: "one which bears the mind of every man toward new thoughts, and the other which voluntarily reduces him to not thinking at all." Thus the American dream finds its alternative in American anti-intellectualism.

In this respect, our culture is by no means unique; it is simply a manifestation of our time, exaggerated by native circumstances; on both sides of the Atlantic, as T. S. Eliot has discovered, "Sweeney guards the hornéd gate." We Americans dream somewhat more of the past and less of the future than our forbears did; yet the views of the Old World are modernized when Mr. Eliot, in one of his early French poems, describes a Byzantine church as a *"vieille usine désaffectée de Dieu."* This is the utterly anti-romantic reversal of Rimbaud's *"mosquée à la place d'une usine";* but of course Mr. Eliot, at this point, is hardly serious; he is no more of an industrialist than Rimbaud was a Mohammedan. He is merely reminding us, as he has done so much more explicitly since, that today it is hard to discern the richest traditions amid the accumulations of rusty machinery. When Renan took his long view from the Acropolis, he saw some truth and some falsehood in every myth. However, he found it harder and harder to tell which was which, in the vast syncretic panorama that the ages had spread out before him. He had come there to pay homage to the Attic goddess of reason, but he was profoundly aware of other beliefs than those comprehended within her philosophy, and the resonance of such Biblical phrases as *tour d'ivoire* confirmed him in his final apostasy. "Les rêves de tous les sages renferment une part de vérité. Tout n'est ici-bas que symbole et que songe." This is truly a far cry from Voltaire, who liked factories much better than mosques, and who had little concern for the mysteries that continue to underlie the human condition.

Is it a vision or a waking dream? For Proust, who explored intensively the limbo between waking and sleeping, it is both at once. To the eye of memory, which was characteristically the Proustian mode, dreams are indistinguishable from realities. Yet the separation between two ways of living, between Swann's familiar way and the Guermantes' remote way, is underlined by renewing the metaphor of two gates, "the low and shameful gate of experience" and "the golden gate of the imagination." The gold, by replacing the ivory, hints that doubt is to be cast on certain worldly values, as well as on certain youthful presuppositions. Proust's great novel follows the pattern of romantic disillusionment, introduced by Cervantes and perfected by Flaubert. But Proust, much more than his predecessors, regards imagination as a means that leads to knowledge, and never completely disengages himself from impressions that have arrived through "the golden gates of the world of dreams." This is why youth retains for him the same nostalgic freshness it held for Hölderlin, who blessed the golden dreams of childhood because they hid the poverty of life:

> Seid gesegnet, goldne Kinderträume,
> Ihr verbargt des Lebens Armut mir.

The way back from the Outland of adulthood to the Elfland of *Sylvie and Bruno* led, for Lewis Carroll, "Through the Ivory Gate." A later stage of life, or of history, would be a sadder one; by definition, it would be disillusioned. But illusion seems to have more of a future today than Freud, in his rationalism, could have predicted. It may be that the cult of the oneiric is a protest against the factual, just as the current rediscovery of symbolism has been a desperate effort to transcend a literal environment in which poets and critics take less and less satisfaction. Once more, then, our path divides; we can only hope our preoccupations guide us, not toward darker states of consciousness, but to further self-knowledge. Perhaps we can take some comfort from an aphorism of Novalis, which Edgar Allan Poe was fond of quoting: "We are near waking when we dream that we dream."

13

Toward a Sociology of the Novel

Here we return through the other gate to a discussion prompted by Lucien Goldmann's special issue of the Revue de l'Institut de Sociologie, *2 (1963), and glancing at several other publications in an important field which is just beginning to be cleared. This review-article appeared in the Journal of the History of Ideas, XXV, 1 (January-March 1965).*

For the past two centuries the novel seems to have predominated over the other literary genres; but it was never accorded much attention or status within the hierarchies of classical criticism; and the discussions of later years have raised a serious question as to its obsolescence, indeed its survival. Its adaptability to changeable conditions, which is the positive side of its resistance to formal analysis, has made it a uniquely sensitive register both for the formulation of personal relationships and for the diffusion of ideas. Most of its critics, when they have not concentrated their efforts on the increasingly self-conscious stratagems of narrative technique, have tended to moralize over or argue about such problems as its subject matter presents. As an object or a mode of knowledge, it has aroused the sporadic interest of social thinkers ever since the Encyclopedists, and has been cited with increasing respect by exponents of what French scholarship — hopefully interlinking the sciences with the humanities — would now designate *les sciences humaines.* It is about two decades since Roger Caillois brought together some Spanish versions of essays on the detective story and kindred manifestations under the rubric of *Sociologia de la novela.* The present number of the *Revue de l'Insititut de Sociologie,* consecrated to *Problèmes d'une sociologie du roman,* marks a more ambitious instauration: a seminar in the sociology of literature at the Free University of Brussels under the direction of Lucien Goldmann. This publication is not primarily a report on the proceedings; nor is it precisely a symposium, since it has not invited contributors to exchange opinions on its set topic. Rather, it is a manifesto wherein the editor has consolidated his own position by flanking it with notable precedent, supporting authority, and congenial exemplification.

Since French thought is inclined to consider nearly everything *dans ses rapports avec les institutions sociales*, and since the French novel has habitually related its immediate concerns to those of society at large, there is nothing especially new in this confrontation. Literary history makes due allowance for what it regards as sociological factors, insofar as the circumstances of authorship may affect a given work; an enterprising handbook by Robert Escarpit, *Sociologie de la littérature*, condenses additional information about the book trade and the reading public; but it remains for the sociologists to lay down a method, if they expect to throw light upon the process as a whole. Some of their German pioneers have been historians of ideas, who could therefore illuminate the formation and transformation of taste. Recent American investigations have been devoted to the behavior of the audience and its responses, generally at the level of popular culture. Academic sociology in France has traditionally been philosophical, rather than historical or empirical, in its methodological orientation. Hence it reflects that belated and somewhat ironic trend whereby, since the last war, French philosophy and its sister disciplines have submitted themselves to the tutelage of German metaphysics. Hegel inspires as much awe in the universities as he did in Germany a century ago, while his Marxian revisionists are taken more seriously than in any other non-Communist climate today. M. Goldmann, as is evident from his interpretation of Racine and Pascal, *Le Dieu caché*, combines an Existentialist stance with a Marxist ideology: his own word is *paramarxiste*. It will be seen that the combination is not a propitious one for the traditional clarity of French style.

M. Goldmann himself provides the general introduction, the final comment, and the longest intervening article — considerably more than half the issue. The article is virtually a monograph, setting forth the conclusions reached by his seminar after a term of concentration upon the novels of André Malraux. Their impact was apparently traced by students through the principal French reviews of the nineteen-twenties and thirties, and an abstract of this provisory documentation is offered by Michel Bernard. Given the contemporaneous spectrum of opinion, the pattern of reaction is pretty much what might have been predicted or even remembered. Certainly so intensive a study could be warranted by the intellectual conflicts surrounding Malraux's writings at every stage. The evolution of his work is closely bound, so M. Goldmann puts it, to the cultural, social, and political history of Western Europe since the end of the First World War. True enough; but most of his contemporaries are linked by such bonds; they do not necessarily make him *"un écrivain particulièrement représentatif."* Conscious of his epoch as he has been, and explicit about it at every turning-point, he has been too extreme an individualist to represent it in the most faithful sense. He has adventured in fiction as he has in archaeology, revolution, war, politics, and esthetics — all of which makes him a great adventurer, but hardly a typical novelist. A certain amount of confusion exists between his fiction and the facts of his career, which literary sociologists might some day help to clarify: for instance, the doubt raised by his controversy with Trotsky, whether his Chinese novels are to be trusted as eye-witness accounts of historic events.

The adjective in M. Goldmann's title, *Introduction à une étude structurale des romans de Malraux,* has become something of an interdisciplinary catchword, with its presumptive model in Lévi-Strauss's structural anthropology and its Germanic equivalent for structure in the untranslatable *Gestalt.* Yet M. Goldmann shows little interest in the elements of novelistic construction, James's "sacred mystery of structure." Arming himself with the cogent precept of Georg Lukács, that the ethic of the novelist turns into an esthetic problem of his work, he surveys what might otherwise be more crudely described as the ideological content of Malraux's books. Proceeding through the sequence with no keener instruments than synopsis, paraphrase, and quotation, he correlates the waxing and waning of the novelist's imagination with his commitment to "certain authentic universal values." *Les Conquérants, La Voie royale,* and the pivotal *Condition humaine* fall properly within the domain of the novel because they reaffirm the individual, whereas the more lyrical *Temps du mépris* and the all but epical *Espoir* stress the countermovement toward a collective outlook. These five novels are preceded and followed by essays and more speculative writing. The abandonment of the fragmentary *Noyers de l'Altenburg* and the subsequent shift to commentaries upon the plastic arts reveal a loss of faith on the part of Malraux, which significantly coincides with a crisis of values on the part of civilization (Values? *Gebrauchswert? Tauschwert?*). Here the unarticulated premise is an equation between his creative period and his *ci-devant* Marxism. The mooted decline of the novel itself is hinged upon the arbitrary decision of a single restless talent to change its field of activity.

This view will not altogether square with Malraux's own conception of art, which places an un-Marxist emphasis upon the power of the human will to challenge and conquer material forces, and which has a good deal in common with the psychology of his fictional revolutions. In any case, he seems unique rather than representative; he may well lend himself more readily to psychological than to sociological inquiry; and his novels are not less interesting because they afford so precarious a basis for generalizations about the novel. If M. Goldmann's capacities as a theorist are jeopardized by his choice of an example, he is much wiser and happier in reviving the unduly neglected theories of a distinguished predecessor, Georg Lukács. *Die Theorie des Romans,* possibly the most penetrating essay that ever addressed itself to that elusive subject, was written fifty years ago in Berlin, where it was first published as a book in 1920. Since its Hungarian author was converted to Marxism shortly afterward, it is not included in his canon as the ablest critic and esthetician of Communist Europe. Nor has it met with the recognition it deserved in the West, where a first French translation is heralded by the two chapters that M. Goldmann has printed. Meanwhile the original edition has lately been reprinted in West Germany, prefaced by a *nihil obstat* from Lukács which is both an apologia and an autocritique. Therein he acknowledges his Hegelian origins, movingly recalls his early efforts under the *geistesgeschichtliche* influence of Wilhelm Dilthey and Max Weber, and — while going through the motions of repudiation — manages to confirm some continuities of the European mind.

The translated chapters deal with the inner form of the novel and with its historico-philosophic conditioning (the terminology is quite as unyielding to English as to French). This, to be sure, is the core of Lukács' argument; but, excerpted from its context, it loses the benefit of his far-ranging perspectives. Having started in classic fashion by contrasting the epic with the novel, he distinguishes between their respective forms by referring them back to the closed and open cultures that produced them. The modern genre has gained maturity at the expense of earlier certainties, so that it must subjectively face its more complex situation. Under the outward semblance of biography, it records the tensions between a problematic individual and a contingent world. These are resolved in an overview transcending the limitations of the protagonist, a final state of enhanced self-awareness which may be termed irony. The term betrays a latent obligation to Friedrich Schlegel and the Romantic theorists. Again, the use of Goethe's term *das Dämonische* to characterize the novelistic *Weltanschauung*, has overtones which hark back to an unseasonable mysticism. When Lukács goes on to sketch a typology of the novel, in the second half of his book, it becomes clear that his conceptual scheme is best suited to the *Bildungsroman* and best satisfied by *Wilhelm Meister* — is limited, in short, by its German vantage point. He was writing, as he now reminds us, before the innovations of Proust, Joyce, and Mann. His further studies have covered more ground and focused more concretely on the many mansions within the house of fiction. Yet *Die Theorie des Romans*, as a theoretical foundation for himself and others to build on, still contains much that is sound and even more that is stimulating.

A similar approach has been currently taken, M. Goldmann points out, by René Girard of the Johns Hopkins University in his paradoxical and provocative *Mensonge romantique et vérité romanesque*. To M. Goldmann's miscellany he contributes seven pages which project a breath-taking span, *De "La Divine Comédie" à la sociologie du roman*. But Professor Girard's destination, as he hints, is not so much a sociology as it is a phenomenology of the novel. His Dantesque starting point is the episode of Paolo and Francesca — a passage which is usually romanticized by its interpreters, as he shows, but which is fraught with sharper implications for those who would understand the dynamics of fiction. The lovers, moved to their adulterous passion by a go-between in the shape of a book, exhibit a sort of paradigm in which the genuine emotion is brought out by the vicarious experience (*"le désir dérivé"*). One is reminded of La Rochefoucauld's maxim that many people would never fall in love if they had not read about it somewhere. The romance of Galeotto, which performs the mediating function in Dante's *Inferno*, seems to have its counterparts within the most characteristic novels: in the romances that move Don Quixote to action or the sentimental reading-matter that conditions the fate of Madame Bovary. Whether we speak in general terms of his Quixotry or of her *Bovarysme* — to which Professor Girard adds such examples as Stendhal's *vanité* and Proust's *snobisme* — there is always an illusory set of ideals to be tested and found wanting through successive encounters with reality. Hence the plot of a novel, be it picaresque or *Bildungsroman*, can be defined as a quest which is discredited (*"une recherche dégradée"*).

Since *recherche* can mean both search and research, it embraces poetic and scientific connotations, and has consequently served as a key-word for French novelists, as in the notably ambiguous *A la recherche du temps perdu*. The economy of the language has had less fortunate consequences in the case of the word *roman* itself, since it must do duty for both *novel* and *romance*. The latter is our cognate term for the more exotic form, and to our ears its name suggests its major theme. The former, which we have gained at the price of having no English designation for *nouvelle*, carries with it suggestions of novelty and modernity, not to say news. To be sure, there are significant affinities between the two, here exemplified in a résumé of a treatise by Professor Erich Köhler of Heidelberg, who has studied the interplay of ideals and realities in the courtly romances of Chrétien de Troyes. But the lack of a verbal category for romance has made it harder to take full cognizance of the transition from epic to novel: to specify such tendencies as the emergence of feminine characters or the increasing preoccupation with private concerns. If we consistently follow Lukács in relating the different modes of fiction to their differing cultural backgrounds, we can differentiate the romance from the novel by underlining the distinction between the knightly and the bourgeois, between the norms of chivalry and of business. A sociology can scarcely afford to overlook the economic aspect of the society that frames its reference, as Lukács was to acknowledge with a vengeance. The strategic importance of *Don Quixote* can be traced to its location at the watershed between the feudal system and free enterprise. Its primacy among novels is based upon the long line of romances that it so poignantly entertains and so pointedly rejects.

Thus it hits upon the basic device for novels to emulate: the rejection of romance (*le romanesque*) — or, as the issues broaden, of romanticism (*le romantique*), of bookish preconceptions and sentimental fantasies in whatever guises they appear. The formula that Charles Sorel devised for imitations of Cervantes, *Anti-roman*, was latterly revived by Jean-Paul Sartre in his preface to the first anti-novel of Nathalie Sarraute; and the cycle has been rounded out by her latest novel, which deals with the reception of a novel, *Les Fruits d'or*. M. Goldmann is far-seeing enough to draw Madame Sarraute into his discussion, along with the other leading practitioner of the *nouveau roman*, Alain Robbe-Grillet. Madame Sarraute, like still another member of the new school, Michel Butor, sees the novelist's task as *une recherche* to the most experimental degree. Just as the physicist could not pursue his researches without assimilating the work of Einstein and Planck, so — she argues — the novelist cannot advance unless he takes account of the revolution brought about by Proust, Joyce, Kafka, and Virginia Woolf. The tradition against which they were revolting, that of Balzac, Flaubert, Tolstoy, and Dostoevsky, had been revolutionary in its day; for the novel strives continually to keep up with changing reality, and all art is an "unceasing movement from the known to the unknown." M. Goldmann would associate Madame Sarraute's own novels with those of the previous generation stressing "the dissolution of character," as opposed to those of M. Robbe-Grillet, which look ahead by asserting "the autonomy of objects." On the other hand, M. Robbe-Grillet, insisting that his objects have their beholders, claims to be no less subjective than his forerunners.

M. Goldmann, whose heated interventions end by casting him in the role of Molière's Maître de Philosophie, comments on *Nouveau Roman et réalité* at greater length than both of its two proponents, whose articles are the texts of lectures delivered at Brussels and elsewhere. He tells us, speaking *"en sociologue,"* that he views them as a physiologist would view a pair of athletes; it is for him to analyze the physiological structures they merely utilize. The comparison is as specious as it is presumptuous. Madame Sarraute and M. Robbe-Grillet, like most good novelists, are better sociologists than most of those who arrogate the profession to themselves. M. Goldmann would make use of them in an attempt to demonstrate a thesis: a correspondence between the condition of the novel and the Marxian concept of surplus value superseding production value, more particularly between the objectivism of Robbe-Grillet and the Fetishism of Commodities as expounded in *Das Kapital*. Now Marx himself, in an appendix to *Zur Kritik der Politischen Ökonomie*, warned against such naïve parallels. The relation between human beings and commodities, which is the very substance of economics, has a specialized and complicated story of its own which touches the novel at numerous crucial points. These are not less impressive when they are undistorted by doctrinaire oversimplification or misplaced concreteness. It is not for nothing that *Robinson Crusoe*, with its idyllic parable of man attaining control over his environment, was the favorite novel of classical economists. But it is Balzac, with his cold-blooded classification of subjects into men, women, and things, who plays the economist among novelists — so thoroughly that M. Goldmann would interpret him, disregarding a well-known letter of Friedrich Engels to the contrary, as an apologist for the bourgeoisie.

If M. Robbe-Grillet is a spokesman for things-in-themselves, he salutes Balzac as the chronicler of a "reassuring world where things were above all the property of man." Looking at that same world some forty years later, Zola saw men and women subordinated to things, and wrote a central chapter in the unhappy chronicle of man's reification. It is surprising that M. Goldmann ignores so important a witness; yet the Marxists, to their disadvantage, have regarded Zola's Naturalism as a deviation from Realism rather than an intensification of it. There is no disagreement about the realistic impetus of the mainstream, and it is no freak of etymology that the word *real* derives from the Latin for thing (*res*). Since things are by definition more real than words, the attempt to embody things in words is bound to be an approximation. Without presuming to define reality, the novelist — like Madame Sarraute — is painfully aware of the clichés and conventions that get in its way, and his clearest means of pushing beyond them is to show up their unreality. Accordingly, the novel involves an exposure; but what it unmasks is inherent within its peculiar nature; deliberately it cultivates a series of illusions in order that it may culminate in a disillusionment. This procedure seems to recapitulate the experience of growing up, as it is recollected by Jean-Paul Sartre in *Les Mots*: ideas hold a priority over things in our book-nurtured minds, and our adolescent idealisms are gradually corrected by the maturing undeceptions that educate us to life. Small wonder then if our surrogate, the novelistic hero, turns out to be a problematic figure; his problems are those conflicting beliefs and exploding assumptions upon which our world is contingent; and though his quest is disillusioning, it leads toward enlightenment.

The history of the novel is coextensive with the hegemony of the middle class, which it both expresses and protests against. This commitment to a kind of liberal opposition should explain how the novelist could be at once *engagé*, in the Sartrian prescription, and detached, on the recommendation of M. Girard; and it may help to account for Balzac's ambivalence. The unprecedented mobility of the period has made for many rapid changes in the apprehension of reality, so that the realism of any novel has a purely relative meaning, dependent not only upon its apprehenders but upon its context both social and literary: that is to say, it can never be literally real, and yet at best it bears a closer resemblance to our notions of actuality than anything we may have encountered among our previous reading. It is not for nothing that fiction means falsehood, that most novels seem palpably untrue, and that the truthful one is a rare exception. That is why its critique of society often begins as a parody of literature. If, in these all too summary remarks, I have rather freely restated certain views of M. Goldmann's colleagues, it is because I am frankly interested in bridging the distance between them and certain tentative ventures of my own toward a sociology of the novel. I must confess, however, that I am put off when M. Goldmann uses the adjectives *relativistic* and *positivistic* as if they were reproaches for scholarship to avoid. When he talks about the need for rigor, we may well sympathize with his hopes. But rigor must be achieved empirically, through a substantive acquaintance with the relevant texts from a technical standpoint, and with the exact relations between imaginative fiction and the socio-cultural facts — not by the imposition of vague absolutes from on high or the importation of categorical sanctions from the east.

M. Robbe-Grillet is, for his part, so thoroughgoing a rigorist that his novels sometimes chill their readers. His critical writings, which scan the situation with thoughtful competence, have just been gathered together under the watchword, *Pour un nouveau roman.* The novel must always be new, if it is to be meaningful, he affirms: it must renew itself for every generation. "Flaubert écrivait le nouveau roman de 1860, Proust le nouveau roman de 1910" — and, though the problem waxes progressively difficult, the nineteen-sixties are highly articulate as well as ingenious in facing it. M. Robbe-Grillet, like his fellow *nouveaux romanciers*, prefers to speak of researches rather than theories. The history of the novel is a continuous evolution, if not a succession of revolutions, for him; it has taken its periodic stands to dispel accumulating illusion, if not to challenge encrusted convention. But the novelist's task has become more refractory as his world has grown less stable, less intelligible, less innocent — in a word, less anthropocentric. Such old-fashioned conceptions as "story" and "character" stood and fell by obsolete conceptions of nature and human nature. Even the "absurdity" of Albert Camus, like the idea of tragedy, presupposes a rational adjustment between the individual and the universe. With the disappearance of fixed landmarks, storytelling becomes impossible. A "passion for describing" has marked the direction from Flaubert to Kafka and beyond; a *nouveau réalisme* should interfuse the naturalism of the one with the "metaphysical oneirism" of the other, incidentally neutralizing such outworn antitheses as *form/content* and *objectivity/subjectivity*. "All writers think they are realists," inasmuch as they seek to recreate reality, and each emergent school displaces its predecessors in the name of realism.

14

Janes and Emilies,
or the Novelist as Heroine

If the following piece were substantial or serious enough to bear the weight of such terminology, I might almost describe it as a practical exercise in the sociology of the novel, with a surmise or two on the psychology of fabulation. It was delivered as the Joseph Warren Beach Memorial Lecture at the University of Minnesota on May 5, 1965, and published in the Southern Review (Autumn 1965).

The controversy that I am being rash enough to rake up was already an old one for Chaucer's Wife of Bath. Her fifth and last and best husband, you remember, happened to be a scholar. True to form, before she managed to tame him, he used to fortify himself by quoting what the sages had said against women. His wife was not the person to be impressed by so pedantic a ploy. She merely retorted: "Who peyntede the lion, tell me who?" Behind her rhetorical question lies an ancient beast-fable; its gist is that our pictures of lions show them as either captives or carcasses because the painters were men, and that — if the lions had done the painting — their portraiture would tell quite another story. The parable can be applied with profit to many a problem which may have been distorted by the vested interest of the informant. Who is responsible for our view of the matter at hand, and how has he refracted it in making us see it his way? What did those scholarly authorities, those benighted misogynists, know about women? They were all men, and most of them had been monkish celibates at that. The other side, after all, has still to be heard from.

> Bigod, if women had writen stories
> As clerkes han within hir oratories,
> They wod han writen of men more wikednesse
> Than al the mark of Adam may redresse.

The situation is not so lopsided as it might initially seem, if we remind ourselves that the author of this passage was likewise a

man, and that Chaucer was gallantly making an ironic counter-
statement on behalf of the daughters of Eve. No one has failed to
be convinced by his portrait of Dame Alisoun; but she, both in her
hostility and in her complicity, has ventured far across the middle
ground between the sexes. Masculine writers have been fairly convincing in their presentation of harridans like Elinor Rumming or
trollops like Moll Flanders, and the Wife of Bath is both. That
has been easy because, as Montaigne says, "It is easier to accuse
one sex than to excuse the other." Literature is richer in such accusations than in such apologies. Before actresses were allowed upon
the stage, when boys played feminine parts, it is not surprising
that they tended to be viragoes like Noah's wife, or that even the
ingénues in Shakespeare were often more at ease when they put on
men's clothes. Such portraits could hardly be acceptable to subjects
who had never really sat for them. The prostitute who speaks in
Villon's *ballade* sees her decaying charms through a man's hostile
eyes, in the opinion of Simone de Beauvoir. And pornography, even
when it purports to be *The Memoirs of a Woman of Pleasure*,
has been traditionally written from the customer's point of view.

I do not mean to imply, because the pen has ordinarily been a
male prerogative throughout the greater part of history, that the
female of the species has been continually traduced or else neglected. To be sure, Aristophanes has shown us an assembly of
Athenian women, the *Thesmophoriasuzae*, passing judgment
against Euripides because they felt — or Aristophanes did — that
he had misrepresented them in his plays. More frequently the
author has gone to the other extreme, placing his heroine upon a
pedestal — or rather, in the instance of Dante's Beatrice, an altar
— beatified after her death into a mystical ideal. Dulcinea may
have been a kitchenmaid, but Don Quixote had a transfiguring
vision of her which historically corresponded to the cult of womanhood in the medieval romances. On a more sensual plane, Homer
visualized Helen through the impact of her presence on men.
Numerous heroines have swept readers off their feet because their
authors had fallen in love with them, as Stendhal obviously did

with his Duchess of Sanseverina. Though the artist's attitude has ranged widely, all the way from reverence to lust, all the way from Pamela (be it Sidney's or Richardson's) to Justine (Sade's or Durrell's), there has never been much doubt who painted the lioness.

Generally, she has been viewed from a distance, more or less; but there has been a continuous endeavor to identify with her viewpoint, whether through the first person or through some other stylistic means. The *Lettres portugaises* were long accepted at their face value, as a firsthand outpouring of passionate reminiscences and embittered reproaches addressed by a Portuguese nun to her French lover who had abandoned her. Recent investigation has confirmed what Rousseau surmised on the grounds of literary artifice: that they were actually composed by the man who pretended to be their translator, the Sieur de Guilleragues. We may wonder whether better-known works of fiction, if their authorship had been disguised or concealed, would have teased and puzzled us in the same fashion. Confronted with an anonymous piece of writing, have we any stylistic criteria for ascertaining the sex of the writer? Richardson was led to become a novelist through his readiness to provide young ladies with models of letter-writing. Perhaps it could be said of him what the critic Marcel Arland said of his French counterpart, Marivaux, that he had a feminine soul, *une âme féminine*. Yet, to be literal, this psychic insight could not result in anything but a female impersonation.

The vaunted closeness of the identification between Flaubert and Madame Bovary (*c'est moi*) ended by infusing virile blood into his heroine's veins, according to his most perceptive reader, Baudelaire. Despite the brilliance of the impersonation, "Madame Bovary has remained a man." Madame de Beauvoir, observing that Stendhal projects himself into the female character of his Lamiel, welcomes that tomboyish incarnation of the Stendhalian hero as a pioneer of feminism. It has been rumored of Proust, for better or worse, that he transposed his acquaintance with certain young men into his portrayal of *jeunes filles en fleur*. The psychological disparities that we detect in such cases might not have been evident in a more formal medium. The requirements of the naturalistic novel impel the writer to present his subject in more and more intimate detail. Edmond de Goncourt, as a middle-aged bachelor, had few qualifications for dealing with the subject of girlhood; but he had a touching confidence in his documentary procedures for authenticating his novels; and he was not too proud to launch, in the preface to *La Faustin,* a direct appeal for help:

Let me explain: I want to write a novel which will be simply a psychological and physiological study of a young girl, growing up and being educated in the hothouse of a big city, a novel founded on *human documents* . . .

Both the italics and the ellipses are Goncourt's, along with the other mannerisms, and he interposes a footnote to claim the italicized formula as one of his contributions to Naturalism.

Well, at the moment of undertaking this work, I find that books about women written by men are lacking — lacking in feminine collaboration. I should be eager to have such collaboration, not from just one woman but from a large number. Yes, I have the ambition of composing my novel with a bit of help and trust from the ladies who do me the honor of reading me. Perchance it is the general impression that I have no need of this. But the impressions of a girl and of a little girl, details about the simultaneous awakening of intelligence and coquettishness, confidences as to that new personage created in the child by her first communion, confessions of being led astray by music, effusions on the sensations of a young woman going out for the first time in society, analyses of unconscious feelings of love, the disclosure of delicate emotions and shy refinements — in a word, all the unknown *femininity* at the depths of a woman, which husbands and lovers spend their lives ignoring, that is what I ask for.

And I appeal to my feminine readers in all countries, requesting them in their hours of idleness, when the past rises within them again in its sorrow or happiness, to set down some of their thoughts on paper by way of recollection, and having done so, to send it off anonymously to the address of my publisher.

Goncourt's correspondents must have disappointed him, for he did not break any precedents in his next and last novel, *Chérie.* In

fact, *The History of a Young Lady's Entrance into the World* had
been anonymously published by just such a young lady, Fanny
Burney, with *Evelina* a century before. Why then should a feminine reader become a research assistant to Edmond de Goncourt,
if on her own she could now be a Colette — or, in a later generation, a Françoise Sagan? At this stage the masculine novelist is
ready to make an admission which is the premise of Dorothy Richardson: that only a woman can give us an inside story, based on
full participation in a woman's consciousness. Unfortunately, Mrs.
Richardson's consciousness is so much less interesting or resourceful than Proust's or Joyce's that not many readers of either sex have
stayed with her through the twelve volumes of her *Pilgrimage*. If
we assume that men cannot draw women, that only women can,
does it follow that women cannot draw men? That is the question
Samuel Butler begged in the most paradoxical of his books, *The
Authoress of the Odyssey*. There he argued for the attribution of
the epic, not to an old man named Homer, but to a young woman
who might have been the original of Nausicaa.

The basis of that argument was the description of men's activities, which Butler considered inept and naïve in contrast with the
knowing treatment of feminine habits and characteristics. His
clinching point was an ungallant inference, an *argumentum ad
feminam*. When the wandering husband returns to the faithful
wife, and they retire to the connubial bed, she tells him what has
happened to her before he tells her what has happened to him.
"I believe," Butler inferred, "a male writer would have made
Ulysses' story come first and Penelope's second." The issue here is
not altogether a competition for precedence; the fact is that the
respective sexes have different tales to unfold. When the romance
broke up between George Sand and Alfred de Musset, she rushed
into print with her novelized version of it, *Elle et lui*. Whereupon
he retaliated with his, *Lui et elle*, and by coming second had the
last word. More than once both parties to such a relationship have,
so to speak, filed libels of divorce in the courts of literature and
publicly exchanged recriminations. Possibly the most instructive

case was that of Madame de Staël and Benjamin Constant. To set her self-portrait in *Corinne* alongside of his in *Adolphe* is to understand the attraction of opposites, as well as their ultimate incompatibility. His book is a concentrated analysis, hers a long-drawn-out rhapsody.

One is tempted to speculate on what it might have been like if Albertine — whoever, whichever she was — had consoled herself by writing a novel about her affair with Marcel. Since we cannot have the whole truth without access to both sides, it is peculiarly fortunate that Madame de La Fayette produced her masterpiece, *La Princess de Clèves*, with the collaboration of her lover, the aphoristic Duc de La Rochefoucauld, so that her tenderness is framed within the perspective of his worldliness. Collaborators in fiction, as in love, inhabit two worlds which vitally overlap, but which are very differently proportioned. The woman cannot rival the man in range of experience, as Madame de Beauvoir ruefully admits in *Le Deuxième Sexe*, her intelligent woman's guide to the battle of the sexes. "This explains why so fine a book as *Middlemarch* does not equal *War and Peace; Wuthering Heights*, in spite of its grandeur, does not have the sweep of *The Brothers Karamazov*." It does not explain why Henry James lacks the sweep of Tolstoy and Dostoevsky. Moreover, if the field of the woman writer has too long been circumscribed by her role in society, it has been enlarged by her emancipation during the modern epoch. Of that enlargement Madame de Beauvoir is assuredly one of the oracles.

When Virginia Woolf was invited to deliver a paper on "Women in Fiction," she turned the problems over in her mind until they took the form of a feminist pamphlet, *A Room of One's Own*. Her speculation on the possibility that Shakespeare had a sister, equally gifted but mutely inglorious, throws light upon *Orlando*, her imaginary biography of a woman of letters who began her — or his — immortal career as a man of letters during the Elizabethan period. Coleridge's declaration that all great minds are androgynous may be the only solution to the dilemma. Falling short of that, one way or the other, we are all prejudiced by our sexual provinciality, whatever its province happens to be. The ideal novelist might well be a kind of spiritual hermaphrodite, combining this man's scope with that woman's sensitivity. Such a combination of gifts is seldom bestowed on anyone except angels like Balzac's heroine, Séraphita, who is also his hero, Séraphitus. Granted the historical limitations, it is possible to demur against Mrs. Woolf that woman — never completely at a loss for words — has never been at a great disadvantage as a storyteller. On the contrary, the art of storytelling was the defense with which Scheherazade preserved her existence against the constant menace of male authority, thereby bringing the *Arabian Nights* into the world.

Women have been universally recognized as experts at interpreting the refinements of love. No man has ever equaled Sappho's lyrical account of its classic symptoms. Past mistresses of romantic narrative such as Lady Murasaki or Marie de France outdid all rivals of their time or place. It is not for nothing that we speak of old wives' tales, or incline to put some faith in them when the teller is a Selma Lagerlöf. Recollections of growing up in the bosom of a family are most sympathetically treated from the sisterly and daughterly angle of a Louisa May Alcott. The universals of living on the soil acquire a particular meaning when they are apprehended through the duties of a farmer's wife and imparted to us by a Willa Cather. The purview of the novel tends to concern itself with — to borrow another subtitle from Fanny Burney — *Female Difficulties*. Neoclassic critics scorned the genre, with Boileau, because they regarded it as an effeminized epic. Furthermore, ever since John Lyly had appealed "to the ladies and gentlewomen of England," it had been directed at a reading public which was predominantly feminine. Its characteristic reader was like Clarissa's friend, Miss Howe, vicariously suffering with the heroine from one breathless letter to the next.

Its arbiter of taste was Lydia Languish, daydreaming on her chaise longue while awaiting her maid's return from the circulating library with such titles as *The Mistakes of the Heart*, *The Tears of*

Sensibility, and *The Delicate Distress.* Only a lady novelist could supply that sort of demand, yet her social position was as marginal and uncertain as the esthetic status of the novel itself. Usually a bluestocking, sometimes an adventuress, she emerged into the nineteenth century as the virtual priestess of an ambiguous rite. It may be a coincidence worth noting that, in France and England alike, the most articulate lionesses assumed the name of George. There was, indeed, something mannish about both George Sand and George Eliot; both of them achieved careers by flouting the domestic conventions of the day. George Sand's personal image, associated with her long line of heroines, evolved from *femme fatale* to matriarch. George Eliot's, after hovering between the fallen woman and the woman preacher of *Adam Bede,* was sublimated into the legend of a latter-day Saint Teresa in *Middlemarch.* For both Aurore Dupin and Mary Ann Evans, the masculine pseudonym was as much a prerequisite of the literary profession as a room of one's own and a bank account would be for Virginia Woolf.

Even when challenging the predominance of the male, the female paid tribute to him by aping his ways, as George Sand did by wearing trousers and smoking cigars. But, in the long run, the disposition for travesty has not been confined to one side. Occasionally, for reasons of their own, men have masked their publications with feminine pseudonyms. Prosper Mérimée attributed his early excursions in drama to a fictitious Spanish actress, Clara Gazul. The minor poet and critic, William Sharp, published his best work — his Scottish tales and sketches — under a pen name which he never acknowledged, Fiona Macleod. When a reviewer of *The Picture of Dorian Gray* remarked, "Oscar Wilde is but the *nom de plume* of a literary lady," that remark was either very obtuse or very subtle, but it underscored a well-established convention. Max Beerbohm once put forward the same suggestion about Rudyard Kipling, arguing that only an authoress would have laid so exaggerated a stress on virility (it is not recorded how Sir Max reacted to Ernest Hemingway). Charlotte Brontë has told us about the decision that she made with her sisters, Emily and Anne, when the three brought out their poems together in a first volume:

Averse to personal publicity, we veiled our own names under those of Currer, Ellis, and Acton Bell; the ambiguous choice being dictated by a sort of conscientious scruple at assuming Christian names positively masculine, while we did not like to declare ourselves women, because — without at that time suspecting that our mode of writing and thinking was not what is called "feminine" — we had a vague impression that authoresses are liable to be looked on with prejudice; we had noticed how critics sometimes use for their chastisement the weapon of personality, and for their reward, a flattery which is not true praise.

The mask of pseudonymity afforded scant protection to *Jane Eyre* — one of whose reviewers announced that, if Currer Bell was not a man, she was a woman who had manifestly forfeited her respectability. It is hard for us, over-enlightened as we are today by the publicized privacies of contemporary fiction, to understand how Charlotte Brontë could ever have scandalized her contemporaries, or for the merest moment been considered unladylike, let alone unfeminine. What apparently shocked them more than Jane Eyre's forward behavior was its impetuous expression, the candor of her femininity: "Reader, I married him." Emily Brontë, on the other hand, must have gained some credence for her unmaidenly disguise; *The North American Review* described Ellis Bell as "a man of uncommon talents, but dogged, brutal, and morose." M. Héger, the Brussels schoolmaster with whom Charlotte seems to have fallen in love, testified that Emily should have been a man; as he somewhat condescendingly put it, she had a head for logic unusual in a woman. It was rather her emotional than her rational qualities that interested Matthew Arnold, when — in his elegy, "Haworth Churchyard" — he compared her with Byron for "might,/Passion, vehemence, grief,/Daring."

The infusion of masculinity served to bring out, with all the less inhibition, the womanly traits. Emily may well have been, in Sydney Dobell's phrase, "not feminine but female"; by Charlotte's testimonial, "stronger than a woman, simpler than a child." Her identification with her hero, which seems uniquely strong in *Wuthering Heights*, is consummated through her heroine, and reinforced by the vehemence, might, grief, and daring of their mutual passion. It is Cathy who exclaims: "I am Heathcliff!" The narration is relayed to us at varying removes, mostly through Nelly Dean, the motherly housekeeper, and wholly through Mr. Lockwood, the man of the world, who is recovering from a seaside flirtation by taking up a retreat on the Yorkshire moors. ("The only failure in the book is the writing it in the person of a gentleman," commented the admiring Lewis Carroll, who was to succeed so conspicuously in identifying with a little girl.) Unlike the artless solo of Jane Eyre's confession, here we listen to a number of voices, and mystery blends into irony. From their children's games among the Gondals — in the imaginary kingdom they conjured up out of a box of toy soldiers — the Brontës had learned to enrich the straitening bleakness of their lives by the projection of fantasies which, to some extent, were shared and, to some extent, were highly individual.

The circumstances that allowed Branwell Brontë to exhaust his energies in petty dissipations, as a man, may not be unconnected with his failure to produce books as his sisters did. Their verbalized imaginings, though they differ greatly in intensity from one sister to another, retrace a generic pattern which might be summed up by slightly misquoting a line from Coleridge: "A woman wailing for her demon-lover." Emily's version of the theme is intensified almost to the point of demonic possession, since the vengeful forces of death and destruction seem to be at least as potent as the provocations and frustrations of Eros. But the basic components throughout — the ruined manor, the sinister squire, the innocent maiden, the tempestuous courtship, the various skeletons in their family closets — belong to the conventional machinery of Gothic romance. From a more skeptical vantage point, where we think inevitably of Jane Austen, the Brontës could be likened to the impressionable Catherine Morland, seeking to impose her own romanticized preconceptions on the cupboards and laundry-bills of

Northanger Abbey. Charlotte Brontë, as we might suspect, had firm reservations about Jane Austen, believing that her shrewdness verged upon shrewishness. She praised her for the "Chinese fidelity" and "miniature delicacy" of her technique, but added:

She ruffles her reader by nothing vehement, disturbs him by nothing profound: the Passions are perfectly unknown to her; she rejects even a speaking acquaintance with that stormy Sisterhood.

In contradistinction to the stormy sisterhood of Haworth Parsonage, she spoke in the well-modulated tones of common sense. Though she too lived out her life in uneventful spinsterhood, her fiction could sufficiently preoccupy itself with calls and cotillions and tactics of matchmaking rather than restless dreams and windswept graves. Consequently it invokes the norms of society, not the estrangements of nature. "Living constantly with right-minded and well-informed people, her heart and understanding had received every advantage of discipline and culture." The internal balance of this self-confident sentence reflects the balanced outlook of Jane Fairfax, who is too much of a paragon to suit Emma Woodhouse. But the impulsive Emma is an anti-heroine, whose Mr. Knightley — in spite of his chivalric name — must play the admonitory part of a governess. Sense and sensibility have their vocal exponents, not just in that novel with Elinor and Marianne Dashwood respectively, but wherever Jane Austen's heroines are confronted with two divergent lines of conduct or responsive attitudes. The usual alternative was sensibility; the average heroine was a *femme moyenne sensible*. Elizabeth Bennet stands out, not merely from her sisters and mother, but from her sex, as their wittiest and most charming spokeswoman of good sense.

It goes without saying that she is more sensible — that is to say, more common-sensical — than the representatives of the other sex in *Pride and Prejudice*, to varying degrees. Jane Austen's men, as Elizabeth Bowen has pointed out, are "present only in their relation to women." This may help to account for their obtuseness, in relation to the acumen of Jane Austen's *persona*. It is harder to account for her anti-heroes in the light of her professed admiration for *Sir Charles Grandison*, that notoriously unbelievable man who can do no wrong. Much of the motivation behind her heroines might be compressed into the unvoiced avowal: "I told him a thing or two!" The prejudice that temporarily blurs the penetration of Elizabeth Bennet is not so innate a defect as the arrogant pride of Fitzwilliam Darcy. In the war of wits between the sexes, on the battleground between Beatrice and Benedick or Millamant and Mirabel, the later couple is more evenly matched than on the moral plane. The author notes of Elizabeth that "she had a lively, playful disposition, which delighted in anything ridiculous." And Elizabeth notes of Mr. Darcy: "He has a very satirical eye, and if I do not begin by being impertinent myself, I shall soon grow afraid of him."

Jane Austen had, above all, a very satirical ear; she could see through her characters, as it were, by taking them off; she is a devastating listener, whose mocking sallies demonstrate that the verb *remark* means both to notice and to comment on what has been noticed. Epigrammatic crispness and worldly wisdom converge in Jane Austen's manipulation of dialogue, which has been refined to chilly austerity in the dialectical exercises of Ivy Compton-Burnett. Elizabeth gets the best of her repartees with Mr. Darcy, inasmuch as he capitulates by turning serious. When he expresses his feelings and proposes to her, it is significant that the narrator reports him indirectly; for once, she looks the other way and shies away from a conversation. Though she is more at ease with the obstacles to love than with its fulfillments, her final chapters do their official duty by marrying off her heroines. Miss Bowen suspects that there may have been more to Darcy than his creator understood. There was certainly more than met Elizabeth's eye, when she thought she saw through him. One might surmise that, as a dashing gentleman of his period, he probably saw himself in a rather more Byronic light. What would the Brontës have made of him? Another Mr. Rochester? A Heathcliff?

And what would have happened to Heathcliff, had he stormed

from the moor into Mrs. Bennet's drawing room? Would his fascinating wildness have been tamed, shrinking into a surly domes-
ticity, and his posturings been taken down a peg? We cannot draw
any parallel from the circumstance that allotted the roles of Darcy
and Heathcliff to the same actor in the film versions of *Pride and
Prejudice* and *Wuthering Heights*, given the versatility of Sir
Laurence Olivier. Yet the difference between the two figures is less
than the difference between two feminine modes of reaction to a
masculine stimulus, one of them building it up and the other
cutting it down to size. Romance, though it stands farther apart
from everyday reality, has a less rigorous outlook than realism.
Emily Brontë's hero-worship may have undertones of animosity,
but it is grounded upon warm emotive attachment. Jane Austen
may be moved to modify her resolve never to be taken in, but her
dominant mood is a cool satiric detachment. This may be more
difficult to achieve, and some would regard it as more of an achievement; others find it too prosaic, as well as too dispassionate. Such
conflicting opinions are quite consistent with its essential modernity, as opposed to a more nostalgic state of mind, which is conceivably more poetic.

The four hundred years between Chaucer and Jane Austen had
greatly augmented the list of literary works by women. Yet they
could not have appreciably squared the account, for *Persuasion*
could repeat the caveat of the Wife of Bath. " 'Yes, yes, if you
please, no reference to examples in books,' " declares Anne Elliott.

"Men have had every advantage of us in telling their own story. Education has been theirs in so much higher a degree; the pen has been in
their hands. I will not allow books to prove anything."

" 'But how shall we prove anything?' " asks Captain Harville respectfully. " 'We never shall,' " Anne replies fatalistically.

"We can never expect to prove anything upon such a point. It is a
difference of opinion which does not admit of proof. We each begin,
probably, with a little bias towards our own sex; and upon that bias
build every circumstance in favour of it which has occurred within our
own circle . . ."

In other words, when the lion learns to paint, it revenges itself by replacing the painter's bias with a leonine bias. We could go on multiplying examples; and they would lend variety, along with richness and solidity, to the portrait gallery through which we have all too hastily been expatiating. But I think they would do nothing to controvert the generalization that women writing novels tend, on the whole, to be one or the other of two perennially contrasting types. These, if I may do so without undue familiarity, I would venture to call the Janes and the Emilies. This is not to suggest that two great novelists can be explained away by any schematic polarization. Relatively speaking, Jane Austen had her brooding intensities, just as Emily Brontë had her analytic moments. Yet there is reason for borrowing their names as convenient labels to distinguish in fiction what might be designated, in optical terms, as a sharp or a soft focus.

If Trollope takes a middle way himself, he indicates the extremes with his Mr. Popular Sentiment and his Dr. Anticant. Such tendencies are not limited to woman writers, of course, though men are seldom as soft as the Emilies or as sharp as the Janes. The former, as I have implied, are probably more numerous than the latter, for all the uniqueness of Emily Brontë herself. The fictional process that engages the reader in a train of vicarious experience usually starts from the close involvement of the author with her characters. She may not confess quite so frankly as Marie Bashkirtseff, "I am my own heroine." But the subject matter is strongly colored by her personal identification with it. Because life is a romance for her, a *roman vécu*, the novel becomes a *vie romancée*, an idealized autobiography not necessarily lived but projected from deep within. Clearly, there is love in this approach. If the term had not been vulgarized by psychoanalysis, we could speak of libido, meaning the sort of emotion that transforms its object by embracing it. The alternative may be the more sophisticated approach, since it is less spontaneous, more guarded. It need not be hatred or aggression; it may or may not harbor an animus; but it is alert at all points in its suspicions. It is experienced enough to expect trouble and look for weaknesses.

Absolute objectivity, the Olympian prospect, the Flaubertian goal of utter impartiality, is not humanly attainable. If it were, it would very likely hold little interest for human beings. But to view an object from the outside is to minimize the risks of subjectivity by inviting the corroboration of other observers. Women have been more disadvantaged in science than in literature; yet they need not be, insofar as they have manifested a special talent for the observation of external details. Madame de Sévigné has had many goddaughters, fully determined never to miss anything, and adept at fusing a sensitive impression with a pointed comparison. Needless to add, it is the Janes who leave us with clear-cut and memorable images, whereas the Emilies put so much of themselves into their depiction that, without them, it would seem diffuse and vague. With them, it can work through the method of empathy. The alternate method is mimicry, which presupposes some distancing and distortion, and which leads rather to caricature than to idealization, utilizing vocal as well as visual effects. Though James Joyce would not furnish an apt example, because he was a man and because he is a nonpareil, he has the knack of illustrating both methods through his use of monologue.

The author of *Ulysses* is personally involved with Stephen Dedalus primarily; the characterization of Leopold Bloom is largely a mimetic effort, while Marion Tweedy Bloom has virtually been created by ear (she does nothing but lie in the dark and soliloquize). As a verbal mimic Joyce went farthest in the chapter devoted to Gerty McDowell, where the sentimentalism of the style is more than a parody of women's magazines; it is a reduction of womankind to absurdity. Ventriloquism, as a weapon of satire, can be exploited by both sides — by the sexes against each other, as Joyce's rasping falsetto seems to remind us. It can also be employed with deadly effect when the antagonism is intrasexual, and the rallying-cry is the Elizabethan proverb: "Women beware women!" Here the object lesson that has lately claimed wide attention is *The Group* by Mary McCarthy. This, we need not go out of our way to recall, is the collective case-history of a self-constituted

élite; eight American college girls during the years between graduation from Vassar in 1933 and the onset of the Second World
War. A witness who graduated from an Eastern men's college in
the class of '33 might be allowed to attest the mixed idealism
and disillusionment of those initiatory years, which would offer
substance for an important *Bildungsroman*.

But though the war and the Great Depression foster a certain
amount of ideological small-talk, it gets quickly lost amid the
welter of more feminine concerns that fill the pages and form the
texture of Miss McCarthy's book: gossip, recipes, window-shopping,
interior decoration, beauty hints, advice to the lovelorn — in short,
the journalistic incidentals of "modern living" as of the nineteen-
thirties. The resulting disproportion may well be an intrinsic part
of the author's design, a calculated protest against women's lot,
all the louder because they would seem to have been emancipated
so little by their higher education. Miss McCarthy has discussed
some of her intentions in a letter to her Danish translator which
was somehow published in *Encounter* for November 1964, and
which differs refreshingly from most of her critical articles in the
whole-heartedness of its appreciation. She pays her respects to the
antifeminist tradition when she generalizes by citing Mozart's title,
Così fan tutte — all women behave that way. By skillfully catching
the intonations of types and the clichés of coteries, and blending
them into a dissonant chorus, she has applied and extended the
Gerty McDowell strategy. When she entitled her collection of
short stories *Cast a Cold Eye*, she took her stand in the most militant vanguard of the Janes.

But Yeats himself, from whom the quotation is borrowed, was
scarcely an unemotional onlooker; and Miss McCarthy can surprise and disarm us by her occasional lapses into an Emily. She
can outdo Thackeray by far, when it comes to writing *A Novel
Without a Hero*, yet she cannot do without heroines. The case of
Polly, the hospital technician, whose tribulations end in the arms
of an understanding young doctor, has overtones of a television
serial. That, however, is an exception to prove the rule that mar-

riages are sinister traps and husbands unworthy of their mates. Though Miss McCarthy's novels are plentifully stocked with anti-heroines, like the fictions of the nineteenth-century Georges they habitually center upon a *femme incomprise*, a superior woman better understood by the novelist than by the others, and hence more tenderly handled than they are, set apart and spared the ironic aspersions that shrivel them up. In *The Group*, which she dominates, her nickname is Lakey, and she is "intellectual, impeccable, disdainful, and . . . rich." Moving "like a young queen," she draws her skirts back from the entanglements of the story and disappears into Europe, whence she returns at the end, along with the revelation that she is a Lesbian. She has succeeded in maintaining her superiority by dispensing with the male of the species, even for purposes of sexual intercourse.

The Group has earned its notoriety by the underlying subversiveness of its revolt against the female condition. Children are coolly eyed as little nuisances, who disrupt and besmirch their mothers' lives with the demands of breast-feeding and toilet-training. With an Amazonian dedication, Miss McCarthy takes the offensive in intersexual conflict and carries the war into the camp of the unforgivable enemy. A candidly circumstantial bedroom scene is for her a *scène à faire*; firmly she insists that her heroines grit their teeth and go through the distasteful business; and the seduction of Dottie in *The Group* is as grim and loveless as the very similar set-pieces in *A Charmed Life* and *The Company She Keeps*. Its symbolic memento is a contraceptive device, and its motivating impulse is a sense of humiliation. We have come a long way from Jane Austen or Emily Brontë or even so free a spirit as Katherine Mansfield. "Truly the books I read nowadays astound me," the last could write in 1930 to John Middleton Murry.

Female writers discovering a freedom, a frankness, a license, to speak their hearts reveal themselves as . . . [*sic*] sex maniacs. There's not a relationship between a man and woman that isn't the one sexual relationship — at its lowest. *Intimacy* is the sexual act. I am terribly ashamed to tell the truth; it's a very horrible exposure.

Freud had meanwhile intervened to overcome such compunctions. Frankness of expression has encouraged an increasing freedom of behavior, and the only limits to that progression have been laid down by the facts of biology. Yet these facts are limiting, and Mary McCarthy's resentments have done no more than Katherine Mansfield's bewilderments for the plight of the heroine.

No one has ever dramatized that plight more incisively than the eighteenth-century soldier of fortune, Choderlos de Laclos, in his *Liaisons dangereuses*, where the nymphomaniac protagonist, Madame de Merteuil, uses the code of gallantry as a weapon of promiscuous vengeance against all males for the subjection of her girlhood and marriage. Men, when all has been said, have done more than women themselves to bring about their liberation. It was Flaubert who discredited those romantic presumptions which, forming the very stuff of feminine fiction in the nineteenth century, have come to be diagnosed as *Bovarysme*. He cured himself of that malady, deeply susceptible to it as he was, by visiting it so heavily on his Emma. Fictional heroes have not infrequently been the victims of similar aberrations and self-deceptions, which — since we trace them back to the anti-hero of the first great novel — we characterize as Quixotry. As a matter of record, the power of fantasy is just as adaptable to a manly guise as to a womanly one. No woman wailing for her demon-lover has paralleled the erotic wish-dreams of frustrated prisoners like the Marquis de Sade and Jean Genet. We realize how distracted Hemingway could become with his own role-playing in *Green Hills of Africa*, when we read the clearer-sighted *Out of Africa* by the Danish baroness who subscribed herself Isak Dinesen.

That Norman Mailer has so frankly proclaimed his latest novel *An American Dream* does not make it any less embarrassing as an exercise in wish-fulfillment. The current vogue of James Bond is as much of an opiate as the romances of chivalry were for Don Quixote. Not that there is anything chivalrous about 007; judged by old-fashioned codes, he would seem to be a perfect bounder. The contrast could not be sharper between his sado-masochistic exhibitions and the leisured and cultured *modus vivendi* of his forerunner Sherlock Holmes, playing the violin, solving a crime by ratiocination, and getting his excitement from a hypodermic needle now and then. Yet, when Ian Fleming's secret agent performs the games and undergoes the rites of manliness, what male reader does not enjoy them with him? The network of international intrigue that is spun around him, wherever he goes, is an unconvincing cover for operations which are intriguing in another sense. What matters is the sport, the drinks, the casual venery, the snobbish luxuries, the commando tricks. If the daydreams suddenly shift into nightmares, this is so that prowess may exert itself. There is always a monster in the offing; it may be suspected of Soviet espionage, but it might as well be Grendel's Mother. "This time it really was St. George and the dragon," we are expressly told in *Goldfinger*.

Those for whom the drug is too exciting may prefer a sedative like Trollope. If we feel alienated from our century, he can make us feel at home in his, by welcoming us to a comfortable place in a settled and familiar society. His cathedral town, his squirearchical county, his recognizable landmarks, his well-appointed houses, his well-connected families, his vistas of the institutions supporting them, seem as real as anything we could imagine between the covers of books. But imagine them we do, and so did he; for the well-organized and substantial world that he presented so matter-of-factly was a dream of order, a mirage of solidity, an oasis of comfort in a desert of anxieties not dissimilar to our own. What loomed behind it for him was not Barchester Towers or Gatherum Castle, but a hard-working bureaucratic routine, a bohemian intellectual background, a bankrupt father, an expatriate brother, and a mother who redeemed lost causes and paid for wildcat schemes by her novel-writing. I do not mean to suggest that Anthony Trollope should be classified with Emily Brontë, with whom I have already been too categorical. More of a satirist than a visionary, he had more in common with Jane Austen, albeit she was better acquainted than he with cathedral towns.

If I have been swerving toward men writers little by little, despite a commitment to concentrate upon women, it is because the same imaginative processes are observable in both, though with considerable variance in degree. They reveal themselves more directly in woman writers because the angle of vision has been more restricted, the intuitions have been nearer the surface. But any writer's invention must depend upon his immediate psychological resources: so much for the Emilies. And the projection of them must be submitted to the standards of social judgment: so much for the Janes. Oscillating more nervously than their male colleagues between these poles, women novelists have naturally been purer in inspiration and less powerful in comprehension. Since we are dealing with people and not with computers, the choice is not the binary *either/or*. Any product of imagination is bound — like life — to be ambivalent, sympathetic in some respects and critical in others, a synthesis which fluctuates with the individual. Tolstoy, after noting that the popularity of Dickens was due to the love that he lavished on his characters, appended a clarifying afterthought: "It is well when an author stands only just outside his subject, so that one continually doubts whether the treatment is subjective or objective."

This is true of Dickens, in the sense that he is both a romantic and a realist, that he mythologizes the commonplace, that the narration of *Bleak House* alternates between the fresh voice of a young girl and the deliberate chill of a clammy impersonality. It is true in other ways of other novelists: of Proust, who moves from egoistic lyricism to sociological drama, or James, who remains himself while infiltrating the minds of his protagonists, or Thomas Mann, who combines the autobiographical with the essayistic. It is true, above all, of Tolstoy. He could portray animals with such sympathy that Turgenev told him he must have been a horse in a previous incarnation. (Had it been he who painted the lion, that question would never have been raised.) Yet he could take so long a historical view that many readers have been put off by the epilogue to *War and Peace*. At his best, which is the best the novel has to show, he fused the intimacy of individual feeling with the pattern of panoramic events. We admire Jane Austen's clear-eyed appraisal from a distance, when Emma Watson goes to the ball. But when Natasha Rostov makes her début, we are there with Tolstoy, to live through the suspense and delectation of her bashful pangs and girlish triumphs.

This was a lecture delivered on several occasions, among them a meeting of the Humanities Association of Canada at Queen's University in Kingston, Ontario, on June 15, 1960. It was published in The Massachusetts Review (August 1960), translated into Italian for Inventario (January-December 1963), and republished in the volume edited by Stanley Burnshaw, Varieties of Literary Experience (New York University Press, 1962), wherein it enjoyed the contiguity of Lionel Trilling's essay "On the Modern Element in Modern Literature."

Mr. Trilling, with characteristic persuasiveness, takes an altogether different view of the matter at hand, and, despite his Arnoldian title, diverges even more completely from Arnold's conception of "intellectual deliverance." Mr. Trilling's modernism would stress "the disenchantment of our culture with culture itself," "the bitter line of hostility to civilization," and "the discovery and canonization of the primal, non-ethical energies." His discussion seems to be grounded upon his pedagogical experience with a specific sequence of "prolegomenal books": Nietzsche, Freud, and Frazer confirm the irrational trend of argument, which draws its literary illustration from such important but atypical works as "Heart of Darkness," "Death in Venice," and the poetry of William Blake. Now I am far from denying the value of that unflinching look into the abyss of the unconscious which writers from Dostoevsky to Kafka have taken; and Mr. Trilling is so reasonable that, had he been concerned with artistic technique or the relevance of scientific thought, I venture to think that he might have placed more weight on the enlargement of consciousness. Our difference could be resolved in historical terms, though it might require some give and take in the terminology. Insofar as we are still moderns, I would argue, we are the children of Humanism and the Enlightenment. To identify and isolate the forces of unreason, in a certain sense, has been a triumph for the intellect. In another sense it has reinforced that anti-intellectual undercurrent which, as it comes to the surface, I would prefer to call post-modern. Labels apart, we might well agree on significances and influences.

Anyone who addresses himself to the moment is reminded, quite soon afterwards, that his animadversions are somewhat outmoded. I wish I could have had the benefit of Stephen Spender's firsthand account, The Struggle of the Modern (Berkeley: University of California Press, 1963) or W. J. Bate's notable essay "The English Poet and the Burden of the Past," in Aspects of the Eighteenth Century (Baltimore: The Johns Hopkins University Press, 1965). My observations were set down at the threshold of the nineteen-sixties; now that we have come halfway through that decade, the London Times Literary Supplement has already seen fit to survey the quinquennium. It is not clear how much illumination can be cast by such short-range appraisals. During the nineteen-twenties the TLS took a dim view of much that was brilliantly going on; today, perhaps by way of compensation in leaner years, its anonymous critics want to be "with it," whatever it may be. But to speak so belatedly of the avant-garde as "the changing guard" is to evoke the sentry-boxes at Whitehall or Buckingham Palace, to impose routine upon the very effort to break away from routine, to shrug off all critical distinctions with "Plus ça change . . ." The knowing advocacy of change for change's sake can be as mindless as the blind opposition to change, and a record of opposition to change for the better is scarcely lived down by favoring change for the worse. Having been chary in its contemporaneous recognition of Joyce and Lawrence, the TLS is anxious not to miss the boat with Allen Ginsberg and Jean Genet.

A more searching question, if we happened to share something of the literary excitement that passed by some of our head-shaking elders a generation ago, is whether indeed we are missing current achievements of comparable importance simply because our own arteries have been hardening in their turn. Since many of the modernists are now recognized as classics, are we not indulging in passéisme when we hesitate to hail the present generation as even more modern, equally gifted but naturally harder to appreciate through first impressions? It is our duty, of course, to be interested in the writers of our time. For obvious reasons our evaluation of them, whether we tend to overrate or to underrate, is notoriously fallible. If I am justified in my high estimate of the twenties, the sixties could fall considerably short of them and yet be extremely interesting. There are objective grounds, I believe, for such a view. If our criteria are technical, we are bound to take note of the more inventive craftsmanship of the earlier period. To some extent, we are still living upon its backlog of experimentation: how much of the nouveau roman could be accounted for as a set of French exercises imparting the methods of Joyce, Faulkner, Hemingway, and Virginia Woolf! To some extent, the will to experiment has given way to a practised deployment of convention: novelists writing in English, perhaps discouraged by the monumental examples of these masters, seem willing to settle for the traditional form, more or less well made, and concentrate upon the documentation. Two of the most remarkable novels of the past decade, The Leopard and Dr. Zhivago, technically are throwbacks to an earlier epoch. One of the most promising new movements, the '47 Group in Germany, is expressly devoted to catching up with the years lost under the Nazi blackout.

The dissociation of the writer from his role as artist, to which I refer, proceeds apace. The vogue of "camp" presupposes a relaxation of serious canons of taste. Open forms, freer verse, looser language — in every sense — register a protest against artistry as well as a gesture for spontaneity. The peculiar sort of Gesamtkunstwerk known as a "happening" may be a reaction against the threat of computerized poetry. William Burroughs' notion of writing books by cutting out or "folding in" random snippets from other books sets a more demoralizing example for would-be writers than his fantasies of drug addiction. The self-exhausting impetus toward novelty, combining with an extended freedom from censorship, has been making thoroughfares out of untrodden paths and conducting guided tours of private underworlds. Hopefully I keep looking for disproof of my generalization that today's novelist shows little concern for the life of the mind. But the recent novel acclaimed most widely, Saul Bellow's Herzog, almost seems devised to clinch the point, with its portrait of a broken-down intellectual clinging to some rather frayed petticoats. Mr. Bellow alleviates the self-pity with a welcome seasoning of self-irony; yet the compulsive pattern is that of all his novels and his single play, the monologue of a slob. To scan the horizon for younger talents is to be impressed by the fluent and finely textured work of John Updike. But here again all fresh departures return to the stumbling-blocks of adolescence — adolescence so institutionalized that the old people's home of The Poorhouse Fair turns out to be merely another high school. Nor does The Centaur, by superimposing mythological parallels à la Joyce, manage to escape from that obsessive and limiting milieu.

This limitation of scale and this retrenchment of variety cannot but seem anticlimactic when contrasted with the sweep and richness of previous attainments. There is no inherent reason why time's noblest offspring should be the last; on the other hand, there is an irrepressible tendency to canonize — at least for a day — the very latest thing; and the resulting confusion of values may have been further confounded by the academic study of contemporary literature. Faute de mieux, our contemporaries have an immediacy for us which their predecessors could never hold, regardless of quality. Yet Beckett, after Joyce, seems thin and strident and monotonous; Miller looks like an amusing but crude burlesque of Lawrence. The catcall, Who's Afraid of Virginia Woolf?, lends voice to an insecure bravado; contrivers of shoddy effects, like Edward Albee, have reason to be afraid of Virginia Woolf. It is difficult not to conclude, if we retain any perspective, that we have fallen among epigones. The image of the man of letters has taken a decided tumble since Goethe sat for it. The hero no longer aspires to be anything more than an anti-hero. The mood, as set by Sartre, is revulsion: La Nausée. These considerations may point to underlying factors, which are located outside of the individual's control. If this seems to be an unpropitious time for the arts, if culture itself lies in extremis as Mr. Trilling suggests, it is because of those desperate urgencies which coerce our world. T. S. Eliot's famous prophecy that the millennium would come with a whimper, not a bang, was reversed just twenty years ago. Meanwhile, in suspense lest we hear that bang, we continue to be assailed by a chorus of whimpers.

A new apartment building in New York City, according to a recent announcement, has been named The Picasso. Though I have not had the pleasure of seeing it, I would suggest that it ought to be hailed as a landmark, indicating that we Americans have smoothly rounded some sort of cultural corner. Heretofore it has been more customary to christen our apartments after the landed estates or the rural counties of England, as if by verbal association to compensate for the rootless transience of metropolitan living. A few years ago the name of Picasso, as household god, would have conjured up notions of a jerrybuilt structure and a bohemian ambience. Prospective tenants, in their perennial quest for comfort and security, would have been put off by a vision of collapsible stairways, rooms without floors, trapezoidal kitchenettes, or neighbors with double faces and blue-green complexions. But in the meanwhile the signature has brought untold wealth and unquestioned prestige to its signer, and now it becomes a warrant of domestic respectability. If this is not an arrival, no painter can ever be said to have arrived. But where? At the latest and strangest phase of a restless career, where previous arrivals have always been points of departure.

We must admit that our eponymous hero has met with more appropriate recognitions, notably the retrospective gathering of Picasso's works, exhibited in several cities on the occasion of his seventy-fifth birthday. That was indeed a retrospect: not only of the productivity wherewith a single man could fill a museum, but of the versatility that enabled him to master such varied styles and numerous media. To follow his progression from room to room and period to period — from drawing and painting to sculpture and ceramics, or from Romanticism and Impressionism to Cubism and Primitivism — was to recapitulate the history of art. Above the labels of the catalogue loomed the dynamic personality of the artist, not merely a school in himself but a whole succession of schools, seeking to outrival his own work at every subsequent stage as well as the work of so many earlier artists. If there was any text he was born to illustrate, it was Ovid's *Metamorphoses*. The conceiving eye that could turn a broken mechanical toy into a monstrous ape or a sacrificial goat, the shaping hand that could transform a terra-cotta pitcher into an archaic goddess of love, such are the faculties that Marcel Proust must have had in mind when he described the impact of great painters as *"une métamorphose des choses."* Emerson, a favorite writer of Proust's, had described the poetic process as "a metamorphosis of things."

Pablo Picasso, who will be eighty next year, is unique in his field, but not in his artistic eminence. In the sister art of music, we think at once of the protean achievement of Igor Stravinsky, his junior by one year. There, with due allowance for technical differences, we seem to note a similar tendency, which some bewildered cataloguers might have labeled Ultraism. This is the will to change, in other words that metamorphic impetus, that systematic deformation, that reshaping spirit which must continually transpose its material and outdistance itself in a dazzling sequence of newer and newest manners. Picasso was asked by a conventional person who admired his classical illustrations, "Since you can draw so beautifully, why do you spend your time making those queer things?" He answered succinctly, "That's why." He might have countered with another question: why retrace familiar lines? Similarly Stravinsky might have replied, to hearers aware that his departures were firmly grounded upon past mastery of his craft: why go on repeating the recognized chords? There are other possible modalities, though they may sound discordant the first time you hear them. The original composer is he who must try them, in the interests of further discovery.

Since more and more combinations have been tried, more and more possibilities have been exhausted, and the problems of experimentation have become harder and harder. The public, of course, is shocked; it prefers the accustomed harmonies to the neoteric experiments, and it finds Cubist projections unrecognizable. However, the development of the arts is registered through a series of shocks to the public — which, after all, in buying cars or clothes, accepts the principle of planned obsolescence. At its own pace, it too is animated by "the need for a constant refreshment," as has been pointed out by James Johnson Sweeney, who as Director of the Guggenheim Museum has done so much to supply that need. The shift of taste fits in with a dialectical pattern of revolution and alternating reaction, as the breaking of outmoded images gives way to the making of fresh ones. Hence the successful iconoclast frequently ends as an image-maker. Witness T. S. Eliot, whose career has been a literary parallel to Stravinsky's or Picasso's. Since his conversion to the Anglican Church and his naturalization as a British subject, we have come to view him as a living embodiment of tradition. Yet he emerged as an experimentalist, whose problematic endeavors startled and puzzled his early readers.

This realignment corresponds with the usual transition from the *enfant terrible*, who is naturally radical, to the elder statesman, who is normally conservative. But it does not explain why such grand old men as Bernard Shaw and André Gide, several years after their respective deaths, still seem so alive and so much younger than their survivors. It does not account for the patricidal attacks, launched against modernism in general and Mr. Eliot in particular, by angry middle-aged men such as Karl Shapiro, whose rallying cry is *In Defence of Ignorance*. It throws no light on the charlatanical fame that has accrued to Picasso's younger compatriot, Salvador Dalí, for turning back his limp and dripping watches. Yet one of the spokesmen for a resurgent conservatism, Peter Viereck, throws out a meaningful hint, when he speaks of "the revolt against revolt." And the Institute of Modern Art at Boston has officially marked the mid-century transition by changing its name to the Institute of Contemporary Art. Now, we are all contemporaries; about that we have no option, so long as we stay alive. But we may choose whether or not we wish to be modern, and the present drift seems to be toward the negative choice and away from the hazards of controversial involvement.

"An intellectual deliverance is the peculiar demand of those ages which are called modern." So Matthew Arnold had declared in his inaugural lecture "On the Modern Element in Literature." But though that lecture was delivered at Oxford in 1857 — the year that inaugurated French modernism by dragging both *Madame*

Bovary and *Les Fleurs du mal* through the lawcourts — it was not much more than another of Arnold's pleas for classicism. By recourse to his criteria, which were those of high civilization, Sophocles and Lucretius could be ranked among the moderns. It remained for the late Edwin Muir to work out the implications of this relativistic conception, applying it also to the Renaissance and to such nineteenth-century prophets as Nietzsche. Muir's sharply pointed paragraphs in *The New Age*, collected under a pseudonym as *We Moderns* in 1918, were republished in the United States two years later with a polemical introduction by H. L. Mencken. Modernity, they argued, does not necessarily mean the very latest thing; rather it is a program of cultural emancipation, "a principle of life itself" which can only be maintained by "constantly struggling." The struggle of the moment was against such reactionaries as G. K. Chesterton and such derivatives as John Galsworthy. The long-range conflict would meet those forces which, recognizing the challenge of modernism, damn it as heresy in every sphere.

Today we live in what has been categorized — by whom but Arnold Toynbee? — as the Post-Modern Period. Looking back toward the Moderns, we may feel as Dryden did when he looked back from the Restoration to the Elizabethans, contrasting earlier strength with later refinement. "Theirs was the giant race before the Flood. . . . The Second Temple was not like the First." But, we may console ourselves by reflecting, there are times of change and times that seek stability; a time for exploring and innovating may well lead into a time for assimilating and consolidating. We may well count ourselves fortunate in that we can so effortlessly enjoy those gains secured by the pangs of our forerunners. Lacking the courage of their convictions, much in our arts and letters simply exploits and diffuses, on a large scale and at a popular level, the results of their experimentalism. F. Scott Fitzgerald, because he managed to catch some of the glamor that finally caught him, has himself been sentimentalized as a hero of biography, fiction, and drama. Compare his own reckless hero of the twenties, the great

and flamboyant Gatsby, with a typical protagonist of the fifties —
the decent, judicious, respectable Arthur Winner in James Gould
Cozzens' *By Love Possessed* — and you can measure how far we
have advanced into the middle age of the twentieth century.

Compare a militant novel of the thirties — let us say John Steinbeck's *Grapes of Wrath* — with a penitent novel of the forties,
Lionel Trilling's *Middle of the Journey*, and you can locate the
turn that came *nel mezzo del cammin*. The Second World War
was the Flood; but the Temple had been crumbling and the giant
race disappearing through what W. H. Auden, retrospectively and
rather too severely, called "a low dishonest decade." Some of the
talents were prematurely sacrificed: Guillaume Apollinaire, García
Lorca. Others survived without honor in their own countries, as
Ezra Pound and Boris Pasternak did for different reasons. Many
of their amiable juniors were led astray by those "enemies of
promise" which Cyril Connolly demurred at but did little to resist. The query "Who killed Dylan Thomas?" has prompted some
maudlin accusations. The poignant fact about James Agee's writing,
much of it published posthumously, is his uneasiness about not
living up to his genuine promise. The gifted J. D. Salinger, who
writes so movingly of adolescent confusions, has yet to free himself from them. Our colleges are full of writers in residence, who
offer courses in "creative" writing, and publish embittered novels
whose principal source of interest is the noncoincidental resemblance between their colleagues and their characters.

Though our Miltons may not be glorious, they are both vocal
and pampered. Poetry has become a caucus-race, where there are
prizes for all the participants and where there are virtually no
spectators. The little magazines that "died to make verse free," as
people used to say, have been resurrected on the campuses, where
they specialize in the stricter Provençal forms. Joyce's books, which
were burned and censored during his lifetime, have become a happy
hunting ground for doctoral candidates; while his disheveled disciple, Samuel Beckett, is the subject of an article in a current issue
of *PMLA*. One of my intermittent nightmares is based on two

tons of Thomas Wolfe's manuscripts now reposing in a vault of the Houghton Library, and the thought that future scholars will gain reputations by putting back what the editors cut out. It is significant that Lawrence Durrell's tetralogy, one of the very few ambitious novels to appear in Britain latterly, takes place in the self-consciously decadent city of Alexandria. "Art," as Thomas Mann announced and illustrated in *Doktor Faustus*, "is becoming criticism." In the same vein John Crowe Ransom, who turned from poet to critic some thirty years ago, lately announced that literature has been moving from an age of creation into an age of criticism.

Mr. Ransom, interviewed on his retirement from his influential chair as teacher and editor at Kenyon College, stressed the happier aspects of the prevailing situation: the necessity for thoughtful rereading, the opportunities for self-cultivation and renewed understanding of the existent classics. An instance might be the revival of Henry James, far more dominant now than he ever was in his day. These are valid and absorbing pursuits, and I am too ingrained an academic myself to deplore the amenities of the Academy. Then too, it must be conceded, there are positive advantages to living in an epoch which technology has enriched with esthetic appliances, so that our acquaintance with music and with the fine arts is vastly augmented by long-playing records and photographic reproductions. But this is reproduction, not production; we are mainly consumers rather than producers of art. We are readers of reprints and connoisseurs of high fidelity, even as we are gourmets by virtue of the expense account and the credit card. For our wide diffusion of culture is geared to the standardizations of our economy, and is peculiarly susceptible to inflationary trends. The independence of our practitioners, when they are not domesticated by institutions of learning, is compromised more insidiously by the circumstances that make art a business.

The prosperous and the established, *The Just and the Unjust*, find their mirror in the novels of Mr. Cozzens, as opposed to that concern for the underprivileged which novelists used to profess. Genius, more understanding than misunderstood, rises to worldly success in the shrewd fiction of C. P. Snow, where science and scholarships provide the means for "the new men" to enter "the corridors of power." From England we hear of young men who are angry, presumably at the various conformities that they sum up in their conception of an Establishment. It is not quite so clear what is beating our so-called beat generation; they seem to be rebels without a cause, born too late in a world too old. Jack Kerouac, in *On the Road*, has produced a document which fills some of us with the wistful feeling that experience must somehow have passed us by. Yet his friends, for all their violent whims, do not seem to be having nearly so good a time as Hemingway's playboys in *The Sun Also Rises*. The school associated with San Francisco, for whatever a personal impression may or may not be worth, looks very much like Greenwich Village transported across the continent long after its heyday. It exemplifies the cultural lag rather than the advance-guard.

As it happens, I have been somewhat associated with the publishing firm known as New Directions, which was founded in the late nineteen-thirties by my college friend, James Laughlin. In spite of its vanguard title, it has been primarily engaged in fighting a rear-guard action. The leading innovators on its list have been Ezra Pound and William Carlos Williams, both of whom are advanced septuagenarians nowadays. The other day I noticed a reference to the annual miscellany, *New Directions*, which was characterized as "the accepted place for off-beat publication." Here is an interesting contradiction in terms, which reveals a deeper contradiction in our standards. Whether it expresses the nonconformist's yearning for conformity or the conformist's urge toward nonconformity, it gives with one hand what it takes away with the other. It weighs the notion of acceptance against the compound *off-beat*, which is so characteristic an expression of the mid-century. The noun *beat* accords with the terminology of jazz; as an ungrammatical participle, the same word carries certain sado-masochistic overtones, e.g. *beat-up*. Rounded off by a Slavic suffix, which may be either affectionate or contemptuous, and which must have been reinforced by the Sputnik, it has become an epithet for the fashion of being flagrantly unfashionable, *beatnik*.

However, its underlying connotation seems to derive from the cop who is off his beat, the man in uniform who has gone off duty and strayed into unfamiliar territory. Thus it subserves the ambivalent curiosity of the denizens of a well-grooved society about whatever may lie beyond its beaten paths. It represents an ineffectual effort to vary the cliché, and probably owes its currency to those whose own beat is Madison Avenue. A cognate phrase, *off-Broadway*, is more concrete in specifying the relationship between that main thoroughfare, the precinct of uniformity, and its bypaths, where novelty may perchance be encountered. Legitimate drama, all but superseded on Broadway by musical comedy, has had to improvise its theaters in devious lofts and makeshift basements. Shaw's *Pygmalion*, in its Broadwayized version of Covent Garden, *My Fair Lady*, is the soaring index of this trend. Like those bland composites to which Hollywood reduces imported ideas, it is an entrepreneurial accomplishment, another by-product of the middleman's pragmatic philosophy as stated by Pope:

> Be not the first by whom the new are tried,
> Nor yet the last to lay the old aside.

That sentiment is reversed paradoxically when an advertisement for *Esquire*, the haberdashery magazine, salutes its *clientèle* as "the aware moderns who are the first to embrace a new idea and speed it upon its way to becoming the popular fashion." Well, we Post-Moderns like to eat our cake and keep it, to take a chance on a sure thing. We tipsters want to call the long shot while hogging the inside track, to take credit for originality without risking unpopularity. Hence we congratulate ourselves upon our broadmindedness because *Lady Chatterley's Lover* is now a best-seller after thirty years of suppression.

Thirty years constitute nature's round number for the span from infancy through maturity, and consequently a kind of basic rhythm for reckoning the progresses and regressions of mankind. Thirty years is just about the age-difference between a playboy and an academician: consider the case history of Jean Cocteau. What is generally regarded as the Irish Renaissance began in 1892 with Yeats's *Countess Cathleen* and terminated in 1922 with Joyce's *Ulysses*. Broader movements, succeeding one another, are comparable in their periodicity. Thus, if we start with Wordsworth's manifesto of 1800, we observe that the Continental triumph of Romanticism dates from 1830. Shortly before the end of another cycle, this gives way to the countertendencies toward Positivism, Realism, and Naturalism; whereas, when we move from the sixties to the nineties, the latest watchwords are Symbolism, Estheticism, and Decadence. It will be seen that a revolutionary generation tends to be succeeded by a reactionary one; to put it less politically and more psychologically, there seems to be a cyclic oscillation between tough and tender minds. That would help to explain the phenomenon of the hard-boiled nineteen-twenties, recoiling as it were from the softness of the *fin du siècle*. It might also set the acknowledged weaknesses of the fifties into clarifying perspective.

But nostalgia for the vigorous youth of our century is a weakness in which we need not indulge ourselves; nor would it serve any purpose to draw invidious comparisons between our immediate contemporaries and our elders. The average life is privileged to span two generations, responding to what Henri Peyre has termed *"le rythme alterné des générations,"* and we live at least in the afterglow of the Moderns. Insofar as they were ahead of their time, we can even claim to be nearer to them. Furthermore, each generation has three decades, in which either to gather momentum after a wavering start, or else to subside from a powerful beginning. Accordingly, the manic twenties declined into the depressive thirties, which yielded in turn to the war-interrupted forties. If the countermovement of the fifties seems to have begun unpromisingly, we may take comfort in expecting the sixties to proceed on a rising plane, looking toward the next watershed in the nineteen-eighties. There George Orwell's object-lesson gives us pause, and we shift with relief to a backward glance and a less complex set of variables. We can examine the material factors, chart the framing conditions, and project the hypothetical curves of artistic activity. Yet we have no means of predicting how the human sensibilities, in their most individualized manifestations, will respond.

The best we can do is to recognize when those responses have occurred with a special resonance. But that point cannot be established by generalizations; let me particularize instead, with a handful of titles and names and dates. Among the latter, 1922 stands out as the year of Proust's death, of the publication of his central volume, *Sodome et Gomorrhe,* and the first appearance of his work in England. English letters had likewise to absorb the twofold shock of *Ulysses* and *The Waste Land.* And if this was not enough for the reviewers, D. H. Lawrence offered them *Aaron's Rod,* Virginia Woolf *Jacob's Room,* and Katherine Mansfield *The Garden Party.* Readers of poetry faced not merely the Georgian Anthology but Hardy's *Late Lyrics and Earlier,* Yeats's *Later Poems,* and Housman's *Last Poems* — it sounded rather autumnal, but the harvest grew with reaping. Lytton Strachey's *Books and Characters* was more narrowly *de l'époque,* while Max Beerbohm's *Rossetti and His Circle* was an antiquarian curio. Among the highlights of the season in France were *Charmes,* Valéry's collection of verse, and the first installment of Martin du Gard's *Les Thibault.* Germany saw Bertolt Brecht's first play, *Baal,* and *Die Sonette an Orpheus* by Rainer Maria Rilke. Americans were reading Sinclair Lewis' *Babbitt* and being scandalized by Eugene O'Neill's *Anna Christie.*

Though I have been highly selective, the list is sufficient to justify an *annus mirabilis* — or would be, if there were not others comparably brilliant. Let us therefore sample another year, jumping arbitrarily to 1924, when Franz Kafka died, scarcely known, since his novels would only be published during the next three years. The greatest event for the critics was Thomas Mann's masterwork, *Der Zauberberg.* The noisiest, perhaps, was the Surrealist Manifesto, which proved to be something of an anticlimax; but

Valéry counterbalanced it with his first collection of critical prose, *Variété*; while Gide braved scandal by signing *Corydon*. America witnessed Sherwood Anderson's autobiography, *A Story-Teller's Story*, Marianne Moore's salient volume of poetic *Observations*, and William Faulkner's first book, also in verse, *The Marble Faun*. In Britain, George Moore waxed more reminiscent than ever with *Conversations in Ebury Street*; T. E. Hulme's posthumous *Speculations* were to have continuing influence on criticism and poetry; each of the three Sitwells contributed to the ebullition by bringing out a book; and Bernard Shaw was inspired to touch his heights by the theme of *Saint Joan*. E. M. Forster's *Passage to India* may have been an omen as well as a milestone; for it was his most important novel to date, and it is the last that Mr. Forster has given us.

Everyone can multiply for himself these modern instances; while students of Russian or Spanish literature can point to additional flowerings which were either transplanted or nipped in the bud. Futurism, as Joyce foresaw, had no future; Marinetti fell in line behind Mussolini; and Hitler was to proscribe Modernism as degenerate art or *Kulturbolschewismus*. We hardly need to underline the pressures or constraints that limited the epoch so poignantly, *entre deux guerres*, to Mr. Forster's "long week-end," 1918–1939. Nor could we blame the generation confronted with the task of continuing to write, if they found it hard to forgive such knowledge. Yet at this distance we can perceive, with increasing clarity, that the modernistic movement comprises one of the most remarkable constellations of genius in the history of the West. And while some of its lights are still among us, before they have all been extinguished, we should ask ourselves why they have burned with such pyrotechnic distinction. What, if anything, have such figures in common, each of them vowed to idiosyncracy, practising a divergent medium, formed in a disparate background? Above all, the elementary circumstance that they happen to be coeval, more or less; that they are all, or would have been, in their eighth decade today. But what, if we are not to beg the question, was the *Zeit-*

geist they shared? What was there in the air they breathed that differed from the intellectual climate of their successors or predecessors?

All of them grew up in the late nineteenth century and matured in the early twentieth, reaching their prime in the period between the wars. The nineteenth was not so well organized as the eighteenth, nor so deeply speculative as the seventeenth, nor so richly magniloquent as the Renaissance. But, as the apogee of middle-class liberalism, it permitted a maximum of leeway for the emergence of individuality; it educated individuals thoroughly; it collected art and fostered science; it cultivated human relationships; it developed temperament and talent. Into its world the Modernists were born, and yet they were not quite shaped by it. To it they often hark back, with that acute sensibility which they have reserved for their own impressions of adolescence. Had they been born any earlier, they might have felt — with Henry Adams — that they had missed a still earlier boat. Had they been mid-Victorians, they might have poured their creative energies into causes that they now could take for granted. If they had reached maturity in the nineties, their views would have inevitably been colored by the outlook of the Decadents. But they took the *fin du siècle* in youthful stride; for them, it was not so much the end of one century as it was the beginning of another.

One of the determining characteristics of modern man, which influences the role he plays and relates him to pre-existing phenomena, is the awareness of chronology. We who are children of the twentieth century never experienced the excitement of welcoming it. Our casual habit of predating centuries makes us insensitive to the West's first realization that its second millennium was now in sight. The bliss that Wordsworth inhaled at the dawning of the French Revolution had been a disillusioning adumbration. "Years of the modern! years of the unperform'd!" Such had been Whitman's prologue to a performance which he anticipated all the more keenly because, as he chanted, "No one knows what will happen next." At all events, things would be happening; and those whose existence falls within the limits of a single century may well envy those who cross temporal boundaries and have a chance to inscribe their names on history's blank pages. How terribly much it must have meant to James Joyce, as an eighteen-year-old university student, to have set his ambitions down on paper and dated them "1900!" Here was the brave new world that had been heralded by his mentor Ibsen, by Nietzsche whose death came that very year, by Tolstoy and those other Proto-Moderns who had been breaking the images that had stood in its way.

One of the assumptions about the First World War was that it had settled history. Its sequel was to teach T. S. Eliot that "History is now and England." But the interval thought of itself in the present tense, separating modernity from history. The past was over; the present was happily more comfortable — though unhappily less colorful, as Miniver Cheevy and other time-snobs lamented. Ernest Hemingway's first book of stories was aptly entitled *In Our Time,* and its grasp of immediacy was heightened by its reminiscences of battle. His intensive concentration on the instant, which imparts a film-like quality to his fiction, is pinpointed in "The Snows of Kilimanjaro," when a polyglot series of synonyms runs through the mind of a dying writer: "Now, *ahora, maintenant, heute.* . . ." Whatever the language, the meaning is imminence; and that "nowness" is a precondition of the search for newness, for what Whitman had termed "the unperform'd." To perform the unperformed! *La Nouvelle Revue Française!* "The Great English Vortex!" The sense of novelty, of potentialities being opened up, does not seem any less eager because it is juxtaposed to the inherited sense of the past and the pleasures of retrospection. Everyman, in his more thoughtful moods, is conscious of his overwhelming patrimony as heir of all the ages; and his relation to them takes the guise of an endless stroll among the masterpieces of their invisible museum.

Time was of the essence, not only for the metaphysician Bergson, but for the innumerable poets, novelists, painters, and scientists who worked in the dimension he formulated. Vainly did Wyndham Lewis assail the time-consciousness of his contemporaries. As the Gracehoper retorted to the Ondt, in Joyce's fable, "Why can't you beat time?" The lifework of Proust was precisely such an attempt, the attempt of an aging dilettante to make up for lost time by recapturing the past, repudiating its ephemeral concerns and crystallizing its highest moments through an appeal to the timelessness of art. Yeats pursued the same objective symbolically, when he pictured himself abandoning the earthbound sphere of nature and setting sail for the timeless art-city, Byzantium. His poet, Michael Robartes, had desired to remember forgotten beauty. The feeling of belatedness has the habitual effect of stimulating the act of memory, along with the stylistic consequence of sounding echoes, evoking reverberations, and playing with *pastiche*. When Pound advised disciples to "make it new," he was repeating a maxim as old as Confucius, and was well aware of the irony; for his studies in the Renaissance had won him insights into the processes of cultural renewal, and shown him how renovation could be innovation — what "the age demanded."

What I have ventured to call the metamorphic impetus seems to have resulted from this paradoxical state of feeling belated and up-to-date simultaneously, and of working experimental transformations into traditional continuities. But there are other preconditions of Modernism, geographical as well as historical. Joyce and Picasso, Eliot and Stravinsky have another trait in common — alas, too common among the uncommon artists of our time. How few of them have lived out their careers in the lands of their origin! To be sure, migration is a civilizing force, and sojourn abroad has been a classic step in the artistic *curriculum vitae*. Unfortunately we have had to learn, through dint of wars, revolutions, and political persecutions, the distinction between expatriation and exile. The hyphenated German-Jewish Czech, Kafka, though he did not live to share it, clairvoyantly sketched the plight of the displaced person. Mann, who was destined to become a transatlantic nomad, had situated his magic mountain in neutral Switzerland. There, in the International Sanitorium Berghof, his Teutonic hero undergoes successive exposure to a Swiss physician, an Italian poet, a Polish priest, a Dutch businessman, and a Russian mistress. Then, having gained an education while regaining his health, he is lost in combat with the Allies.

The catchphrase employed by Continental architects, "The International Style," might be very appropriately extended to other works of the twenties. Many of them were composed in Paris, the capital of between-the-wars cosmopolitanism. "The School of Paris" — a topographical designation for unacademic painting — was presided over by our expatriate Spaniard, Picasso, who now has his monument in New York. Paris was the inevitable headquarters for those Russian dancers, designers, and choreographers who staged Stravinsky's ballets. It was where a famous generation of Americans got temporarily lost, under the Sybilline tutelage of Gertrude Stein. Meanwhile, in an apartment near the Etoile, the self-exiled Irishman Joyce was carefully elaborating the most minute and comprehensive account that any city has ever received from literature — his account of his native Dublin. *Ulysses* is of its time, in endeavoring to arrest the eighteen hours of time it exhaustively chronicles. Nineteenth-century novelists, especially Balzac, had set forth the complexities of the metropolis, but through a sequence of loosely connected novels where more or less conventional narrative was filled in with sharply detailed observation. Joyce's unexampled contribution was a gigantic yet rigorously experimental design, which controlled the accumulating details as they fell into place.

It is the metamorphic impetus that provides this controlling device: the transmutation of Dublin citizens into mythical archetypes out of the *Odyssey*. In the novel, as Naturalism had left it, the environment came dangerously close to swamping the personages. That was not the fault of the Naturalists, but of the situations with which they dealt. The dehumanization of art, if I may build upon a useful phrase from Ortega y Gasset, mirrors the dehumanization of life. Joyce, by resorting to metamorphosis and even to mock-apotheosis, was trying to rehumanize his characters;

and he succeeded in giving them contour, if not stature. Journalistic novelists like John Dos Passos and Jean-Paul Sartre, seeking a panoramic or kaleidoscopic approach to the urban scene, have imitated Joyce's structural methods. But the problem, to which the French *Unanimistes* and the German proponents of the *Gesamtkunstwerk* have also addressed themselves, goes beyond — or else within — the matter of structure. If the object is unity, that must bear an organic connection to the multiplicity; its collective pattern must be revealed and confirmed through individual lives; its outward view of social interaction must be combined with an inner focus on psychological motivation.

Hence the old-fashioned type of rounded fictional character, standing between the narrator and the reader, seems to dissolve in the stream of consciousness, which directly and transparently conveys a flow of impression and sensation from the external world. Though the novelist need not utilize the internal monologue, increasingly he approximates to the voice and the viewpoint of his protagonist. The very completeness of the ensuing intimacy forces him to fall back upon the raw materials of his own autobiography, refining them into self-portraiture of the artist. The intensity of Proust's introspection pushed him to the point where he disclosed an abyss between the *moi* and everything else. Gide, by writing his novel about a novelist writing a novel, *Les Faux-monnayeurs,* including his novelist's journal, and then publishing the journal he kept while writing that novel, *Le Journal des Faux-monnayeurs,* demonstrated that first-person narrative may become a double mirror reflecting infinity. Fiction was spurred to such feats of self-consciousness by the revelations of psychoanalysis: the Freudian probing for unconscious motives, the Jungian search for universal patterns. It may be an exaggeration to argue that human nature changed in 1910, but Virginia Woolf was bold enough to do so, though probably unaware that the International Psychoanalytical Association had been founded in that year.

That argument was a measured overstatement, put forward in defending the new Georgian novelists against such Edwardians as Arnold Bennett. Mrs. Woolf knew that it would have just about as much validity as the assertion that sunsets have changed since Monet and the Impressionists undertook to paint them. It was true, in the sense that characterization had changed, that people too were being visualized through the eyes of other people, and that another metamorphosis was thereby being effected. The author of *Orlando* understood that permutations so subtle and subjective might have a circumscribing effect on the novel. Most flexible of genres, it readily focuses either upon the recesses of the self or the expanses of society; and the twenties took it to both extremes, sometimes at once, with their mental analyses and their monumental constructs. Here is where Ultraism may have attained its *ne plus ultra*. Joyce himself could go no farther than *Finnegans Wake;* few others could get that far; and later novelists have understandably made no attempt to press beyond *Ulysses.* This has stirred some critics to announce that the novel is an obsolete or dying form. One cannot deny that it seems to be regressing toward the plane of documentary realism, where at best it may be indistinguishable from reportage or good journalism.

But fiction is doomed to failure in its competition with fact. What it possesses that nonfiction lacks is fantasy — that is to say, the projective power of the imagination, which confers value and significance on the stuff of our everyday apprehension by rearranging and transmuting it. Thus the apparent sordidness and purposelessness of our day with Leopold Bloom in Dublin are transmuted into a symbolic re-enactment of Homer's epic. Some of those cross-references seem farfetched, and others grimly ironic; yet, as a whole, they interpret for us data which would otherwise be meaningless. Joyce's use of myth makes the past a key to the present. More than that, wrote T. S. Eliot in his review of *Ulysses*, "It has the importance of a scientific discovery." Future writers would take advantage of it, as he predicted; and even then he had just finished his *Waste Land*, which abounded in flashbacks and parallels. In that least heroic and most fragmentary of epics, he exorcized the blight of contemporaneous London by tracing through it the outline of a quest for the Holy Grail. A timeless ritual, a timely critique, I. A. Richards commented that it completed the severance between poetry and belief. But, in the long run, it proved to be a station on Mr. Eliot's pilgrimage toward faith.

It is not surprising that Modernism, the product of cities, should be so impelled to recreate the image of cities. One of the greatest Modernists, in this respect, is Charlie Chaplin, who has so brilliantly rendered the metropolis in all its frustrations and incongruities. For T. S. Eliot, London is "unreal"; but its apparition is that of Vienna, Athens, Jerusalem, or Alexandria; and his elegiac vision becomes prophetic when he imagines "falling towers." The prophecy was apocalyptically fulfilled by the bombings of the next war, which Mr. Eliot — combining his own observation as air-raid warden with a reminiscence from Dante's *Inferno* — has powerfully invoked in the last of his *Four Quartets*. That he should proceed by musical analogy, finding his inspiration in the austere but imposing string quartets of the later Beethoven, is still another trait of his generation. Poets' poets and novelists' novelists, painters' painters and musicians' musicians, they were profoundly versed in their own particular crafts, and so wholeheartedly devoted to craftsmanship that they attempted to transfer it from one art to another. Writers borrowed thematic techniques from Wagner, who himself had aimed at a synesthesia, to be induced by music in conjunction with other arts. Poetry encompassed painting and music, when Wallace Stevens presented — after Picasso — his *Man with a Blue Guitar*.

The thought that a man of letters should consider himself a practitioner of the fine arts, or that he should be designated professionally as an artist, is a legacy from Flaubert's generation which is not likely to outlast Joyce's by long. The cult of intransigent artistry, which both men practised as devoutly as if it were their religious vocation, is embodied in and elucidated by the latter's *Portrait of the Artist as a Young Man*, where the archetypal figure is Daedalus, the fabulous Greek artificer, and the epigraph is a line about him from Ovid's *Metamorphoses*: "*Et ignotas animum dimittit in artes.*" Joyce was clearly inviting the application to himself: "And so he turned his mind to unknown arts." Paul Valéry discerned a historical prototype in the artist-engineer of the Italian Renaissance, and paid his homage in two essays upon the method of Leonardo da Vinci. He made his own apologia through the personage of M. Teste (M. Tête, Mr. Head), whose cerebral soliloquies begin with the unabashed admission: "*La bêtise n'est pas mon fort.*" Stupidity has decidedly not been the forte of the Modernists; they have left that virtue to their Post-Modern attackers, who can now write in defence of ignorance. If M. Teste seems arrogant, let them make the most of that last infirmity. He was just as firm, in refusing to suffer fools, as they are weak in appealing to philistines.

Though recent literature prides itself upon its outspokenness, there remains one organ of the body which it is almost taboo to mention, and that is the brain. What may seem a sin, on the part of the Moderns, is that they were preoccupied with the minds of their characters, and — what is worse — that they make serious demands upon the minds of their readers. This cannot be lightly forgiven by an era whose culture-heroes are persistently mindless — whether they be the good-hearted goons of John Steinbeck, the epicene slobs of Tennessee Williams, or the analphabetic gladiators of the later Hemingway. But popularity was excluded, by definition, from the aims of the writers I have been discussing; their names did not figure upon the best-seller lists of their day; many others did, which are now forgotten. The aura of obscurity or unintelligibility which may still occasionally tinge these intellectuals, in some degree, emanates from their refusal to advertise themselves or to talk down to their audience in the hope of enlarging it. That, for them, would indeed have been a treason of the clerks. Their ultimate quality, which pervades their work to the very marrow, is its uncompromising intellectuality. Like the intelligentsia of old Russia or the class of mandarins in China, they looked upon letters as a way of life.

But this may have presupposed, along with their own dedication, other conditions which may no longer be possible. The extraordinary spread of higher learning has lowered it, and introduced a large amount of dilution. The highbrows and the lowbrows have intermarried, and their children are — exactly what Virginia Woolf dreaded most — all middlebrows. Instead of a tension between the uncomprehending majority and the saving remnant — or, if you will, between sensible citizens and longhaired coteries — there has been a *détente*, a relaxation, and a collaboration for mutual profit between the formerly intractable artist and the no longer hostile bourgeoisie. Out of it there seems to be emerging a middlebrow synthesis, the moderated expression of our mid-century. But that is a subject notoriously better appreciated by professors of sociology and experts on mass communication than it is by old-fashioned scholars or modernist critics. Nor do I wish to imply that all of our talents, responding to technological pressure and economic attraction, have become mere purveyors of entertainment. On the contrary, many of them profess an engagement of the sincerest kind to the responsibilities of common welfare. The Modernists did not have to make such commitments, because they were not threatened by such urgencies. Hence they could strive for artistic perfection in singleminded detachment.

Alfred North Whitehead was strongly convinced that the early twentieth century was one of the greatest epochs in the march of intellect. Though he was thinking basically of mathematics and physics, he held a lively belief in the interplay between the sciences and the humanities. He concurred with the opinion that Wordsworth, writing from the opposite vantage point, had expressed in the opening year of the nineteenth century:

If the labours of Men of science should ever create any material revolution, direct or indirect, in our condition, and in the impressions which we habitually receive, the Poet will sleep then no more than at present;

he will be ready to follow the steps of the Man of science, not only in those general indirect effects, but he will be at his side, carrying sensation into the midst of the objects of the science itself.

Certainly such a material revolution has taken place; the arts have struggled to adapt themselves to it; and we gain a fuller comprehension of the modern artist, if we envision him — in Wordsworth's terms — at the side of the scientist. The partnership, however uneasy, has intensified his curiosity and sharpened his preoccupation with his own technique. He has been encouraged to experiment, not by blindly accepting hypotheses as Zola did in his *roman expérimental,* but rather as Valéry did in transferring to poetry the lessons he had learned from geometry, or in taking for his motto *"ars non stagnat."* Successful experiment involves trial and error and much incidental waste before verification, as scientists well know. This is a necessary function performed, upon the fringes of the arts, by that continued ferment of willed eccentricity whose products we can usually dismiss. But "the two cultures," as Sir Charles Snow has lately reminded us, are still too far apart. What should draw them together, more than anything else, is the shared recognition that conjointly they cover an area which man has set aside for the free play of painstaking intelligence.

Science no longer underprops our world view with rationalistic or positivistic reassurances. It has undergone a modernist phase of its own, and seen its solid premises subverted by such concepts as relativity and indeterminacy. Where, then, can we turn for illumination? Can we come to no more helpful conclusion than the message that E. M. Forster discerned in the Marabar Caves of India? "Everything exists; nothing has value." Critics of the Moderns have accused them of being deficient in a sense of values, of believing in nothing beyond that negativistic credo. However, to reread Eliot's "Fire Sermon," or Kafka's "Parable of the Law," or Mann's farewell to his soldier-hero, or Proust's commemoration of a great writer's death, or Joyce's hallucinating encounter between a sonless father and a fatherless son, is to feel the glow of ethical insight. A younger and more plain-spoken writer whom we have lost much too soon, Albert Camus, received the Nobel Prize three years ago for having "illuminated the problems of the human conscience in our time." That citation recalls the warning of an earlier French moralist, Rabelais, at the very dawn of modernity, that *"science sans conscience"* would bring ruin to the soul. Joyce's young artist, Stephen Dedalus, pledged himself to create the "un-created conscience" of his people. Has it not been the endeavor of his generation to have created a conscience for a scientific age?

This article is the latest in the present collection, having appeared in The Atlantic Monthly for February 1966, slightly abridged for reasons of space. The process of emancipation it traces goes farther each day; indeed it seems to have come full circle with the new anthology of M. Girodias, which spares the prurient reader the effort of thumbing his way through many books in search of the mooted passages. At the moment, the issue stands again before the Supreme Court. The basic problems of censorship or noncensorship now, as I tried to indicate, are social and psychological rather than legal and ethical. But I have been interested in the subject primarily as a special case for the problem of realism — the extension of the literary franchise to planes of experience heretofore unexpressed because of official taboos.

I

When I was a freshman at Harvard, a Cambridge bookseller was jailed for selling a copy of Joyce's *Ulysses* to a customer who turned out to be an agent from the Watch and Ward Society of Massachusetts. The issue was brought home to some of us — if not to the court — when our most admired instructor, F. O. Matthiessen, testified in vain for the defense. Not that we had got as far as Harvard in innocence of the banned book. During a previous summer, like hundreds of other Americans, I had bought my own copy from the publisher, Sylvia Beach, at her little Paris bookshop on the Rue de l'Odéon. To pack it wrapped in laundry and smuggle it past the U. S. customs inspectors, thereby involving ourselves in what was called "booklegging," gave us an easy thrill of complicity with the embattled author and his courageous champions. It also widened our sense of a rift existing between true culture and the Establishment.

Four years afterward, in 1933, soon after Prohibition had been repealed by the emergent New Deal, the ban on *Ulysses* was lifted. The critical decision, which opened the way for an American edition the following year, was handed down by Judge John M. Woolsey of the U. S. District Court for Southern New York. His incisive opinion acted as a great watershed, since it reversed the trend of earlier opinions and would be frequently cited in later ones. Specifically, books had been condemned on the basis of passages which sounded offensive when taken out of context and without concern for the author's design. Moreover, the determining question had been — in the reverberating phraseology of the so-called Hicklin Rule — whether the reading of such books would tend to "deprave and corrupt" those into whose hands they were likely to fall, regardless of — or rather, with special regard for — their immaturity.

Some of the world's acknowledged classics could be adjudged obscene, and had been, by such procedures. The freedom to read had been abridged, for educated adults, because a mooted book might fall into the hands of children. Mr. Podsnap's cautionary principle of Victorian morality had become a legal criterion: "Would it bring a blush into the cheek of a young person?" Instead of the *jeune fille* as final arbiter of the book's effect, Judge Woolsey proposed "what the French would call *l'homme moyen sensuel.*" The law now seems to recognize this concept of the normal adult reader, "a person with average sex instincts," as the counterpart to its "reasonable man" in matters of practical judgment. Curiously enough, the French expression — more correctly *l'homme sensuel moyen* — is never used in the sensual land of France. It seems to have been invented by Matthew Arnold, who, to be sure, was writing about George Sand.

As for the dishing-up of salacious titbits carefully chosen to nauseate the courtroom, it is now general practice to consider a work of literature as a whole. Taking the trouble to master Joyce's demanding technique, Judge Woolsey found that *Ulysses* presented modern life in elaborate cross-section. Its round of daily activities included the library and concert-hall, as well as the bedroom and bathroom. Sexual and other bodily functions occupied no larger place than they might in ordinary lives. The same extenuation could scarcely be urged for *Lady Chatterley's Lover*, which is overwhelmingly preoccupied with sex. That may help to explain why it remained unpublishable in the United States until 1959 and in Great Britain until 1961, a generation after Lawrence's death. Nor could it be argued by his admirers that this intense last novel was his masterpiece, as *Ulysses* was Joyce's. Obviously, D. H. Lawrence was less the dispassionate artist than James Joyce.

But Lawrence was a passionate moralist, who preached his unorthodox message with evangelical fervor, and therein lay the strength that could be rallied to his support when *Lady Chatterley's Lover* went on trial at the Old Bailey. The intervening years had seen drastic changes, if not in sexual habits or morals, then in the frankness and sincerity with which they could be publicly discussed. The voice in the wilderness had been amplified into a posthumous cause, while losing none of its militant solemnity. The very name of the case, *Regina v. Penguin*, suggesting as it does a chapter from *Alice in Wonderland*, aptly announced the procession of church dignitaries, lady dons, schoolmasters, librarians, editors, critics, and publicists who took the witness stand. Against those thirty-five respectable experts the prosecution could produce no adverse testimony, except for a fastidiously skeptical judgment by Katherine Anne Porter, which Lawrence's defenders promptly impugned.

After a meticulous rereading, John Sparrow would contend that Lady Chatterley's gamekeeper was not such a model of heterosexual normality as witnesses had claimed. But Penguin had already won its case, and was circulating 200,000 paperbacks at three shillings and sixpence apiece. In retrospect it seems particularly significant that, unlike other trials which have led to the unbanning of suppressed books, this one had been decided by a jury. The prosecution, trying to extend the obsolete Hicklin Rule, had asked the jurymen: "Is it a book that you would even wish your wife or your servants to read?" And the defense had taken that point by reminding them that they lived in a democratic society, characterized by equal rights for women, the decline of the servant class, and the production of Penguin Books. The vindication of *Lady Chatterley's Lover* spoke, like the novel itself, for the social as well as the sexual revolution.

II

Regina v. Penguin Books Limited was the test case under the
new Obscene Publications Act of 1959. Thus it rounded off a cycle,
the century of the Hicklin Rule, which in turn had been based on
Lord Campbell's Obscene Publications Act of 1857. By a coincidence which may be worth noting, that year likewise marked the
interdiction of *Madame Bovary*, and it is certainly worth noting
that Flaubert was acquitted. The idea of suppressing literature,
on suspicion of its demoralizing potentialities, is at least as old as
Plato. Through the course of history, however, censorship has
mainly been exerted against religious heresy or political subversion.
The *Index Librorum Prohibitorum* was an instrument of the
Church's Counter-Reformation. The censor as guardian of private
morality is essentially a mid-Victorian figure. His period of dominance in Anglo-American culture was unconscionably prolonged,
with such untoward results as can be read in the lives and works
of Hardy, George Moore, and Shaw, or Whitman, Mark Twain,
and Dreiser.

The brilliant writers of the early twentieth century grew up in an
atmosphere of libertarian protest against what Lawrence called
"the censor-morons" — whom we might recognize, under a court-
lier phrase, as H. L. Mencken's *"virtuosi* of virtue." Joyce and
Lawrence, each in his unique way, could realize their talents only
through expatriation. Both *Ulysses* and *Lady Chatterley's Lover*
could have been first published only in France, where tradition has
been especially tolerant to books printed in English and destined
for illegal export. The judicial decisions that naturalized these two
novels into the body of English literature, all too belatedly, had
to square them with prevailing moral standards. Judge Woolsey
concluded his decision, with an epigrammatic flourish, by stating
that the effect of *Ulysses*, while somewhat emetic, was not aphrodisiac. *Lady Chatterley's Lover* could not be so easily exonerated
from the charge of undue eroticism; but, given its preoccupation,
it is clearly a tract for reform.

The volume that comes next on our shelf of literary contraband, though it has also been legitimatized by the courts, takes us into more problematic areas of discussion. *Tropic of Cancer* has not the high dedication of the two books we smuggled in before it. Indeed its utter laxity is a source of its appeal to a later generation which, perhaps, may feel more kinship with underground man than with the intransigent intellectual. Nor does the stature of Henry Miller begin to compare with that of Joyce or Lawrence; yet his critical reputation has profited from the confusions that have surrounded theirs. When compared with Joyce, as George Orwell pointed out in his farsighted essay "Inside the Whale," Miller hardly seems an artist at all. As a would-be moralist he stands at the opposite pole from Lawrence, who would have been more outraged than anyone else by the loveless fornications of *Tropic of Cancer*.

Insofar as there are degrees of vulnerability to attacks from more conventional moralists, this is a harder book to defend than its predecessors. Yet Miller has an undeniable talent, a kind of raffish gusto, as a braggart storyteller in the picaresque mode. While his monologue drifts along the gutters of Paris, it turns up some memorable flotsam. Unfortunately, and increasingly in his other work, this authentic vein of pungent humor is adulterated by messianic rhapsodies — *Leaves of Grass* gone to seed — which prove rather more embarrassing. Nevertheless, the seriousness of their intentions cannot be denied. Consequently in 1961, when the Attorney General of Massachusetts sought to ban the recent American edition of *Tropic of Cancer*, several critics were on hand to testify in its behalf. The case was heard in the Superior Court, where the judge decreed the book to be "obscene, indecent, and impure." That decree was subsequently reversed by the Supreme Judicial Court of the Commonwealth.

When I reread this decision, and see my testimony quoted, I must confess that my feelings are somewhat mixed. I had ventured to say — in effect — that the book's predominant mood was "one of sexual revulsion," and that its self-conscious morbidity reflected a sense of cultural decadence. Of course I stand by this view, and feel honored that some of the justices evidently concurred with it. But I cannot help wondering whether the book or I would have had their approval if the suggested line of interpretation had emphasized the joys of the flesh. The puritanical implication is that a writer may concern himself with sex if he treats it as a bad thing, or so long as his treatment of it is emetic rather than aphrodisiac. As a matter of fact, my fellow witnesses found Miller's outlook healthier than I did. One of them even introduced a fascinating comparison between *Tropic of Cancer* and *Huckleberry Finn*.

My colleagues, whom I respect, may conceivably be right. In any case, as professors of literature, we are used to critical disagreements. I trust that the judges allow for this variance, and do not take our personal opinions for absolute verities simply because we are consulted as "experts" offering "evidence as to the literary, cultural, or educational character" of the writings in question. What surprised me, in the *Tropic of Cancer* affair, was that no evidence could be admitted from psychiatrists and social workers. Similarly, in *Regina v. Penguin*, where the court listened so patiently to schoolmistresses and theologians, the defense could get no hearing for doctors and "people who deal with those who are sexually depraved or corrupted." Granted that such expertise is hard to come by, that the behavioral sciences are far from exact in their application. We are all left in the dark on the crucial point: the actual impact of the alleged means of corruption.

III

With regard to obscenity, the law has modified itself so extensively in recent years that the interested layman is bewildered — and not less so when he finds himself suddenly called upon as an expert by the courts. Bewilderments are bound to arise from questions which lie open at both ends; and, though a book is an objective artifact, the intent of its author is subjective, and so is its effect upon the reader. As the Director of Public Prosecutions said, in discussing the Obscene Publications Bill, " 'Intent' is a difficult word." There is even a school of formalistic critics which would rule out "the intentional fallacy." Judge Woolsey supplied his colleagues on the bench with another epigram, which they have used to test the purity of a writer's motives, when he spoke of "dirt for dirt's sake." The late Justice Frankfurter, characteristically asking for more precision, suggested that the phrase be changed to "dirt for money's sake."

But to speak of dirt is to beg a subtle question. And if the practice of writing for money is generally approved, why should it be specially enjoined against when the subject matter happens to be the important matter of sex? Is it because of the possible effect? Then we shift our ground, and the lawyers begin to talk about provoking lustful thoughts or appealing to prurient interest. Ordinarily we praise a writer when, in dealing with any other subject, he manages to convey sensations and stimulate reactions. Advertisers vie with one another, using a directly visual stimulus, to inject an erotic flavor into the most irrelevant situations. We cannot walk through our day without encountering dozens of random excitations which, if we are healthy, ought to arouse our susceptibilities. "A state of mind is not enough," Mr. Justice Douglas has written, "it is the relationship of that state of mind to overt action that would seem to be critical."

It is humbling to realize how little is known about the nature of that relationship, and how widely the trains of speculation diverge. Literature is full of stories that demonstrate — and possibly exaggerate — the influence of literature on behavior, such as Dante's poignant example of Paolo and Francesca, who became lovers after reading a romance together. Specialists in children's problems earnestly and endlessly debate over comic books: whether they are a major cause of juvenile delinquency or a valid inoculation against it. Classicists and psychoanalysts alike believe in catharsis, the notion that the mind can be purged of its antisocial tendencies by participating in vicarious passions. Tragedy has been exhibiting crimes on the stage for centuries, and its after-effects are usually regarded as elevating rather than conducive to further crime.

Books that dwell on sexual episodes might be just as likely to relieve tensions as to incite lewd and lascivious conduct.

At all events, we must have broader experience, keener observation, and more systematic investigation before we can make confident assumptions as to how a given piece of reading-matter would affect an unforeseen variety of readers. It may be that the Kinsey Institute, which has assembled an impressive library of erotica, will carry its researches into this limbo and bring us back some antiseptic answers. In the meantime, the reading public has been enjoying an unprecedented latitude. The battles for Joyce (inclusion of sex as part of the all-round picture), Lawrence (emphasis on sex as a means of salvation), and Miller (obsession with sex as a nihilistic gesture) have opened the floodgates. After *Ulysses*, *Lady Chatterley's Lover*, and *Tropic of Cancer*, what then? Irreversibly the progression moves on, impelled by its own momentum, a sheer need for the next revelation to outstrip the last one. Having exploited the themes of normal sexuality, it seeks new disclosures by turning to perversion and inversion.

Censorship has backed down with less and less struggle, as Vladimir Nabokov's *Lolita* or William Burroughs' *Naked Lunch* has bridged the rapid transition from the Parisian bookleggers to a New York imprimatur — and, what is more, to a *nihil obstat* in Boston. Nabokov would be an exception in any grouping, a displaced mandarin from a more elegant age, and his flirtation with vice is merely another whim of his idiosyncrasy. Burroughs continues Miller's sodden bohemianism well into its gangrenescent stage. He finds his material by wallowing deeper and deeper, and relies on drugs to give it an imaginative lift. Yet even *Naked Lunch* pays tribute to moralism in a preface and in an appended article written for *The British Journal of Addiction*. Therein Burroughs observes the convention of gallows literature, where the condemned man edifies the crowd by warning them against his particular fate. So Nabokov, tongue in cheek as usual, palms off *Lolita* as a psychiatric case-history.

The quest for sensation has been approaching the line between serious literature and pornography, if indeed that borderline is still discernible. Joyce and Lawrence both drew it very sharply, since their artistic integrity depended upon it. "Genuine pornography is almost always underworld," Lawrence could write, "it doesn't come into the open." Manifestly, we live in another epoch. The notorious *Memoirs of a Woman of Pleasure*, which has won greater notoriety as *Fanny Hill*, earned John Cleland a reprimand from the Privy Council when he brought it out in the year of *Tom Jones*. Its transatlantic distribution led, in 1821, to the first American suppression for obscenity. Notwithstanding, it has gained and held a place in Anglo-American culture, quite properly a surreptitious place among bookdealers' *curiosa*. Lately it has been brought out from under the counter and commended to a waiting world by Nabokov's publisher, the reputable old firm that published Washington Irving and Herman Melville.

IV

In the light of these developments, we can appreciate the historic irony of the recent announcement by Maurice Girodias, head of the Olympia Press and original publisher of the once-prohibited books by Miller, Nabokov, and Burroughs. His remarkable list includes Samuel Beckett, Lawrence Durrell, and other English-writing luminaries of the current international twilight, along with certain titles which might still be classified somewhere as "hard-core pornography." M. Girodias has declared his intention of moving his operations from Paris to the United States, as soon as he can disentangle them from his present difficulties with the French government. We have come a long way from the days of Sylvia Beach; and so has France, presumably, in the other direction. M. Girodias has reason to envy the Grove Press of New York, which has been so successful in domesticating many of the works that are giving him trouble, notably the English translation of Genet's *Notre-Dame des Fleurs*.

Jean Genet is a writer of unquestioned power, whose style alone would set his books apart from the pornographic confessions they often resemble, and from those American novels and stories which have recently been putting us into close touch with the homosexual *demimonde*. Yet it would be uncritical to think that Genet was not obscene, and his verbose apologist, Jean-Paul Sartre, argues the contrary: obscenity is the stance for Genet's virulent critique of modern society. In this respect, as in others, he is an heir to the Marquis de Sade, that pariah of the eighteenth century who has become a culture-hero today and whose most provocative writings have just been handsomely republished by the Grove Press. Since Mr. Justice Brennan has ruled in the Roth case of 1957 that "all ideas having even the slightest redeeming social importance" are entitled to constitutional protection, the needle's eye would seem to be large enough for the passage of such camels.

Not much room has been left for any working definition of pornography; its hard core has been softened, at any rate. Its etymological meaning, "writing about prostitution," should have some bearing on *Fanny Hill* (banned by the Massachusetts court that unbanned *Tropic of Cancer*), where every page invites what long ago Judge Woolsey called "the leer of the sensualist." But a book like *Candy* works both sides of the street by offering itself as a parody of the pornographic genre (pornography being itself a parody of more serious fiction). Rarities formerly locked in the librarians' Inferno are available in paperback, sometimes in competing editions where the sanctions of copyright fail to apply. It could be suspected that, whereas the old-fashioned censor-morons confounded art with pornography, we are now being invited to accept pornography as art. However, the old distinctions no longer serve. Those who might once have been stigmatized as purveyors of smut, "dirt for money's sake," are hailed as benefactors of civil liberties, *virtuosi* of virtue at a profit.

Established novelists do their best — and worst — to keep up with the subterranean movement, and to keep on the best-seller lists, by providing their characters with more detailed bedroom histories. Norman Mailer asserted in 1959 that sex was "perhaps the last remaining frontier of the novel which has not been exhausted by the nineteenth and early twentieth century novelists." One might have assumed that this territory was not altogether virgin before *An American Dream*, but Mailer is amply justified in his pioneering metaphor. From its first emergence, with the breakthrough of the middle class into literature, the novel has been explicitly committed to the enlargement of human experience. Its great practitioners have all been realists, in the sense that they had to cut through conventions and fight against hypocrisies, while striving to capture some segment of reality which has hitherto gone unexpressed. Hence they scandalized the authorities of their day, who retorted with repressive tactics.

Flaubert, Dostoevsky, even the Brontës — no less than Lawrence, Joyce, and their successors — all arrived by *succès de scandale*. Invariably contemporaries are shocked by innovation in the arts, and commonly accuse the innovators of being sensation-mongers — which from time to time they must be. But the shock wears off with habituation, and what is no longer new can thereupon be judged by whether or not it seems true. It was shocking to see the forbidden monosyllables in print while *Ulysses* was proscribed, though they might not have offended in masculine conversation or in feminine stream of consciousness. Nowadays we have merely to ask ourselves whether or not they fit into the fictional contexts in which they so freely appear. The convention of using asterisks or dashes seems as quaint as Ernest Hemingway's substitution of the word "obscenity" for the Spanish oaths in *For Whom the Bell Tolls*. Profanity derives its peculiar force from the violation of a taboo; expletives become meaningless once the taboos lose their hold.

When the Berkeley students shouted dirty words from a public platform, they confirmed the proprieties against which they were protesting. If speech were completely free, no words would bring a blush to a young person's cheek or raise the eyebrows of an older one. As with the language, so with the contents of books. Descriptions of sexual intimacy, if we get used to reading them, ought to provoke no special titillation. We should be able to take them or leave them, depending on whether they carry honest conviction. When everything has been said, we can focus on how it is said. We may still need safeguards for the immature; but for adults so much is already permitted that not much can consistently be excluded. Our freedom to read, as guaranteed by the law, is virtually complete. Free speech and due process, the First and Fourteenth Amendments to the Constitution as reinterpreted by Justice Brennan, reaffirm the humanism of Terence: "I am a human being, and therefore consider nothing human alien to me."

Accordingly, when writers are allowed to write anything they please and publishers to put it in circulation, then the great responsibility for discrimination rests with the reader. Art in itself may be neither moral nor immoral, as Oscar Wilde insisted; but, since we are potentially both, the courts stand ready to correct our overt immorality. Meanwhile it remains for us to determine the uses of art. If we abandon censorship, we depend all the more imperatively upon criticism. If we agree that books are neither dirty nor clean, we must be sure to remember that they are bad or good, and must not be distracted into ignoring that difference. After all, it has never been too difficult to tell a potboiler from a work of art, and it should be even simpler with potboilers that concentrate upon sex to the point of monotony. To criticize them is to discriminate between artistic imagination and autistic fantasy. One of the wholesome results of our hard-won candor is that it could end by driving the pornographers out of business.

Like the preceding essay, but nineteen years before it, the following essay was also published in The Atlantic Monthly (January 1947). A critical fantasia on a psychological theme, it is by far the oldest piece in this volume. I reprint it after some hesitation as a kind of period piece, bespeaking the reader's tolerance for allusions no longer topical or speculations which have since become commonplaces: see the chapter on "the rejected father" in Geoffrey Gorer's American People (1948). Its original appearance provoked a certain amount of correspondence, some of it from psychoanalysts who — flatteringly but incorrectly — assumed that I was either a professional colleague or a former analysand. More to my regret, I received two or three letters from Catholics objecting to the term "Mariolatry." I hastened to answer that I appreciated the basis of their objection, as well as the theological distinction between their church's veneration of Mary and the Virgin-worship of which it has sometimes been accused by Protestant controversialists. However, it was precisely that accusation to which my discussion alluded, historically and not unsympathetically. Meanwhile the record of Life with Father, my starting-point, has been outdistanced on Broadway by My Fair Lady: to analyze its success would be quite another story, probably involving that cultural arrivisme and that middlebrow synthesis which I have ventured to discuss in "What Was Modernism?" The concept of alternating generations, which is suggested there, might find its motivating principle in the relationship that is dwelt on here. I might add, as I look about our campuses today and watch a new generation of young iconoclasts, that I feel more optimistic than I did when I wrote this article long ago.

I

When a play runs for several seasons, we may justifiably assume that it performs some kind of public ritual. Thus *Uncle Tom's Cabin*, which scored the longest run in the annals of our stage, re-enacts the tensest issue in our history. Comparably, within much narrower precincts, the appeal of *Abie's Irish Rose* was grounded upon its stage-managed relaxations of racial tension. More recently *Tobacco Road* has been sending its audiences home to their kitchenette apartments with renewed confidence in the metropolitan way of life. And *Oklahoma!*, seen through the other end of the opera glass, has revived the city dweller's pastoral dream — that sempiternal urge toward folksiness which produces royal milkmaids in one age and drugstore cowboys in another. In realistic drama the only escape, known as catharsis to Aristotelians and Freudians alike, comes at the exit to the theater. A more popular formula, neatly achieved in the Theatre Guild's horse-operetta, uses the proscenium to frame our fantasies. The question is whether we are escaping from, or escaping to, ourselves.

Now there is an escapism in time as well as place, and it is most effective when it carries us back to the period where our memories begin. This may fluctuate anywhere between Only Yesterday and the Gay Nineties. (What, by the way, was so terribly gay about them? To one who cannot judge them except by their works, they seem rather pessimistic and consciously decadent). Out of the past half-century there can scarcely be a corny song or a gingerbread gadget, an eccentric character or an outmoded costume, that has not been resurrected on stage, screen, and radio, re-exploited in fiction, nonfiction, and advertising. Few epochs can have sentimentalized their immediate predecessors so fulsomely. Why? Because Prohibition created a cultural gap which Repeal filled in with beery reminiscence? Possibly. Because the Second World War re-created the emotional atmosphere of the First? To some extent. But the elemental reason is that we now look back — through both wars and the intervening crises — toward our lost youth, our native innocence, our unchallenged security.

Hence *Life with Father* has gradually reached the proportions of a national institution. Several generations of child-actors have outgrown their parts; a whole dynasty has mugged its way through the title role; and, although the play itself has not yet faded into retrospect, it is being gloriously reprocessed by the nostalgia mills of Hollywood. Crowds will long continue to apply at the box office for admission, as it were, to the family circle. There they will enjoy a twofold satisfaction, not less intense because it is self-contradictory. The first response is not unlike the condescending reception that we sometimes vouchsafe to dime novels or old-fashioned melodramas: it reinforces our sense of superiority, superficially confirms our belief in progress. At last, after all these years, we have grown up. Father is dead, and we can laugh at all the things he used to take so seriously. How small the world is, and how big we are! Yet we cannot claim to have profited from the discovery that there is no Santa Claus.

The second response is touched off somewhere within the deeper recesses of our experience. Here is Father again, larger than life and more opinionated than ever, making up our minds for us with the same irascible gusto, sheltering us from the world with all the old substantial comforts! Blending the professional sophistication of the *New Yorker* school with the childlike sensibility of a chronic invalid, Clarence Day was specially endowed to attain and sustain this highly ambivalent mood. His adapters, Messrs. Crouse and Lindsay, by concentrating upon the episode of Father's baptism, follow the most deeply rooted of dramatic traditions; for the mystery plays too were based on the sacraments, and Father's relationship with God — like Abraham's — is peculiarly direct and personal. *Life with Father* therefore transcends our crazy domestic drama. The walls may fall down in *The Skin of Our Teeth*, but Father's house is still standing. The family may go dizzily to pieces in *You Can't Take It with You*, but Father remains untouched by the Depression.

For Father, all-wise and all-powerful, was above all a good provider. If he has become the culture hero of our time, it is because — like the Fool in *King Lear* — he lived before our time. Hounded on every side by doubts and insecurities, we posthumously venerate him because we very poignantly miss him. But we must admit that his apotheosis has come too late to help us. In earlier and more hard-boiled repertories, we must remember, he played an ignominiously comic role: the cuckold, the heavy, the pantaloon, deceived by his wife, defied by his children, defrauded by servants and parasites. It must have been his success in business which, sooner or later, earned him a more respectful treatment: in Molière's comedies, even as in *Bringing Up Father*, he is the bourgeois spokesman for common sense, sturdily resisting the affectations of his blue-stocking wife and his social-climbing daughters. Here, as Voltaire pointed out, was a man of tremendous potentialities: *"Un père de famille est capable de tout. . . ."*

Yet the father-image is ultimately a tragic conception. It centers upon a protagonist who, owing his position to his seniority, stands closer to death than those whose lives he dominates. Their tragedy commences where his leaves off. Once his rivals, now his heirs, they temper their grief with a certain degree of relief, which in turn is mingled with consciousness of guilt. Reproaching themselves, they trace a whole grim train of consequences to the destiny that Oedipus so vainly tried to avoid — the murder of a father. The classic myth, in which psychoanalysis would discern the very pattern of children's attitudes toward their parents, grossly exaggerates the situation. Such impulses can fortunately be cushioned in private life; the function of drama, however, is to bring them out. "And the rude son shall strike the father dead," warns Ulysses in *Troilus and Cressida.* Synge's poltroon cannot be a hero, in *The Playboy of the Western World,* until he has "destroyed his da." Thereupon his triumph is short-lived. Nemesis soon reappears in the shape of the indestructible old man, a battered god in a tragicomic machine.

II

These ties and conflicts, which originally assert themselves within the bosom of the family, are repeated by society at large, thereby setting the larger patterns of loyalty and disaffection. Periods of social stability, of feudal hierarchies or Chinese dynasties, rest upon a substructure of filial obedience. Beneath the restless individualism of the moderns, the accelerating effort of each new generation to outdistance the last, lies a fundamental questioning of paternal authority. A hundred years ago Balzac, diagnosing this trend as a consequence of the French Revolution, illustrated it with his unforgettable portraits of old men in decline and young men on the make. Appropriately in 1859, the year of Darwin's *Origin of Species*, Meredith's *Ordeal of Richard Feverel* depicted the breakdown of a rigidly paternalistic system, frustrated by the perennially youthful forces of nature. Two or three years later, in *Fathers and Sons*, Turgenev brought the antagonism to a head by arranging a duel between an old-fashioned liberal and a callow nihilist. That issue, never settled, is fought again on an international scale by the rival ideologues of Mann's *Magic Mountain*.

Movements and manifestoes, revolutions and counterrevolutions, are thus propelled by the cycle of crabbed age and youth: the juniors repudiating their elders, then waxing middle-aged and academic, and being repudiated by ever brighter juniors. Generation succeeds generation with mounting rivalry as the twentieth century succeeds the nineteenth. The unfilial impiety of Samuel Butler supplies a posthumous postscript, *The Way of All Flesh*, which Bernard Shaw described as "patricide and matricide long drawn out." Matricide is perhaps the best description of our retrospective attitude toward the age of Queen Victoria. Lytton Strachey, by immolating the eminent Victorians, inaugurated the debunking of the twenties. Today the *enfants terribles* who survived that decade are older but not yet mature. The characteristic heroes of English literature, from A. E. Housman to P. G. Wodehouse, have been golden lads, mamma's boys, playboys who never grew up. On the playing fields, they seem to have acquired, not the humanistic wisdom of their forefathers, but the paradoxical whimsey of their bachelor uncles — the Lewis Carrolls and Edward Lears.

It is life with Mother, apparently, that obsesses our British contemporaries. They no longer even struggle against it as D. H. Lawrence did in *Sons and Lovers*. The fatherly refugee of *Prater Violet* tells the narrator, Christopher Isherwood, that too many Englishmen are in love with their mothers. Cyril Connolly, in his intimate journal, tells the public that his notion of happiness is "a womb with a view." This is, to put it mildly, a retrogressive position; this is second childhood with a vengeance. Whereas paternity is largely a cultural influence, which should lead via education toward independence, maternity is the explicit symbol of the child's dependence on the parent, since it embodies their biological connection. But that is another story, closely related and perversely complicated — a long-drawn-out story which Proust would call "the profanation of the mother." And Proust, whose most revealing essay is called "Filial Sentiments of a Parricide," was himself the most devoted of sons. Such devotion, transferred from his family to his art, remains the one absolute in his world of shifting appearances and corrupted values.

Oscar Wilde is quoted as saying, *"Il faut toujours tuer son père."* Our sketch of the artist as a parricide, killing the things he loves, finds its most impressive model in Dostoevsky, whose own father was actually murdered by rebellious serfs, and whose lifework is consequently overcast by the mood of self-accusation. Transferring his sense of guilt from a personal to a political sphere, he repented in Siberia for having conspired against — whom but the Little Father of Russia, the Tsar? It is this abrupt transition from revolution to reaction, from rationalism to mysticism, from Western to Eastern ideals, that makes his fiction a casebook for our times. The skeptical Ivan assumes the moral responsibility for the murder of old Karamazov, while the youngest brother, Alyosha, seeks another father in the saintly Zossima and another home in the Orthodox Church. The Satanic, the Titanic, the Byronic archetypes of intellectual rebellion — theirs is the tragic pride that goes before a fall. After the fall — which is accompanied, in Dostoevsky's case, by symptoms of "the falling sickness" — comes a humility too abject to be elevated by anything short of Divine Grace.

But Dostoevsky is peculiarly dynamic because he embraces extremes; he juxtaposes the icon and the iconoclast. Before we agree with the many discerning critics who maintain that his twentieth-century successor is Franz Kafka, we must make one significant reservation. Where Dostoevsky's heroes both act and suffer, Kafka's merely suffer; where the former are ruthless experimentalists, the latter are sleepwalking masochists. This means, of course, that the forces of opposition have increased; that the opposing authorities have become more unfathomable and overwhelming than ever. Though Kafka is likewise preoccupied with family matters, his diffident scions no longer dare to oppose their stern progenitors. In a typical story, "The Judgment," a son informs his father of his engagement, is thereupon ordered to kill himself, and ends by dutifully complying. All of his stories, Kafka said, could be summed up as an attempt to escape from his father. Yet he never completely escaped, for his apologia takes the form of a "Letter to My Father." Life without him was quite as impossible as life with him.

As a consumptive Jew, a German writer in a Slavic country, an uprooted artist among entrenched burghers, Kafka was well qualified to represent the displaced person, to present the Central European nightmare. Few of his fragmentary writings were published during his brief career; most of them, dating from the First World War and its aftermath, prophetically foreshadow the causes and effects of the Second. Homeless, his characters wander through abandoned streets; helpless, they are shunted into prison camps. Officers, officials, detectives, judges, domineer at every level of the bureaucracy — from father to *Führer*. A salesman, suddenly turning into an insect, worries chiefly about his boss's disapproval. An educated ape congratulates himself on escaping from the intolerable freedom of the jungle to the restrictions of civilization. A telephone rings, but somehow communication is never established. A prisoner is summoned, but the charge against him is never specified. The ironic parable that consummates *The Trial* has many meanings: one of them, surely, is that we are weak-kneed fools to let an officious doorkeeper prevent us from entering an open door.

III

In the face of augmenting combinations of circumstance which seem to defy all rational human control, the stature of the individual has shrunk pathetically. This process of attrition is reflected throughout modern fiction — most powerfully in the novels and stories of Kafka, perhaps, but not less ubiquitously in the little magazines and the comic strips. Albert Camus has suggested that we model our composite hero upon Sisyphus, the classical prototype of futility, rolling his absurd stone up an endless hill. Whatever his name or disguise — Leopold Bloom, Miss Lonelyhearts, Caspar Milquetoast — he is recognizably the Little Man. Fatherless and father-ridden, childless and childlike, he is old enough but not wise enough for parenthood; he carries into his adult years the frustrations and hesitations of adolescence. Against a sea of troubles, on his own initiative, he is incapable of taking arms; but he can muddle through his appointed task, like the Sad Sack, whenever the Sergeant stands *in loco parentis.*

Turning from war to religion, he discovers that the theologians have already debated his problem. The controversy that most sharply divided the churches of the East and the West involved the filial-paternal relationship under its most universal aspect. Characteristically the Patriarchate insisted on the primacy of the Father, while Catholics upheld the doctrine of *filioque,* which implies an equal status for the Son. Though Protestants rejected the cult of the Madonna, and attacked the Mariolatry of the Roman Church, the central tradition of Western Christianity has been its humanized conception of Jesus Christ: the Son of man to whom a heavenly Father has given "authority to execute judgment." Latter-day religious thinkers, however, have re-emphasized the concept of fatherhood — not so much the benign providence of the Paternoster as the terrifying and inscrutable Jehovah of the Old Testament. In *Fear and Trembling,* a book which profoundly influenced Kafka, the Danish philosopher Kierkegaard envisages man's relation to God in Abraham's sacrifice of Isaac. But Isaac is happily saved by divine intervention; where in Oriental versions of the theme, notably in the story of Sohrab and Rustum, the son is fated to be slain by the father.

Our range of awareness extends from the first man we know, whose impact ordinarily determines our relations with our fellow men, to the ultimately unknowable, which we anthropomorphically drape with paternal attributes. At historical intervals, like the names of begetters in Biblical genealogies, our horizon is peopled with quasi-paternal figures: prophets and priests, sages and saints, captains and kings, emperors and popes. To the extent that they receive our veneration and reward our prayers, they satisfy our tribal need for an intercessor. On the political plane, in a somewhat oversimplified form, the *patria potestas* is known as "the leader principle," and is equally valid for ward bosses and Roman Senators. His clients or heelers, whom he calls "the boys," refer to their leader as "the old man." His fatherland, if he happens to be its eldest statesman, proudly salutes him as the Father of his Country. If he has taken part in the framing of its constitution, his fame is enshrined among the ashes of the Founding Fathers.

Much of the greatness of the late President Roosevelt was due to his superb interpretation in the sympathetic role of Paterfamilias. This was evident, not merely in his own large family and fatherly presence, but particularly in his mastery of radio technique. That reassuring voice, at every crisis for more than a dozen years, penetrated millions of homes, dominated millions of firesides, left millions with the feeling that their personal interests were not being neglected. The most widespread response to the shock of his death was: "I feel as if I had lost a father." Winston Churchill, admirably performing a similar part, combined the inflections of his eighteenth-century ancestors with the conventional gestures of John Bull. Significantly, these Great White Fathers of wartime have now been replaced by two incarnate Little Men. And, if Messrs. Truman and Attlee are less authoritative than their precursors, they are also more democratic, since they more directly represent our uncertainties and weaknesses. In a house divided, lacking domestic supervision, the Boy Debaters emerge, the Deweys and Stassens, aping the mannerisms of the departed sire.

Where in this scheme of things can we place the Hitlers, the Mussolinis, the fascist dictators? Obviously, they are the Wicked Stepfathers of folklore and legend. Originally the black sheep, the scapegrace sons, they become the heads of households through some default, and retain the uneasy psychology of the interloper. They press their authoritarian claims without fulfilling their parental responsibilities; instead they seek broader and ever more destructive channels for their adolescent aggressiveness. Without quite daring to apply their own genetic theories, we might declare them unfit for fatherhood. At the other extreme we encounter the clinching case of Stalin, who — whatever he isn't — is indeed a patriarch. Hence he is the most puissant ruler in the world today. Doubtless his priestly training and Tsarist backdrop have served to accentuate the paternalism of his regime. Certainly his icon has pervaded Russian thought as the views of the iconoclastic Trotsky could never have done. Behind them both looms the Marxist tradition, parricidal in its revolutionary origins, patriarchal in its social consequences.

It is scarcely a coincidence that the socialist movement and the psychoanalytic school should follow the same pattern of development: an initial revelation, an apostolic succession, division among the disciples, revision of the master's teaching. Freud may look darkly backward toward Moses while Marx looks hopefully ahead to the Messiah, but each attains his particular comprehensiveness by treating all mankind as one big unhappy family. Both are increasingly influential because, in an epoch of collective irresponsibility, they stress the bonds between men as well as the barriers. May we not conclude, in the light of these comparative patristics, that every man is potentially a father-slayer and a father-seeker? Whether he proceeds in a radical or conservative direction will depend upon the repulsions and attractions that authority exerts for him. Wherever he confronts vested interests, strained prerogatives, undue repressions, he welcomes change. Wherever he meets scanted obligations, crumbling institutions, maladjusted efforts, he longs for permanence. He thereby reduces the ups and downs of history to the dimensions of a family quarrel.

IV

Every moment may be unique in its way, just as every age is an age of transition; but there are certain factors, converging upon the present moment, which make it uniquely transitional. The impetus of liberalism, strengthened during the nineteenth century by science, seems to have spent itself in the period of critical realism between the two wars. The recent war, with its temporary dictatorships, has established a far from stable equilibrium: still another could start a chain reaction which would end in total explosion. Totalitarianism, far from being extinguished, comes closer to home than before. Meanwhile a so-called failure of nerve has been driving prodigal sons back to their respective hearths and sanctuaries. The air is heavy with conversion and recantation. In the absence of original artistic creations, reprints and revivals flourish. We reread the novels of Trollope, and relive the warmth and comfort of the mid-Victorians. Only a literary businessman, who had to live down his mother's radicalism and his father's improvidence, could have conjured up such substantial fantasies. Two of our most individualistic poets, E. E. Cummings and Dylan Thomas, have devoted two of their finest poems to their respective fathers.

The homelessness of this postwar generation is not confined to the spiritual realm; it is a desperately practical problem. Small wonder that tree-lined vistas of prewar villages, back yards and front porches, Burchfield houses and period pieces, should harbor such elusive charm. Our nostalgia culminates in the homage we pay to Clarence Day's only begetter. Orphaned like David Copperfield, our world is torn between competing foster-fathers: between the grim efficiency of an autocratic Mr. Murdstone and the genial incompetence of a democratic Mr. Micawber. The plight we share with Kafka's waif-like characters, the avoidance of responsibility at all costs, has been well analyzed by Erich Fromm in a volume suggestively entitled *Escape from Freedom*. If our escapes to the past were purely imaginary, they would simply be harmless escapades. But we have lately been reminded that Greece, though never able to get along with its king, has been unable to get along without him. And we have educators who solemnly aver that, since Saint Thomas Aquinas could answer the questions he himself propounded, he offers a solution to all of our perplexities.

The demand for an up-to-date universal doctor is variously supplied (Father Divine, "Pappy" O'Daniel, Mr. Anthony). It's a wise child that knows, in this pandemonium of free advice, whom to listen for. The filial instinct seems so deeply ingrained that it is bound to find some expression or other. Even in tribes where mother-right prevails, anthropologists inform us, the father's perquisites are accorded to the maternal uncle. In more complex societies, church and state organize the means of appeal to higher authority. Roman Catholicism and Soviet Communism, perhaps because both are constructed on the bedrock of paternalistic discipline, are among the few institutions that command much devotion today. Conversely, each turns out its unfilial quota of heretics and rebels. But apostasy is usually the beginning of a private quest for confessors or commissars. Samuel Butler, having committed his symbolic patricide, made a tutelary deity of Darwin, whom he later discarded in favor of Lamarck. Stendhal, having disinherited his natural father, deified Napoleon; and, forswearing politics when his idol fell, set up a new pantheon of artists and writers.

Since we must look up toward something, our constant effort is to discover objects worthy of admiration: other men's fathers if not our own, heroes if not divinities. The pitfalls of indiscriminate hero-worship, in the Century of the Common Man, hardly need to be pointed out. Wistfully we contemplate the elderly demigods of the schoolroom, the bearded poets and side-whiskered statesmen. What sort of confidence can our household gods, our boyish crooners and beardless pitchers, inspire? Our actors — those who perchance do not play Father — remain juveniles until late in life. Our copywriters bask in their golden legends of eternal youth. Only our whiskey advertisers seem willing to recognize the capabilities of middle age. Most precocious of all, however, our atomic scientists, appalled by the results of their latest mischief, show sudden promise of accepting the leadership their guilty knowledge imposes upon them. Their humanistic colleagues, gathering the experiences of countless generations of fathers, must bring it to bear upon our contemporary needs.

Every dilemma has two ways out. Thus the continuous path that leads through adolescence to maturity is education. We like

to recall, as we revise our curricula, that the teacher is the traditional surrogate for the parent. Yet there is another consideration
which, since it invokes a law of nature, is still more fundamental.
Children do grow up; sons in their turn become fathers; and cultural changes revolve with the biological cycle. Literature offers
few more striking illustrations that the career of James Joyce. A be-
bellious young artist, he portrayed himself as Icarus, the son who
presumptuously tried his father's wings. When his trial flight succeeded, the rebel identified himself with the creator, Daedalus, who
devised among other things a notorious labyrinth. *Ulysses* expounds
the heresy that every son should become his own father. Assuming
gigantic stature in *Finnegans Wake*, Joyce could still express childish bewilderment: "Carry me along, taddy, like you done through
the toy fair!" But the dominant image is the father comforting his
child at night (and, incidentally, the exile remembering Ireland):
"Sonly all in your imagination, dim. Poor little brittle magic nation, dim of mind!"

The search is predestined, then, to guide us to ourselves; and for
this conclusion we are not altogether prepared. Schools have prolonged our infancy, sports have promoted our infantilism, publicists
have kept us in a state of arrested development. Our own novelists,
from Hemingway to Steinbeck, have dealt with problem children
rather than adults, with white mice rather than men. While there
are youth and experiment, there ought to be hope — hope for what
Van Wyck Brooks, before he became an ancestor-worshiper, called
"America's Coming-of-Age." But the rites of passage cannot be
delayed much longer; no indulgent father stands ready to bear
the responsibilities we shirk; and we ourselves are old enough to
know better. The king is dead, long live the king! The armored
figure that stalks across the battlement, after all, is only a ghost.
The young prince, if he would come into his kingdom, must learn
to make his own decisions, to think and act for himself. And,
unless he acts quickly, his vacant throne may be occupied by some
usurper.

18

Irving Babbitt and

the Teaching of Literature

This inaugural lecture explains itself — a little too explicitly, perhaps, for any other context than the occasion on which it was pronounced at Harvard University on November 7, 1960. It was published as a brochure shortly afterward by the University, the fourth section having appeared in the Harvard Alumni Bulletin (November 26, 1960) under the title "Irving Babbitt and the New Humanism." Happily it is no longer true, as it was when I made the statement, that there are none of Babbitt's documents in the Harvard College Library. I have since had the privilege of examining, through the kindness of his daughter, Mrs. George Howe, a transcript of his correspondence with Paul Elmer More — an important interchange which should see the light of publication. What, if any, relationship exists between this essay and the preceding one it is not for me to say.

I

When James Russell Lowell was being persuaded to undertake the Smith Professorship of the French and Spanish Languages in 1855, Francis James Child held out to him "the privilege of free speech on the great themes of modern literature." Personally, I cannot imagine a more congenial privilege, especially when it is reinforced by the freedom of the Harvard College Library and the stimulus of an audience second to none in its avid concern for books and ideas. I am also poignantly aware that such incumbents as Lowell and Child himself, who relinquished the Boylston Professorship of Rhetoric and Oratory to become Harvard's first Professor of English in 1876, are no longer within calling distance; while, on the other hand, professorships have been proliferating through recent years, in accordance with trends of cultural inflation which have diffused and diluted college degrees, upgrading agricultural colleges into state universities and promoting freshmen from sections to seminars. As long ago as 1911, *The Nation,* committed in those days to hierarchical principles, ran an editorial proposing a "Super-Professorate." This was immediately countered by a

321

sharply reasoned letter to the editor, questioning the criteria by which superprofessors were likely to be selected, and expressing a well-grounded fear that intellectual discipline might count for less than enthusiastic popularization. The letter-writer, whose students could have recognized him even if he had not appended his signature, knew whereof he spoke. He was Irving Babbitt; he was then in his forty-sixth year; and he was still an Assistant Professor of French in Harvard University.

It was not until the following year, after he had been offered a post at a Midwestern university, that President Lowell named him as a Professor of French Literature. His colleague, the shrewd and assiduous J. D. M. Ford, though eight years younger than Babbitt, had been appointed to a full professorship five years before him. Whether this conspicuous neglect had been due to his forthright criticisms of President Eliot's policies, to the opposition of senior colleagues protecting a scholarly regimen which Babbitt had already challenged, or to his own deliberate refusal to fall in with the requirements of the doctoral degree, it is now too late for speculation. But it is not surprising that he came to regard a faculty of arts and sciences as "an aggregate of mutually repellent particles" — perhaps, as such, a greater source of energy for him than it was for those who took a more static and self-satisfied view of it. What would our academic communities be if, in their continual process of reproducing themselves, they did not produce their monitors of dissent? How saliently the thought of Thorstein Veblen, who could not keep a professorial job, stands out from the dim apologetics of his conformable rivals! How necessary it must have been for our pioneering literary historian, V. L. Parrington, or for our leading Shakespearean commentator, E. E. Stoll — both of them disaffected Harvard alumni — to assume a controversial stance! What a loss for everyone when such productive tensions are cut short by protesting resignations, like those of Joel Elias Spingarn or Charles A. Beard from a sister institution!

Harvard has not been invulnerable to losses of that description.

George Ticknor, despite his success in establishing the study of modern languages, felt balked in his further efforts here and resigned in mid-career. Little credit accrues to the University for its brief and marginal appointments of such brilliant figures as John Fiske and Charles Sanders Peirce. The self-searching chapter entitled "Failure" in *The Education of Henry Adams*, which deals with the autobiographer's seven-year assistant professorship, may well serve as a standing admonition to any member of our faculty who has managed to pass beyond that rank. And yet it was Henry Adams who proudly affirmed that "a teacher affects eternity; he can never tell where his influence stops." Babbitt's very resistance to current doctrines generated an apostolic zeal which indoctrinated a growing band of disciples. His pedagogical ascendancy, first asserted over his fellow graduate student, Paul Elmer More, naturally made most of its converts among younger teachers and future educators. However, in refutation of the later charge that Babbitt's influence stopped at the edge of the campus, if not of the Yard, it will not be forgotten that he was called master by our most eminent Anglo-American man of letters. "To have once been a pupil of Babbitt's was to remain always in that position," T. S. Eliot has attested, "and to be grateful for (in my case) a very much qualified approval." Talented pupils were bound to diverge in their mature accomplishments; but "the magnitude of the debt" remained; and Van Wyck Brooks paused to acknowledge it parenthetically in his radical manifesto, *Letters and Leadership*.

The loyalties that Babbitt commanded — not to say pieties — may be gauged from the testimonial volume edited by Frederick T. Manchester and Odell Shepherd. Even more interesting would be the recollections of those who reacted from his teaching as divergently as Walter Lippmann, Gilbert Seldes, Crane Brinton, David McCord, Newton Arvin, Granville Hicks, Charles Wyzanski, David Riesman, and Ralph Kirkpatrick. Those who shrugged it off as merely parochial or anachronistic might have been surprised to come across some of its European affinities: with T. E.

Hulme and Wyndham Lewis in England, with Charles Maurras and Julien Benda in France. Doctoral dissertations in various countries have been addressed to problems raised by this scholar who refused to write a thesis. His position, as he saw it, was less ambiguous than that of Charles W. Eliot, who represented the Puritan temperament at its best, and who had lent an air of respectability to the relaxation of educational standards. Hence it required a maverick to present the case for tradition, to wage a vehement polemic on behalf of the moderate virtues, to oppose a bland subversiveness with a cantankerous decorum, to campaign for restraint. Small wonder if Babbitt's intentions, so far as they had been bruited beyond the classroom, were misunderstood and resented. The precedent of Socrates had taught him that gadflies court disfavor, to say the least. At a time when the profession of letters stood farther apart from the halls of learning than it does today, he became a bugbear for the bohemians, an advocate of the dead against the living, the arch-reactionary who comes out flatly against everything that matters. As irony would have it, his very surname — or rather, his homonym, used for a novel by Sinclair Lewis — became synonymous with philistine.

Latterly there have been signs to indicate that the reputation of Irving Babbitt might be emerging from its interval of eclipse. Though his cause seemed a losing one to his opponents, it is not yet lost a generation afterward. On the contrary, their causes — precisely because they seemed so up-to-date — have dated more than his old-fashioned values. If he dwelt in an ivory tower, it had windows which looked out and down on a clear and broad perspective. Thus he could warn international-minded readers against the futility of the League of Nations, the danger of uncontrolled military explosives, and "our growing unpopularity abroad." In 1924 he speculated:

Let us ask ourselves again whether the chances of a clash between America and Japan are likely to diminish if Japan becomes more democratic, if, in other words, the popular will is substituted for the will of a small group of "elder statesmen." Any one who knows what the

Japanese sensational press has already done to foment suspicion against America is justified in harboring doubts on this point.

Back on the domestic front, as early as 1908, he had made this trenchant comment on the disparity between underprivileged citizens and predatory businessmen:

The eager efforts of our philanthropists to do something for the Negro and the newsboy are well enough in their way; but a society that hopes to be saved by what it does for its Negroes and its newsboys is a society that is trying to lift itself by its own boot-straps. Our real hope of safety lies in our being able to induce our future Harrimans and Rockefellers to liberalize their own souls, in other words to get themselves rightly educated.

Higher education was Babbitt's point of departure and point of return; on that ground his prophetic challenges were most fully justified and have been most squarely met. What he called "the Philological Syndicate" has been toppled by the sheer unbalanced poundage of its Germanized scholarship. Though the Ph.D. has not been abolished, it has been considerably humanized. Babbitt's plea for a teaching degree like the French *agrégation*, emphasizing wide reflection instead of narrow research, accords with the latest recommendations from our graduate deans. Meanwhile the decline of the classics seems, in Harvard at least, to have been shored. In 1925, Babbitt lamented, there were 12 graduate students in Ancient Languages to 216 in Modern; thirty-five years later, we have 37 in Ancient to 237 students in Modern Languages (excluding Radcliffe, where the respective enrollments have increased much more than proportionately). As for the colleges and their programs of undergraduate instruction, they have been inclining away from the lecture hall and toward the tutorial conference; General Education, with its core of great books, has moderated the chaos of free electives; and indeed there are some institutions where Aristotle rules with as heavy a hand as in the Middle Ages. Whether or not this reversion would have pleased Babbitt may be open to doubt. Citing Coleridge's remark that every man is either a Platonist or an Aristotelian, he used to add with characteristic pungency: "In my opinion, Coleridge was far too complimentary to the average man."

II

The voice of reason that cried out so passionately in a wilderness of distractions had its retarded impact, which in turn has its fitting acknowledgment. "And thus the whirligig of time brings in his revenges." Since Babbitt was above all a teacher's teacher, his memorial takes a pedagogical form. One of his most devoted former pupils, as it so happily turns out, is presiding over our present era of development and revaluation at Harvard; and President Pusey has seen fit to mark Babbitt's contribution with a chair which will perpetuate his name. This recognition is double; for it not only honors a prophet within his own parish at last; it strengthens our relations with the larger Republic of Letters by sponsoring, as he unofficially did, the hopeful subject of Comparative Literature. At this point my professional enthusiasm is overtaken by my sense of personal limitation. The first incumbent of the Babbitt Professorship may boast of having been one of Professor Babbitt's last students; but "last" might also mean laggard in the pursuit of Babbitt's acquirements or hesitant in the acceptance of his tenets. Nor could I claim a laying-on of hands without recalling a publication I have long tried to forget, a paper written originally for his course in Romanticism. When he heard that it would be published in a series of undergraduate essays — well, I will not do his memory the injustice of trying to quote him verbatim. His approval was qualified, of course, though he was generally encouraging and specifically helpful. I particularly remember the pensive statement that he himself had not published a book until well into his forties, along with the sobering query whether I was really old enough to practise as a critic.

I am now in a better position than I was then to appreciate the wisdom of such doubts, though I must add that they do not meet much agreement when I pass them on to my own students. The advantage that age exerts over youth is, at best, a temporary one; and it tends to decrease in a civilization which prides itself upon abridging all time-spans; yet the consequent advantage gained by youth is likewise, in its very nature, temporary. The cycle of generations regulates the habitual rhythms of education, insofar as humane learning must be accumulated before it can be imparted. Babbitt's preference for maturity was not a matter of calendar age or primarily of relative experience; it was a question of gaining a critic's license by getting to know one's business, so to speak, by mastering a complex and voluminous body of material. How could one judge or discriminate or generalize or trace relevant connections or, in short, make valid interpretations without such groundwork? Babbitt was, as detractors complained, an opinionated man; but no man ever took more pains to document his opinion. In effect, his teaching was premised upon the importance of holding definite opinions and — what is still more important — of earning the right to hold them through patient study and rigorous cogitation. Brash criticasters, bypassing those prerequisites, could — and do — arrive at quick and arresting conclusions; but Babbitt would have us examine their credentials before we mistake them for serious practitioners. Erudite scholars, at the other extreme, could be so overwhelmed by the tasks of accumulation and organization that they would all but abandon the hope of reaching any conclusion.

Babbitt, as usual, found the middle way more arduous than the extremes. Wtih the curricular shift from ancient to modern languages, *litterae humaniores* had given place to philology; and philology, having made its linguistic and textual contributions, faced its point of diminishing returns. Lacking a direction of their own but influenced by the concurrent investigations of science, the philologists went on collecting and compiling with little regard for value or significance, and ended by subjecting the graduate schools to a pedantic cult of trivial detail. On the undergraduate level, the reaction to this esoteric professionalism was to make a classroom oracle of the literary dilettante, with his vague appreciations and studied mannerisms. Yet Babbitt, who had even less in common with a Copeland than with a Kittredge, impartially damned the feuding houses of impressionism and antiquarianism. Scholarship was the precondition of criticism, for him, as criticism was the consummation of scholarship. "The encyclopedia facts," as he regularly announced, were presupposed in his lectures and tested by his examinations. Repeatedly he reminded his listeners that "rounded estimates" of the works he cited would have had to put more stress upon their esthetic merits. But he frankly concentrated upon the transmission of ideas, and his pithy citations were carefully chosen to reveal the authors in their own phrases. Often the change of context introduced a harsher light; anything they had said, one suspected, might be held against them. However, the system was inclusive enough to be roughly equable in the long run. Everything that everyone had said was neatly filed away in some mental drawer, ready to be pulled out in response to some pertinent inquiry.

Babbitt the pedagogue is so vivid a ghost that I can never enter Sever 11 without envisioning that patriarchal white head, those Roman features, and those ponderous shoulders brooding over a desk he has just strewn with books in many languages. As he rustles through them, translating here and annotating there, his monologue becomes a dialogue in which the minds of all the ages participate. On a plane beneath his notice, it also became a lottery; for, during his sequence of quotations and references, he would mention between fifty and a hundred different names in the interim of a single hour; so that his more enterprising and less dedicated students could pool their pennies and draw lots for what might prove to be the final number, keeping check on the margins of their notebooks. Most of us, however, came to realize that we had a larger stake in the dialectical interplay. Mr. Babbitt's courses usually started with a *bibliographie raisonnée*, where the listed authorities came alive, and began to jostle for position, as soon as he had dictated their titles and dates. He proceeded, in Socratic fashion, by defining a series of basic terms: words providing the keys to fundamental concepts, retraced across the length and breadth of history through exhilarating semantic excursions. Frequently he brought his points home with topical allusions: timely newspaper clippings or public utterances, constituting a sort of *sottisier* or scrapbook of contemporary fatuities. But the farther he went back into the past, the wiser seemed the bywords with which he returned. His pedagogy admitted us to a pantheon of thinkers — classical, scriptural, scholastic, humanistic, oriental — whose views were canvassed, and messages conveyed, for our special benefit.

Knowledge was not a collective abstraction for Babbitt; it existed concretely and individually, wherever precept became example through the life and work of a sage. Each of us, he counselled, quoting Spinoza, should bear in mind an exemplar of human nature: *"idea hominis, tamquam naturae humanae exemplar."* The prototype to whom we invariably compared him, for reasons not far to seek, was Dr. Johnson. But it seems more deeply suggestive that the two portraits he placed in his Widener study were those of Sainte-Beuve and Charles Eliot Norton. Norton, who had been the friendliest among his teachers, incarnated the last refinement of an earlier Harvard, highly cultivated and many-minded yet somewhat amateurish and provincial. Given his friendship with Carlyle and Ruskin, or his services to archaeology and the study of Dante, he has been rather superciliously evoked by George Santayana in a broadside attack on "the genteel tradition":

Old Harvard men will remember the sweet sadness of Professor Norton. He would tell his classes, shaking his head with a slight sigh, that the Greeks did not play football. In America there had been no French cathedrals, no Venetian school of painting, no theater, and even no gentlemen, but only gentlemanly citizens.

Santayana's list of what was lacking reads like a parody of Henry James's famous lament on the flatness of the American scene; but the caricature makes clear, at any rate, why the role of the gentleman or *honnête homme* was so very strategic in Babbitt's thought. Though the rugged young Midwesterner had no pretensions to the sort of gentility personified by the elderly Bostonian, still it was an attenuated link with the humanists of the Renaissance. What had been an elegiac reminiscence for Norton was transformed by Babbitt into a militant criterion. To implement it he turned more directly toward Europe, and toward a critical mentor as unlike the high-minded Norton as possible and no more like himself, the worldly and professional Sainte-Beuve. Babbitt was impressed by the penetrating psychology that could expertly sketch so vast a gallery of personalities; and his two principal courses in French literature were devoted to the writers Sainte-Beuve had studied at fullest length, Pascal and Chateaubriand. From Sainte-Beuve, too, Babbitt drew his method of exemplification through self-revealing passages. Sainte-Beuve is the veritable hero of Babbitt's most affirmative book, *The Masters of Modern French Criticism*, and is all but designated there as the universal doctor of the nineteenth century. But his range of sympathies, alas, is traceable to his century's lack of standards. Babbitt can accept his eclecticism, but not his relativism, when Sainte-Beuve confesses:

My curiosity, my desire to see everything, to look on everything at close quarters, my extreme pleasure at finding the relative truth of everything, involved me in this series of experiments, which have been for me only a long course in moral physiology.

And when he goes on to analyze and "botanize," professing himself "a naturalist of souls," he loses his American disciple. Babbitt returns intuitively to Norton's master, Emerson, who has redressed so many balances because he reconciles so many attitudes. The ideal critic, Babbitt decides, significantly noting that Sainte-Beuve's picture hung in Emerson's study at Concord, would combine the Frenchman's flexibility with the American's elevation.

                    III

Ralph Waldo Emerson was a strikingly untraditional thinker; but his conception of the American scholar is by now a tradition in itself, to be saluted in passing on these occasions, and emulated all the more earnestly by outlanders migrating from the Midwest to New England. Babbitt, though descended from Plymouth colonists, had been born in 1865 at Dayton, Ohio. Though he was suspicious of the quest for origins, and too proud to welcome an intimate scrutiny of his background, it is always illuminating to find latent sources of inspiration more profound than the entries in a *curriculum vitae*. He was, it would seem, a chary correspondent; our archives have no document in his hand. Yet by a strangely ironic coincidence, which cannot embarrass his inherent dignity at this stage, we do possess two letters from his father. The first is addressed to Professor Henry W. Longfellow in 1847 from a youth of nineteen, who is teaching country school in Missouri, learning Spanish by himself, and anxious to study at Harvard. As a specimen of his potentialities, he submits two cantos of a would-be romantic poem, "Gem of the Sea." Longfellow need not have been impressed; the young poet did not get a scholarship; and he seems to have moved on in other directions. The second letter is dated from Los Angeles in 1898, when the writer was seventy and his unmentioned son was an instructor at Harvard. The recipient was Professor William James, whose approbation the elder Babbitt besought for his many discoveries and for a vaunted message to the world. This time his enclosure was part of a set of books titled *Human Culture and Cure*, replete with testimonials and illustrations, including a diagram of the author's brain.

Edwin Dwight Babbitt signed himself M.D.; but whether those initials stood for doctor of medicine or doctor of magnetism is uncertain; and that uncertainty may have awakened his son's skepticism about academic degrees. Dr. Babbitt, who could be consulted by mail, practised in the light of hypnotism, spiritualism, phrenology, clairvoyance, massages, sun-baths, electrical treatments, inhabited planets, and utopian socialism. He claimed to see bodily aura, and to have a consultant who saw atoms with the naked eye. As author, publisher, and bookseller, he brought out such items as

Babbitt's Health Guide, Vital Magnetism, the Fountain of Life,
and *Marriage, with Sexual and Social Up-Building.* Among the fly-
leaves he advertised such inventions as Psychomized Paper, the
Chromo Disk, and the Grand Thermalume. But he remained what
he had been, a teacher, managing a business school when Irving
was a boy, and winding up in California as dean of an institution
which styled itself the College of Fine Forces. Inasmuch as his
advice to families was predicated upon "the innate nobility which
every child possesses," this incorrigible reformer may have been
a Wordsworthian — if not a Micawberish — parent. His own child
grew up to harbor an intensive distrust of that assumption, together
with a comprehensive disbelief in nature's remedies. William
James, so bright and distant a luminary in the father's astral firmament, was the son's Cambridge neighbor and philosophical target;
his *Varieties of Religious Experience* was tartly rechristened by
Irving Babbitt as *Wild Religions I Have Known.* It may be that
Babbitt's early exposure to pseudoscience at its wildest set his teeth
on edge, and inoculated him against more substantial manifestations of the modern spirit.

Edwin Babbitt may have been a crackpot; but he was not a
quack, since he so transparently believed in the schemes, contraptions, and panaceas he so volubly dispensed; and since his transcendental confidence does not seem to have been shared by the
public, his enterprise did not even succeed materially in providing
a stable home for his wife and five children. "Breaking up house-
keeping" seems to have been their commonest childhood remembrance. Irving's mother died when he was eleven; though he was
helped by uncles, he was soon on his own. During a sojourn in
New York he sold papers; his incidental reference to newsboys
and Negroes is by no means unfeeling. He worked on a farm in
Ohio, a ranch in Wyoming, and — as police reporter — a newspaper in Cincinnati. He had a varied acquaintance with American
life before he graduated from high school, where he specialized in
chemistry and civil engineering, to matriculate at college slightly
older than his classmates, who considered him reserved and shy. To

come to Harvard was not only to realize Edwin Babbitt's thwarted ambition; it was to recoil from the atmosphere of New Thought by embracing traditionalism. He concentrated in Classics, with high honors as a sophomore and plain honors on graduation in 1889, having incurred the displeasure of the Greek grammarian, William Watson Goodwin, through a belated composition. For the next two years, he taught Greek and Latin at the University of Montana. With his savings he fulfilled his plan of returning to Europe, where he had spent a strenuous junior year on a walking trip with a classmate; and in Paris, under Sylvain Lévi, he studied Sanscrit and Indian philosophy.

Notwithstanding these institutional associations, he had inherited from his self-taught father the autodidactic temperament. Avoiding the sanctioned routines by which *Homo academicus* is molded and rounded and polished, he lived the maxim that true education is self-education; and his educational goals were too far-reaching to fit within a departmental program. His formal training terminated with a master's degree from the Harvard Graduate School in 1893. Thence, after a year of teaching Romance Languages at Williams College, he gravitated back to the Harvard department, where for the next two decades his main assignments were undergraduate classes in the French language. Little by little he came to lecture in the interdepartmental field of Comparative Literature, taking over Lewis Gates's courses in the Romantic Movement and the History of Criticism, and introducing the course that became his uniquely personal vehicle: Rousseau and His Influence. Settled on Kirkland Road with a family of his own, his way of life could hardly have been more simple or methodical. Most of his social energies were held in reserve for the war of ideas he daily waged in the classroom. Accordingly, as one French visitor put it, he was "pedagogic in the drawing room." Though he was visiting professor for a term at the Sorbonne, he seldom resumed his European journeying. Having once seen the museums and cathedrals, a traveling companion reports, Babbitt preferred to read and write at his hotel. Nor could he ever be lured to the Orient, in spite of his

lifelong interest in its culture and of Mrs. Babbitt's birth and up-
bringing in China. His orbit was Cambridge as Kant's had been
Königsberg. To accompany our peripatetic upon his local walks
was, I may say, a vigorous exercise physically as well as intel-
lectually.

Babbitt judged — and would have wanted others to judge him
— by final causes, not beginnings but ends. His own end was an
exemplary fulfillment of his belief in self-control, an enactment of
Montaigne's adage that to philosophize is to learn how to die. His
latter years were overshadowed by a wasting disease. Punctiliously
he kept up with his academic responsibilities through the final
examinations of 1933. Stoically he lingered on for five weeks as an
invalid, setting his domestic affairs in order and working as much
as he could on his translation of *The Dhammapada*. On one occasion, endeavoring to take his mind off the pain, Mrs. Babbitt suggested reading a detective story. This was a licensed indulgence
for Paul Elmer More; but, as Babbitt may have remembered, it
was also the esthetic passion of George Lyman Kittredge and the
Philological Syndicate. Babbitt — who reread Homer in Greek for
his own recreation — had characterized their specialistic researches
as mere detective-work, and had alluded to John Livingston Lowes
— his ablest antagonist in the battle over the Romantics — as "the
most accomplished of literary sleuths." Hence, from his virtual
deathbed, Babbitt rallied to answer his wife's suggestion firmly:
"Detective stories? Good Lord, no! I can still meditate." The key
to those ultimate thoughts was thought itself, unmitigated by
anodynes. From his Buddhist text, to be posthumously published,
he had translated:

Through meditation wisdom is won, through lack of meditation wisdom is lost; let a man who knows this double path of gain and loss so
conduct himself that wisdom may grow.

The pervasive theme of *The Dhammapada* is the growth of wisdom
as embodied in the earnest strivings of the wise man, the medita-
tive Brahman who has attained the highest end, the leader not
led by others who remains unshaken in the midst of praise or blame.

If you see an intelligent man who detects faults and blames what is
blame-worthy, follow that wise man as though he were a revealer of
(hidden) treasures.
Let him admonish, let him teach, let him forbid what is improper! —
he will be beloved of the good, by the bad he will be hated.

All of us may secretly long for the guidance of such a sage, especially during our formative period, when we first seek it in the
paternal image. Irving Babbitt must have been soon disappointed
by the exemplar or *idea hominis* presented in Edwin Babbitt,
whose pretensions formed an object-lesson in the need for common
sense. It could be said of the son that he continued the father's
examination of mental phenomena, dramatically forewarned of
the tangents and heading straight for a center. It was a central
path that brought Irving Babbitt to Harvard University. The
elders he encountered there — Eliot and James, Goodwin and Kittredge — were models of sounder learning; yet he found them
immersed in a *Zeitgeist* which had fostered the feckless tinkering
he knew so well; they were specialized investigators rather than
universal doctors; they were rather sleuths than sages. He liked to
point out that the term "scholar" meant, etymologically speaking,
a man of leisure; and the use of that leisure, he insisted, was not
for revery but for reflection. The crown of meditation was mediation; scholarly contemplation should lead to action, which ought
not to be confused with the hustling of committees. Babbitt's objective was the "spiritual strenuousness" of Buddha under the tree
of perfect knowledge. Finding it unrealized elsewhere, he sought
it through his own character and conviction. Gradually he became
a guide for other seekers. From the East itself they came to Cambridge, as one Chinese scholar has recollected, "to sit at the feet
of the new sage."

IV

Babbitt, according to More, was "greater as a teacher than a
writer," and possibly greatest of all as a talker. His writing, often
dictated to his wife, catches the firmness of his voice for those who

heard it, though it misses the timing of his wit. Like other talkers, especially lecturers, he could be discursive and repetitious; but he held us by the richness of his anecdotal illustrations and epigrammatic comments; while he underscored his exposition, in Matthew Arnold's manner, with telling catchwords. Babbitt's seven books, largely based upon his lectures and articles, are integrated through his underlying preoccupations. Their emphasis ranges from esthetics to politics via philosophy. Their pattern is varied by the endless mosaic of apophthegms and instances. The hidden treasures they reveal are nothing more nor less than the great commonplaces, which have been made increasingly uncommon by the novelties of material progress. The extracts that Babbitt prescribes are drawn from the distillations of human experience. The authorities whom he cites, approached as a body, constitute that very principle of authority which he invokes. This testament of wisdom is not limited to the Western hemisphere, grand as the Greco-Roman tradition of *paideia* has been; one of Babbitt's most farsighted contributions was his insistence that an enlightened world view must come to terms with Asiatic thought. Nor was he, in his running critique of "a cheap contemporaneousness," an uncritical praiser of the ancients; he described himself as "a modern of moderns," though decidedly not a modernist, yet a thoroughgoing individualist; and, in describing his philosophical outlook, he employed such words as "positive," "empirical," and even "experimental." His whole endeavor with the past was to make it live in the present, to learn and teach the lessons of history.

Babbitt took his educational stand in that slowly ripened first book of his, *Literature and the American College: Essays in Defense of the Humanities*. His opening chapter, "What Is Humanism?," propounded a question he had raised as early as 1895, in a guest lecture at the University of Wisconsin, and would pursue to the point where it instigated a public controversy thirty-five years afterward. His epigraph was a passage from Emerson, which he found many further occasions to quote, distinguishing between two irreconcilable laws: "Law for man, and law for thing." It was the

age-old distinction recognized by the Greeks between νόμος and
φύσις, custom and nature. The consequences of flouting it have
been labeled by sociologists as *anomie*, and are somewhat more
humanely set forth by the Emersonian poet, Robert Frost:

> As long on earth
> As our comparisons were stoutly upward
> With gods and angels, we were men at least,
> But little lower than the gods and angels.
> But once comparisons were yielded downward
> Once we began to see our images
> Reflected in the mud and even dust,
> 'Twas disillusion upon disillusion.
> We were lost piecemeal to the animals,
> Like people thrown out to delay the wolves.

Thus the human condition may be located midway in the hierarchy
of being, whence it may look upward toward the supernatural or
downward toward the naturalistic level. The humanism of the
Renaissance, prompted by the rediscovery of the classics, rescued
man from the dizzying aspirations and rarefied altitudes of medieval theology. But this descent did not stop at the half-way house
where he was most at home, in Babbitt's interpretation; it went
on by reducing civilization to the plane of things and animals.
Existence was traced, by philosophers like Bergson, to a vital urge
from the depths of the unconscious, *élan vital*. Babbitt would have
centered the process on a *frein vital* — or, to repeat the phrase he
borrowed from Emerson, who had borrowed the notion from his
oriental reading, an "inner check." The moral issue was whether
the intricate compound of human nature should be dominated
by its human or by its natural component. The tendency toward
dehumanization, for Babbitt, coincided historically with the Romantic Movement. Romanticism, as he redefined it, was the Pandora's box that had released all the other -isms to harass our world
— beginning with humanitarianism, which he considered a travesty
of humanism. The most persuasive ideologue of the movement,
Jean-Jacques Rousseau, was Babbitt's personal devil. That omni-

present role was warranted by the scope of Rousseau's influence, if not by Babbitt's own habit of pointing out awful examples. Rousseau exemplified the sentimentalist, whose cultivation and exhibition of impulse had undermined the strict self-discipline of the sages, revolutionizing for the worst the *idea hominis*.

This was a situation, not a doctrine, as Ramon Fernandez could observe from a distance. The diagnosis was acute enough, though the prescription becomes more problematic. Babbitt was fundamentally a moralist, like the Existentialists of today; like them, he sought a metaphysical groundwork for his ethics. But, as his Swedish expositor, Folke Leander, concludes, "For Babbitt the epistemological problem . . . finally runs into the ethical problem." So, we should add, does every other problem. His concept of an inner check, or higher will, approximates what Protestants would call conscience and Freudians would term the superego. Some of his fellow travelers traveled farther than he, notably More and T. S. Eliot, in coming to believe that the ethical problem could be solved only by adopting a religious position. They confronted Babbitt with a dilemma: to be either a naturalist or a supernaturalist, either to ally himself with the enemy or to join his allies on a pilgrimage to Canterbury or Rome. Here was no excluded middle for him; rather, it was the central span of his dualism; and he did not need the shelter of dogma to keep his metaphysics warm. Like Sainte-Beuve, he could emerge with respect and regret from the vanished spiritual retreat of Port-Royal. "Speaking . . . not as an orthodox Christian but simply as a psychological observer," Babbitt was keenly interested in Christianity, utterly fascinated by Buddhism, and probably most sympathetic to the secular creed of Confucius. "Professor Babbitt knows too much," wrote Mr. Eliot frankly — too much about comparative religion to be converted by particular articles of faith. He remained the self-reliant individualist, who — with Vigny's isolated thinker — might have professed: "Le vrai Dieu, le Dieu fort, est le Dieu des idées!" The humanist, as a skeptic yet not an agnostic, would pay equal attention to both lines of Pope's well-balanced couplet:

> Know then thyself, presume not God to scan,
> The proper study of mankind is man.

Facing the dilemma's other horn, naturalism, an unimpaled Babbitt made common cause with Anglo-Catholics, Neo-Thomists, and other religionists, as well as skeptical traditionalists. The real gulf was the one that yawned like Pascal's whenever communication was attempted between the academic world and contemporary letters. When Babbitt's energetic disciple, Stuart P. Sherman, resigned from his professorship of English at the University of Illinois to become editor of the *New York Herald-Tribune's* weekly book-review, his old teacher told him he was trying to build a bridge between Irving and George F. Babbitt. Sherman died all too prematurely; yet during the later twenties the catchphrase "New Humanism," was more and more in the air; and Babbitt's increasingly vocal disciples acquired a monthly organ, *The Bookman*. Finally, on May 9, 1930, the master himself "invaded New York, the stronghold of his enemies," — to echo the patriotic account in the *New York Times* — and submitted his views to a debate with Carl Van Doren and Henry Seidel Canby. Symbolically, the amplifiers at Carnegie Hall broke down; but it is clear that Babbitt was his intransigent self, and that the audience overwhelmingly favored his easy-going antagonists. "Though it was a very warm day," Babbitt conceded, back in Cambridge, "the occasion might be described as a frost." Yet the *Kulturkampf* raged on in the periodicals, reaching its climax that same year when the quasi-official symposium, *Humanism and America*, provoked a counter-attack from dissenting critics, *The Critique of Humanism*. The latter, we must admit, was the livelier volume: Edmund Wilson carried the battle of books into Babbitt's camp by accusing him of turning Sophocles into a "Harvard humanist." However, there was no genuine meeting of minds. The Humanists argued for a timeless ethic, the free-lances for a timely esthetic — neither successfully, as it turned out.

That discussion ushered in the thirties, with their prevailing trend toward social criticism. Insofar as this called for moral com-

mitment, Neo-Humanism may have prepared the way. The new
Marxism was hardly the Great Awakening preached by the professorial doctrinaires. But Babbitt had consistently warned them
against expecting their kind of revival; once humanism was taken
up as a fad, it was bound to go the way of all -isms. He was glad to
see it revert to the Academy, where its continuing function is to
transcend the ephemeral. The date of his death was so pivotal that,
in retrospect, we cannot wish he had survived it; for 1933 brought
a wave of authoritarianism which caught up some of his more
reactionary followers. Babbitt had expressed discomfort over the
political extremism of his French *confrères* associated with the
Action Française; and in *Democracy and Leadership* he criticized
American society from the reasonable vantage point of Burke's
independent conservatism. Like most of our respectable conserva-
tives, he thought of himself as a genuine liberal. Never professing
to be wholly orthodox, he could not apply the stigma of heresy to
his opponents, as the more fanatical have subsequently done. Temperamentally, Stuart Sherman remarked, he may have been a radical out of his time. Had he been born into a classical age, Austin
Warren suggests, he might have opposed its orthodoxy: "was not
his real role that of adversary?" If we seek Mr. Eliot's detached
opinion, we might turn to that infernal passage where the poet
encounters the spirit of "some dead master," who tells him:

> I am not eager to rehearse
> My thought and theory which you have forgotten.
> These things have served their purpose: let them be . . .
> For last year's words belong to last year's language
> And next year's words await another voice.

Our climate has so changed in the last generation that it seems
vain to interrogate the dead. And it is with private relief that I
refrain from asking Sainte-Beuve's question: what would our predecessors have thought of us? The situations Babbitt deplored have,
in some respects, been aggravated. Commercialization has flourished; standardization has certainly not decreased; menacing techniques of popular manipulation have been devised. Culture itself

is projected and interconnected through networks infinitely more efficient and powerful than the system of amplification that failed in 1930 at Carnegie Hall; we are more dependent than ever on gadgets and slogans, more estranged from "a sense of the inner life." Our spokesmen still take that "quantitative view of life" which Babbitt reprehended, and the quantities may have affected the qualities for the worse. We live in a world of science fiction come true, where George F. Babbitt may bask in a Grand Thermalume; where Edwin Babbitt, with his Vital Magnetism, might seem less of a crank than Irving Babbitt, with his Inner Check. Law for Thing has provided utilitarianism with an unanswerable argument in the shape of a mushroom cloud. The ideal of the gentleman seems hopelessly outmoded, at a moment when the prime qualification for our highest office — so millions are reported to feel — is the ability to talk back to Premier Khrushchev. Babbitt's censure may indeed be more pertinent than ever before. But we pay him small tribute by echoing his formulas. We should do much better by emulating the moral courage he showed in withstanding the drift of circumstances.

V

It is the merit of the innovator, which Babbitt wryly granted Rousseau, to ask the right questions though he may give the wrong answers. It is the merit of the traditionalist to give the right answers to questions no longer moot, which ought nonetheless to be reconsidered and more broadly reformulated. Thus Babbitt's approach to the cultural crisis of modernity was adapted from Arnold's, and Arnold had already been conducting a rear-guard defense of a waning tradition. Culture — for both critics — was a certain type of education, admittedly the best, and nearly everything else was anarchy. But culture, so defined, has meanwhile almost withered away; while anarchy, in need of redefinition, has organized itself and set up vast subcultures of its own. Babbitt, more than fifty years ago, could refer nostalgically to "the almost

lost art of reading." He could not have foreseen a technological
revolution, no less consequential than the development of the
printed book, which it may now be supplanting with audiovisual
media. Yet he had taken issue with the Romanticists because he
feared their hostility to book-learning. Wordsworth had dismissed
"those barren leaves" in favor of nature's greenery and the "spontaneous wisdom" of the wood, which — he maintained in "The
Tables Turned" — could teach us so much more than "the med-
dling intellect" of "all the sages." Therein the poet was answering
his friend, whose more traditional attitude had been stated at the
outset of the preceding poem, "Expostulation and Reply." It might
be said of Babbitt that he turned the tables back again, and that
his life-work was an expostulation against the romantic reply to
the neoclassicists. Man was not born yesterday, after all; but our
forebears will have lived in vain unless we take advantage of their
bequest, which is the sole guarantee of our children's enlightenment.

> "Where are your books? — that light bequeathed
> To Beings else forlorn and blind?
> Up! up! and drink the spirit breathed
> From dead men to their kind.

> "You look round on your Mother Earth,
> As if she for no purpose bore you;
> As if you were her first-born birth,
> And none had lived before you!"

In America, the land of innovation, there have been pragmatic
reasons for scanning the horizon so naïvely. There has also been,
on the part of an augmenting minority, keen awareness of tradition. Emerson's alignment, the party of hope, has always won the
majorities in its intermittent dialectic with the party of memory.
Consequently, the task of the adversary has become all the more
urgently needful and useful. Babbitt was sometimes accused of
being a destructive critic, who ignored beauties in order to stigma-
tize faults; and it is true, to adopt his quizzical expression, that his
gustos were less memorable than his disgustos. His library was

crammed with such unexpected authors as André Gide, whose pages were not merely cut and thumbed but crisply underlined and emphatically annotated. To whatever came his way, Babbitt's response was wholeheartedly critical, generally involving a conflict of principle and tending more often than not toward an adverse judgment. To blame what was blameworthy, he believed, was the only means of maturely resisting our national disposition to be "childishly uncritical." Where the Everlasting Yea had too many partisans, and the Spirit of Denial all too few, the man of moral stature would be he who — as Melville wrote — says no in thunder, though the devil bids him say yes. Babbitt's dissidence had made him apt at framing military metaphors, especially in scholastic contexts. When some of us told him that we had invited John Dewey to address the Harvard Classical Club, his mock-heroic comment was: "You have let the enemy into the citadel." After that alert, it was slightly anticlimactic when Dewey read us an unexceptionably conventional paper about the Pre-Socratics; but it may have foreshadowed the dialectical process that is now leading our educators up, up from the pastures of permissiveness and back toward the citadels of discipline.

Babbitt might himself have become a classical scholar, had not his undergraduate experience discouraged him, and had he not been temperamentally inclined to polemic rather than apologia. In his negatively humorous moods, he deprecated his own subject, French, as "a cheap and nasty substitute for Latin." More positively and seriously, he regarded France as the center of modern civilization, on the particular grounds that criticism was so express and characteristic a trait of its literature. Yet as he declared in his preface to *The New Laokoon*, it was "one-sided" to study "one literature"; an acquaintance with several, in their interrelationship, was prerequisite for any understanding of genres and movements; indeed Rousseau had attained his peculiar predominance through what Joseph Texte, the first official French *comparatiste*, has termed "literary cosmopolitanism." Hence Babbitt was instrumental in efforts to humanize the college curriculum by establishing an honors program in Classics and Allied Subjects, and by examining students of Modern Languages in the Bible, Shakespeare, and Ancient Authors. Given his interests and abilities, it was inevitable that he become identified with Comparative Literature. Not so much a field as a perspective, our subject — or rather, our object — owes its existence to the pooled resources of various departments, contributed with a magnanimity which — I hope — will continue to be perennial. At Harvard, professors have offered courses in Comparative Literature since 1892; since 1904 there has been a department offering graduate degrees. Understandably, the original focus was upon the vernacular literatures of the Middle Ages. Babbitt enlarged it to comprehend the prospect opened up by Arnold in his inaugural lecture of 1857 at Oxford:

. . . everywhere there is connection, everywhere there is illustration; no single event, no single literature, is adequately comprehended except in its relation to other events, to other literatures. The literature of ancient Greece, the literature of the Christian Middle Age, so long as they are regarded as two isolated literatures, two isolated growths of the human spirit, are not adequately comprehended; and it is adequate comprehension which is the demand of the present age.

This vision of cultural relatedness, of an intellectual continuum extending through time and space, beckons us toward that realm of Goethe's promise, *Weltliteratur*. In a world which strains at the boundaries of nationalism, why should they be perpetuated by literature, which has crossed them so freely in the past? Arnold moves on by quoting Prince Albert, whose choice of words inadvertently helps to strengthen the meaning of our problematic term, "comparative":

"We must compare," — the illustrious Chancellor of Cambridge said the other day to his hearers at Manchester, — "we must compare the works of other ages with those of our own age and country; that, while we feel proud of the immense development of knowledge and power of production which we possess, we may learn humility in contemplating the refinement of feeling and intensity of thought manifested in the works of the older schools."

Verily, the study of Comparative Literature should inculcate the lesson of humility. Given the limitations that languages sooner or later lay down, no one would presume to take all of letters for his province; one simply tries to counteract one's innate provinciality, and to obtain a more objective view of what one may know, by relevant comparisons with whatever one can learn. To be a humanist, alas, has come to mean little more than not to be a scientist, and occasionally to defend one's interests by attacking those of one's colleagues. Meanwhile the humanities, like the sciences, have perforce been chopped up and thrown to the specialists, though there is an observable reaction in favor of Babbitt's catholicity. On the other hand, the scientific viewpoint has been broadened and chastened to an extent which may outdate some of his reservations. Faced with the dilemma between naturalism and supernaturalism, those who cannot embrace a supernatural credo — as he could not —may find their working solution in a concept of nature tempered by humanity: of Law for Man refining on Law for Thing, which it is man's privilege to comprehend, if not altogether to control. A naturalist, so long as he is preoccupied with souls, can still be humane. If there is a distribution of academic labor between "the two cultures," there should be — as C. P. Snow has lately argued — a sharing of intellectual responsibility. To what has proved an unproductive debate, President Eliot may well be allowed the last word: "This University recognizes no real antagonism between literature and science." Each of them has too much to learn from the other.

Much has been happening within the sphere of literary studies, however delimited. The locution "creative," which used to make Babbitt wince, has become the staple of English departments, where it designates a mode of writing that is virtually neoclassical in its dependence on imitation. The chronological emphasis has shifted all the way from the medieval to the modern period: from one extreme of unripeness to another, in Babbitt's estimation. Though he broke down barriers between criticism and scholarship, we cannot imagine him hailing a revival of criticism unsupported by scholarship. J. E. Spingarn, the one contemporary whose achievement might have been comparable, if his scholarly career had not been interrupted, clashed with Babbitt over esthetics and called for a "New Criticism." That call was answered by a later generation of teacher-critics, many of them tradition-conscious Southerners, whose cardinal virtue was Babbitt's chief deficiency, a concern with form. Babbitt's main concern had been explicit in the title of his Dartmouth address, "On Teaching the Intellectual Content of Literature"; and it seems appropriate that he wrote a pamphlet on French writers for the introductory series entitled "Reading with a Purpose." Reading for pleasure, and with a perceptive eye for stylistic effect, was undeniably subordinated to the more austere demands of humanistic pedagogy. Nowadays the pendulum of taste has swung so far in the formalistic direction that such purposefulness is apt to be condemned as heretical or fallacious. Yet a narrowly rhetorical method is no more conducive to rounded estimates than what has come to be known as content-analysis. Babbitt had taken the opposite course in reaction from belletristic colleagues, whose appreciation of books — as he lamented in his Twenty-Five-Year Class Report — was "insufficiently vivified by ideas." Style, he reflected in a last address to the American Academy of Arts and Letters, "bears a relation to one's total outlook on life." Even John Keats, after all, when pausing in contemplation before a certain well-wrought urn, permitted himself to speculate about the lives and thoughts of the youths and maidens depicted thereon. Beauty is not invariably truth, and it is for the critic to press the distinction. To be truly positive and empirical, he must bring historical consciousness to his formal analysis; his understanding of the text must be grounded in its context of signification.

If newer critics have narrowed their scope and lowered their sights, we now have a broader category for what Babbitt practised, in the grand manner of Arnold's criticism of life or the *politiques et moralistes* of nineteenth-century France. His terrain, which bordered on so many others, was basically the history of ideas, the middle ground between literature and philosophy. In cultivating it, he was less dispassionate or systematic than the professional philosopher, Arthur Lovejoy, with whom he engaged in a stimulating controversy. It was, in fact, Babbitt's passionate sense of involvement which enabled him to reanimate the play of intellectual forces so vividly and concretely. Romanticism was the causal nexus explaining the modern epoch, to him and his students, because it had captured men's minds and altered their values on an unprecedented scale. From his standpoint, it had blurred clear and distinct ideas into confusing and seductive images. Those who responded more sympathetically rejected his strictures as unimaginative; yet it was the power of imagination which preoccupied him beyond all other themes; and he frequently recurred to Pascal's insight that "the imagination disposes of everything," or to Napoleon's acknowledgment that "imagination rules the world." At a date when historians stressed material factors and leaned heavily upon economic determinism, Babbitt's belief that man should be master of things must have seemed quixotically bookish. But the subsequent rise of revolutionary Communism has demonstrated, contrary to the implications of Marx's own dialectical materialism, that Law for Thing can be overmastered by ideology. The idea itself, in the struggle for man's future, will be a more potent weapon than the atom or the dollar. Against the mounting pressures that encroach from all sides upon the autonomy of the individual, the single stratagem Babbitt would recommend is to exercise "the ethical imagination": the will to resist what seems evil in the name of what seems good. As for the delicate and difficult matter of judging between them, what, if not Law for Man, can teach us that ultimate mode of discrimination? And where should we be looking for it, if not at the very heart of the educational process?

Index